The Java EE 7 Tutorial
Volume 2

Fifth Edition

The Java EE 7 Tutorial

Volume 2

Fifth Edition

Eric Jendrock
Ricardo Cervera-Navarro
Ian Evans
Kim Haase
William Markito

✦ Addison-Wesley

Upper Saddle River, NJ ● Boston ● Indianapolis ● San Francisco
New York ● Toronto ● Montreal ● London ● Munich ● Paris ● Madrid
Capetown ● Sydney ● Tokyo ● Singapore ● Mexico City

Many of the designations used by manufacturers and sellers to distinguish their products are claimed as trademarks. Where those designations appear in this book, and the publisher was aware of a trademark claim, the designations have been printed with initial capital letters or in all capitals.

Oracle and Java are registered trademarks of Oracle and/or its affiliates. Other names may be trademarks of their respective owners.

The authors and publishers have taken care in the preparation of this book, but make no expressed or implied warranty of any kind and assume no responsibility for errors or omissions. No liability is assumed for incidental or consequential damages in connection with or arising out of the use of the information or programs contained herein.

This document is provided for information purposes only and the contents hereof are subject to change without notice. This document is not warranted to be error-free, nor subject to any other warranties or conditions, whether expressed orally or implied in law, including implied warranties and conditions of merchantability or fitness for a particular purpose. We specifically disclaim any liability with respect to this document and no contractual obligations are formed either directly or indirectly by this document. This document may not be reproduced or transmitted in any form or by any means, electronic or mechanical, for any purpose, without our prior written permission.

For information about buying this title in bulk quantities, or for special sales opportunities (which may include electronic versions; custom cover designs; and content particular to your business, training goals, marketing focus, or branding interests), please contact our corporate sales department at corpsales@pearsoned.com or at (800) 382-3419.

For government sales inquiries, please contact governmentsales@pearsoned.com.

For questions about sales outside the United States, please contact international@pearsoned.com.

Visit us on the Web: informit.com/aw

Library of Congress control Number: 2014933972

ISBN-13: 978-0-321-98008-3
ISBN-10: 0-321-98008-5
Text printed in the United States on recycled paper at Edwards Brothers Malloy in Ann Arbor, Michigan.
First printing, May 2014

Contents

12   Creating and Using String-Based Criteria Queries

13   Controlling Concurrent Access to Entity Data with Locking

14   Creating Fetch Plans with Entity Graphs

Contents

25   Using Java EE Interceptors 497

26   Batch Processing 511

Contents

30   Duke's Forest Case Study Example 595

Index 615

Preface

This tutorial is a guide to developing enterprise applications for the Java Platform, Enterprise Edition 7 (Java EE 7), using GlassFish Server Open Source Edition.

GlassFish Server Open Source Edition is the leading open-source and open-community platform for building and deploying next-generation applications and services. GlassFish Server Open Source Edition, developed by the GlassFish project open-source community at `https://glassfish.java.net/`, is the first compatible implementation of the Java EE 7 platform specification. This lightweight, flexible, and open-source application server enables organizations not only to leverage the new capabilities introduced within the Java EE 7 specification, but also to add to their existing capabilities through a faster and more streamlined development and deployment cycle. GlassFish Server Open Source Edition is hereafter referred to as GlassFish Server.

The following topics are addressed here:

- Audience
- Before You Read This Book
- Related Documentation
- The Oracle Accessibility Program
- Conventions
- Default Paths and File Names
- Acknowledgments

Audience

This tutorial is intended for programmers interested in developing and deploying Java EE 7 applications. It covers the technologies comprising the Java EE platform and describes how to develop Java EE components and deploy them on the Java EE Software Development Kit (SDK).

Before You Read This Book

Before proceeding with this book, you should be familiar with Volume 1 of this tutorial. Both volumes assume that you have a good knowledge of the Java programming language. A good way to get to that point is to work through the Java Tutorials (http://docs.oracle.com/javase/tutorial/).

Related Documentation

The Java EE 7 Tutorial, Volume 1 covers Java EE 7 technologies not included in this volume, including JavaServer Faces, Java Servlets, Bean Validation, Contexts and Dependency Injection for Java EE, and web services.

The GlassFish Server documentation set describes deployment planning and system installation. To obtain documentation for GlassFish Server Open Source Edition, go to https://glassfish.java.net/docs/.

The Java EE 7 API specification can be viewed at http://docs.oracle.com/javaee/7/api/ and is also provided in the Java EE 7 SDK.

Additionally, the Java EE Specifications at http://www.oracle.com/technetwork/java/javaee/tech/index.html might be useful.

For information about creating enterprise applications in the NetBeans Integrated Development Environment (IDE), see https://netbeans.org/kb/.

For information about the Java DB database for use with GlassFish Server, see http://www.oracle.com/technetwork/java/javadb/overview/.

The GlassFish Samples project is a collection of sample applications that demonstrate a broad range of Java EE technologies. The GlassFish Samples are bundled with the Java EE Software Development Kit (SDK) and are also available from the GlassFish Samples project page at https://glassfish-samples.java.net/.

The Oracle Accessibility Program

For information about Oracle's commitment to accessibility, visit the Oracle Accessibility Program website at `http://www.oracle.com/pls/topic/lookup?ctx=acc&id=docacc`.

Conventions

The following table describes the typographic conventions that are used in this book.

Convention	Meaning	Example
Boldface	Boldface type indicates graphical user interface elements associated with an action or terms defined in text.	From the **File** menu, choose **Open Project**. A **cache** is a copy that is stored locally.
`Monospace`	Monospace type indicates the names of files and directories, commands within a paragraph, URLs, code in examples, text that appears on the screen, or text that you enter.	Edit your `.login` file. Use `ls -a` to list all files. `machine_name% you have mail.`
Italic	Italic type indicates book titles, emphasis, or placeholder variables for which you supply particular values.	Read Chapter 6 in the *User's Guide*. Do *not* save the file. The command to remove a file is `rm` *filename*.

Default Paths and File Names

The following table describes the default paths and file names that are used in this book.

Placeholder	Description	Default Value
as-install	Represents the base installation directory for GlassFish Server or the SDK of which GlassFish Server is a part.	Installations on the Solaris operating system, Linux operating system, and Mac operating system: *user's-home-directory*`/glassfish4/glassfish` Windows, all installations: *SystemDrive*`:\glassfish4\glassfish`

Placeholder	Description	Default Value
as-install-parent	Represents the parent of the base installation directory for GlassFish Server.	Installations on the Solaris operating system, Linux operating system, and Mac operating system: *user's-home-directory*/glassfish4 Windows, all installations: *SystemDrive*:\glassfish4
tut-install	Represents the base installation directory for the *Java EE Tutorial* after you install GlassFish Server or the SDK and run the Update Tool.	*as-install-parent*/docs/javaee-tutorial
domain-dir	Represents the directory in which a domain's configuration is stored.	*as-install*/domains/domain1

Acknowledgments

The Java EE tutorial team would like to thank the Java EE specification leads: Linda DeMichiel, Bill Shannon, Emmanuel Bernard, Ed Burns, Shing Wai Chan, Kin-Man Chung, Danny Coward, Nigel Deakin, Rod Johnson, Roger Kitain, Jitendra Kotamraju, Anthony Lai, Bob Lee, Ron Monzillo, Rajiv Mordani, Pete Muir, Paul Parkinson, Santiago Pericas-Geertsen, Marek Potociar, Sivakumar Thyagarajan, Marina Vatkina, and Chris Vignola.

We would also like to thank the Java EE 7 SDK team, especially Snjezana Sevo-Zenzerovic, Adam Leftik, Michael Chen, and John Clingan.

The JavaServer Faces technology chapters benefited greatly from suggestions by Manfred Riem as well as by the spec leads.

We would like to thank our manager, Alan Sommerer, for his support and steadying influence.

We also thank Jordan Douglas and Dawn Tyler for developing and updating the illustrations. Edna Elle provided invaluable help with tools. Sheila Cepero helped smooth our path in many ways.

Finally, we would like to express our profound appreciation to Greg Doench, Elizabeth Ryan, Caroline Senay, and the production team at Addison-Wesley for graciously seeing our manuscript to publication.

Part I

Introduction

Part I introduces the platform, the tutorial, and the examples. This part contains the following chapters:

- Chapter 1, "Overview"
- Chapter 2, "Using the Tutorial Examples"

1

Overview

This chapter introduces you to Java EE enterprise application development. Here you will review development basics, learn about the Java EE architecture and APIs, become acquainted with important terms and concepts, and find out how to approach Java EE application programming, assembly, and deployment.

Developers today increasingly recognize the need for distributed, transactional, and portable applications that leverage the speed, security, and reliability of server-side technology. **Enterprise applications** provide the business logic for an enterprise. They are centrally managed and often interact with other enterprise software. In the world of information technology, enterprise applications must be designed, built, and produced for less money, with greater speed, and with fewer resources.

With the Java Platform, Enterprise Edition (Java EE), development of Java enterprise applications has never been easier or faster. The aim of the Java EE platform is to provide developers with a powerful set of APIs while shortening development time, reducing application complexity, and improving application performance.

The Java EE platform is developed through the Java Community Process (JCP), which is responsible for all Java technologies. Expert groups composed of interested parties have created Java Specification Requests (JSRs) to define the various Java EE technologies. The work of the Java Community under the JCP program helps to ensure Java technology's standards of stability and cross-platform compatibility.

The Java EE platform uses a simplified programming model. XML deployment descriptors are optional. Instead, a developer can simply enter the information as an **annotation** directly into a Java source file, and the Java EE server will configure the component at deployment and runtime. These annotations are generally used to embed in a program data that would otherwise be furnished in a deployment descriptor. With annotations, you put the specification information in your code next to the program element affected.

In the Java EE platform, dependency injection can be applied to all resources a component needs, effectively hiding the creation and lookup of resources from application code. Dependency injection can be used in Enterprise JavaBeans (EJB) containers, web containers, and application clients. Dependency injection allows the Java EE container to automatically insert references to other required components or resources, using annotations.

This tutorial uses examples to describe the features available in the Java EE platform for developing enterprise applications. Whether you are a new or experienced enterprise developer, you should find the examples and accompanying text a valuable and accessible knowledge base for creating your own solutions.

The following topics are addressed here:

- Java EE 7 Platform Highlights
- Java EE Application Model
- Distributed Multitiered Applications
- Java EE Containers
- Web Services Support
- Java EE Application Assembly and Deployment
- Development Roles
- Java EE 7 APIs
- Java EE 7 APIs in the Java Platform, Standard Edition 7
- GlassFish Server Tools

1.1 Java EE 7 Platform Highlights

The most important goal of the Java EE 7 platform is to simplify development by providing a common foundation for the various kinds of components in the Java EE platform. Developers benefit from productivity improvements with more annotations and less XML configuration, more Plain Old Java Objects (POJOs), and simplified packaging. The Java EE 7 platform includes the following new features:

- New technologies, including the following:
    - Batch Applications for the Java EE Platform (see Section 1.8.21)
    - Concurrency Utilities for Java EE (see Section 1.8.20)
    - Java API for JSON Processing (JSON-P) (see Section 1.8.19)
    - Java API for WebSocket (see Section 1.8.18)
- New features for EJB components (see Section 1.8.1, "Enterprise JavaBeans Technology," for details)
- New features for servlets (see Section 1.8.2, "Java Servlet Technology," for details)
- New features for JavaServer Faces components (see Section 1.8.3, "JavaServer Faces Technology," for details)
- New features for the Java Message Service (JMS) (see Section 1.8.13, "Java Message Service API," for details)

1.2 Java EE Application Model

The Java EE application model begins with the Java programming language and the Java virtual machine. The proven portability, security, and developer productivity they provide form the basis of the application model. Java EE is designed to support applications that implement enterprise services for customers, employees, suppliers, partners, and others who make demands on or contributions to the enterprise. Such applications are inherently complex, potentially accessing data from a variety of sources and distributing applications to a variety of clients.

To better control and manage these applications, the business functions to support these various users are conducted in the middle tier. The middle tier represents an environment that is closely controlled by an enterprise's information technology department. The middle tier is typically run on dedicated server hardware and has access to the full services of the enterprise.

The Java EE application model defines an architecture for implementing services as multitier applications that deliver the scalability, accessibility, and manageability needed by enterprise-level applications. This model partitions the work needed to implement a multitier service into the following parts:

- The business and presentation logic to be implemented by the developer

- The standard system services provided by the Java EE platform

The developer can rely on the platform to provide solutions for the hard systems-level problems of developing a multitier service.

1.3 Distributed Multitiered Applications

The Java EE platform uses a distributed multitiered application model for enterprise applications. Application logic is divided into components according to function, and the application components that make up a Java EE application are installed on various machines depending on the tier in the multitiered Java EE environment to which the application component belongs.

Figure 1–1 shows two multitiered Java EE applications divided into the tiers described in the following list. The Java EE application parts shown in Figure 1–1 are presented in Section 1.3.2, "Java EE Components."

- Client-tier components run on the client machine.

- Web-tier components run on the Java EE server.

- Business-tier components run on the Java EE server.

- Enterprise information system (EIS)-tier software runs on the EIS server.

Although a Java EE application can consist of all tiers shown in Figure 1–1, Java EE multitiered applications are generally considered to be three-tiered applications because they are distributed over three locations: client machines, the Java EE server machine, and the database or legacy machines at the back end. Three-tiered applications that run in this way extend the standard two-tiered client-and-server model by placing a multithreaded application server between the client application and back-end storage.

Figure 1–1   Multitiered Applications

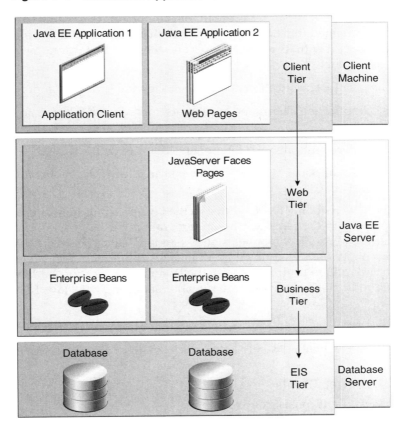

1.3.1 Security

Although other enterprise application models require platform-specific security measures in each application, the Java EE security environment enables security constraints to be defined at deployment time. The Java EE platform makes applications portable to a wide variety of security implementations by shielding application developers from the complexity of implementing security features.

The Java EE platform provides standard declarative access control rules that are defined by the developer and interpreted when the application is deployed on the server. Java EE also provides standard login mechanisms so that application developers do not have to implement these mechanisms in their applications. The same application works in a variety of security environments without changing the source code.

1.3.2 Java EE Components

Java EE applications are made up of components. A **Java EE component** is a self-contained functional software unit that is assembled into a Java EE application with its related classes and files and that communicates with other components.

The Java EE specification defines the following Java EE components:

- Application clients and applets are components that run on the client.
- Java Servlet, JavaServer Faces, and JavaServer Pages (JSP) technology components are web components that run on the server.
- EJB components (enterprise beans) are business components that run on the server.

Java EE components are written in the Java programming language and are compiled in the same way as any program in the language. The differences between Java EE components and "standard" Java classes are that Java EE components are assembled into a Java EE application, they are verified to be well formed and in compliance with the Java EE specification, and they are deployed to production, where they are run and managed by the Java EE server.

1.3.3 Java EE Clients

A Java EE client is usually either a web client or an application client.

1.3.3.1 Web Clients

A **web client** consists of two parts:

- Dynamic web pages containing various types of markup language (HTML, XML, and so on), which are generated by web components running in the web tier
- A web browser, which renders the pages received from the server

A web client is sometimes called a **thin client**. Thin clients usually do not query databases, execute complex business rules, or connect to legacy applications. When you use a thin client, such heavyweight operations are off-loaded to enterprise beans executing on the Java EE server, where they can leverage the security, speed, services, and reliability of Java EE server-side technologies.

1.3.3.2 Application Clients

An **application client** runs on a client machine and provides a way for users to handle tasks that require a richer user interface than can be provided by a markup language. An application client typically has a graphical user interface (GUI) created from the Swing API or the Abstract Window Toolkit (AWT) API, but a command-line interface is certainly possible.

Application clients directly access enterprise beans running in the business tier. However, if application requirements warrant it, an application client can open an HTTP connection to establish communication with a servlet running in the web tier. Application clients written in languages other than Java can interact with Java EE servers, enabling the Java EE platform to interoperate with legacy systems, clients, and non-Java languages.

1.3.3.3 Applets

A web page received from the web tier can include an embedded applet. Written in the Java programming language, an **applet** is a small client application that executes in the Java virtual machine installed in the web browser. However, client systems will likely need the Java Plug-in and possibly a security policy file for the applet to successfully execute in the web browser.

Web components are the preferred API for creating a web client program because no plug-ins or security policy files are needed on the client systems. Also, web components enable cleaner and more modular application design because they provide a way to separate applications programming from web page design. Personnel involved in web page design thus do not need to understand Java programming language syntax to do their jobs.

1.3.3.4 The JavaBeans Component Architecture

The server and client tiers might also include components based on the JavaBeans component architecture (JavaBeans components) to manage the data flow between the following:

- An application client or applet and components running on the Java EE server

- Server components and a database

JavaBeans components are not considered Java EE components by the Java EE specification.

JavaBeans components have properties and have `get` and `set` methods for accessing those properties. JavaBeans components used in this way are typically simple in design and implementation but should conform to the naming and design conventions outlined in the JavaBeans component architecture.

1.3.3.5 Java EE Server Communications

Figure 1–2 shows the various elements that can make up the client tier. The client communicates with the business tier running on the Java EE server either directly or, as in the case of a client running in a browser, by going through web pages or servlets running in the web tier.

Figure 1–2   Server Communication

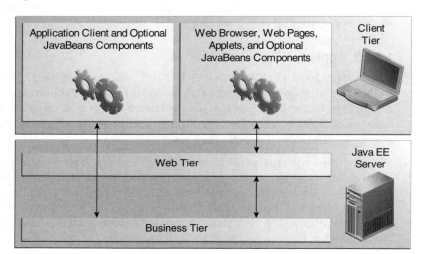

1.3.4 Web Components

Java EE web components are either servlets or web pages created using JavaServer Faces technology and/or JSP technology (JSP pages). **Servlets** are Java programming language classes that dynamically process requests and construct responses. **JSP pages** are text-based documents that execute as servlets but allow a more natural approach to creating static content. **JavaServer Faces technology** builds on servlets and JSP technology and provides a user interface component framework for web applications.

Static HTML pages and applets are bundled with web components during application assembly but are not considered web components by the Java EE specification. Server-side utility classes can also be bundled with web components and, like HTML pages, are not considered web components.

As shown in Figure 1–3, the web tier, like the client tier, might include a JavaBeans component to manage the user input and send that input to enterprise beans running in the business tier for processing.

Figure 1–3   Web Tier and Java EE Applications

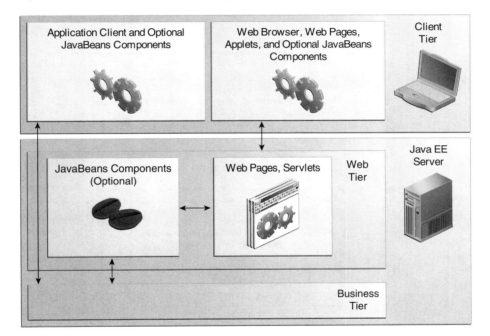

1.3.5 Business Components

Business code, which is logic that solves or meets the needs of a particular business domain such as banking, retail, or finance, is handled by enterprise beans running in either the business tier or the web tier. Figure 1–4 shows how an enterprise bean receives data from client programs, processes it (if necessary), and sends it to the enterprise information system tier for storage. An enterprise bean also retrieves data from storage, processes it (if necessary), and sends it back to the client program.

Figure 1–4   Business and EIS Tiers

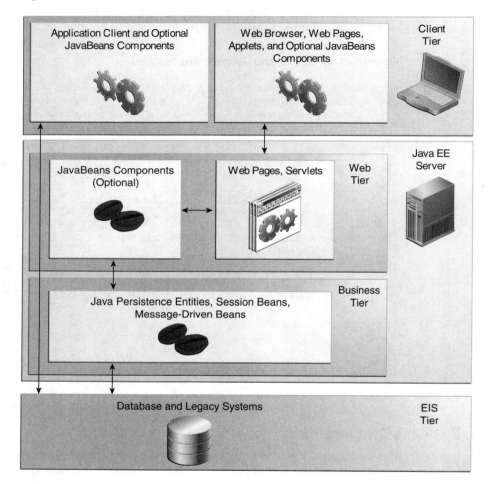

1.3.6 Enterprise Information System Tier

The enterprise information system tier handles EIS software and includes enterprise infrastructure systems, such as enterprise resource planning (ERP), mainframe transaction processing, database systems, and other legacy information systems. For example, Java EE application components might need access to enterprise information systems for database connectivity.

1.4 Java EE Containers

Normally, thin-client multitiered applications are hard to write because they involve many lines of intricate code to handle transaction and state management, multithreading, resource pooling, and other complex low-level details. The component-based and platform-independent Java EE architecture makes applications easy to write because business logic is organized into reusable components. In addition, the Java EE server provides underlying services in the form of a container for every component type. Because you do not have to develop these services yourself, you are free to concentrate on solving the business problem at hand.

1.4.1 Container Services

Containers are the interface between a component and the low-level, platform-specific functionality that supports the component. Before it can be executed, a web, enterprise bean, or application client component must be assembled into a Java EE module and deployed into its container.

The assembly process involves specifying container settings for each component in the Java EE application and for the Java EE application itself. Container settings customize the underlying support provided by the Java EE server, including such services as security, transaction management, Java Naming and Directory Interface (JNDI) API lookups, and remote connectivity. Here are some of the highlights.

- The Java EE security model lets you configure a web component or enterprise bean so that system resources are accessed only by authorized users.

- The Java EE transaction model lets you specify relationships among methods that make up a single transaction so that all methods in one transaction are treated as a single unit.

- JNDI lookup services provide a unified interface to multiple naming and directory services in the enterprise so that application components can access these services.

- The Java EE remote connectivity model manages low-level communications between clients and enterprise beans. After an enterprise bean is created, a client invokes methods on it as if it were in the same virtual machine.

Because the Java EE architecture provides configurable services, components within the same application can behave differently based on where they are deployed. For example, an enterprise bean can have security settings that allow it a certain level of access to database data in one production environment and another level of database access in another production environment.

The container also manages nonconfigurable services, such as enterprise bean and servlet lifecycles, database connection resource pooling, data persistence, and access to the Java EE platform APIs (see Section 1.8, "Java EE 7 APIs").

1.4.2 Container Types

The **deployment** process installs Java EE application components in the Java EE containers, as illustrated in Figure 1–5.

Figure 1–5   Java EE Server and Containers

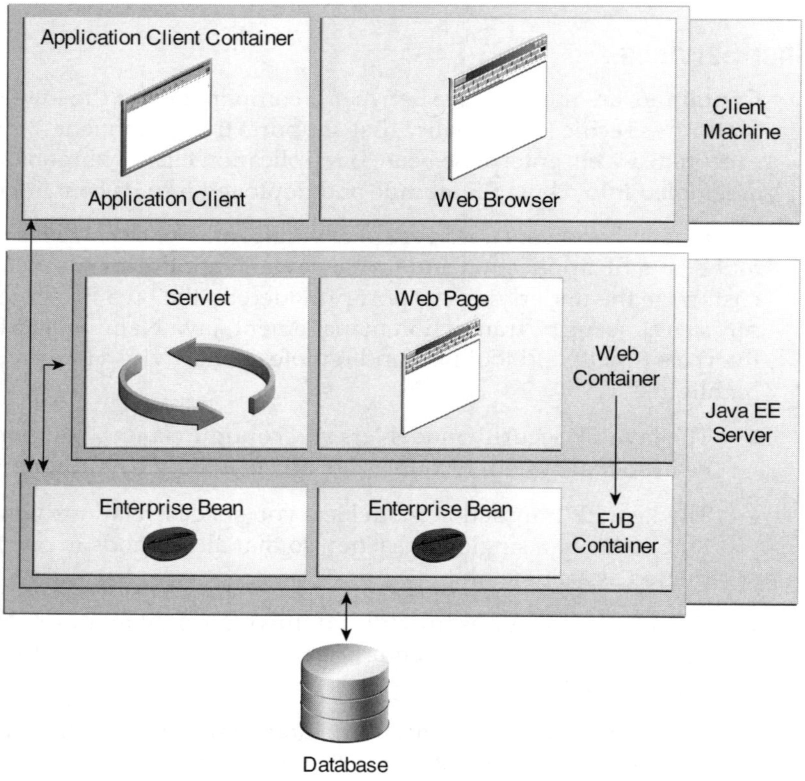

The server and containers are as follows:

- **Java EE server**: The runtime portion of a Java EE product. A Java EE server provides EJB and web containers.

- **EJB container**: Manages the execution of enterprise beans for Java EE applications. Enterprise beans and their container run on the Java EE server.

- **Web container**: Manages the execution of web pages, servlets, and some EJB components for Java EE applications. Web components and their container run on the Java EE server.

- **Application client container**: Manages the execution of application client components. Application clients and their container run on the client.

- **Applet container**: Manages the execution of applets. Consists of a web browser and a Java Plug-in running on the client together.

1.5 Web Services Support

Web services are web-based enterprise applications that use open, XML-based standards and transport protocols to exchange data with calling clients. The Java EE platform provides the XML APIs and tools you need to quickly design, develop, test, and deploy web services and clients that fully interoperate with other web services and clients running on Java-based or non-Java-based platforms.

To write web services and clients with the Java EE XML APIs, all you need to do is pass parameter data to the method calls and process the data returned; for document-oriented web services, you send documents containing the service data back and forth. No low-level programming is needed because the XML API implementations do the work of translating the application data to and from an XML-based data stream that is sent over the standardized XML-based transport protocols. These XML-based standards and protocols are introduced in the following sections.

The translation of data to a standardized XML-based data stream is what makes web services and clients written with the Java EE XML APIs fully interoperable. This does not necessarily mean that the data being transported includes XML tags, because the transported data can itself be plain text, XML data, or any kind of binary data, such as audio, video, maps, program files, computer-aided design (CAD) documents, and the like. The next section introduces XML and explains how parties doing business can use XML tags and schemas to exchange data in a meaningful way.

1.5.1 XML

Extensible Markup Language (XML) is a cross-platform, extensible, text-based standard for representing data. Parties that exchange XML data can create their own tags to describe the data, set up schemas to specify which tags can be used in a particular kind of XML document, and use XML style sheets to manage the display and handling of the data.

For example, a web service can use XML and a schema to produce price lists, and companies that receive the price lists and schema can have their own style sheets to handle the data in a way that best suits their needs. Here are examples.

- One company might put XML pricing information through a program to translate the XML into HTML so that it can post the price lists to its intranet.

- A partner company might put the XML pricing information through a tool to create a marketing presentation.

- Another company might read the XML pricing information into an application for processing.

1.5.2 SOAP Transport Protocol

Client requests and web service responses are transmitted as Simple Object Access Protocol (SOAP) messages over HTTP to enable a completely interoperable exchange between clients and web services, all running on different platforms and at various locations on the Internet. HTTP is a familiar request-and-response standard for sending messages over the Internet, and SOAP is an XML-based protocol that follows the HTTP request-and-response model.

The SOAP portion of a transported message does the following:

- Defines an XML-based envelope to describe what is in the message and explain how to process the message

- Includes XML-based encoding rules to express instances of application-defined data types within the message

- Defines an XML-based convention for representing the request to the remote service and the resulting response

1.5.3 WSDL Standard Format

The Web Services Description Language (WSDL) is a standardized XML format for describing network services. The description includes the name of the service, the location of the service, and ways to communicate with the service. WSDL service descriptions can be published on the Web. GlassFish Server provides a tool for generating the WSDL specification of a web service that uses remote procedure calls to communicate with clients.

1.6 Java EE Application Assembly and Deployment

A Java EE application is packaged into one or more standard units for deployment to any Java EE platform-compliant system. Each unit contains

- A functional component or components, such as an enterprise bean, web page, servlet, or applet

- An optional deployment descriptor that describes its content

Once a Java EE unit has been produced, it is ready to be deployed. Deployment typically involves using a platform's deployment tool to specify location-specific information, such as a list of local users who can access it and the name of the local database. Once deployed on a local platform, the application is ready to run.

1.7 Development Roles

Reusable modules make it possible to divide the application development and deployment process into distinct roles so that different people or companies can perform different parts of the process.

The first two roles, Java EE product provider and tool provider, involve purchasing and installing the Java EE product and tools. After the software is purchased and installed, Java EE components can be developed by application component providers, assembled by application assemblers, and deployed by application deployers. In a large organization, each of these roles might be executed by different individuals or teams. This division of labor works because each of the earlier roles outputs a portable file that is the input for a subsequent role. For example, in the application component development phase, an enterprise bean software developer delivers EJB JAR files. In the application assembly role, another developer may combine these EJB JAR files into a Java EE application and save it in an EAR file. In the application deployment role, a system administrator at the customer site uses the EAR file to install the Java EE application into a Java EE server.

The different roles are not always executed by different people. If you work for a small company, for example, or if you are prototyping a sample application, you might perform tasks in every phase.

1.7.1 Java EE Product Provider

The Java EE product provider is the company that designs and makes available for purchase the Java EE platform APIs and other features defined in the Java EE specification. Product providers are typically application server vendors that implement the Java EE platform according to the Java EE 7 platform specification.

1.7.2 Tool Provider

The tool provider is the company or person who creates development, assembly, and packaging tools used by component providers, assemblers, and deployers.

1.7.3 Application Component Provider

The application component provider is the company or person who creates web components, enterprise beans, applets, or application clients for use in Java EE applications.

1.7.3.1 Enterprise Bean Developer

An enterprise bean developer performs the following tasks to deliver an EJB JAR file that contains one or more enterprise beans:

- Writes and compiles the source code

- Specifies the deployment descriptor (optional)

- Packages the .class files and the deployment descriptor into the EJB JAR file

1.7.3.2 Web Component Developer

A web component developer performs the following tasks to deliver a WAR file containing one or more web components:

- Writes and compiles servlet source code

- Writes JavaServer Faces, JSP, and HTML files

- Specifies the deployment descriptor (optional)

- Packages the .class, .jsp, and .html files and the deployment descriptor into the WAR file

1.7.3.3 Application Client Developer

An application client developer performs the following tasks to deliver a JAR file containing the application client:

- Writes and compiles the source code
- Specifies the deployment descriptor for the client (optional)
- Packages the `.class` files and the deployment descriptor into the JAR file

1.7.4 Application Assembler

The application assembler is the company or person who receives application modules from component providers and may assemble them into a Java EE application EAR file. The assembler or deployer can edit the deployment descriptor directly or can use tools that correctly add XML tags according to interactive selections.

A software developer performs the following tasks to deliver an EAR file containing the Java EE application:

- Assembles EJB JAR and WAR files created in the previous phases into a Java EE application (EAR) file
- Specifies the deployment descriptor for the Java EE application (optional)
- Verifies that the contents of the EAR file are well formed and comply with the Java EE specification

1.7.5 Application Deployer and Administrator

The application deployer and administrator is the company or person who configures and deploys application clients, web applications, Enterprise JavaBeans components, and Java EE applications; administers the computing and networking infrastructure where Java EE components and applications run; and oversees the runtime environment. Duties include setting transaction controls and security attributes and specifying connections to databases.

During configuration, the deployer follows instructions supplied by the application component provider to resolve external dependencies, specify security settings, and assign transaction attributes. During installation, the deployer moves the application components to the server and generates the container-specific classes and interfaces.

A deployer or system administrator performs the following tasks to install and configure a Java EE application or Java EE components:

- Configures the Java EE application or components for the operational environment

- Verifies that the contents of the EAR, JAR, and/or WAR files are well formed and comply with the Java EE specification

- Deploys (installs) the Java EE application or components into the Java EE server

1.8 Java EE 7 APIs

Figure 1–6 shows the relationships among the Java EE containers.

Figure 1–6   Java EE Containers

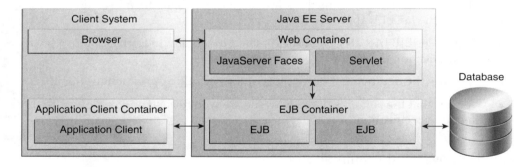

Figure 1–7 shows the availability of the Java EE 7 APIs in the web container.

Figure 1–7   Java EE APIs in the Web Container

Web Container	WebSocket	Java SE
	Concurrency Utilities	
	Batch	
	JSON-P	
	Bean Validation	
	EJB Lite	
	EL	
Servlet	JavaMail	
	JSP	
	Connectors	
JavaServer Faces	Java Persistence	
	JMS	
	Management	
	WS Metadata	
	Web Services	
	JACC	
	JASPIC	
	JAX-RS	
	JAX-WS	
	JSTL	
	JTA	
	CDI	
	Dependency Injection	

New in Java EE 7

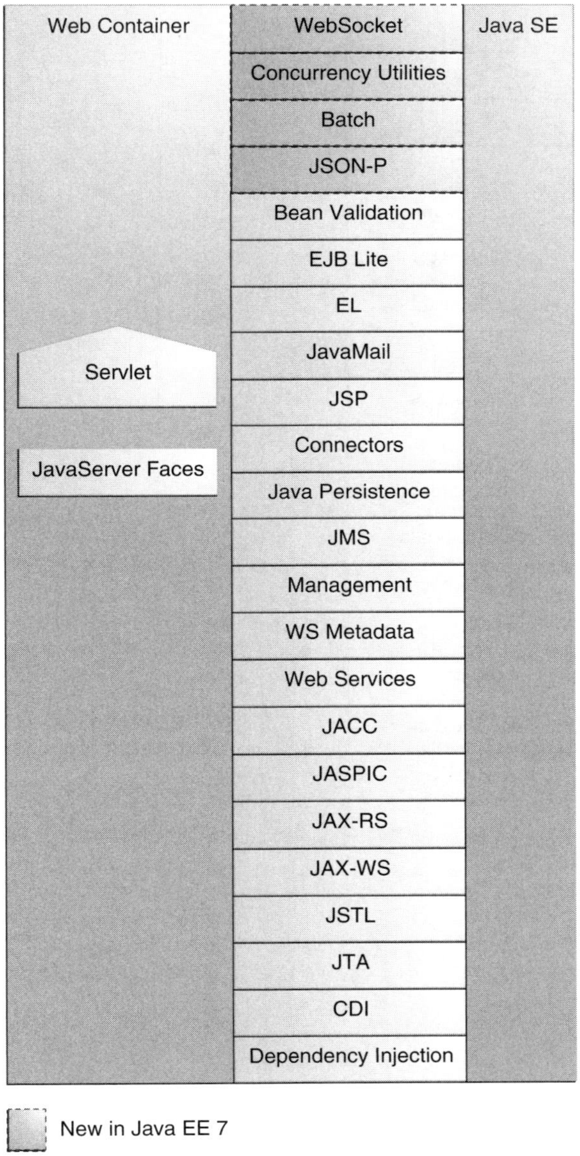

Figure 1–8 shows the availability of the Java EE 7 APIs in the EJB container.

Figure 1–8   Java EE APIs in the EJB Container

EJB Container	Concurrency Utilities	Java SE
	Batch	
	JSON-P	
	CDI	
	Dependency Injection	
	JavaMail	
	Java Persistence	
	JTA	
	Connectors	
	JMS	
EJB	Management	
	WS Metadata	
	Web Services	
	JACC	
	JASPIC	
	Bean Validation	
	JAX-RS	
	JAX-WS	

New in Java EE 7

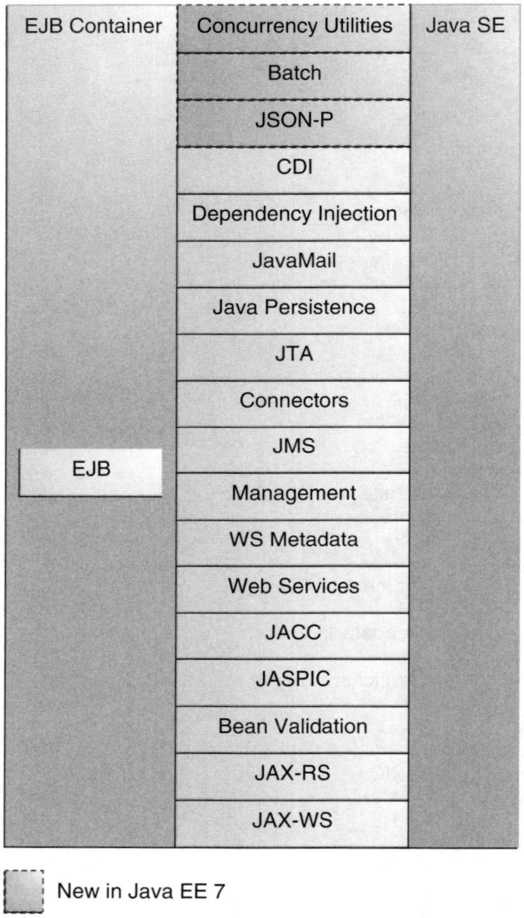

Figure 1–9 shows the availability of the Java EE 7 APIs in the application client container.

Figure 1–9   Java EE APIs in the Application Client Container

Application Client Container	Java Persistence	Java SE
	Management	
	WS Metadata	
	Web Services	
Application Client	JSON-P	
	JMS	
	JAX-WS	
	Bean Validation	
	JavaMail	
	CDI	
	Dependency Injection	

New in Java EE 7

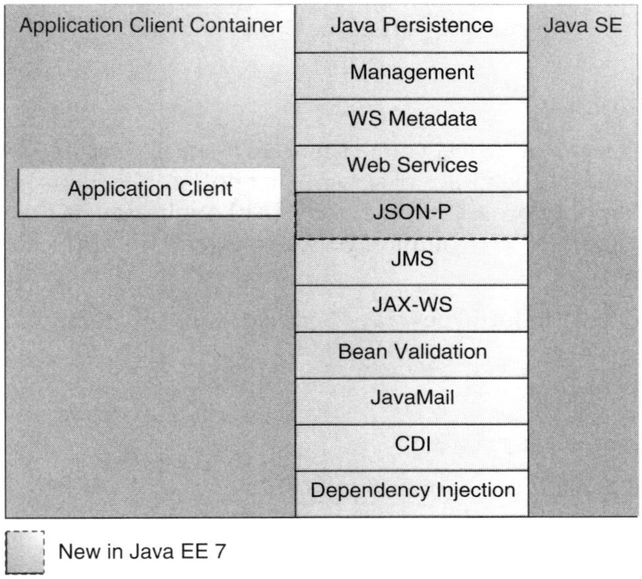

The following sections give a brief summary of the technologies required by the Java EE platform and the APIs used in Java EE applications.

1.8.1 Enterprise JavaBeans Technology

An **Enterprise JavaBeans (EJB) component**, or **enterprise bean**, is a body of code that has fields and methods to implement modules of business logic. You can think of an enterprise bean as a building block that can be used alone or with other enterprise beans to execute business logic on the Java EE server.

Enterprise beans are either session beans or message-driven beans.

- A **session bean** represents a transient conversation with a client. When the client finishes executing, the session bean and its data are gone.

- A **message-driven bean** combines features of a session bean and a message listener, allowing a business component to receive messages asynchronously. Commonly, these are Java Message Service (JMS) messages.

In the Java EE 7 platform, new enterprise bean features include the following:

- Asynchronous local session beans in EJB Lite
- Nonpersistent timers in EJB Lite

The Java EE 7 platform requires Enterprise JavaBeans 3.2 and Interceptors 1.2. The Interceptors specification is part of the EJB specification.

1.8.2 Java Servlet Technology

Java Servlet technology lets you define HTTP-specific servlet classes. A servlet class extends the capabilities of servers that host applications accessed by way of a request-response programming model. Although servlets can respond to any type of request, they are commonly used to extend the applications hosted by web servers.

In the Java EE 7 platform, new Java Servlet technology features include the following:

- Nonblocking I/O
- HTTP protocol upgrade

The Java EE 7 platform requires Servlet 3.1.

1.8.3 JavaServer Faces Technology

JavaServer Faces technology is a user interface framework for building web applications. The main components of JavaServer Faces technology are as follows:

- A GUI component framework.
- A flexible model for rendering components in different kinds of HTML or different markup languages and technologies. A `Renderer` object generates the markup to render the component and converts the data stored in a model object to types that can be represented in a view.
- A standard `RenderKit` for generating HTML 4.01 markup.

The following features support the GUI components:

- Input validation
- Event handling
- Data conversion between model objects and components
- Managed model object creation

- Page navigation configuration
- Expression Language (EL)

All this functionality is available using standard Java APIs and XML-based configuration files.

In the Java EE 7 platform, new features of JavaServer Faces technology include the following:

- HTML5-friendly markup
- Faces Flows
- Resource library contracts

The Java EE 7 platform requires JavaServer Faces 2.2 and Expression Language 3.0.

1.8.4 JavaServer Pages Technology

JavaServer Pages (JSP) technology lets you put snippets of servlet code directly into a text-based document. A JSP page is a text-based document that contains two types of text:

- Static data, which can be expressed in any text-based format, such as HTML or XML
- JSP elements, which determine how the page constructs dynamic content

For information about JSP technology, see the *The Java EE 5 Tutorial* at `http://docs.oracle.com/javaee/5/tutorial/doc/`.

The Java EE 7 platform requires JavaServer Pages 2.3 for compatibility with earlier releases but recommends the use of Facelets as the display technology in new applications.

1.8.5 JavaServer Pages Standard Tag Library

The JavaServer Pages Standard Tag Library (JSTL) encapsulates core functionality common to many JSP applications. Instead of mixing tags from numerous vendors in your JSP applications, you use a single, standard set of tags. This standardization allows you to deploy your applications on any JSP container that supports JSTL and makes it more likely that the implementation of the tags is optimized.

JSTL has iterator and conditional tags for handling flow control, tags for manipulating XML documents, internationalization tags, tags for accessing databases using SQL, and tags for commonly used functions.

The Java EE 7 platform requires JSTL 1.2.

1.8.6 Java Persistence API

The Java Persistence API (JPA) is a Java standards–based solution for persistence. Persistence uses an object/relational mapping approach to bridge the gap between an object-oriented model and a relational database. The Java Persistence API can also be used in Java SE applications outside of the Java EE environment. Java Persistence consists of the following areas:

- The Java Persistence API

- The query language

- Object/relational mapping metadata

The Java EE 7 platform requires Java Persistence API 2.1.

1.8.7 Java Transaction API

The Java Transaction API (JTA) provides a standard interface for demarcating transactions. The Java EE architecture provides a default auto commit to handle transaction commits and rollbacks. An auto commit means that any other applications that are viewing data will see the updated data after each database read or write operation. However, if your application performs two separate database access operations that depend on each other, you will want to use the JTA API to demarcate where the entire transaction, including both operations, begins, rolls back, and commits.

The Java EE 7 platform requires Java Transaction API 1.2.

1.8.8 Java API for RESTful Web Services

The Java API for RESTful Web Services (JAX-RS) defines APIs for the development of web services built according to the Representational State Transfer (REST) architectural style. A JAX-RS application is a web application that consists of classes packaged as a servlet in a WAR file along with required libraries.

The Java EE 7 platform requires JAX-RS 2.0.

1.8.9 Managed Beans

Managed Beans, lightweight container-managed objects (POJOs) with minimal requirements, support a small set of basic services, such as resource injection, lifecycle callbacks, and interceptors. Managed Beans represent a generalization of the managed beans specified by JavaServer Faces technology and can be used anywhere in a Java EE application, not just in web modules.

The Managed Beans specification is part of the Java EE 7 platform specification (JSR 342). The Java EE 7 platform requires Managed Beans 1.0.

1.8.10 Contexts and Dependency Injection for Java EE

Contexts and Dependency Injection for Java EE (CDI) defines a set of contextual services, provided by Java EE containers, that make it easy for developers to use enterprise beans along with JavaServer Faces technology in web applications. Designed for use with stateful objects, CDI also has many broader uses, allowing developers a great deal of flexibility to integrate different kinds of components in a loosely coupled but typesafe way.

The Java EE 7 platform requires CDI 1.1.

1.8.11 Dependency Injection for Java

Dependency Injection for Java defines a standard set of annotations (and one interface) for use on injectable classes.

In the Java EE platform, CDI provides support for Dependency Injection. Specifically, you can use injection points only in a CDI-enabled application.

The Java EE 7 platform requires Dependency Injection for Java 1.0.

1.8.12 Bean Validation

The Bean Validation specification defines a metadata model and API for validating data in JavaBeans components. Instead of distributing validation of data over several layers, such as the browser and the server side, you can define the validation constraints in one place and share them across the different layers.

The Java EE 7 platform requires Bean Validation 1.1.

1.8.13 Java Message Service API

The Java Message Service (JMS) API is a messaging standard that allows Java EE application components to create, send, receive, and read messages. It enables distributed communication that is loosely coupled, reliable, and asynchronous.

In the platform, new features of JMS include the following:

- A new, simplified API offers a simpler alternative to the previous API. This API includes a `JMSContext` object that combines the functions of a `Connection` and a `Session`.

- All objects with a `close` method implement the `java.lang.Autocloseable` interface so that they can be used in a Java SE 7 `try`-with-resources block.

The Java EE 7 platform requires JMS 2.0.

1.8.14 Java EE Connector Architecture

The Java EE Connector Architecture is used by tools vendors and system integrators to create resource adapters that support access to enterprise information systems that can be plugged in to any Java EE product. A **resource adapter** is a software component that allows Java EE application components to access and interact with the underlying resource manager of the EIS. Because a resource adapter is specific to its resource manager, a different resource adapter typically exists for each type of database or enterprise information system.

The Java EE Connector Architecture also provides a performance-oriented, secure, scalable, and message-based transactional integration of Java EE platform–based web services with existing EISs that can be either synchronous or asynchronous. Existing applications and EISs integrated through the Java EE Connector Architecture into the Java EE platform can be exposed as XML-based web services by using JAX-WS and Java EE component models. Thus JAX-WS and the Java EE Connector Architecture are complementary technologies for enterprise application integration (EAI) and end-to-end business integration.

The Java EE 7 platform requires Java EE Connector Architecture 1.7.

1.8.15 JavaMail API

Java EE applications use the JavaMail API to send email notifications. The JavaMail API has two parts:

- An application-level interface used by the application components to send mail

- A service provider interface

The Java EE platform includes the JavaMail API with a service provider that allows application components to send Internet mail.

The Java EE 7 platform requires JavaMail 1.5.

1.8.16 Java Authorization Contract for Containers

The Java Authorization Contract for Containers (JACC) specification defines a contract between a Java EE application server and an authorization policy provider. All Java EE containers support this contract.

The JACC specification defines `java.security.Permission` classes that satisfy the Java EE authorization model. The specification defines the binding of container-access decisions to operations on instances of these permission classes. It defines the semantics of policy providers that use the new permission classes to address the authorization requirements of the Java EE platform, including the definition and use of roles.

The Java EE 7 platform requires JACC 1.5.

1.8.17 Java Authentication Service Provider Interface for Containers

The Java Authentication Service Provider Interface for Containers (JASPIC) specification defines a service provider interface (SPI) by which authentication providers that implement message authentication mechanisms may be integrated in client or server message-processing containers or runtimes. Authentication providers integrated through this interface operate on network messages provided to them by their calling containers. The authentication providers transform outgoing messages so that the source of each message can be authenticated by the receiving container, and the recipient of the message can be authenticated by the message sender. Authentication providers authenticate each incoming message and return to their calling containers the identity established as a result of the message authentication.

The Java EE 7 platform requires JASPIC 1.1.

1.8.18 Java API for WebSocket

WebSocket is an application protocol that provides full-duplex communications between two peers over TCP. The Java API for WebSocket enables Java EE applications to create endpoints using annotations that specify the configuration parameters of the endpoint and designate its lifecycle callback methods.

The WebSocket API is new to the Java EE 7 platform. The Java EE 7 platform requires Java API for WebSocket 1.0.

1.8.19 Java API for JSON Processing

JSON is a text-based data exchange format derived from JavaScript that is used in web services and other connected applications. The Java API for JSON Processing

(JSON-P) enables Java EE applications to parse, transform, and query JSON data using the object model or the streaming model.

JSON-P is new to the Java EE 7 platform. The Java EE 7 platform requires JSON-P 1.0.

1.8.20 Concurrency Utilities for Java EE

Concurrency Utilities for Java EE is a standard API for providing asynchronous capabilities to Java EE application components through the following types of objects: managed executor service, managed scheduled executor service, managed thread factory, and context service.

Concurrency Utilities for Java EE is new to the Java EE 7 platform. The Java EE 7 platform requires Concurrency Utilities for Java EE 1.0.

1.8.21 Batch Applications for the Java Platform

Batch jobs are tasks that can be executed without user interaction. The Batch Applications for the Java Platform specification is a batch framework that provides support for creating and running batch jobs in Java applications. The batch framework consists of a batch runtime, a job specification language based on XML, a Java API to interact with the batch runtime, and a Java API to implement batch artifacts.

Batch Applications for the Java Platform is new to the Java EE 7 platform. The Java EE 7 platform requires Batch Applications for the Java Platform 1.0.

1.9 Java EE 7 APIs in the Java Platform, Standard Edition 7

Several APIs that are required by the Java EE 7 platform are included in the Java Platform, Standard Edition 7 (Java SE 7) and are thus available to Java EE applications.

1.9.1 Java Database Connectivity API

The Java Database Connectivity (JDBC) API lets you invoke SQL commands from Java programming language methods. You use the JDBC API in an enterprise bean when you have a session bean access the database. You can also use the JDBC API from a servlet or a JSP page to access the database directly without going through an enterprise bean.

The JDBC API has two parts:

- An application-level interface used by the application components to access a database
- A service provider interface to attach a JDBC driver to the Java EE platform

The Java SE 7 platform requires JDBC 4.1.

1.9.2 Java Naming and Directory Interface API

The Java Naming and Directory Interface (JNDI) API provides naming and directory functionality, enabling applications to access multiple naming and directory services, such as LDAP, DNS, and NIS. The JNDI API provides applications with methods for performing standard directory operations, such as associating attributes with objects and searching for objects using their attributes. Using JNDI, a Java EE application can store and retrieve any type of named Java object, allowing Java EE applications to coexist with many legacy applications and systems.

Java EE naming services provide application clients, enterprise beans, and web components with access to a JNDI naming environment. A **naming environment** allows a component to be customized without the need to access or change the component's source code. A container implements the component's environment and provides it to the component as a JNDI **naming context**.

The naming environment provides four logical namespaces: java:comp, java:module, java:app, and java:global for objects available to components, modules, or applications or shared by all deployed applications. A Java EE component can access named system-provided and user-defined objects. The names of some system-provided objects, such as a default JDBC DataSource object, a default JMS connection factory, and a JTA UserTransaction object, are stored in the java:comp namespace. The Java EE platform allows a component to name user-defined objects, such as enterprise beans, environment entries, JDBC DataSource objects, and messaging destinations.

A Java EE component can also locate its environment naming context by using JNDI interfaces. A component can create a javax.naming.InitialContext object and look up the environment naming context in InitialContext under the name java:comp/env. A component's naming environment is stored directly in the environment naming context or in any of its direct or indirect subcontexts.

1.9.3 JavaBeans Activation Framework

The JavaBeans Activation Framework (JAF) is used by the JavaMail API. JAF provides standard services to determine the type of an arbitrary piece of data, encapsulate access to it, discover the operations available on it, and create the appropriate JavaBeans component to perform those operations.

1.9.4 Java API for XML Processing

The Java API for XML Processing (JAXP), part of the Java SE platform, supports the processing of XML documents using Document Object Model (DOM), Simple API for XML (SAX), and Extensible Stylesheet Language Transformations (XSLT). JAXP enables applications to parse and transform XML documents independently of a particular XML-processing implementation.

JAXP also provides namespace support, which lets you work with schemas that might otherwise have naming conflicts. Designed to be flexible, JAXP lets you use any XML-compliant parser or XSL processor from within your application and supports the Worldwide Web Consortium (W3C) schema. You can find information on the W3C schema at `http://www.w3.org/XML/Schema`.

1.9.5 Java Architecture for XML Binding

The Java Architecture for XML Binding (JAXB) provides a convenient way to bind an XML schema to a representation in Java language programs. JAXB can be used independently or in combination with JAX-WS, in which case it provides a standard data binding for web service messages. All Java EE application client containers, web containers, and EJB containers support the JAXB API.

The Java EE 7 platform requires JAXB 2.2.

1.9.6 Java API for XML Web Services

The Java API for XML Web Services (JAX-WS) specification provides support for web services that use the JAXB API for binding XML data to Java objects. The JAX-WS specification defines client APIs for accessing web services as well as techniques for implementing web service endpoints. The Implementing Enterprise Web Services specification describes the deployment of JAX-WS-based services and clients. The EJB and Java Servlet specifications also describe aspects of such deployment. JAX-WS-based applications can be deployed using any of these deployment models.

The JAX-WS specification describes the support for message handlers that can process message requests and responses. In general, these message handlers execute in the same container and with the same privileges and execution context as the JAX-WS client or endpoint component with which they are associated. These message handlers have access to the same JNDI namespace as their associated component. Custom serializers and deserializers, if supported, are treated in the same way as message handlers.

The Java EE 7 platform requires JAX-WS 2.2.

1.9.7 SOAP with Attachments API for Java

The SOAP with Attachments API for Java (SAAJ) is a low-level API on which JAX-WS depends. SAAJ enables the production and consumption of messages that conform to the SOAP 1.1 and 1.2 specifications and the SOAP with Attachments note. Most developers do not use the SAAJ API, instead using the higher-level JAX-WS API.

1.9.8 Java Authentication and Authorization Service

The Java Authentication and Authorization Service (JAAS) provides a way for a Java EE application to authenticate and authorize a specific user or group of users to run it.

JAAS is a Java programming language version of the standard Pluggable Authentication Module (PAM) framework, which extends the Java platform security architecture to support user-based authorization.

1.9.9 Common Annotations for the Java Platform

Annotations enable a declarative style of programming in the Java platform.

The Java EE 7 platform requires Common Annotations for the Java Platform 1.2.

1.10 GlassFish Server Tools

GlassFish Server is a compliant implementation of the Java EE 7 platform. In addition to supporting all the APIs described in the previous sections, GlassFish Server includes a number of Java EE tools that are not part of the Java EE 7 platform but are provided as a convenience to the developer.

This section briefly summarizes the tools that make up GlassFish Server. Instructions for starting and stopping GlassFish Server, starting the Administration Console, and starting and stopping the Java DB server are in Chapter 2, "Using the Tutorial Examples."

GlassFish Server contains the tools listed in Table 1–1. Basic usage information for many of the tools appears throughout the tutorial. For detailed information, see the online help in the GUI tools.

Table 1–1   **GlassFish Server Tools**

Tool	Description
Administration Console	A web-based GUI GlassFish Server administration utility. Used to stop GlassFish Server and to manage users, resources, and applications.
asadmin	A command-line GlassFish Server administration utility. Used to start and stop GlassFish Server and to manage users, resources, and applications.
appclient	A command-line tool that launches the application client container and invokes the client application packaged in the application client JAR file.
capture-schema	A command-line tool to extract schema information from a database, producing a schema file that GlassFish Server can use for container-managed persistence.
package-appclient	A command-line tool to package the application client container libraries and JAR files.
Java DB database	A copy of the Java DB server.
xjc	A command-line tool to transform, or bind, a source XML schema to a set of JAXB content classes in the Java programming language.
schemagen	A command-line tool to create a schema file for each namespace referenced in your Java classes.
wsimport	A command-line tool to generate JAX-WS portable artifacts for a given WSDL file. After generation, these artifacts can be packaged in a WAR file with the WSDL and schema documents, along with the endpoint implementation, and then deployed.
wsgen	A command-line tool to read a web service endpoint class and generate all the required JAX-WS portable artifacts for web service deployment and invocation.

2

Using the Tutorial Examples

This chapter tells you everything you need to know to install, build, and run the examples.

The following topics are addressed here:

- Required Software
- Starting and Stopping GlassFish Server
- Starting the Administration Console
- Starting and Stopping the Java DB Server
- Building the Examples
- Tutorial Example Directory Structure
- Java EE 7 Maven Archetypes in the Tutorial
- Getting the Latest Updates to the Tutorial
- Debugging Java EE Applications

2.1 Required Software

The following software is required to run the examples:

- Java Platform, Standard Edition (see Section 2.1.2)
- Java EE 7 Software Development Kit (see Section 2.1.1)
- Java EE 7 Tutorial Component (see Section 2.1.3)

- NetBeans IDE (see Section 2.1.4)

- Apache Maven (see Section 2.1.5)

2.1.1 Java EE 7 Software Development Kit

GlassFish Server Open Source Edition 4 is targeted as the build and runtime environment for the tutorial examples. To build, deploy, and run the examples, you need a copy of GlassFish Server and, optionally, NetBeans IDE. To obtain GlassFish Server, you must install the Java EE 7 Software Development Kit (SDK), which you can download from http://www.oracle.com/technetwork/java/javaee/downloads/. Make sure that you download the Java EE 7 SDK, not the Java EE 7 Web Profile SDK. There are distributions of the Java EE 7 SDK with and without the Java Platform, Standard Edition 7 Development Kit.

2.1.1.1 SDK Installation Tips

Do the following during the installation of the SDK.

- Allow the installer to download and configure the Update Tool. If you access the Internet through a firewall, provide the proxy host and port.

- Configure the GlassFish Server administration user name as admin, and specify no password. This is the default setting.

- Accept the default port values for the Admin Port (4848) and the HTTP Port (8080).

- Do not select the check box to create an operating system service for the domain.

You can leave the check box to start the domain after creation selected if you wish, but this is not required.

This tutorial refers to *as-install-parent*, the directory where you install GlassFish Server. For example, the default installation directory on Microsoft Windows is C:\glassfish4, so *as-install-parent* is C:\glassfish4. GlassFish Server itself is installed in *as-install*, the glassfish directory under *as-install-parent*. So on Microsoft Windows, *as-install* is C:\glassfish4\glassfish.

After you install GlassFish Server, add the following directories to your PATH to avoid having to specify the full path when you use commands:

```
as-install-parent/bin
as-install/bin
```

2.1.2 Java Platform, Standard Edition

To build, deploy, and run the examples, you need a copy of the Java Platform, Standard Edition 7 Development Kit (JDK 7). Some distributions of the Java EE 7 SDK include JDK 7. You can download JDK 7 software separately from `http://www.oracle.com/technetwork/java/javase/downloads/`.

2.1.3 Java EE 7 Tutorial Component

The tutorial example source is contained in the tutorial component. To obtain the tutorial component, use the Update Tool.

2.1.3.1 To Obtain the Tutorial Component Using the Update Tool

1. Start the Update Tool by performing one of the following actions.

   - From the command line, enter the command `updatetool`.

   - On a Windows system, from the Start menu, choose **All Programs**, then select **Java EE 7 SDK**, then select **Start Update Tool**.

2. Expand the **Java EE 7 SDK** node.

3. Select **Available Updates**.

4. From the list, select the **Java EE 7 Tutorial** check box.

5. Click **Install**.

6. Accept the license agreement.

   After installation, the Java EE 7 Tutorial appears in the list of installed components. The tool is installed in the *as-install-parent*/`docs/javaee-tutorial` directory, which is referred to throughout the tutorial as *tut-install*. This directory contains two subdirectories: `docs` and `examples`. The `examples` directory contains subdirectories for each of the technologies discussed in the tutorial.

Next Steps

Updates to the Java EE 7 Tutorial are published periodically. For details on obtaining these updates, see Section 2.8, "Getting the Latest Updates to the Tutorial."

2.1.4 NetBeans IDE

The NetBeans integrated development environment (IDE) is a free, open-source IDE for developing Java applications, including enterprise applications. NetBeans

IDE supports the Java EE platform. You can build, package, deploy, and run the tutorial examples from within NetBeans IDE.

To run the tutorial examples, you need the latest version of NetBeans IDE. You can download NetBeans IDE from `https://netbeans.org/downloads/`. Make sure that you download the Java EE bundle.

2.1.4.1 To Install NetBeans IDE without GlassFish Server

When you install NetBeans IDE, do not install the version of GlassFish Server that comes with NetBeans IDE. To skip the installation of GlassFish Server, follow these steps.

1. On the first page of the NetBeans IDE Installer wizard, deselect the check box for GlassFish Server and click **OK**.

2. Accept both the License Agreement and the Junit License Agreement.

   A few of the tutorial examples use the Junit library, so you should install it.

3. Continue with the installation of NetBeans IDE.

2.1.4.2 To Add GlassFish Server as a Server Using NetBeans IDE

To run the tutorial examples in NetBeans IDE, you must add your GlassFish Server as a server in NetBeans IDE. Follow these instructions to add GlassFish Server to NetBeans IDE.

1. From the **Tools** menu, choose **Servers**.

2. In the Servers wizard, click **Add Server**.

3. Under **Choose Server**, select **GlassFish Server** and click **Next**.

4. Under **Server Location**, browse to the location of the Java EE 7 SDK and click **Next**.

5. Under **Domain Location**, select **Register Local Domain**.

6. Click **Finish**.

2.1.5 Apache Maven

Maven is a Java technology–based build tool developed by the Apache Software Foundation and is used to build, package, and deploy the tutorial examples. To run the tutorial examples from the command line, you need Maven 3.0 or higher. If you do not already have Maven, you can install it from:

```
http://maven.apache.org
```

Be sure to add the *maven-install*/bin directory to your path.

If you are using NetBeans IDE to build and run the examples, it includes a copy of Maven.

2.2 Starting and Stopping GlassFish Server

You can start and stop GlassFish Server using either NetBeans IDE or the command line.

2.2.1 To Start GlassFish Server Using NetBeans IDE

1. Click the **Services** tab.

2. Expand **Servers**.

3. Right-click the GlassFish Server instance and select **Start**.

2.2.2 To Stop GlassFish Server Using NetBeans IDE

To stop GlassFish Server using NetBeans IDE, right-click the GlassFish Server instance and select **Stop**.

2.2.3 To Start GlassFish Server Using the Command Line

To start GlassFish Server from the command line, open a terminal window or command prompt and execute the following:

```
asadmin start-domain --verbose
```

A **domain** is a set of one or more GlassFish Server instances managed by one administration server. The following elements are associated with a domain.

- **The GlassFish Server port number**: The default is 8080.

- **The administration server's port number**: The default is 4848.

- **An administration user name and password**: The default user name is admin, and by default no password is required.

You specify these values when you install GlassFish Server. The examples in this tutorial assume that you chose the default ports as well as the default user name and lack of password.

With no arguments, the start-domain command initiates the default domain, which is domain1. The --verbose flag causes all logging and debugging output to appear on the terminal window or command prompt. The output also goes into the server log, which is located in *domain-dir*/logs/server.log.

Or, on Windows, from the **Start** menu, choose **All Programs**, then choose **Java EE 7 SDK**, then choose **Start Application Server**.

2.2.4 To Stop GlassFish Server Using the Command Line

To stop GlassFish Server, open a terminal window or command prompt and execute:

```
asadmin stop-domain domain1
```

Or, on Windows, from the **Start** menu, choose **All Programs**, then choose **Java EE 7 SDK**, then choose **Stop Application Server**.

2.3 Starting the Administration Console

To administer GlassFish Server and manage users, resources, and Java EE applications, use the Administration Console tool. GlassFish Server must be running before you invoke the Administration Console. To start the Administration Console, open a browser at http://localhost:4848/.

Or, on Windows, from the **Start** menu, choose **All Programs**, then choose **Java EE 7 SDK**, then choose Administration Console.

2.3.1 To Start the Administration Console Using NetBeans IDE

1. Click the **Services** tab.

2. Expand **Servers**.

3. Right-click the GlassFish Server instance and select **View Domain Admin Console**.

> **Note:** NetBeans IDE uses your default web browser to open the Administration Console.

2.4 Starting and Stopping the Java DB Server

GlassFish Server includes the Java DB database server.

To start the Java DB server from the command line, open a terminal window or command prompt and execute:

```
asadmin start-database
```

To stop the Java DB server from the command line, open a terminal window or command prompt and execute:

```
asadmin stop-database
```

For information about the Java DB included with GlassFish Server, see http://www.oracle.com/technetwork/java/javadb/overview/.

2.4.1 To Start the Database Server Using NetBeans IDE

When you start GlassFish Server using NetBeans IDE, the database server starts automatically. If you ever need to start the server manually, however, follow these steps.

1. Click the **Services** tab.

2. Expand **Databases**.

3. Right-click **Java DB** and select **Start Server**.

Next Steps

To stop the database using NetBeans IDE, right-click **Java DB** and select **Stop Server**.

2.5 Building the Examples

The tutorial examples are distributed with a configuration file for either NetBeans IDE or Maven. Either NetBeans IDE or Maven may be used to build, package, deploy, and run the examples. Directions for building the examples are provided in each chapter.

2.6 Tutorial Example Directory Structure

To facilitate iterative development and keep application source files separate from compiled files, the tutorial examples use the Maven application directory structure.

Each application module has the following structure:

- `pom.xml`: Maven build file
- `src/main/java`: Java source files for the module
- `src/main/resources`: configuration files for the module, with the exception of web applications
- `src/main/webapp`: web pages, style sheets, tag files, and images (web applications only)
- `src/main/webapp/WEB-INF`: configuration files for web applications (web applications only)

When an example has multiple application modules packaged into an EAR file, its submodule directories use the following naming conventions:

- *example-name*-`app-client`: application clients
- *example-name*-`ejb`: enterprise bean JAR files
- *example-name*-`war`: web applications
- *example-name*-`ear`: enterprise applications
- *example-name*-`common`: library JAR containing components, classes, and files used by other modules

The Maven build files (`pom.xml`) distributed with the examples contain goals to compile and assemble the application into the `target` directory and deploy the archive to GlassFish Server.

2.7 Java EE 7 Maven Archetypes in the Tutorial

Some of the chapters have instructions on how to build an example application using Maven archetypes. **Archetypes** are templates for generating a particular Maven project. The Tutorial includes several Maven archetypes for generating Java EE 7 projects.

2.7.1 Installing the Tutorial Archetypes

You must install the included Maven archetypes into your local Maven repository before you can create new projects based on the archetypes. You can install the archetypes using NetBeans IDE or Maven.

2.7.1.1 Installing the Tutorial Archetypes Using NetBeans IDE

1. From the **File** menu, choose **Open Project**.

2. In the Open Project dialog box, navigate to:

   tut-install/examples

3. Select the archetypes folder.

4. Click **Open Project**.

5. In the **Projects** tab, right-click the archetypes project and select **Build**.

2.7.1.2 Installing the Tutorial Archetypes Using Maven

1. In a terminal window, go to:

   tut-install/examples/archetypes/

2. Enter the following command:

   ```
   mvn install
   ```

2.8 Getting the Latest Updates to the Tutorial

Check for any updates to the tutorial by using the Update Tool included with the Java EE 7 SDK.

2.8.1 To Update the Tutorial Using NetBeans IDE

1. Open the **Services** tab in NetBeans IDE and expand **Servers**.

2. Right-click the GlassFish Server instance and select **View Domain Update Center** to display the Update Tool.

3. Select **Available Updates** in the tree to display a list of updated packages.

4. Look for updates to the Java EE 7 Tutorial (javaee-tutorial) package.

5. If there is an updated version of the Tutorial, select **Java EE 7 Tutorial** (javaee-tutorial) and click **Install**.

2.8.2 To Update the Tutorial Using the Command Line

1. Open a terminal window and enter the following command to display the Update Tool:

   ```
   updatetool
   ```

2. Select **Available Updates** in the tree to display a list of updated packages.

3. Look for updates to the Java EE 7 Tutorial (javaee-tutorial) package.

4. If there is an updated version of the Tutorial, select **Java EE 7 Tutorial** (javaee-tutorial) and click **Install**.

2.9 Debugging Java EE Applications

This section explains how to determine what is causing an error in your application deployment or execution.

2.9.1 Using the Server Log

One way to debug applications is to look at the server log in *domain-dir*/logs/ server.log. The log contains output from GlassFish Server and your applications. You can log messages from any Java class in your application with System.out.println and the Java Logging APIs (documented at http://docs.oracle.com/javase/7/docs/technotes/guides/ logging/) and from web components with the ServletContext.log method.

If you use NetBeans IDE, logging output appears in the Output window as well as the server log.

If you start GlassFish Server with the --verbose flag, all logging and debugging output will appear on the terminal window or command prompt and the server log. If you start GlassFish Server in the background, debugging information is available only in the log. You can view the server log with a text editor or with the Administration Console log viewer.

2.9.1.1 To Use the Administration Console Log Viewer

1. Select the GlassFish Server node.

2. Click **View Log Files**.

   The log viewer opens and displays the last 40 entries.

3. To display other entries, follow these steps.

   a. Click **Modify Search**.

   b. Specify any constraints on the entries you want to see.

   c. Click **Search** at the top of the log viewer.

2.9.2 Using a Debugger

GlassFish Server supports the Java Platform Debugger Architecture (JPDA). With JPDA, you can configure GlassFish Server to communicate debugging information using a socket.

2.9.2.1 To Debug an Application Using a Debugger

1. Follow these steps to enable debugging in GlassFish Server using the Administration Console:

   a. Expand the **Configurations** node, then expand the **server-config** node.

   b. Select the **JVM Settings** node. The default debug options are set to:

   ```
   -agentlib:jdwp=transport=dt_socket,server=y,suspend=n,address=9009
   ```

   As you can see, the default debugger socket port is 9009. You can change it to a port not in use by GlassFish Server or another service.

   c. Select the **Debug Enabled** check box.

   d. Click **Save**.

2. Stop GlassFish Server and then restart it.

Part II

Enterprise Beans

Part II explores Enterprise JavaBeans components. This part contains the following chapters:

- Chapter 3, "Enterprise Beans"
- Chapter 4, "Getting Started with Enterprise Beans"
- Chapter 5, "Running the Enterprise Bean Examples"
- Chapter 6, "Using the Embedded Enterprise Bean Container"
- Chapter 7, "Using Asynchronous Method Invocation in Session Beans"

3

Enterprise Beans

Enterprise beans are Java EE components that implement Enterprise JavaBeans (EJB) technology. Enterprise beans run in the EJB container, a runtime environment within GlassFish Server (see Section 1.4.2, "Container Types"). Although transparent to the application developer, the EJB container provides system-level services, such as transactions and security, to its enterprise beans. These services enable you to quickly build and deploy enterprise beans, which form the core of transactional Java EE applications.

The following topics are addressed here:

- What Is an Enterprise Bean?
- What Is a Session Bean?
- What Is a Message-Driven Bean?
- Accessing Enterprise Beans
- The Contents of an Enterprise Bean
- Naming Conventions for Enterprise Beans
- The Lifecycles of Enterprise Beans
- Further Information about Enterprise Beans

3.1 What Is an Enterprise Bean?

Written in the Java programming language, an enterprise bean is a server-side component that encapsulates the business logic of an application. The **business logic** is the code that fulfills the purpose of the application. In an inventory control application, for example, the enterprise beans might implement the business logic in methods called `checkInventoryLevel` and `orderProduct`. By invoking these methods, clients can access the inventory services provided by the application.

3.1.1 Benefits of Enterprise Beans

For several reasons, enterprise beans simplify the development of large, distributed applications. First, because the EJB container provides system-level services to enterprise beans, the bean developer can concentrate on solving business problems. The EJB container, rather than the bean developer, is responsible for system-level services, such as transaction management and security authorization.

Second, because the beans rather than the clients contain the application's business logic, the client developer can focus on the presentation of the client. The client developer does not have to code the routines that implement business rules or access databases. As a result, the clients are thinner, a benefit that is particularly important for clients that run on small devices.

Third, because enterprise beans are portable components, the application assembler can build new applications from existing beans. Provided that they use the standard APIs, these applications can run on any compliant Java EE server.

3.1.2 When to Use Enterprise Beans

You should consider using enterprise beans if your application has any of the following requirements.

- The application must be scalable. To accommodate a growing number of users, you may need to distribute an application's components across multiple machines. Not only can the enterprise beans of an application run on different machines, but also their location will remain transparent to the clients.

- Transactions must ensure data integrity. Enterprise beans support transactions, the mechanisms that manage the concurrent access of shared objects.

- The application will have a variety of clients. With only a few lines of code, remote clients can easily locate enterprise beans. These clients can be thin, various, and numerous.

3.1.3 Types of Enterprise Beans

Table 3–1 summarizes the two types of enterprise beans. The following sections discuss each type in more detail.

Table 3–1   Enterprise Bean Types

Enterprise Bean Type	Purpose
Session	Performs a task for a client; optionally, may implement a web service
Message-driven	Acts as a listener for a particular messaging type, such as the Java Message Service API

3.2 What Is a Session Bean?

A **session bean** encapsulates business logic that can be invoked programmatically by a client over local, remote, or web service client views. To access an application that is deployed on the server, the client invokes the session bean's methods. The session bean performs work for its client, shielding it from complexity by executing business tasks inside the server.

A session bean is not persistent. (That is, its data is not saved to a database.)

For code samples, see Chapter 5, "Running the Enterprise Bean Examples."

3.2.1 Types of Session Beans

Session beans are of three types: stateful, stateless, and singleton.

3.2.1.1 Stateful Session Beans

The state of an object consists of the values of its instance variables. In a **stateful session bean**, the instance variables represent the state of a unique client/bean session. Because the client interacts ("talks") with its bean, this state is often called the **conversational state**.

As its name suggests, a session bean is similar to an interactive session. A session bean is not shared; it can have only one client, in the same way that an interactive session can have only one user. When the client terminates, its session bean appears to terminate and is no longer associated with the client.

The state is retained for the duration of the client/bean session. If the client removes the bean, the session ends and the state disappears. This transient nature of the state is not a problem, however, because when the conversation between the client and the bean ends, there is no need to retain the state.

3.2.1.2 Stateless Session Beans

A **stateless session bean** does not maintain a conversational state with the client. When a client invokes the methods of a stateless bean, the bean's instance variables may contain a state specific to that client but only for the duration of the invocation. When the method is finished, the client-specific state should not be retained. Clients may, however, change the state of instance variables in pooled stateless beans, and this state is held over to the next invocation of the pooled stateless bean. Except during method invocation, all instances of a stateless bean are equivalent, allowing the EJB container to assign an instance to any client. That is, the state of a stateless session bean should apply across all clients.

Because they can support multiple clients, stateless session beans can offer better scalability for applications that require large numbers of clients. Typically, an application requires fewer stateless session beans than stateful session beans to support the same number of clients.

A stateless session bean can implement a web service, but a stateful session bean cannot.

3.2.1.3 Singleton Session Beans

A **singleton session bean** is instantiated once per application and exists for the lifecycle of the application. Singleton session beans are designed for circumstances in which a single enterprise bean instance is shared across and concurrently accessed by clients.

Singleton session beans offer similar functionality to stateless session beans but differ from them in that there is only one singleton session bean per application, as opposed to a pool of stateless session beans, any of which may respond to a client request. Like stateless session beans, singleton session beans can implement web service endpoints.

Singleton session beans maintain their state between client invocations but are not required to maintain their state across server crashes or shutdowns.

Applications that use a singleton session bean may specify that the singleton should be instantiated upon application startup, which allows the singleton to perform initialization tasks for the application. The singleton may perform cleanup tasks on application shutdown as well, because the singleton will operate throughout the lifecycle of the application.

3.2.2 When to Use Session Beans

Stateful session beans are appropriate if any of the following conditions are true.

- The bean's state represents the interaction between the bean and a specific client.

- The bean needs to hold information about the client across method invocations.

- The bean mediates between the client and the other components of the application, presenting a simplified view to the client.

- Behind the scenes, the bean manages the work flow of several enterprise beans.

To improve performance, you might choose a stateless session bean if it has any of these traits.

- The bean's state has no data for a specific client.

- In a single method invocation, the bean performs a generic task for all clients. For example, you might use a stateless session bean to send an email that confirms an online order.

- The bean implements a web service.

Singleton session beans are appropriate in the following circumstances.

- State needs to be shared across the application.

- A single enterprise bean needs to be accessed by multiple threads concurrently.

- The application needs an enterprise bean to perform tasks upon application startup and shutdown.

- The bean implements a web service.

3.3 What Is a Message-Driven Bean?

A **message-driven bean** is an enterprise bean that allows Java EE applications to process messages asynchronously. This type of bean normally acts as a JMS message listener, which is similar to an event listener but receives JMS messages instead of events. The messages can be sent by any Java EE component (an application client, another enterprise bean, or a web component) or by a JMS application or system that does not use Java EE technology. Message-driven beans can process JMS messages or other kinds of messages.

3.3.1 What Makes Message-Driven Beans Different from Session Beans?

The most visible difference between message-driven beans and session beans is that clients do not access message-driven beans through interfaces. Interfaces are described in Section 3.4, "Accessing Enterprise Beans." Unlike a session bean, a message-driven bean has only a bean class.

In several respects, a message-driven bean resembles a stateless session bean.

- A message-driven bean's instances retain no data or conversational state for a specific client.

- All instances of a message-driven bean are equivalent, allowing the EJB container to assign a message to any message-driven bean instance. The container can pool these instances to allow streams of messages to be processed concurrently.

- A single message-driven bean can process messages from multiple clients.

The instance variables of the message-driven bean instance can contain some state across the handling of client messages, such as a JMS API connection, an open database connection, or an object reference to an enterprise bean object.

Client components do not locate message-driven beans and invoke methods directly on them. Instead, a client accesses a message-driven bean through, for example, JMS by sending messages to the message destination for which the message-driven bean class is the `MessageListener`. You assign a message-driven bean's destination during deployment by using GlassFish Server resources.

Message-driven beans have the following characteristics.

- They execute upon receipt of a single client message.

- They are invoked asynchronously.

- They are relatively short-lived.

- They do not represent directly shared data in the database, but they can access and update this data.

- They can be transaction-aware.

- They are stateless.

When a message arrives, the container calls the message-driven bean's `onMessage` method to process the message. The `onMessage` method normally casts the message to one of the five JMS message types and handles it in accordance with the application's business logic. The `onMessage` method can call helper methods or can invoke a session bean to process the information in the message or to store it in a database.

A message can be delivered to a message-driven bean within a transaction context, so all operations within the onMessage method are part of a single transaction. If message processing is rolled back, the message will be redelivered. For more information, see Section 17.6, "Receiving Messages Asynchronously Using a Message-Driven Bean," and Chapter 22, "Transactions."

3.3.2 When to Use Message-Driven Beans

Session beans allow you to send JMS messages and to receive them synchronously but not asynchronously. To avoid tying up server resources, do not to use blocking synchronous receives in a server-side component; in general, JMS messages should not be sent or received synchronously. To receive messages asynchronously, use a message-driven bean.

3.4 Accessing Enterprise Beans

> **Note:** The material in this section applies only to session beans and not to message-driven beans. Because they have a different programming model, message-driven beans do not have interfaces or no-interface views that define client access.

Clients access enterprise beans either through a no-interface view or through a business interface. A **no-interface view** of an enterprise bean exposes the public methods of the enterprise bean implementation class to clients. Clients using the no-interface view of an enterprise bean may invoke any public methods in the enterprise bean implementation class or any superclasses of the implementation class. A **business interface** is a standard Java programming language interface that contains the business methods of the enterprise bean.

A client can access a session bean only through the methods defined in the bean's business interface or through the public methods of an enterprise bean that has a no-interface view. The business interface or no-interface view defines the client's view of an enterprise bean. All other aspects of the enterprise bean (method implementations and deployment settings) are hidden from the client.

Well-designed interfaces and no-interface views simplify the development and maintenance of Java EE applications. Not only do clean interfaces and no-interface views shield the clients from any complexities in the EJB tier, but they also allow the enterprise beans to change internally without affecting the clients. For example, if you change the implementation of a session bean business method, you won't have to alter the client code. But if you were to change the method definitions in the interfaces, you might have to modify the client code as well. Therefore, it is important that you design the interfaces and no-interface views carefully to isolate your clients from possible changes in the enterprise beans.

Session beans can have more than one business interface. Session beans should, but are not required to, implement their business interface or interfaces.

3.4.1 Using Enterprise Beans in Clients

The client of an enterprise bean obtains a reference to an instance of an enterprise bean through either **dependency injection**, using Java programming language annotations, or **JNDI lookup**, using the Java Naming and Directory Interface syntax to find the enterprise bean instance.

Dependency injection is the simplest way of obtaining an enterprise bean reference. Clients that run within a Java EE server-managed environment, JavaServer Faces web applications, JAX-RS web services, other enterprise beans, or Java EE application clients support dependency injection using the `javax.ejb.EJB` annotation.

Applications that run outside a Java EE server-managed environment, such as Java SE applications, must perform an explicit lookup. JNDI supports a global syntax for identifying Java EE components to simplify this explicit lookup.

3.4.1.1 Portable JNDI Syntax

Three JNDI namespaces are used for portable JNDI lookups: `java:global`, `java:module`, and `java:app`.

- The `java:global` JNDI namespace is the portable way of finding remote enterprise beans using JNDI lookups. JNDI addresses are of the following form:

  `java:global[/application-name]/module-name/`
  `enterprise-bean-name[/interface-name]`

  Application name and module name default to the name of the application and module minus the file extension. Application names are required only if the application is packaged within an EAR. The interface name is required only if the enterprise bean implements more than one business interface.

- The `java:module` namespace is used to look up local enterprise beans within the same module. JNDI addresses using the `java:module` namespace are of the following form:

  `java:module/enterprise-bean-name/[interface-name]`

The interface name is required only if the enterprise bean implements more than one business interface.

- The `java:app` namespace is used to look up local enterprise beans packaged within the same application. That is, the enterprise bean is packaged within an EAR file containing multiple Java EE modules. JNDI addresses using the `java:app` namespace are of the following form:

  ```
  java:app[/module-name]/enterprise-bean-name[/interface-name]
  ```

  The module name is optional. The interface name is required only if the enterprise bean implements more than one business interface.

For example, if an enterprise bean, `MyBean`, is packaged within the web application archive `myApp.war`, the module name is `myApp`. The portable JNDI name is `java:module/MyBean`. An equivalent JNDI name using the `java:global` namespace is `java:global/myApp/MyBean`.

3.4.2 Deciding on Remote or Local Access

When you design a Java EE application, one of the first decisions you make is the type of client access allowed by the enterprise beans: remote, local, or web service.

Whether to allow local or remote access depends on the following factors.

- **Tight or loose coupling of related beans**: Tightly coupled beans depend on one another. For example, if a session bean that processes sales orders calls a session bean that emails a confirmation message to the customer, these beans are tightly coupled. Tightly coupled beans are good candidates for local access. Because they fit together as a logical unit, they typically call each other often and would benefit from the increased performance that is possible with local access.

- **Type of client**: If an enterprise bean is accessed by application clients, it should allow remote access. In a production environment, these clients almost always run on machines other than those on which GlassFish Server is running. If an enterprise bean's clients are web components or other enterprise beans, the type of access depends on how you want to distribute your components.

- **Component distribution**: Java EE applications are scalable because their server-side components can be distributed across multiple machines. In a distributed application, for example, the server that the web components run on may not be the one on which the enterprise beans they access are deployed. In this distributed scenario, the enterprise beans should allow remote access.

- **Performance**: Owing to such factors as network latency, remote calls may be slower than local calls. On the other hand, if you distribute components among different servers, you may improve the application's overall performance. Both of these statements are generalizations; performance can vary in different operational environments. Nevertheless, you should keep in mind how your application design might affect performance.

If you aren't sure which type of access an enterprise bean should have, choose remote access. This decision gives you more flexibility. In the future, you can distribute your components to accommodate the growing demands on your application.

Although it is uncommon, it is possible for an enterprise bean to allow both remote and local access. If this is the case, either the business interface of the bean must be explicitly designated as a business interface by being decorated with the `@Remote` or `@Local` annotations, or the bean class must explicitly designate the business interfaces by using the `@Remote` and `@Local` annotations. The same business interface cannot be both a local and a remote business interface.

3.4.3 Local Clients

A local client has these characteristics.

- It must run in the same application as the enterprise bean it accesses.
- It can be a web component or another enterprise bean.
- To the local client, the location of the enterprise bean it accesses is not transparent.

The no-interface view of an enterprise bean is a local view. The public methods of the enterprise bean implementation class are exposed to local clients that access the no-interface view of the enterprise bean. Enterprise beans that use the no-interface view do not implement a business interface.

The **local business interface** defines the bean's business and lifecycle methods. If the bean's business interface is not decorated with `@Local` or `@Remote`, and if the bean class does not specify the interface using `@Local` or `@Remote`, the business interface is by default a local interface.

To build an enterprise bean that allows only local access, you may, but are not required to, do one of the following.

- Create an enterprise bean implementation class that does not implement a business interface, indicating that the bean exposes a no-interface view to clients. For example:

```
@Session
public class MyBean { ... }
```

- Annotate the business interface of the enterprise bean as a `@Local` interface. For example:

```
@Local
public interface InterfaceName { ... }
```

- Specify the interface by decorating the bean class with `@Local` and specify the interface name. For example:

```
@Local(InterfaceName.class)
public class BeanName implements InterfaceName { ... }
```

3.4.3.1 Accessing Local Enterprise Beans Using the No-Interface View

Client access to an enterprise bean that exposes a local, no-interface view is accomplished through either dependency injection or JNDI lookup.

- To obtain a reference to the no-interface view of an enterprise bean through dependency injection, use the `javax.ejb.EJB` annotation and specify the enterprise bean's implementation class:

```
@EJB
ExampleBean exampleBean;
```

- To obtain a reference to the no-interface view of an enterprise bean through JNDI lookup, use the `javax.naming.InitialContext` interface's `lookup` method:

```
ExampleBean exampleBean = (ExampleBean)
        InitialContext.lookup("java:module/ExampleBean");
```

Clients *do not* use the `new` operator to obtain a new instance of an enterprise bean that uses a no-interface view.

3.4.3.2 Accessing Local Enterprise Beans That Implement Business Interfaces

Client access to enterprise beans that implement local business interfaces is accomplished through either dependency injection or JNDI lookup.

- To obtain a reference to the local business interface of an enterprise bean through dependency injection, use the `javax.ejb.EJB` annotation and specify the enterprise bean's local business interface name:

```
@EJB
Example example;
```

- To obtain a reference to a local business interface of an enterprise bean through JNDI lookup, use the `javax.naming.InitialContext` interface's `lookup` method:

```
ExampleLocal example = (ExampleLocal)
        InitialContext.lookup("java:module/ExampleLocal");
```

3.4.4 Remote Clients

A remote client of an enterprise bean has the following traits.

- It can run on a different machine and a different JVM from the enterprise bean it accesses. (It is not required to run on a different JVM.)

- It can be a web component, an application client, or another enterprise bean.

- To a remote client, the location of the enterprise bean is transparent.

- The enterprise bean must implement a business interface. That is, remote clients *may not* access an enterprise bean through a no-interface view.

To create an enterprise bean that allows remote access, you must either

- Decorate the business interface of the enterprise bean with the `@Remote` annotation:

```
@Remote
public interface InterfaceName { ... }
```

- Or decorate the bean class with `@Remote`, specifying the business interface or interfaces:

```
@Remote(InterfaceName.class)
public class BeanName implements InterfaceName { ... }
```

The **remote interface** defines the business and lifecycle methods that are specific to the bean. For example, the remote interface of a bean named BankAccountBean might have business methods named `deposit` and `credit`. Figure 3–1 shows how the interface controls the client's view of an enterprise bean.

Figure 3–1   Interfaces for an Enterprise Bean with Remote Access

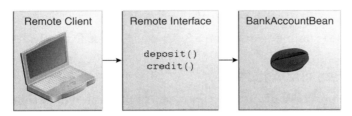

Client access to an enterprise bean that implements a remote business interface is accomplished through either dependency injection or JNDI lookup.

- To obtain a reference to the remote business interface of an enterprise bean through dependency injection, use the `javax.ejb.EJB` annotation and specify the enterprise bean's remote business interface name:

```
@EJB
Example example;
```

- To obtain a reference to a remote business interface of an enterprise bean through JNDI lookup, use the `javax.naming.InitialContext` interface's `lookup` method:

```
ExampleRemote example = (ExampleRemote)
        InitialContext.lookup("java:global/myApp/ExampleRemote");
```

3.4.5 Web Service Clients

A web service client can access a Java EE application in two ways. First, the client can access a web service created with JAX-WS. (For more information on JAX-WS, see Chapter 28, "Building Web Services with JAX-WS," in *The Java EE 7 Tutorial, Volume 1*.) Second, a web service client can invoke the business methods of a stateless session bean. Message beans cannot be accessed by web service clients.

Provided that it uses the correct protocols (SOAP, HTTP, WSDL), any web service client can access a stateless session bean, whether or not the client is written in the Java programming language. The client doesn't even "know" what technology implements the service: stateless session bean, JAX-WS, or some other technology. In addition, enterprise beans and web components can be clients of web services. This flexibility enables you to integrate Java EE applications with web services.

A web service client accesses a stateless session bean through the bean's web service endpoint implementation class. By default, all public methods in the bean class are accessible to web service clients. The @WebMethod annotation may be used to customize the behavior of web service methods. If the @WebMethod annotation is used to decorate the bean class's methods, only those methods decorated with @WebMethod are exposed to web service clients.

For a code example, see Section 5.3, "A Web Service Example: helloservice."

3.4.6 Method Parameters and Access

The type of access affects the parameters of the bean methods that are called by clients. The following sections apply not only to method parameters but also to method return values.

3.4.6.1 Isolation

The parameters of remote calls are more isolated than those of local calls. With remote calls, the client and the bean operate on different copies of a parameter object. If the client changes the value of the object, the value of the copy in the bean does not change. This layer of isolation can help protect the bean if the client accidentally modifies the data.

In a local call, both the client and the bean can modify the same parameter object. In general, you should not rely on this side effect of local calls. Perhaps someday you will want to distribute your components, replacing the local calls with remote ones.

As with remote clients, web service clients operate on different copies of parameters than does the bean that implements the web service.

3.4.6.2 Granularity of Accessed Data

Because remote calls are likely to be slower than local calls, the parameters in remote methods should be relatively coarse-grained. A coarse-grained object contains more data than a fine-grained one, so fewer access calls are required. For the same reason, the parameters of the methods called by web service clients should also be coarse-grained.

3.5 The Contents of an Enterprise Bean

To develop an enterprise bean, you must provide the following files.

- **Enterprise bean class**: Implements the business methods of the enterprise bean and any lifecycle callback methods.

- **Business interfaces**: Define the business methods implemented by the enterprise bean class. A business interface is not required if the enterprise bean exposes a local, no-interface view.

- **Helper classes**: Other classes needed by the enterprise bean class, such as exception and utility classes.

Package the programming artifacts in the preceding list either into an EJB JAR file (a stand-alone module that stores the enterprise bean) or within a web application archive (WAR) module. For more information, see Section 5.2.1, "Packaging Enterprise Beans in EJB JAR Modules," and Section 5.2.2, "Packaging Enterprise Beans in WAR Modules," both in *The Java EE 7 Tutorial, Volume 1.*

3.6 Naming Conventions for Enterprise Beans

Because enterprise beans are composed of multiple parts, it's useful to follow a naming convention for your applications. Table 3–2 summarizes the conventions for the example beans in this tutorial.

Table 3–2   Naming Conventions for Enterprise Beans

Item	Syntax	Example
Enterprise bean name	*name*Bean	AccountBean
Enterprise bean class	*name*Bean	AccountBean
Business interface	*name*	Account

3.7 The Lifecycles of Enterprise Beans

An enterprise bean goes through various stages during its lifetime, or lifecycle. Each type of enterprise bean (stateful session, stateless session, singleton session, or message-driven) has a different lifecycle.

The descriptions that follow refer to methods that are explained along with the code examples in the next two chapters. If you are new to enterprise beans, you should skip this section and run the code examples first.

3.7.1 The Lifecycle of a Stateful Session Bean

Figure 3–2 illustrates the stages that a stateful session bean passes through during its lifetime. The client initiates the lifecycle by obtaining a reference to a stateful session bean. The container performs any dependency injection and then invokes the method annotated with @PostConstruct, if any. The bean is now ready to have its business methods invoked by the client.

Figure 3–2   Lifecycle of a Stateful Session Bean

① Create

② Dependency injection, if any

③ PostConstruct callback, if any

④ Init method, or ejbCreate<METHOD>, if any

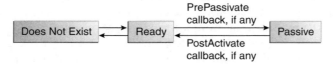

① Remove

② PreDestroy callback, if any

While in the ready stage, the EJB container may decide to deactivate, or **passivate**, the bean by moving it from memory to secondary storage. (Typically, the EJB container uses a least-recently-used algorithm to select a bean for passivation.) The EJB container invokes the method annotated @PrePassivate, if any, immediately before passivating it. If a client invokes a business method on the bean while it is in the passive stage, the EJB container activates the bean, calls the method annotated @PostActivate, if any, and then moves it to the ready stage.

At the end of the lifecycle, the client invokes a method annotated @Remove, and the EJB container calls the method annotated @PreDestroy, if any. The bean's instance is then ready for garbage collection.

Your code controls the invocation of only one lifecycle method: the method annotated @Remove. All other methods in Figure 3–2 are invoked by the EJB container. See Chapter 23, "Resource Adapters and Contracts," for more information.

3.7.2 The Lifecycle of a Stateless Session Bean

Because a stateless session bean is never passivated, its lifecycle has only two stages: nonexistent and ready for the invocation of business methods. Figure 3–3 illustrates the stages of a stateless session bean.

Figure 3–3   Lifecycle of a Stateless or Singleton Session Bean

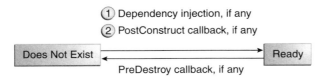

The EJB container typically creates and maintains a pool of stateless session beans, beginning the stateless session bean's lifecycle. The container performs any dependency injection and then invokes the method annotated @PostConstruct, if it exists. The bean is now ready to have its business methods invoked by a client.

At the end of the lifecycle, the EJB container calls the method annotated @PreDestroy, if it exists. The bean's instance is then ready for garbage collection.

3.7.3 The Lifecycle of a Singleton Session Bean

Like a stateless session bean, a singleton session bean is never passivated and has only two stages, nonexistent and ready for the invocation of business methods, as shown in Figure 3–3.

The EJB container initiates the singleton session bean lifecycle by creating the singleton instance. This occurs upon application deployment if the singleton is annotated with the @Startup annotation. The container performs any dependency injection and then invokes the method annotated @PostConstruct, if it exists. The singleton session bean is now ready to have its business methods invoked by the client.

At the end of the lifecycle, the EJB container calls the method annotated @PreDestroy, if it exists. The singleton session bean is now ready for garbage collection.

3.7.4 The Lifecycle of a Message-Driven Bean

Figure 3–4 illustrates the stages in the lifecycle of a message-driven bean.

Figure 3–4   Lifecycle of a Message-Driven Bean

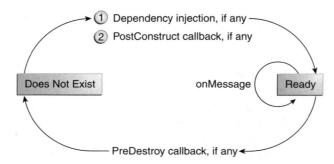

The EJB container usually creates a pool of message-driven bean instances. For each instance, the EJB container performs these tasks.

1. If the message-driven bean uses dependency injection, the container injects these references before instantiating the instance.

2. The container calls the method annotated @PostConstruct, if any.

Like a stateless session bean, a message-driven bean is never passivated and has only two states: nonexistent and ready to receive messages.

At the end of the lifecycle, the container calls the method annotated @PreDestroy, if any. The bean's instance is then ready for garbage collection.

3.8 Further Information about Enterprise Beans

For more information on Enterprise JavaBeans technology, see

- Enterprise JavaBeans 3.2 specification:

    http://www.jcp.org/en/jsr/detail?id=345

- Enterprise JavaBeans 3.2 specification project:

    https://java.net/projects/ejb-spec/

4

Getting Started with Enterprise Beans

This chapter shows how to develop, deploy, and run a simple Java EE application named `converter` that uses an EJB for its business logic. The purpose of `converter` is to calculate currency conversions among Japanese yen, euros, and US dollars. The `converter` application consists of an enterprise bean, which performs the calculations, and a web client.

Here's an overview of the steps you'll follow in this chapter.

1. Create the enterprise bean: `ConverterBean`.

2. Create the web client.

3. Deploy `converter` onto the server.

4. Using a browser, run the web client.

Before proceeding, make sure that you've done the following:

- Read Chapter 1, "Overview"

- Become familiar with enterprise beans (see Chapter 3, "Enterprise Beans")

- Started the server (see Section 2.2, "Starting and Stopping GlassFish Server")

The following topics are addressed here:

- Creating the Enterprise Bean

- Modifying the Java EE Application

4.1 Creating the Enterprise Bean

The enterprise bean in our example is a stateless session bean called
ConverterBean. The source code for ConverterBean is in the *tut-install*/examples/
ejb/converter/src/main/java/ directory.

Creating ConverterBean requires these steps:

1. Coding the bean's implementation class (the source code is provided)

2. Compiling the source code

4.1.1 Coding the Enterprise Bean Class

The enterprise bean class for this example is called ConverterBean. This class
implements two business methods: dollarToYen and yenToEuro. Because the
enterprise bean class doesn't implement a business interface, the enterprise bean
exposes a local, no-interface view. The public methods in the enterprise bean class
are available to clients that obtain a reference to ConverterBean. The source code
for the ConverterBean class is as follows:

```
package javaeetutorial.converter.ejb;

import java.math.BigDecimal;
import javax.ejb.Stateless;

@Stateless
public class ConverterBean {
    private final BigDecimal yenRate = new BigDecimal("83.0602");
    private final BigDecimal euroRate = new BigDecimal("0.0093016");

    public BigDecimal dollarToYen(BigDecimal dollars) {
        BigDecimal result = dollars.multiply(yenRate);
        return result.setScale(2, BigDecimal.ROUND_UP);
    }

    public BigDecimal yenToEuro(BigDecimal yen) {
        BigDecimal result = yen.multiply(euroRate);
        return result.setScale(2, BigDecimal.ROUND_UP);
    }
}
```

Note the @Stateless annotation decorating the enterprise bean class. This
annotation lets the container know that ConverterBean is a stateless session bean.

4.1.2 Creating the converter Web Client

The web client is contained in the following servlet class under the *tut-install/* `examples/ejb/converter/src/main/java/` directory:

`converter/web/ConverterServlet.java`

A Java servlet is a web component that responds to HTTP requests.

The `ConverterServlet` class uses dependency injection to obtain a reference to `ConverterBean`. The `javax.ejb.EJB` annotation is added to the declaration of the private member variable `converter`, which is of type `ConverterBean`. `ConverterBean` exposes a local, no-interface view, so the enterprise bean implementation class is the variable type:

```
@WebServlet(urlPatterns="/")
public class ConverterServlet extends HttpServlet {
  @EJB
  ConverterBean converter;
  ...
}
```

When the user enters an amount to be converted to yen and euro, the amount is retrieved from the request parameters; then the `ConverterBean.dollarToYen` and the `ConverterBean.yenToEuro` methods are called:

```
...
try {
  String amount = request.getParameter("amount");
  if (amount != null && amount.length()> 0) {
    // convert the amount to a BigDecimal from the request parameter
    BigDecimal d = new BigDecimal(amount);
    // call the ConverterBean.dollarToYen() method to get the amount
    // in Yen
    BigDecimal yenAmount = converter.dollarToYen(d);

    // call the ConverterBean.yenToEuro() method to get the amount
    // in Euros
    BigDecimal euroAmount = converter.yenToEuro(yenAmount);
    ...
  }
  ...
}
```

The results are displayed to the user.

4.1.3 Running the converter Example

Now you are ready to compile the enterprise bean class (`ConverterBean.java`) and the servlet class (`ConverterServlet.java`) and to package the compiled classes into a WAR file. You can use either NetBeans IDE or Maven to build, package, deploy, and run the `converter` example.

4.1.3.1 To Run the converter Example Using NetBeans IDE

1. Make sure that GlassFish Server has been started (see Section 2.2, "Starting and Stopping GlassFish Server").

2. From the **File** menu, choose **Open Project**.

3. In the Open Project dialog box, navigate to:

   tut-install/examples/ejb

4. Select the `converter` folder.

5. Click **Open Project**.

6. In the **Projects** tab, right-click the `converter` project and select **Build**.

7. Open a web browser to the following URL:

   http://localhost:8080/converter

8. On the Servlet ConverterServlet page, enter `100` in the field and click **Submit**.

   A second page opens, showing the converted values.

4.1.3.2 To Run the converter Example Using Maven

1. Make sure that GlassFish Server has been started (see Section 2.2, "Starting and Stopping GlassFish Server").

2. In a terminal window, go to:

   tut-install/examples/ejb/converter/

3. Enter the following command:

   mvn install

   This command compiles the source files for the enterprise bean and the servlet, packages the project into a WAR module (`converter.war`), and deploys the WAR to the server. For more information about Maven, see Section 2.5, "Building the Examples."

4. Open a web browser to the following URL:

`http://localhost:8080/converter`

5. On the Servlet ConverterServlet page, enter `100` in the field and click **Submit**.

A second page opens, showing the converted values.

4.2 Modifying the Java EE Application

GlassFish Server supports iterative development. Whenever you make a change to a Java EE application, you must redeploy the application.

4.2.1 To Modify a Class File

To modify a class file in an enterprise bean, you change the source code, recompile it, and redeploy the application. For example, to update the exchange rate in the `dollarToYen` business method of the `ConverterBean` class, you would follow these steps.

To modify `ConverterServlet`, the procedure is the same.

1. Edit `ConverterBean.java` and save the file.

2. Recompile the source file.

   ■ To recompile `ConverterBean.java` in NetBeans IDE, right-click the `converter` project and select **Run**.

   This recompiles the `ConverterBean.java` file, replaces the old class file in the build directory, and redeploys the application to GlassFish Server.

   ■ Recompile `ConverterBean.java` using Maven:

   a. In a terminal window, go to the *tut-install*/`examples/ejb/converter/` directory.

   b. Enter the following command:

   `mvn install`

   This command repackages and deploys the application.

5

Running the Enterprise Bean Examples

This chapter describes the EJB examples. Session beans provide a simple but powerful way to encapsulate business logic within an application. They can be accessed from remote Java clients, web service clients, and components running in the same server.

In Chapter 4, "Getting Started with Enterprise Beans," you built a stateless session bean named `ConverterBean`. This chapter examines the source code of four more session beans:

- `CartBean`: a stateful session bean that is accessed by a remote client

- `CounterBean`: a singleton session bean

- `HelloServiceBean`: a stateless session bean that implements a web service

- `TimerSessionBean`: a stateless session bean that sets a timer

The following topics are addressed here:

- The cart Example

- A Singleton Session Bean Example: counter

- A Web Service Example: helloservice

- Using the Timer Service

- Handling Exceptions

5.1 The cart Example

The cart example represents a shopping cart in an online bookstore and uses a stateful session bean to manage the operations of the shopping cart. The bean's client can add a book to the cart, remove a book, or retrieve the cart's contents. To assemble `cart`, you need the following code:

- Session bean class (`CartBean`)
- Remote business interface (`Cart`)

All session beans require a session bean class. All enterprise beans that permit remote access must have a remote business interface. To meet the needs of a specific application, an enterprise bean may also need some helper classes. The `CartBean` session bean uses two helper classes, `BookException` and `IdVerifier`, which are discussed in Section 5.1.4, "Helper Classes."

The source code for this example is in the *tut-install*/examples/ejb/cart/ directory.

5.1.1 The Business Interface

The `Cart` business interface is a plain Java interface that defines all the business methods implemented in the bean class. If the bean class implements a single interface, that interface is assumed to the business interface. The business interface is a local interface unless it is annotated with the `javax.ejb.Remote` annotation; the `javax.ejb.Local` annotation is optional in this case.

The bean class may implement more than one interface. In that case, the business interfaces must either be explicitly annotated `@Local` or `@Remote` or be specified by decorating the bean class with `@Local` or `@Remote`. However, the following interfaces are excluded when determining whether the bean class implements more than one interface:

- `java.io.Serializable`
- `java.io.Externalizable`
- Any of the interfaces defined by the `javax.ejb` package

The source code for the `Cart` business interface is as follows:

```
package javaeetutorial.cart.ejb;

import cart.util.BookException;
import java.util.List;
import javax.ejb.Remote;

@Remote
public interface Cart {
    public void initialize(String person) throws BookException;
    public void initialize(String person, String id) throws BookException;
    public void addBook(String title);
```

```
    public void removeBook(String title) throws BookException;
    public List<String> getContents();
    public void remove();
}
```

5.1.2 Session Bean Class

The session bean class for this example is called CartBean. Like any stateful session bean, the CartBean class must meet the following requirements.

- The class is annotated @Stateful.

- The class implements the business methods defined in the business interface.

Stateful session beans may also do the following.

- Implement the business interface, a plain Java interface. It is good practice to implement the bean's business interface.

- Implement any optional lifecycle callback methods, annotated @PostConstruct, @PreDestroy, @PostActivate, and @PrePassivate.

- Implement any optional business methods annotated @Remove.

The source code for the CartBean class is as follows:

```
package javaeetutorial.cart.ejb;

import java.io.Serializable;
import java.util.ArrayList;
import java.util.List;
import javaeetutorial.cart.util.BookException;
import javaeetutorial.cart.util.IdVerifier;
import javax.ejb.Remove;
import javax.ejb.Stateful;

@Stateful
public class CartBean implements Cart {
    String customerId;
    String customerName;
    List<String> contents;

    @Override
    public void initialize(String person) throws BookException {
        if (person == null) {
            throw new BookException("Null person not allowed.");
        } else {
            customerName = person;
        }
```

```
            customerId = "0";
            contents = new ArrayList<>();
        }

        @Override
        public void initialize(String person, String id)
                    throws BookException {
            if (person == null) {
                throw new BookException("Null person not allowed.");
            } else {
                customerName = person;
            }

            IdVerifier idChecker = new IdVerifier();
            if (idChecker.validate(id)) {
                customerId = id;
            } else {
                throw new BookException("Invalid id: " + id);
            }

            contents = new ArrayList<>();
        }

        @Override
        public void addBook(String title) {
            contents.add(title);
        }

        @Override
        public void removeBook(String title) throws BookException {
            boolean result = contents.remove(title);
            if (result == false) {
                throw new BookException("\"" + title + " not in cart.");
            }
        }

        @Override
        public List<String> getContents() {
            return contents;
        }

        @Remove
        @Override
        public void remove() {
            contents = null;
        }
    }
```

5.1.2.1 Lifecycle Callback Methods

A method in the bean class may be declared as a lifecycle callback method by annotating the method with the following annotations.

- `javax.annotation.PostConstruct`: Methods annotated with `@PostConstruct` are invoked by the container on newly constructed bean instances after all dependency injection has completed and before the first business method is invoked on the enterprise bean.

- `javax.annotation.PreDestroy`: Methods annotated with `@PreDestroy` are invoked after any method annotated `@Remove` has completed and before the container removes the enterprise bean instance.

- `javax.ejb.PostActivate`: Methods annotated with `@PostActivate` are invoked by the container after the container moves the bean from secondary storage to active status.

- `javax.ejb.PrePassivate`: Methods annotated with `@PrePassivate` are invoked by the container before it passivates the enterprise bean, meaning that the container temporarily removes the bean from the environment and saves it to secondary storage.

Lifecycle callback methods must return `void` and have no parameters.

5.1.2.2 Business Methods

The primary purpose of a session bean is to run business tasks for the client. The client invokes business methods on the object reference it gets from dependency injection or JNDI lookup. From the client's perspective, the business methods appear to run locally, although they run remotely in the session bean. The following code snippet shows how the `CartClient` program invokes the business methods:

```
cart.initialize("Duke DeEarl", "123");
...
cart.addBook("Bel Canto");
...
List<String> bookList = cart.getContents();
...
cart.removeBook("Gravity's Rainbow");
```

The `CartBean` class implements the business methods in the following code:

```
@Override
public void addBook(String title) {
   contents.add(title);
}
```

```
@Override
public void removeBook(String title) throws BookException {
    boolean result = contents.remove(title);
    if (result == false) {
        throw new BookException("\"" + title + "not in cart.");
    }
}

@Override
public List<String> getContents() {
    return contents;
}
```

The signature of a business method must conform to these rules.

- The method name must not begin with ejb, to avoid conflicts with callback methods defined by the EJB architecture. For example, you cannot call a business method ejbCreate or ejbActivate.

- The access control modifier must be public.

- If the bean allows remote access through a remote business interface, the arguments and return types must be legal types for the Java Remote Method Invocation (RMI) API.

- If the bean is a JAX-WS web service endpoint, the arguments and return types for the methods annotated @WebMethod must be legal types for JAX-WS.

- If the bean is a JAX-RS resource, the arguments and return types for the resource methods must be legal types for JAX-RS.

- The modifier must not be static or final.

The throws clause can include exceptions that you define for your application. The removeBook method, for example, throws a BookException if the book is not in the cart.

To indicate a system-level problem, such as the inability to connect to a database, a business method should throw a javax.ejb.EJBException. The container will not wrap application exceptions, such as BookException. Because EJBException is a subclass of RuntimeException, you do not need to include it in the throws clause of the business method.

5.1.3 The @Remove Method

Business methods annotated with javax.ejb.Remove in the stateful session bean class can be invoked by enterprise bean clients to remove the bean instance. The container will remove the enterprise bean after a @Remove method completes, either normally or abnormally.

In CartBean, the remove method is a @Remove method:

```
@Remove
@Override
public void remove() {
    contents = null;
}
```

5.1.4 Helper Classes

The CartBean session bean has two helper classes: BookException and IdVerifier. The BookException is thrown by the removeBook method, and the IdVerifier validates the customerId in one of the create methods. Helper classes may reside in an EJB JAR file that contains the enterprise bean class; a WAR file if the enterprise bean is packaged within a WAR; or an EAR file that contains an EJB JAR file, a WAR file, or a separate library JAR file. In cart, the helper classes are included in a library JAR used by the application client and the EJB JAR file.

5.1.5 Running the cart Example

Now you are ready to compile the remote interface (Cart.java), the enterprise bean class (CartBean.java), the client class (CartClient.java), and the helper classes (BookException.java and IdVerifier.java).

You can use either NetBeans IDE or Maven to build, package, deploy, and run the cart application.

5.1.5.1 To Run the cart Example Using NetBeans IDE

1. Make sure that GlassFish Server has been started (see Section 2.2, "Starting and Stopping GlassFish Server").

2. From the **File** menu, choose **Open Project**.

3. In the Open Project dialog box, navigate to:

   tut-install/examples/ejb

4. Select the cart folder.

5. Select the **Open Required Projects** check box.

6. Click **Open Project**.

7. In the **Projects** tab, right-click the `cart` project and select **Build**.

   This builds and packages the application into `cart.ear`, located in *tut-install/*
   `examples/ejb/cart/cart-ear/target/`, and deploys this EAR file to your
   GlassFish Server instance.

   You will see the output of the `cart-app-client` application client in the
   Output tab:

   ```
   . . .
   Retrieving book title from cart: Infinite Jest
   Retrieving book title from cart: Bel Canto
   Retrieving book title from cart: Kafka on the Shore
   Removing "Gravity's Rainbow" from cart.
   Caught a BookException: "Gravity's Rainbow" not in cart.
   ```

5.1.5.2 To Run the cart Example Using Maven

1. Make sure that GlassFish Server has been started (see Section 2.2, "Starting
   and Stopping GlassFish Server").

2. In a terminal window, go to:

   tut-install/examples/ejb/cart/

3. Enter the following command:

   ```
   mvn install
   ```

   This command compiles and packages the application into an EAR file,
   `cart.ear`, located in the `target` directory, and deploys the EAR to your
   GlassFish Server instance.

   Then, the client stubs are retrieved and run. This is equivalent to running the
   following command:

   ```
   appclient -client cart-ear/target/cart-earClient.jar
   ```

   The client JAR, `cart-earClient.jar`, contains the application client class, the
   helper class `BookException`, and the `Cart` business interface.

   When you run the client, the application client container injects any
   component references declared in the application client class, in this case the
   reference to the `Cart` enterprise bean.

   You will see the output of the `cart-app-client` application client in the
   terminal window:

   ```
   . . .
   Retrieving book title from cart: Infinite Jest
   ```

```
Retrieving book title from cart: Bel Canto
Retrieving book title from cart: Kafka on the Shore
Removing "Gravity's Rainbow" from cart.
Caught a BookException: "Gravity's Rainbow" not in cart.
```

5.2 A Singleton Session Bean Example: counter

The counter example demonstrates how to create a singleton session bean.

5.2.1 Creating a Singleton Session Bean

The javax.ejb.Singleton annotation is used to specify that the enterprise bean implementation class is a singleton session bean:

```
@Singleton
public class SingletonBean { ... }
```

5.2.1.1 Initializing Singleton Session Beans

The EJB container is responsible for determining when to initialize a singleton session bean instance unless the singleton session bean implementation class is annotated with the javax.ejb.Startup annotation. In this case, sometimes called **eager initialization**, the EJB container must initialize the singleton session bean upon application startup. The singleton session bean is initialized before the EJB container delivers client requests to any enterprise beans in the application. This allows the singleton session bean to perform, for example, application startup tasks.

The following singleton session bean stores the status of an application and is eagerly initialized:

```
@Startup
@Singleton
public class StatusBean {
  private String status;

  @PostConstruct
  void init {
    status = "Ready";
  }
  ...
}
```

Sometimes multiple singleton session beans are used to initialize data for an application and therefore must be initialized in a specific order. In these cases, use the javax.ejb.DependsOn annotation to declare the startup dependencies of the singleton session bean. The `@DependsOn` annotation's `value` attribute is one or more strings that specify the name of the target singleton session bean. If more than one dependent singleton bean is specified in `@DependsOn`, the order in which they are listed is not necessarily the order in which the EJB container will initialize the target singleton session beans.

The following singleton session bean, `PrimaryBean`, should be started up first:

```
@Singleton
public class PrimaryBean { ... }
```

`SecondaryBean` depends on `PrimaryBean`:

```
@Singleton
@DependsOn("PrimaryBean")
public class SecondaryBean { ... }
```

This guarantees that the EJB container will initialize `PrimaryBean` before `SecondaryBean`.

The following singleton session bean, `TertiaryBean`, depends on `PrimaryBean` and `SecondaryBean`:

```
@Singleton
@DependsOn({"PrimaryBean", "SecondaryBean"})
public class TertiaryBean { ... }
```

`SecondaryBean` explicitly requires `PrimaryBean` to be initialized before it is initialized, through its own `@DependsOn` annotation. In this case, the EJB container will first initialize `PrimaryBean`, then `SecondaryBean`, and finally `TertiaryBean`.

If, however, `SecondaryBean` did not explicitly depend on `PrimaryBean`, the EJB container may initialize either `PrimaryBean` or `SecondaryBean` first. That is, the EJB container could initialize the singletons in the following order: `SecondaryBean`, `PrimaryBean`, `TertiaryBean`.

5.2.1.2 Managing Concurrent Access in a Singleton Session Bean

Singleton session beans are designed for **concurrent access**, situations in which many clients need to access a single instance of a session bean at the same time. A singleton's client needs only a reference to a singleton in order to invoke any business methods exposed by the singleton and doesn't need to worry about any other clients that may be simultaneously invoking business methods on the same singleton.

When creating a singleton session bean, concurrent access to the singleton's business methods can be controlled in two ways: container-managed concurrency and bean-managed concurrency.

The `javax.ejb.ConcurrencyManagement` annotation is used to specify container-managed or bean-managed concurrency for the singleton. With `@ConcurrencyManagement`, a type attribute must be set to either `javax.ejb.ConcurrencyManagementType.CONTAINER` or `javax.ejb.ConcurrencyManagementType.BEAN`. If no `@ConcurrencyManagement` annotation is present on the singleton implementation class, the EJB container default of container-managed concurrency is used.

Container-Managed Concurrency

If a singleton uses **container-managed concurrency**, the EJB container controls client access to the business methods of the singleton. The `javax.ejb.Lock` annotation and a `javax.ejb.LockType` type are used to specify the access level of the singleton's business methods or `@Timeout` methods. The `LockType` enumerated types are READ and WRITE.

Annotate a singleton's business or timeout method with `@Lock(LockType.READ)` if the method can be concurrently accessed, or shared, with many clients. Annotate the business or timeout method with `@Lock(LockType.WRITE)` if the singleton session bean should be locked to other clients while a client is calling that method. Typically, the `@Lock(LockType.WRITE)` annotation is used when clients are modifying the state of the singleton.

Annotating a singleton class with `@Lock` specifies that all the business methods and any timeout methods of the singleton will use the specified lock type unless they explicitly set the lock type with a method-level `@Lock` annotation. If no `@Lock` annotation is present on the singleton class, the default lock type, `@Lock(LockType.WRITE)`, is applied to all business and timeout methods.

The following example shows how to use the `@ConcurrencyManagement`, `@Lock(LockType.READ)`, and `@Lock(LockType.WRITE)` annotations for a singleton that uses container-managed concurrency.

Although by default singletons use container-managed concurrency, the `@ConcurrencyManagement(CONTAINER)` annotation may be added at the class level of the singleton to explicitly set the concurrency management type:

```
@ConcurrencyManagement(ConcurrencyManagementType.CONTAINER)
@Singleton
public class ExampleSingletonBean {
  private String state;

  @Lock(LockType.READ)
  public String getState() { return state; }
```

```
@Lock(LockType.WRITE)
public void setState(String newState) { state = newState; }
}
```

The getState method can be accessed by many clients at the same time because it is annotated with @Lock(LockType.READ). When the setState method is called, however, all the methods in ExampleSingletonBean will be locked to other clients because setState is annotated with @Lock(LockType.WRITE). This prevents two clients from attempting to simultaneously change the state variable of ExampleSingletonBean.

The getData and getStatus methods in the following singleton are of type READ, and the setStatus method is of type WRITE:

```
@Singleton
@Lock(LockType.READ)
public class SharedSingletonBean {
  private String data;
  private String status;

  public String getData() {
    return data;
  }

  public String getStatus() {
    return status;
  }

  @Lock(LockType.WRITE)
  public void setStatus(String newStatus) {
    status = newStatus;
  }
}
```

If a method is of locking type WRITE, client access to all the singleton's methods is blocked until the current client finishes its method call or an access timeout occurs. When an access timeout occurs, the EJB container throws a javax.ejb.ConcurrentAccessTimeoutException. The javax.ejb.AccessTimeout annotation is used to specify the number of milliseconds before an access timeout occurs. If added at the class level of a singleton, @AccessTimeout specifies the access timeout value for all methods in the singleton unless a method explicitly overrides the default with its own @AccessTimeout annotation.

The @AccessTimeout annotation can be applied to both @Lock(LockType.READ) and @Lock(LockType.WRITE) methods. The @AccessTimeout annotation has one required element, value, and one optional element, unit. By default, the value is specified in milliseconds. To change the value unit, set unit to one of the java.util.concurrent.TimeUnit constants: NANOSECONDS, MICROSECONDS, MILLISECONDS, or SECONDS.

The following singleton has a default access timeout value of 120,000 milliseconds, or 2 minutes. The doTediousOperation method overrides the default access timeout and sets the value to 360,000 milliseconds, or 6 minutes:

```
@Singleton
@AccessTimeout(value=120000)
public class StatusSingletonBean {
  private String status;

  @Lock(LockType.WRITE)
  public void setStatus(String new Status) {
    status = newStatus;
  }

  @Lock(LockType.WRITE)
  @AccessTimeout(value=360000)
  public void doTediousOperation {
    ...
  }
}
```

The following singleton has a default access timeout value of 60 seconds, specified using the TimeUnit.SECONDS constant:

```
@Singleton
@AccessTimeout(value=60, unit=TimeUnit.SECONDS)
public class StatusSingletonBean { ... }
```

Bean-Managed Concurrency

Singletons that use **bean-managed concurrency** allow full concurrent access to all the business and timeout methods in the singleton. The developer of the singleton is responsible for ensuring that the state of the singleton is synchronized across all clients. Developers who create singletons with bean-managed concurrency are allowed to use the Java programming language synchronization primitives, such as synchronization and volatile, to prevent errors during concurrent access.

Add a @ConcurrencyManagement annotation with the type set to ConcurrencyManagementType.BEAN at the class level of the singleton to specify bean-managed concurrency:

```
@ConcurrencyManagement(ConcurrencyManagementType.BEAN)
@Singleton
public class AnotherSingletonBean { ... }
```

5.2.1.3 Handling Errors in a Singleton Session Bean

If a singleton session bean encounters an error when initialized by the EJB container, that singleton instance will be destroyed.

Unlike other enterprise beans, once a singleton session bean instance is initialized, it is not destroyed if the singleton's business or lifecycle methods cause system exceptions. This ensures that the same singleton instance is used throughout the application lifecycle.

5.2.2 The Architecture of the counter Example

The counter example consists of a singleton session bean, CounterBean, and a JavaServer Faces Facelets web front end.

CounterBean is a simple singleton with one method, getHits, that returns an integer representing the number of times a web page has been accessed. Here is the code of CounterBean:

```
package javaeetutorial.counter.ejb;

import javax.ejb.Singleton;

/**
 * CounterBean is a simple singleton session bean that records the number
 * of hits to a web page.
 */
@Singleton
public class CounterBean {
    private int hits = 1;

    // Increment and return the number of hits
    public int getHits() {
        return hits++;
    }
}
```

The @Singleton annotation marks CounterBean as a singleton session bean. CounterBean uses a local, no-interface view.

CounterBean uses the EJB container's default metadata values for singletons to simplify the coding of the singleton implementation class. There is no @ConcurrencyManagement annotation on the class, so the default of container-managed concurrency access is applied. There is no @Lock annotation on the class or business method, so the default of @Lock(WRITE) is applied to the only business method, getHits.

The following version of `CounterBean` is functionally equivalent to the preceding version:

```
package javaeetutorial.counter.ejb;

import javax.ejb.Singleton;
import javax.ejb.ConcurrencyManagement;
import static javax.ejb.ConcurrencyManagementType.CONTAINER;
import javax.ejb.Lock;
import javax.ejb.LockType.WRITE;

/**
 * CounterBean is a simple singleton session bean that records the number
 * of hits to a web page.
 */
@Singleton
@ConcurrencyManagement(CONTAINER)
public class CounterBean {
    private int hits = 1;

    // Increment and return the number of hits
    @Lock(WRITE)
    public int getHits() {
        return hits++;
    }
}
```

The web front end of `counter` consists of a JavaServer Faces managed bean, `Count.java`, that is used by the Facelets XHTML files `template.xhtml` and `index.xhtml`. The `Count` JavaServer Faces managed bean obtains a reference to `CounterBean` through dependency injection. `Count` defines a `hitCount` JavaBeans property. When the `getHitCount` getter method is called from the XHTML files, `CounterBean`'s `getHits` method is called to return the current number of page hits.

Here's the `Count` managed bean class:

```
@Named
@ConversationScoped
public class Count implements Serializable {
    @EJB
    private CounterBean counterBean;
    private int hitCount;

    public Count() {
        this.hitCount = 0;
    }
```

```
        public int getHitCount() {
            hitCount = counterBean.getHits();
            return hitCount;
        }

        public void setHitCount(int newHits) {
            this.hitCount = newHits;
        }
}
```

The `template.xhtml` and `index.xhtml` files are used to render a Facelets view that displays the number of hits to that view. The `index.xhtml` file uses an expression language statement, `#{count.hitCount}`, to access the `hitCount` property of the `Count` managed bean. Here is the content of `index.xhtml`:

```
<html lang="en"
      xmlns="http://www.w3.org/1999/xhtml"
      xmlns:ui="http://xmlns.jcp.org/jsf/facelets"
      xmlns:h="http://xmlns.jcp.org/jsf/html">
    <ui:composition template="/template.xhtml">
        <ui:define name="title">
            This page has been accessed #{count.hitCount} time(s).
        </ui:define>
        <ui:define name="body">
            Hooray!
        </ui:define>
    </ui:composition>
</html>
```

5.2.3 Running the counter Example

You can use either NetBeans IDE or Maven to build, package, deploy, and run the counter example.

5.2.3.1 To Run the counter Example Using NetBeans IDE

1. Make sure that GlassFish Server has been started (see Section 2.2, "Starting and Stopping GlassFish Server").

2. From the **File** menu, choose **Open Project**.

3. In the Open Project dialog box, navigate to:

   tut-install/examples/ejb

4. Select the counter folder.

5. Click **Open Project**.

6. In the **Projects** tab, right-click the `counter` project and select **Run**.

   A web browser will open the URL `http://localhost:8080/counter`, which displays the number of hits.

7. Reload the page to see the hit count increment.

5.2.3.2 To Run the counter Example Using Maven

1. Make sure that GlassFish Server has been started (see Section 2.2, "Starting and Stopping GlassFish Server").

2. In a terminal window, go to:

   tut-install/examples/ejb/counter/

3. Enter the following command:

   ```
   mvn install
   ```

   This will build and deploy `counter` to your GlassFish Server instance.

4. In a web browser, enter the following URL:

   ```
   http://localhost:8080/counter
   ```

5. Reload the page to see the hit count increment.

5.3 A Web Service Example: helloservice

This example demonstrates a simple web service that generates a response based on information received from the client. `HelloServiceBean` is a stateless session bean that implements a single method: `sayHello`. This method matches the `sayHello` method invoked by the client described in Section 28.1.5, "A Simple JAX-WS Application Client," in *The Java EE 7 Tutorial, Volume 1*.

5.3.1 The Web Service Endpoint Implementation Class

`HelloServiceBean` is the endpoint implementation class, typically the primary programming artifact for enterprise bean web service endpoints. The web service endpoint implementation class has the following requirements.

- The class must be annotated with either the `javax.jws.WebService` or the `javax.jws.WebServiceProvider` annotation.

- The implementing class may explicitly reference an SEI through the `endpointInterface` element of the `@WebService` annotation but is not required to do so. If no endpointInterface is specified in @WebService, an SEI is implicitly defined for the implementing class.

■ The business methods of the implementing class must be public and must not be declared static or final.

■ Business methods that are exposed to web service clients must be annotated with javax.jws.WebMethod.

■ Business methods that are exposed to web service clients must have JAXB-compatible parameters and return types. See the list of JAXB default data type bindings in Section 28.2, "Types Supported by JAX-WS," in *The Java EE 7 Tutorial, Volume 1*.

■ The implementing class must not be declared final and must not be abstract.

■ The implementing class must have a default public constructor.

■ The endpoint class must be annotated @Stateless.

■ The implementing class must not define the finalize method.

■ The implementing class may use the javax.annotation.PostConstruct or javax.annotation.PreDestroy annotations on its methods for lifecycle event callbacks.

The @PostConstruct method is called by the container before the implementing class begins responding to web service clients.

The @PreDestroy method is called by the container before the endpoint is removed from operation.

5.3.2 Stateless Session Bean Implementation Class

The HelloServiceBean class implements the sayHello method, which is annotated @WebMethod. The source code for the HelloServiceBean class is as follows:

```
package javaeetutorial.helloservice.ejb;

import javax.ejb.Stateless;
import javax.jws.WebMethod;
import javax.jws.WebService;

@Stateless
@WebService
public class HelloServiceBean {
    private final String message = "Hello, ";
```

```
public void HelloServiceBean() {}

@WebMethod
public String sayHello(String name) {
    return message + name + ".";
}
```

5.3.3 Running the helloservice Example

You can use either NetBeans IDE or Maven to build, package, and deploy the `helloservice` example. You can then use the Administration Console to test the web service endpoint methods.

5.3.3.1 To Build, Package, and Deploy the helloservice Example Using NetBeans IDE

1. Make sure that GlassFish Server has been started (see Section 2.2, "Starting and Stopping GlassFish Server").

2. From the **File** menu, choose **Open Project**.

3. In the Open Project dialog box, navigate to:

   tut-install/examples/ejb

4. Select the `helloservice` folder.

5. Click **Open Project**.

6. In the **Projects** tab, right-click the `helloservice` project and select **Build**.

   This builds and packages the application into `helloservice.ear`, located in *tut-install*/examples/ejb/helloservice/target/, and deploys this EAR file to GlassFish Server.

5.3.3.2 To Build, Package, and Deploy the helloservice Example Using Maven

1. Make sure that GlassFish Server has been started (see Section 2.2, "Starting and Stopping GlassFish Server").

2. In a terminal window, go to:

   tut-install/examples/ejb/helloservice/

3. Enter the following command:

   ```
   mvn install
   ```

This compiles the source files and packages the application into an EJB JAR file located at *tut-install*/examples/ejb/helloservice/target/helloservice.jar. Then the EJB JAR file is deployed to GlassFish Server.

Upon deployment, GlassFish Server generates additional artifacts required for web service invocation, including the WSDL file.

5.3.3.3 To Test the Service without a Client

The GlassFish Server Administration Console allows you to test the methods of a web service endpoint. To test the sayHello method of HelloServiceBean, follow these steps.

1. Open the Administration Console by opening the following URL in a web browser:

   http://localhost:4848/

2. In the navigation tree, select the **Applications** node.

3. In the **Applications** table, click the helloservice link.

4. In the **Modules and Components** table, click the **View Endpoint** link.

5. On the Web Service Endpoint Information page, click the **Tester** link:

   /HelloServiceBeanService/HelloServiceBean?Tester

6. On the Web Service Test Links page, click the non-secure link (the one that specifies port 8080).

7. On the HelloServiceBeanService Web Service Tester page, under **Methods**, enter a name as the parameter to the sayHello method.

8. Click **sayHello**.

   The sayHello Method invocation page opens. Under **Method returned**, you'll see the response from the endpoint.

5.4 Using the Timer Service

Applications that model business work flows often rely on timed notifications. The timer service of the enterprise bean container enables you to schedule timed notifications for all types of enterprise beans except for stateful session beans. You can schedule a timed notification to occur according to a calendar schedule, at a specific time, after a duration of time, or at timed intervals. For example, you could set timers to go off at 10:30 a.m. on May 23, in 30 days, or every 12 hours.

Enterprise bean timers are either programmatic timers or automatic timers. **Programmatic timers** are set by explicitly calling one of the timer creation methods of the `TimerService` interface. **Automatic timers** are created upon the successful deployment of an enterprise bean that contains a method annotated with the `javax.ejb.Schedule` or `javax.ejb.Schedules` annotations.

5.4.1 Creating Calendar-Based Timer Expressions

Timers can be set according to a calendar-based schedule, expressed using a syntax similar to the UNIX `cron` utility. Both programmatic and automatic timers can use calendar-based timer expressions. Table 5–1 shows the calendar-based timer attributes.

Table 5–1   *Calendar-Based Timer Attributes*

Attribute	Description	Default Value	Allowable Values and Examples
second	One or more seconds within a minute	0	0 to 59. For example: `second="30"`.
minute	One or more minutes within an hour	0	0 to 59. For example: `minute="15"`.
hour	One or more hours within a day	0	0 to 23. For example: `hour="13"`.
dayOfWeek	One or more days within a week	*	0 to 7 (both 0 and 7 refer to Sunday). For example: `dayOfWeek="3"`. `Sun, Mon, Tue, Wed, Thu, Fri, Sat`. For example: `dayOfWeek="Mon"`.
dayOfMonth	One or more days within a month	*	1 to 31. For example: `dayOfMonth="15"`. -7 to -1 (a negative number means the nth day or days before the end of the month). For example: `dayOfMonth='-3'`. `Last`. For example: `dayOfMonth="Last"`. [`1st, 2nd, 3rd, 4th, 5th, Last`] [`Sun, Mon, Tue, Wed, Thu, Fri, Sat`]. For example: `dayOfMonth="2nd Fri"`.

Table 5–1   (Cont.) Calendar-Based Timer Attributes

Attribute	Description	Default Value	Allowable Values and Examples
`month`	One or more months within a year	*	1 to 12. For example: `month="7"`.
			Jan, Feb, Mar, Apr, May, Jun, Jul, Aug, Sep, Oct, Nov, Dec. For example: `month="July"`.
`year`	A particular calendar year	*	A four-digit calendar year. For example: `year="2011"`.

5.4.1.1 Specifying Multiple Values in Calendar Expressions

You can specify multiple values in calendar expressions, as described in the following sections.

Using Wildcards in Calendar Expressions

Setting an attribute to an asterisk symbol (*) represents all allowable values for the attribute.

The following expression represents every minute:

```
minute="*"
```

The following expression represents every day of the week:

```
dayOfWeek="*"
```

Specifying a List of Values

To specify two or more values for an attribute, use a comma (,) to separate the values. A range of values is allowed as part of a list. Wildcards and intervals, however, are not allowed.

Duplicates within a list are ignored.

The following expression sets the day of the week to Tuesday and Thursday:

```
dayOfWeek="Tue, Thu"
```

The following expression represents 4:00 a.m., every hour from 9:00 a.m. to 5:00 p.m. using a range, and 10:00 p.m.:

```
hour="4,9-17,22"
```

Specifying a Range of Values

Use a dash character (-) to specify an inclusive range of values for an attribute. Members of a range cannot be wildcards, lists, or intervals. A range of the form x-x, is equivalent to the single-valued expression x. A range of the form x-y where x is greater than y is equivalent to the expression x-*maximumvalue*, *minimumvalue*-y. That is, the expression begins at x, rolls over to the beginning of the allowable values, and continues up to y.

The following expression represents 9:00 a.m. to 5:00 p.m.:

```
hour="9-17"
```

The following expression represents Friday through Monday:

```
dayOfWeek="5-1"
```

The following expression represents the twenty-fifth day of the month to the end of the month, and the beginning of the month to the fifth day of the month:

```
dayOfMonth="25-5"
```

It is equivalent to the following expression:

```
dayOfMonth="25-Last,1-5"
```

Specifying Intervals

The forward slash (/) constrains an attribute to a starting point and an interval and is used to specify every N seconds, minutes, or hours within the minute, hour, or day. For an expression of the form x/y, x represents the starting point and y represents the interval. The wildcard character may be used in the x position of an interval and is equivalent to setting x to 0.

Intervals may be set only for second, minute, and hour attributes.

The following expression represents every 10 minutes within the hour:

```
minute="*/10"
```

It is equivalent to:

```
minute="0,10,20,30,40,50"
```

The following expression represents every 2 hours starting at noon:

```
hour="12/2"
```

5.4.2 Programmatic Timers

When a programmatic timer expires (goes off), the container calls the method annotated @Timeout in the bean's implementation class. The @Timeout method contains the business logic that handles the timed event.

5.4.2.1 The @Timeout Method

Methods annotated @Timeout in the enterprise bean class must return void and optionally take a javax.ejb.Timer object as the only parameter. They may not throw application exceptions.

```
@Timeout
public void timeout(Timer timer) {
    System.out.println("TimerBean: timeout occurred");
}
```

5.4.2.2 Creating Programmatic Timers

To create a timer, the bean invokes one of the create methods of the TimerService interface. These methods allow single-action, interval, or calendar-based timers to be created.

For single-action or interval timers, the expiration of the timer can be expressed as either a duration or an absolute time. The duration is expressed as a the number of milliseconds before a timeout event is triggered. To specify an absolute time, create a java.util.Date object and pass it to the TimerService.createSingleActionTimer or the TimerService.createTimer method.

The following code sets a programmatic timer that will expire in 1 minute (60,000 milliseconds):

```
long duration = 60000;
Timer timer =
    timerService.createSingleActionTimer(duration, new TimerConfig());
```

The following code sets a programmatic timer that will expire at 12:05 p.m. on May 1, 2015, specified as a java.util.Date:

```
SimpleDateFormatter formatter =
    new SimpleDateFormatter("MM/dd/yyyy 'at' HH:mm");
Date date = formatter.parse("05/01/2015 at 12:05");
Timer timer = timerService.createSingleActionTimer(date, new TimerConfig());
```

For calendar-based timers, the expiration of the timer is expressed as a javax.ejb.ScheduleExpression object, passed as a parameter to the TimerService.createCalendarTimer method. The ScheduleExpression class represents calendar-based timer expressions and has methods that correspond to the attributes described in Section 5.4.1, "Creating Calendar-Based Timer Expressions."

The following code creates a programmatic timer using the `ScheduleExpression` helper class:

```
ScheduleExpression schedule = new ScheduleExpression();
schedule.dayOfWeek("Mon");
schedule.hour("12-17, 23");
Timer timer = timerService.createCalendarTimer(schedule);
```

For details on the method signatures, see the `TimerService` API documentation at `http://docs.oracle.com/javaee/7/api/javax/ejb/TimerService.html`.

The bean described in Section 5.4.7, "The timersession Example," creates a timer as follows:

```
Timer timer = timerService.createTimer(intervalDuration,
        "Created new programmatic timer");
```

In the `timersession` example, the method that calls `createTimer` is invoked in a business method, which is called by a client.

Timers are persistent by default. If the server is shut down or crashes, persistent timers are saved and will become active again when the server is restarted. If a persistent timer expires while the server is down, the container will call the `@Timeout` method when the server is restarted.

Nonpersistent programmatic timers are created by calling `TimerConfig.setPersistent(false)` and passing the `TimerConfig` object to one of the timer-creation methods.

The `Date` and `long` parameters of the `createTimer` methods represent time with the resolution of milliseconds. However, because the timer service is not intended for real-time applications, a callback to the `@Timeout` method might not occur with millisecond precision. The timer service is for business applications, which typically measure time in hours, days, or longer durations.

5.4.3 Automatic Timers

Automatic timers are created by the EJB container when an enterprise bean that contains methods annotated with the `@Schedule` or `@Schedules` annotations is deployed. An enterprise bean can have multiple automatic timeout methods, unlike a programmatic timer, which allows only one method annotated with the `@Timeout` annotation in the enterprise bean class.

Automatic timers can be configured through annotations or through the `ejb-jar.xml` deployment descriptor.

Adding a @Schedule annotation on an enterprise bean marks that method as a timeout method according to the calendar schedule specified in the attributes of @Schedule.

The @Schedule annotation has elements that correspond to the calendar expressions detailed in Section 5.4.1, "Creating Calendar-Based Timer Expressions," and the persistent, info, and timezone elements.

The optional persistent element takes a Boolean value and is used to specify whether the automatic timer should survive a server restart or crash. By default, all automatic timers are persistent.

The optional timezone element is used to specify that the automatic timer is associated with a particular time zone. If set, this element will evaluate all timer expressions in relation to the specified time zone, regardless of the time zone in which the EJB container is running. By default, all automatic timers set are in relation to the default time zone of the server.

The optional info element is used to set an informational description of the timer. A timer's information can be retrieved later by using Timer.getInfo.

The following timeout method uses @Schedule to set a timer that will expire every Sunday at midnight:

```
@Schedule(dayOfWeek="Sun", hour="0")
public void cleanupWeekData() { ... }
```

The @Schedules annotation is used to specify multiple calendar-based timer expressions for a given timeout method.

The following timeout method uses the @Schedules annotation to set multiple calendar-based timer expressions. The first expression sets a timer to expire on the last day of every month. The second expression sets a timer to expire every Friday at 11:00 p.m.:

```
@Schedules ({
    @Schedule(dayOfMonth="Last"),
    @Schedule(dayOfWeek="Fri", hour="23")
})
public void doPeriodicCleanup() { ... }
```

5.4.4 Canceling and Saving Timers

Timers can be cancelled by the following events.

- When a single-event timer expires, the EJB container calls the associated timeout method and then cancels the timer.

- When the bean invokes the `cancel` method of the `Timer` interface, the container cancels the timer.

If a method is invoked on a cancelled timer, the container throws the `javax.ejb.NoSuchObjectLocalException`.

To save a `Timer` object for future reference, invoke its `getHandle` method and store the `TimerHandle` object in a database. (A `TimerHandle` object is serializable.) To reinstantiate the `Timer` object, retrieve the handle from the database and invoke `getTimer` on the handle. A `TimerHandle` object cannot be passed as an argument of a method defined in a remote or web service interface. In other words, remote clients and web service clients cannot access a bean's `TimerHandle` object. Local clients, however, do not have this restriction.

5.4.5 Getting Timer Information

In addition to defining the `cancel` and `getHandle` methods, the `Timer` interface defines methods for obtaining information about timers:

```
public long getTimeRemaining();
public java.util.Date getNextTimeout();
public java.io.Serializable getInfo();
```

The `getInfo` method returns the object that was the last parameter of the `createTimer` invocation. For example, in the `createTimer` code snippet of the preceding section, this information parameter is a `String` object with the value `created timer`.

To retrieve all of a bean's active timers, call the `getTimers` method of the `TimerService` interface. The `getTimers` method returns a collection of `Timer` objects.

5.4.6 Transactions and Timers

An enterprise bean usually creates a timer within a transaction. If this transaction is rolled back, the timer creation also is rolled back. Similarly, if a bean cancels a timer within a transaction that gets rolled back, the timer cancellation is rolled back. In this case, the timer's duration is reset as if the cancellation had never occurred.

In beans that use container-managed transactions, the `@Timeout` method usually has the `Required` or `RequiresNew` transaction attribute to preserve transaction integrity. With these attributes, the EJB container begins the new transaction before calling the `@Timeout` method. If the transaction is rolled back, the container will call the `@Timeout` method at least one more time.

5.4.7 The timersession Example

The source code for this example is in the *tut-install*/examples/ejb/ timersession/src/main/java/ directory.

TimerSessionBean is a singleton session bean that shows how to set both an automatic timer and a programmatic timer. In the source code listing of TimerSessionBean that follows, the setTimer and @Timeout methods are used to set a programmatic timer. A TimerService instance is injected by the container when the bean is created. Because it's a business method, setTimer is exposed to the local, no-interface view of TimerSessionBean and can be invoked by the client. In this example, the client invokes setTimer with an interval duration of 8,000 milliseconds, or 8 seconds. The setTimer method creates a new timer by invoking the createTimer method of TimerService. Now that the timer is set, the EJB container will invoke the programmaticTimeout method of TimerSessionBean when the timer expires, in about 8 seconds:

```
. . .
    public void setTimer(long intervalDuration) {
        logger.log(Level.INFO,
            "Setting a programmatic timeout for {0} milliseconds from now.",
            intervalDuration);
        Timer timer = timerService.createTimer(intervalDuration,
            "Created new programmatic timer");
    }

    @Timeout
    public void programmaticTimeout(Timer timer) {
        this.setLastProgrammaticTimeout(new Date());
        logger.info("Programmatic timeout occurred.");
    }
. . .
```

TimerSessionBean also has an automatic timer and timeout method, automaticTimeout. The automatic timer is set to expire every 1 minute and is set by using a calendar-based timer expression in the @Schedule annotation:

```
. . .
    @Schedule(minute = "*/1", hour = "*", persistent = false)
    public void automaticTimeout() {
        this.setLastAutomaticTimeout(new Date());
        logger.info("Automatic timeout occured");
    }
. . .
```

TimerSessionBean also has two business methods: getLastProgrammaticTimeout and getLastAutomaticTimeout. Clients call these methods to get the date and time of the last timeout for the programmatic timer and automatic timer, respectively.

Here's the source code for the `TimerSessionBean` class:

```
package javaeetutorial.timersession.ejb;

import java.util.Date;
import java.util.logging.Level;
import java.util.logging.Logger;
import javax.annotation.Resource;
import javax.ejb.Schedule;
import javax.ejb.Singleton;
import javax.ejb.Startup;
import javax.ejb.Timeout;
import javax.ejb.Timer;
import javax.ejb.TimerService;

@Singleton
@Startup
public class TimerSessionBean {
    @Resource
    TimerService timerService;

    private Date lastProgrammaticTimeout;
    private Date lastAutomaticTimeout;

    private static final Logger logger =
            Logger.getLogger("timersession.ejb.TimerSessionBean");

    public void setTimer(long intervalDuration) {
        logger.log(Level.INFO,
                "Setting a programmatic timeout for {0} milliseconds from now.",
                intervalDuration);
        Timer timer = timerService.createTimer(intervalDuration,
                "Created new programmatic timer");
    }

    @Timeout
    public void programmaticTimeout(Timer timer) {
        this.setLastProgrammaticTimeout(new Date());
        logger.info("Programmatic timeout occurred.");
    }

    @Schedule(minute = "*/1", hour = "*", persistent = false)
    public void automaticTimeout() {
        this.setLastAutomaticTimeout(new Date());
```

```
            logger.info("Automatic timeout occured");
    }

    public String getLastProgrammaticTimeout() {
        if (lastProgrammaticTimeout != null) {
            return lastProgrammaticTimeout.toString();
        } else {
            return "never";
        }
    }

    public void setLastProgrammaticTimeout(Date lastTimeout) {
        this.lastProgrammaticTimeout = lastTimeout;
    }

    public String getLastAutomaticTimeout() {
        if (lastAutomaticTimeout != null) {
            return lastAutomaticTimeout.toString();
        } else {
            return "never";
        }
    }

    public void setLastAutomaticTimeout(Date lastAutomaticTimeout) {
        this.lastAutomaticTimeout = lastAutomaticTimeout;
    }
}
```

Note: GlassFish Server has a default minimum timeout value of 1,000 milliseconds, or 1 second. If you need to set the timeout value lower than 1,000 milliseconds, change the value of the Minimum Delivery Interval setting in the Administration Console. To modify the minimum timeout value, in the Administration Console expand **Configurations**, then expand **server-config**, select **EJB Container**, and click the **EJB Timer Service** tab. Enter a new timeout value under **Minimum Delivery Interval** and click **Save**. The lowest practical value for minimum-delivery-interval-in-millis is around 10 milliseconds, owing to virtual machine constraints.

5.4.8 Running the timersession Example

You can use either NetBeans IDE or Maven to build, package, deploy, and run the timersession example.

5.4.8.1 To Run the timersession Example Using NetBeans IDE

1. Make sure that GlassFish Server has been started (see Section 2.2, "Starting and Stopping GlassFish Server").

2. From the **File** menu, choose **Open Project**.

3. In the Open Project dialog box, navigate to:

   tut-install/examples/ejb

4. Select the timersession folder.

5. Click **Open Project**.

6. From the **Run** menu, choose **Run Project**.

   This builds and packages the application into a WAR file located at *tut-install*/examples/ejb/timersession/target/timersession.war, deploys this WAR file to your GlassFish Server instance, and then runs the web client.

5.4.8.2 To Build, Package, and Deploy the timersession Example Using Maven

1. Make sure that GlassFish Server has been started (see Section 2.2, "Starting and Stopping GlassFish Server").

2. In a terminal window, go to:

   tut-install/examples/ejb/timersession/

3. Enter the following command:

   mvn install

   This builds and packages the application into a WAR file located at *tut-install*/examples/ejb/timersession/target/timersession.war and deploys this WAR file to your GlassFish Server instance.

5.4.8.3 To Run the Web Client

1. Open a web browser to the following URL:

   http://localhost:8080/timersession

2. Click **Set Timer** to set a programmatic timer.

3. Wait for a while and click the browser's **Refresh** button.

   You will see the date and time of the last programmatic and automatic timeouts.

To see the messages that are logged when a timeout occurs, open the server.log file located in *domain-dir*/logs/.

5.5 Handling Exceptions

The exceptions thrown by enterprise beans fall into two categories: system and application.

A **system exception** indicates a problem with the services that support an application. For example, a connection to an external resource cannot be obtained, or an injected resource cannot be found. If it encounters a system-level problem, your enterprise bean should throw a javax.ejb.EJBException. Because the EJBException is a subclass of RuntimeException, you do not have to specify it in the throws clause of the method declaration. If a system exception is thrown, the EJB container might destroy the bean instance. Therefore, a system exception cannot be handled by the bean's client program, but instead requires intervention by a system administrator.

An **application exception** signals an error in the business logic of an enterprise bean. Application exceptions are typically exceptions that you've coded yourself, such as the BookException thrown by the business methods of the CartBean example. When an enterprise bean throws an application exception, the container does not wrap it in another exception. The client should be able to handle any application exception it receives.

If a system exception occurs within a transaction, the EJB container rolls back the transaction. However, if an application exception is thrown within a transaction, the container does not roll back the transaction.

6

Using the Embedded Enterprise Bean Container

This chapter demonstrates how to use the embedded enterprise bean container to run enterprise bean applications in the Java SE environment, outside of a Java EE server.

The following topics are addressed here:

- Overview of the Embedded Enterprise Bean Container
- Developing Embeddable Enterprise Bean Applications
- The standalone Example Application

6.1 Overview of the Embedded Enterprise Bean Container

The embedded enterprise bean container is used to access enterprise bean components from client code executed in a Java SE environment. The container and the client code are executed within the same virtual machine. The embedded enterprise bean container is typically used for testing enterprise beans without having to deploy them to a server.

Most of the services present in the enterprise bean container in a Java EE server are available in the embedded enterprise bean container, including injection, container-managed transactions, and security. Enterprise bean components execute similarly in both embedded and Java EE environments, and therefore the same enterprise bean can be easily reused in both standalone and networked applications.

6.2 Developing Embeddable Enterprise Bean Applications

All embeddable enterprise bean containers support the features listed in Table 6–1.

Table 6–1   Required Enterprise Bean Features in the Embeddable Container

Enterprise Bean Feature	Description
Local session beans	Local and no-interface view stateless, stateful, and singleton session beans. All method access is synchronous. Session beans must not be web service endpoints.
Transactions	Container-managed and bean-managed transactions.
Security	Declarative and programmatic security.
Interceptors	Class-level and method-level interceptors for session beans.
Deployment descriptor	The optional ejb-jar.xml deployment descriptor, with the same overriding rules for the enterprise bean container in Java EE servers.

Container providers are allowed to support the full set of features in enterprise beans, but applications that use the embedded container will not be portable if they use enterprise bean features not listed in Table 6–1, such as the timer service, session beans as web service endpoints, or remote business interfaces.

6.2.1 Running Embedded Applications

The embedded container, the enterprise bean components, and the client all are executed in the same virtual machine using the same classpath. As a result, developers can run an application that uses the embedded container just like a typical Java SE application, as follows:

```
java -classpath mySessionBean.jar:containerProviderRuntime.jar:myClient.jar \
com.example.ejb.client.Main
```

In the above example, mySessionBean.jar is an EJB JAR containing a local stateless session bean, containerProviderRuntime.jar is a JAR file supplied by the enterprise bean provider that contains the needed runtime classes for the embedded container, and myClient.jar is a JAR file containing a Java SE application that calls the business methods in the session bean through the embedded container.

In GlassFish Server, the runtime JAR that includes the classes for the embedded container is glassfish-embedded-all.jar.

6.2.2 Creating the Enterprise Bean Container

The `javax.ejb.embedded.EJBContainer` abstract class represents an instance of the enterprise bean container and includes factory methods for creating a container instance. The `EJBContainer.createEJBContainer` method is used to create and initialize an embedded container instance.

The following code snippet shows how to create an embedded container that is initialized with the container provider's default settings:

```
EJBContainer ec = EJBContainer.createEJBContainer();
```

By default, the embedded container will search the virtual machine classpath for enterprise bean modules: directories containing a `META-INF/ejb-jar.xml` deployment descriptor, directories containing a class file with one of the enterprise bean component annotations (such as `@Stateless`), or JAR files containing an `ejb-jar.xml` deployment descriptor or class file with an enterprise bean annotation. Any matching entries are considered enterprise bean modules within the same application. Once all the valid enterprise bean modules have been found in the classpath, the container will begin initializing the modules. When the `createEJBContainer` method successfully returns, the client application can obtain references to the client view of any enterprise bean module found by the embedded container.

An alternate version of the `EJBContainer.createEJBContainer` method takes a `Map` of properties and settings for customizing the embeddable container instance:

```
Properties props = new Properties();
props.setProperty(...);
...
EJBContainer ec = EJBContainer.createEJBContainer(props);
```

6.2.2.1 Explicitly Specifying Enterprise Bean Modules to Be Initialized

Developers can specify exactly which enterprise bean modules the embedded container will initialize. To explicitly specify the enterprise bean modules initialized by the embedded container, set the `EJBContainer.MODULES` property.

The modules may be located either in the virtual machine classpath in which the embedded container and client code run, or alternately outside the virtual machine classpath.

To specify modules in the virtual machine classpath, set `EJBContainer.MODULES` to a `String` to specify a single module name, or a `String` array containing the module names. The embedded container searches the virtual machine classpath for enterprise bean modules matching the specified names.

```
Properties props = new Properties();
props.setProperty(EJBContainer.MODULES, "mySessionBean");
EJBContainer ec = EJBContainer.createEJBContainer(props);
```

To specify enterprise bean modules outside the virtual machine classpath, set
EJBContainer.MODULES to a java.io.File object or an array of File objects. Each
File object refers to an EJB JAR file, or a directory containing an expanded EJB
JAR file:

```
Properties props = new Properties();
File ejbJarFile = new File(...);
props.setProperty(EJBContainer.MODULES, ejbJarFile);
EJBContainer ec = EJBContainer.createEJBContainer(props);
```

6.2.3 Looking Up Session Bean References

To look up session bean references in an application using the embedded
container, use an instance of EJBContainer to retrieve a javax.naming.Context
object. Call the EJBContainer.getContext method to retrieve the Context object:

```
EJBContainer ec = EJBContainer.createEJBContainer();
Context ctx = ec.getContext();
```

References to session beans can then be obtained using the portable JNDI syntax
detailed in Section 3.4.1.1, "Portable JNDI Syntax." For example, to obtain a
reference to MySessionBean, a local session bean with a no-interface view, use the
following code:

```
MySessionBean msb = (MySessionBean)
            ctx.lookup("java:global/mySessionBean/MySessionBean");
```

6.2.4 Shutting Down the Enterprise Bean Container

From the client, call the close method of the instance of EJBContainer to shut
down the embedded container:

```
EJBContainer ec = EJBContainer.createEJBContainer();
...
ec.close();
```

While clients are not required to shut down EJBContainer instances, doing so
frees resources consumed by the embedded container. This is particularly
important when the virtual machine under which the client application is running
has a longer lifetime than the client application.

6.3 The standalone Example Application

The standalone example application demonstrates how to create an instance of the embedded enterprise bean container in a JUnit test class and call a session bean business method. Testing the business methods of an enterprise bean in a unit test allows developers to exercise the business logic of an application separately from the other application layers, such as the presentation layer, and without having to deploy the application to a Java EE server.

The standalone example has two main components: StandaloneBean, a stateless session bean, and StandaloneBeanTest, a JUnit test class that acts as a client to StandaloneBean using the embedded container.

StandaloneBean is a simple session bean exposing a local, no-interface view with a single business method, returnMessage, which returns "Greetings!" as a String:

```
@Stateless
public class StandaloneBean {

    private static final String message = "Greetings!";

    public String returnMessage() {
        return message;
    }

}
```

StandaloneBeanTest calls StandaloneBean.returnMessage and tests that the returned message is correct. First, an embedded container instance and initial context are created within the setUp method, which is annotated with org.junit.Before to indicate that the method should be executed before the test methods:

```
@Before
public void setUp() {
    ec = EJBContainer.createEJBContainer();
    ctx = ec.getContext();
}
```

The testReturnMessage method, annotated with org.junit.Test to indicate that the method includes a unit test, obtains a reference to StandaloneBean through the Context instance, and calls StandaloneBean.returnMessage. The result is compared with the expected result using a JUnit assertion, assertEquals. If the string returned from StandaloneBean.returnMessage is equal to "Greetings!" the test passes.

```
@Test
public void testReturnMessage() throws Exception {
    logger.info("Testing standalone.ejb.StandaloneBean.returnMessage()");
    StandaloneBean instance = (StandaloneBean)
            ctx.lookup("java:global/classes/StandaloneBean");
    String expResult = "Greetings!";
    String result = instance.returnMessage();
    assertEquals(expResult, result);
}
```

Finally, the `tearDown` method, annotated with `org.junit.After` to indicate that the method should be executed after all the unit tests have run, closes the embedded container instance:

```
@After
public void tearDown() {
    if (ec != null) {
        ec.close();
    }
}
```

6.3.1 To Run the standalone Example Application Using NetBeans IDE

1. Make sure that GlassFish Server has been started (see Section 2.2, "Starting and Stopping GlassFish Server").

2. From the **File** menu, choose **Open Project**.

3. In the Open Project dialog box, navigate to:

   tut-install/examples/ejb

4. Select the `standalone` folder and click **Open Project**.

5. In the **Projects** tab, right-click the `standalone` project and select **Test**.

   This will execute the JUnit test class `StandaloneBeanTest`. The **Output** tab shows the progress of the test and the output log.

6.3.2 To Run the standalone Example Application Using Maven

1. Make sure that GlassFish Server has been started (see Section 2.2, "Starting and Stopping GlassFish Server").

2. In a terminal window, go to:

   tut-install/examples/ejb/standalone/

3. Enter the following command:

```
mvn install
```

This command compiles and packages the application into an JAR file, and executes the JUnit test class StandaloneBeanTest.

7

Using Asynchronous Method Invocation in Session Beans

This chapter discusses how to implement asynchronous business methods in session beans and call them from enterprise bean clients.

The following topics are addressed here:

- Asynchronous Method Invocation
- The async Example Application

7.1 Asynchronous Method Invocation

Session beans can implement **asynchronous methods**, business methods where control is returned to the client by the enterprise bean container before the method is invoked on the session bean instance. Clients may then use the Java SE concurrency API to retrieve the result, cancel the invocation, and check for exceptions. Asynchronous methods are typically used for long-running operations, for processor-intensive tasks, for background tasks, to increase application throughput, or to improve application response time if the method invocation result isn't required immediately.

When a session bean client invokes a typical non-asynchronous business method, control is not returned to the client until the method has completed. Clients calling asynchronous methods, however, immediately have control returned to them by the enterprise bean container. This allows the client to perform other tasks while the method invocation completes. If the method returns a result, the result is an implementation of the `java.util.concurrent.Future<V>` interface, where "V" is the result value type. The `Future<V>` interface defines methods the client may use to check whether the computation is completed, wait for the invocation to complete, retrieve the final result, and cancel the invocation.

7.1.1 Creating an Asynchronous Business Method

Annotate a business method with `javax.ejb.Asynchronous` to mark that method as an asynchronous method, or apply `@Asynchronous` at the class level to mark all the business methods of the session bean as asynchronous methods. Session bean methods that expose web services can't be asynchronous.

Asynchronous methods must return either `void` or an implementation of the `Future<V>` interface. Asynchronous methods that return `void` can't declare application exceptions, but if they return `Future<V>`, they may declare application exceptions. For example:

```
@Asynchronous
public Future<String> processPayment(Order order) throws PaymentException {
    ...
}
```

This method will attempt to process the payment of an order, and return the status as a `String`. Even if the payment processor takes a long time, the client can continue working, and display the result when the processing finally completes.

The `javax.ejb.AsyncResult<V>` class is a concrete implementation of the `Future<V>` interface provided as a helper class for returning asynchronous results. `AsyncResult` has a constructor with the result as a parameter, making it easy to create `Future<V>` implementations. For example, the `processPayment` method would use `AsyncResult` to return the status as a `String`:

```
@Asynchronous
public Future<String> processPayment(Order order) throws PaymentException {
    ...
    String status = ...;
    return new AsyncResult<>(status);
}
```

The result is returned to the enterprise bean container, not directly to the client, and the enterprise bean container makes the result available to the client. The session bean can check whether the client requested that the invocation be cancelled by calling the `javax.ejb.SessionContext.wasCancelled` method. For example:

```
@Asynchronous
public Future<String> processPayment(Order order) throws PaymentException {
    ...
```

```
        if (SessionContext.wasCancelled()) {
            // clean up
        } else {
            // process the payment
        }
        ...
}
```

7.1.2 Calling Asynchronous Methods from Enterprise Bean Clients

Session bean clients call asynchronous methods just like non-asynchronous business methods. If the asynchronous method returns a result, the client receives a Future<V> instance as soon as the method is invoked. This instance can be used to retrieve the final result, cancel the invocation, check whether the invocation has completed, check whether any exceptions were thrown during processing, and check whether the invocation was cancelled.

7.1.2.1 Retrieving the Final Result from an Asynchronous Method Invocation

The client may retrieve the result using one of the Future<V>.get methods. If processing hasn't been completed by the session bean handling the invocation, calling one of the get methods will result in the client halting execution until the invocation completes. Use the Future<V>.isDone method to determine whether processing has completed before calling one of the get methods.

The get() method returns the result as the type specified in the type value of the Future<V> instance. For example, calling Future<String>.get() will return a String object. If the method invocation was cancelled, calls to get() result in a java.util.concurrent.CancellationException being thrown. If the invocation resulted in an exception during processing by the session bean, calls to get() result in a java.util.concurrent.ExecutionException being thrown. The cause of the ExecutionException may be retrieved by calling the ExecutionException.getCause method.

The get(long timeout, java.util.concurrent.TimeUnit unit) method is similar to the get() method, but allows the client to set a timeout value. If the timeout value is exceeded, a java.util.concurrent.TimeoutException is thrown. See the API documentation for the TimeUnit class for the available units of time to specify the timeout value.

7.1.2.2 Cancelling an Asynchronous Method Invocation

Call the cancel(boolean mayInterruptIfRunning) method on the Future<V> instance to attempt to cancel the method invocation. The cancel method returns true if the cancellation was successful and false if the method invocation cannot be cancelled.

When the invocation cannot be cancelled, the mayInterruptIfRunning parameter is used to alert the session bean instance on which the method invocation is running that the client attempted to cancel the invocation. If mayInterruptIfRunning is set to true, calls to SessionContext.wasCancelled by the session bean instance will return true. If mayInterruptIfRunning is to set false, calls to SessionContext.wasCancelled by the session bean instance will return false.

The Future<V>.isCancelled method is used to check whether the method invocation was cancelled before the asynchronous method invocation completed by calling Future<V>.cancel. The isCancelled method returns true if the invocation was cancelled.

7.1.2.3 Checking the Status of an Asynchronous Method Invocation

The Future<V>.isDone method returns true if the session bean instance completed processing the method invocation. The isDone method returns true if the asynchronous method invocation completed normally, was cancelled, or resulted in an exception. That is, isDone indicates only whether the session bean has completed processing the invocation.

7.2 The async Example Application

The async example demonstrates how to define an asynchronous business method on a session bean and call it from a web client. This example contains two modules.

- A web application (async-war) that contains a stateless session bean and a JavaServer Faces interface. The MailerBean stateless session bean defines an asynchronous method, sendMessage, which uses the JavaMail API to send an email to an specified email address.

- An auxiliary Java SE program (async-smtpd) that simulates an SMTP server. This program listens on TCP port 25 for SMTP requests and prints the email messages to the standard output (instead of delivering them).

The following section describes the architecture of the async-war module.

7.2.1 Architecture of the async-war Module

The async-war module consists of a single stateless session bean, MailerBean, and a JavaServer Faces web application front end that uses Facelets tags in XHTML files to display a form for users to enter the email address for the recipient of an email. The status of the email is updated when the email is finally sent.

The MailerBean session bean injects a JavaMail resource used to send an email message to an address specified by the user. The message is created, modified, and sent using the JavaMail API. The session bean looks like this:

```
@Named
@Stateless
public class MailerBean {
    @Resource(name="mail/myExampleSession")
    private Session session;
    private static final Logger logger =
            Logger.getLogger(MailerBean.class.getName());

    @Asynchronous
    public Future<String> sendMessage(String email) {
        String status;
        try {
            Message message = new MimeMessage(session);
            message.setFrom();
            message.setRecipients(Message.RecipientType.TO,
                    InternetAddress.parse(email, false));
            message.setSubject("Test message from async example");
            message.setHeader("X-Mailer", "JavaMail");
            DateFormat dateFormatter = DateFormat
                    .getDateTimeInstance(DateFormat.LONG, DateFormat.SHORT);
            Date timeStamp = new Date();
            String messageBody = "This is a test message from the async "
                    + "example of the Java EE Tutorial. It was sent on "
                    + dateFormatter.format(timeStamp)
                    + ".";
            message.setText(messageBody);
            message.setSentDate(timeStamp);
            Transport.send(message);
            status = "Sent";
            logger.log(Level.INFO, "Mail sent to {0}", email);
        } catch (MessagingException ex) {
            logger.severe("Error in sending message.");
            status = "Encountered an error: " + ex.getMessage();
            logger.severe(ex.getMessage());
        }
        return new AsyncResult<>(status);
    }
}
```

The injected JavaMail resource can be configured through the GlassFish Server Administration Console, through a GlassFish Server administrative command, or through a resource configuration file packaged with the application. The resource configuration can be modified at runtime by the GlassFish Server administrator to use a different mail server or transport protocol.

The web client consists of a Facelets template, `template.xhtml`; two Facelets clients, `index.xhtml` and `response.xhtml`; and a JavaServer Faces managed bean, `MailerManagedBean`. The `index.xhtml` file contains a form for the target email address. When the user submits the form, the `MailerManagedBean.send` method is called. This method uses an injected instance of the `MailerBean` session bean to call `MailerBean.sendMessage`. The result is sent to the `response.xhtml` Facelets view.

7.2.2 Running the async Example

You can use either NetBeans IDE or Maven to build, package, deploy, and run the async example.

7.2.2.1 To Run the async Example Application Using NetBeans IDE

1. Make sure that GlassFish Server has been started (see Section 2.2, "Starting and Stopping GlassFish Server").

2. From the **File** menu, choose **Open Project**.

3. In the Open Project dialog box, navigate to:

   `tut-install/examples/ejb`

4. Select the async folder, select **Open Required Projects**, and click **Open Project**.

5. In the **Projects** tab, right-click the `async-smtpd` project and select **Run**.

   The SMTP server simulator starts accepting connections. The **async-smtpd** output tab shows the following message:

   `[Test SMTP server listening on port 25]`

6. In the **Projects** tab, right-click the `async-war` project and select **Build**.

   This command configures the JavaMail resource using a GlassFish Server administrative command and builds, packages, and deploys the `async-war` module.

7. Open the following URL in a web browser window:

   `http://localhost:8080/async-war`

8. In the web browser window, enter an email address and click **Send email**.

   The `MailerBean` stateless bean uses the JavaMail API to deliver an email to the SMTP server simulator. The **async-smptd** output window in NetBeans IDE shows the resulting email message, including its headers.

9. To stop the SMTP server simulator, click the **X** button on the right side of the status bar in NetBeans IDE.

10. Delete the JavaMail session resource.

    a. In the **Services** tab, expand the **Servers** node, then expand the **GlassFish Server** node.

    b. Expand the **Resources** node, then expand the **JavaMail Sessions** node.

    c. Right-click **mail/myExampleSession** and select **Unregister**.

7.2.2.2 To Run the async Example Application Using Maven

1. Make sure that GlassFish Server has been started (see Section 2.2, "Starting and Stopping GlassFish Server").

2. In a terminal window, go to:

   tut-install/examples/ejb/async/async-smtpd/

3. Enter the following command to build and package the SMTP server simulator:

   ```
   mvn install
   ```

4. Enter the following command to start the STMP server simulator:

   ```
   mvn exec:java
   ```

   The following message appears:

   ```
   [Test SMTP server listening on port 25]
   ```

   Keep this terminal window open.

5. In a new terminal window, go to:

   tut-install/examples/ejb/async/async-war

6. Enter the following command to configure the JavaMail resource and to build, package, and deploy the `async-war` module:

   ```
   mvn install
   ```

7. Open the following URL in a web browser window:

    ```
    http://localhost:8080/async-war
    ```

8. In the web browser window, enter an email address and click **Send email**.

    The `MailerBean` stateless bean uses the JavaMail API to deliver an email to the SMTP server simulator. The resulting email message appears on the first terminal window, including its headers.

9. To stop the SMTP server simulator, close the terminal window in which you issued the command to start the STMP server simulator.

10. To delete the JavaMail session resource, type the following command:

    ```
    asadmin delete-javamail-resource mail/myExampleSession
    ```

Part III

Persistence

Part III explores the Java Persistence API. This part contains the following chapters:

- Chapter 8, "Introduction to the Java Persistence API"
- Chapter 9, "Running the Persistence Examples"
- Chapter 10, "The Java Persistence Query Language"
- Chapter 11, "Using the Criteria API to Create Queries"
- Chapter 12, "Creating and Using String-Based Criteria Queries"
- Chapter 13, "Controlling Concurrent Access to Entity Data with Locking"
- Chapter 14, "Creating Fetch Plans with Entity Graphs"
- Chapter 15, "Using a Second-Level Cache with Java Persistence API Applications"

8

Introduction to the Java Persistence API

The Java Persistence API provides Java developers with an object/relational mapping facility for managing relational data in Java applications. Java Persistence consists of four areas:

- The Java Persistence API
- The query language
- The Java Persistence Criteria API
- Object/relational mapping metadata

The following topics are addressed here:

- Entities
- Entity Inheritance
- Managing Entities
- Querying Entities
- Database Schema Creation
- Further Information about Persistence

8.1 Entities

An entity is a lightweight persistence domain object. Typically, an entity represents a table in a relational database, and each entity instance corresponds to a row in that table. The primary programming artifact of an entity is the entity class, although entities can use helper classes.

The persistent state of an entity is represented through either persistent fields or persistent properties. These fields or properties use object/relational mapping annotations to map the entities and entity relationships to the relational data in the underlying data store.

8.1.1 Requirements for Entity Classes

An entity class must follow these requirements.

- The class must be annotated with the `javax.persistence.Entity` annotation.

- The class must have a public or protected, no-argument constructor. The class may have other constructors.

- The class must not be declared `final`. No methods or persistent instance variables must be declared `final`.

- If an entity instance is passed by value as a detached object, such as through a session bean's remote business interface, the class must implement the `Serializable` interface.

- Entities may extend both entity and non-entity classes, and non-entity classes may extend entity classes.

- Persistent instance variables must be declared private, protected, or package-private and can be accessed directly only by the entity class's methods. Clients must access the entity's state through accessor or business methods.

8.1.2 Persistent Fields and Properties in Entity Classes

The persistent state of an entity can be accessed through either the entity's instance variables or properties. The fields or properties must be of the following Java language types:

- Java primitive types

- `java.lang.String`

- Other serializable types, including:

    - Wrappers of Java primitive types

    - `java.math.BigInteger`

    - `java.math.BigDecimal`

    - `java.util.Date`

- — java.util.Calendar
- — java.sql.Date
- — java.sql.Time
- — java.sql.TimeStamp
- — User-defined serializable types
- — byte[]
- — Byte[]
- — char[]
- — Character[]

- Enumerated types
- Other entities and/or collections of entities
- Embeddable classes

Entities may use persistent fields, persistent properties, or a combination of both. If the mapping annotations are applied to the entity's instance variables, the entity uses persistent fields. If the mapping annotations are applied to the entity's getter methods for JavaBeans-style properties, the entity uses persistent properties.

8.1.2.1 Persistent Fields

If the entity class uses persistent fields, the Persistence runtime accesses entity-class instance variables directly. All fields not annotated javax.persistence.Transient or not marked as Java transient will be persisted to the data store. The object/relational mapping annotations must be applied to the instance variables.

8.1.2.2 Persistent Properties

If the entity uses persistent properties, the entity must follow the method conventions of JavaBeans components. JavaBeans-style properties use getter and setter methods that are typically named after the entity class's instance variable names. For every persistent property *property* of type *Type* of the entity, there is a getter method get*Property* and setter method set*Property*. If the property is a Boolean, you may use is*Property* instead of get*Property*. For example, if a Customer entity uses persistent properties and has a private instance variable called firstName, the class defines a getFirstName and setFirstName method for retrieving and setting the state of the firstName instance variable.

The method signatures for single-valued persistent properties are as follows:

```
Type getProperty()
void setProperty(Type type)
```

The object/relational mapping annotations for persistent properties must be applied to the getter methods. Mapping annotations cannot be applied to fields or properties annotated @Transient or marked transient.

8.1.2.3 Using Collections in Entity Fields and Properties

Collection-valued persistent fields and properties must use the supported Java collection interfaces regardless of whether the entity uses persistent fields or properties. The following collection interfaces may be used:

- java.util.Collection
- java.util.Set
- java.util.List
- java.util.Map

If the entity class uses persistent fields, the type in the preceding method signatures must be one of these collection types. Generic variants of these collection types may also be used. For example, if it has a persistent property that contains a set of phone numbers, the Customer entity would have the following methods:

```
Set<PhoneNumber> getPhoneNumbers() { ... }
void setPhoneNumbers(Set<PhoneNumber>) { ... }
```

If a field or property of an entity consists of a collection of basic types or embeddable classes, use the javax.persistence.ElementCollection annotation on the field or property.

The two attributes of @ElementCollection are targetClass and fetch. The targetClass attribute specifies the class name of the basic or embeddable class and is optional if the field or property is defined using Java programming language generics. The optional fetch attribute is used to specify whether the collection should be retrieved lazily or eagerly, using the javax.persistence.FetchType constants of either LAZY or EAGER, respectively. By default, the collection will be fetched lazily.

The following entity, Person, has a persistent field, nicknames, which is a collection of String classes that will be fetched eagerly. The targetClass element is not required, because it uses generics to define the field.

```
@Entity
public class Person {
    ...
    @ElementCollection(fetch=EAGER)
    protected Set<String> nickname = new HashSet();
    ...
}
```

Collections of entity elements and relationships may be represented by `java.util.Map` collections. A `Map` consists of a key and a value.

When using `Map` elements or relationships, the following rules apply.

- The `Map` key or value may be a basic Java programming language type, an embeddable class, or an entity.

- When the `Map` value is an embeddable class or basic type, use the `@ElementCollection` annotation.

- When the `Map` value is an entity, use the `@OneToMany` or `@ManyToMany` annotation.

- Use the `Map` type on only one side of a bidirectional relationship.

If the key type of a `Map` is a Java programming language basic type, use the annotation `javax.persistence.MapKeyColumn` to set the column mapping for the key. By default, the `name` attribute of `@MapKeyColumn` is of the form *RELATIONSHIP-FIELD/PROPERTY-NAME*_KEY. For example, if the referencing relationship field name is `image`, the default `name` attribute is `IMAGE_KEY`.

If the key type of a `Map` is an entity, use the `javax.persistence.MapKeyJoinColumn` annotation. If the multiple columns are needed to set the mapping, use the annotation `javax.persistence.MapKeyJoinColumns` to include multiple `@MapKeyJoinColumn` annotations. If no `@MapKeyJoinColumn` is present, the mapping column name is by default set to *RELATIONSHIP-FIELD/PROPERTY-NAME*_KEY. For example, if the relationship field name is `employee`, the default `name` attribute is `EMPLOYEE_KEY`.

If Java programming language generic types are not used in the relationship field or property, the key class must be explicitly set using the `javax.persistence.MapKeyClass` annotation.

If the `Map` key is the primary key or a persistent field or property of the entity that is the `Map` value, use the `javax.persistence.MapKey` annotation. The `@MapKeyClass` and `@MapKey` annotations cannot be used on the same field or property.

If the Map value is a Java programming language basic type or an embeddable class, it will be mapped as a collection table in the underlying database. If generic types are not used, the @ElementCollection annotation's targetClass attribute must be set to the type of the Map value.

If the Map value is an entity and part of a many-to-many or one-to-many unidirectional relationship, it will be mapped as a join table in the underlying database. A unidirectional one-to-many relationship that uses a Map may also be mapped using the @JoinColumn annotation.

If the entity is part of a one-to-many/many-to-one bidirectional relationship, it will be mapped in the table of the entity that represents the value of the Map. If generic types are not used, the targetEntity attribute of the @OneToMany and @ManyToMany annotations must be set to the type of the Map value.

8.1.2.4 Validating Persistent Fields and Properties

The Java API for JavaBeans Validation (Bean Validation) provides a mechanism for validating application data. Bean Validation is integrated into the Java EE containers, allowing the same validation logic to be used in any of the tiers of an enterprise application.

Bean Validation constraints may be applied to persistent entity classes, embeddable classes, and mapped superclasses. By default, the Persistence provider will automatically perform validation on entities with persistent fields or properties annotated with Bean Validation constraints immediately after the PrePersist, PreUpdate, and PreRemove lifecycle events.

Bean Validation constraints are annotations applied to the fields or properties of Java programming language classes. Bean Validation provides a set of constraints as well as an API for defining custom constraints. Custom constraints can be specific combinations of the default constraints, or new constraints that don't use the default constraints. Each constraint is associated with at least one validator class that validates the value of the constrained field or property. Custom constraint developers must also provide a validator class for the constraint.

Bean Validation constraints are applied to the persistent fields or properties of persistent classes. When adding Bean Validation constraints, use the same access strategy as the persistent class. That is, if the persistent class uses field access, apply the Bean Validation constraint annotations on the class's fields. If the class uses property access, apply the constraints on the getter methods.

Table 21–1 in *The Java EE 7 Tutorial, Volume 1* lists Bean Validation's built-in constraints, defined in the javax.validation.constraints package.

All the built-in constraints listed in Table 21–1 in *The Java EE 7 Tutorial, Volume 1* have a corresponding annotation, *ConstraintName*.List, for grouping multiple constraints of the same type on the same field or property. For example, the following persistent field has two @Pattern constraints:

```
@Pattern.List({
    @Pattern(regexp="..."),
    @Pattern(regexp="...")
})
```

The following entity class, Contact, has Bean Validation constraints applied to its persistent fields:

```
@Entity
public class Contact implements Serializable {
    @Id
    @GeneratedValue(strategy = GenerationType.AUTO)
    private Long id;
    @NotNull
    protected String firstName;
    @NotNull
    protected String lastName;
    @Pattern(regexp = "[a-z0-9!#$%&'*+/=?^_`{|}~-]+(?:\\."
            + "[a-z0-9!#$%&'*+/=?^_`{|}~-]+)*@"
            + "(?:[a-z0-9](?:[a-z0-9-]*[a-z0-9])?\\.)+[a-z0-9]"
            + "(?:[a-z0-9-]*[a-z0-9])?",
            message = "{invalid.email}")
    protected String email;
    @Pattern(regexp = "^\\(?(\\d{3})\\)?[- ]?(\\d{3})[- ]?(\\d{4})$",
            message = "{invalid.phonenumber}")
    protected String mobilePhone;
    @Pattern(regexp = "^\\(?(\\d{3})\\)?[- ]?(\\d{3})[- ]?(\\d{4})$",
            message = "{invalid.phonenumber}")
    protected String homePhone;
    @Temporal(javax.persistence.TemporalType.DATE)
    @Past
    protected Date birthday;
    ...
}
```

The @NotNull annotation on the firstName and lastName fields specifies that those fields are now required. If a new Contact instance is created where firstName or lastName have not been initialized, Bean Validation will throw a validation error. Similarly, if a previously created instance of Contact has been modified so that firstName or lastName are null, a validation error will be thrown.

The `email` field has a `@Pattern` constraint applied to it, with a complicated regular expression that matches most valid email addresses. If the value of `email` doesn't match this regular expression, a validation error will be thrown.

The `homePhone` and `mobilePhone` fields have the same `@Pattern` constraints. The regular expression matches 10 digit telephone numbers in the United States and Canada of the form (*xxx*) *xxx*-*xxxx*.

The `birthday` field is annotated with the `@Past` constraint, which ensures that the value of `birthday` must be in the past.

8.1.3 Primary Keys in Entities

Each entity has a unique object identifier. A customer entity, for example, might be identified by a customer number. The unique identifier, or **primary key**, enables clients to locate a particular entity instance. Every entity must have a primary key. An entity may have either a simple or a composite primary key.

Simple primary keys use the `javax.persistence.Id` annotation to denote the primary key property or field.

Composite primary keys are used when a primary key consists of more than one attribute, which corresponds to a set of single persistent properties or fields. Composite primary keys must be defined in a primary key class. Composite primary keys are denoted using the `javax.persistence.EmbeddedId` and `javax.persistence.IdClass` annotations.

The primary key, or the property or field of a composite primary key, must be one of the following Java language types:

- Java primitive types
- Java primitive wrapper types
- `java.lang.String`
- `java.util.Date` (the temporal type should be DATE)
- `java.sql.Date`
- `java.math.BigDecimal`
- `java.math.BigInteger`

Floating-point types should never be used in primary keys. If you use a generated primary key, only integral types will be portable.

A primary key class must meet these requirements.

- The access control modifier of the class must be `public`.

- The properties of the primary key class must be `public` or `protected` if property-based access is used.

- The class must have a public default constructor.

- The class must implement the `hashCode()` and `equals(Object other)` methods.

- The class must be serializable.

- A composite primary key must be represented and mapped to multiple fields or properties of the entity class or must be represented and mapped as an embeddable class.

- If the class is mapped to multiple fields or properties of the entity class, the names and types of the primary key fields or properties in the primary key class must match those of the entity class.

The following primary key class is a composite key, and the `customerOrder` and `itemId` fields together uniquely identify an entity:

```java
public final class LineItemKey implements Serializable {
    private Integer customerOrder;
    private int itemId;

    public LineItemKey() {}

    public LineItemKey(Integer order, int itemId) {
        this.setCustomerOrder(order);
        this.setItemId(itemId);
    }

    @Override
    public int hashCode() {
        return ((this.getCustomerOrder() == null
                ? 0 : this.getCustomerOrder().hashCode())
                ^ ((int) this.getItemId()));
    }

    @Override
    public boolean equals(Object otherOb) {
        if (this == otherOb) {
            return true;
        }
```

```
        if (!(otherOb instanceof LineItemKey)) {
            return false;
        }
        LineItemKey other = (LineItemKey) otherOb;
        return ((this.getCustomerOrder() == null
                ? other.getCustomerOrder() == null : this.getCustomerOrder()
                .equals(other.getCustomerOrder()))
                && (this.getItemId() == other.getItemId()));
    }

    @Override
    public String toString() {
        return "" + getCustomerOrder() + "-" + getItemId();
    }
    /* Getters and setters */
}
```

8.1.4 Multiplicity in Entity Relationships

Multiplicities are of the following types.

- **One-to-one**: Each entity instance is related to a single instance of another entity. For example, to model a physical warehouse in which each storage bin contains a single widget, StorageBin and Widget would have a one-to-one relationship. One-to-one relationships use the javax.persistence.OneToOne annotation on the corresponding persistent property or field.

- **One-to-many**: An entity instance can be related to multiple instances of the other entities. A sales order, for example, can have multiple line items. In the order application, CustomerOrder would have a one-to-many relationship with LineItem. One-to-many relationships use the javax.persistence.OneToMany annotation on the corresponding persistent property or field.

- **Many-to-one**: Multiple instances of an entity can be related to a single instance of the other entity. This multiplicity is the opposite of a one-to-many relationship. In the example just mentioned, the relationship to CustomerOrder from the perspective of LineItem is many-to-one. Many-to-one relationships use the javax.persistence.ManyToOne annotation on the corresponding persistent property or field.

- **Many-to-many**: The entity instances can be related to multiple instances of each other. For example, each college course has many students, and every student may take several courses. Therefore, in an enrollment application, Course and Student would have a many-to-many relationship.

Many-to-many relationships use the `javax.persistence.ManyToMany` annotation on the corresponding persistent property or field.

8.1.5 Direction in Entity Relationships

The direction of a relationship can be either bidirectional or unidirectional. A bidirectional relationship has both an owning side and an inverse side. A unidirectional relationship has only an owning side. The owning side of a relationship determines how the Persistence runtime makes updates to the relationship in the database.

8.1.5.1 Bidirectional Relationships

In a **bidirectional** relationship, each entity has a relationship field or property that refers to the other entity. Through the relationship field or property, an entity class's code can access its related object. If an entity has a related field, the entity is said to "know" about its related object. For example, if `CustomerOrder` knows what `LineItem` instances it has and if `LineItem` knows what `CustomerOrder` it belongs to, they have a bidirectional relationship.

Bidirectional relationships must follow these rules.

- The inverse side of a bidirectional relationship must refer to its owning side by using the `mappedBy` element of the `@OneToOne`, `@OneToMany`, or `@ManyToMany` annotation. The `mappedBy` element designates the property or field in the entity that is the owner of the relationship.

- The many side of many-to-one bidirectional relationships must not define the `mappedBy` element. The many side is always the owning side of the relationship.

- For one-to-one bidirectional relationships, the owning side corresponds to the side that contains the corresponding foreign key.

- For many-to-many bidirectional relationships, either side may be the owning side.

8.1.5.2 Unidirectional Relationships

In a **unidirectional** relationship, only one entity has a relationship field or property that refers to the other. For example, `LineItem` would have a relationship field that identifies `Product`, but `Product` would not have a relationship field or property for `LineItem`. In other words, `LineItem` knows about `Product`, but `Product` doesn't know which `LineItem` instances refer to it.

8.1.5.3 Queries and Relationship Direction

Java Persistence query language and Criteria API queries often navigate across relationships. The direction of a relationship determines whether a query can navigate from one entity to another. For example, a query can navigate from LineItem to Product but cannot navigate in the opposite direction. For CustomerOrder and LineItem, a query could navigate in both directions because these two entities have a bidirectional relationship.

8.1.5.4 Cascade Operations and Relationships

Entities that use relationships often have dependencies on the existence of the other entity in the relationship. For example, a line item is part of an order; if the order is deleted, the line item also should be deleted. This is called a cascade delete relationship.

The javax.persistence.CascadeType enumerated type defines the cascade operations that are applied in the cascade element of the relationship annotations. Table 8–1 lists the cascade operations for entities.

Table 8–1   Cascade Operations for Entities

Cascade Operation	Description
ALL	All cascade operations will be applied to the parent entity's related entity. All is equivalent to specifying cascade={DETACH, MERGE, PERSIST, REFRESH, REMOVE}
DETACH	If the parent entity is detached from the persistence context, the related entity will also be detached.
MERGE	If the parent entity is merged into the persistence context, the related entity will also be merged.
PERSIST	If the parent entity is persisted into the persistence context, the related entity will also be persisted.
REFRESH	If the parent entity is refreshed in the current persistence context, the related entity will also be refreshed.
REMOVE	If the parent entity is removed from the current persistence context, the related entity will also be removed.

Cascade delete relationships are specified using the cascade=REMOVE element specification for @OneToOne and @OneToMany relationships. For example:

```
@OneToMany(cascade=REMOVE, mappedBy="customer")
public Set<CustomerOrder> getOrders() { return orders; }
```

8.1.5.5 Orphan Removal in Relationships

When a target entity in a one-to-one or one-to-many relationship is removed from the relationship, it is often desirable to cascade the remove operation to the target entity. Such target entities are considered "orphans," and the orphanRemoval attribute can be used to specify that orphaned entities should be removed. For example, if an order has many line items and one of them is removed from the order, the removed line item is considered an orphan. If orphanRemoval is set to true, the line item entity will be deleted when the line item is removed from the order.

The orphanRemoval attribute in @OneToMany and @oneToOne takes a Boolean value and is by default false.

The following example will cascade the remove operation to the orphaned order entity when the customer entity is deleted:

```
@OneToMany(mappedBy="customer", orphanRemoval="true")
public List<CustomerOrder> getOrders() { ... }
```

8.1.6 Embeddable Classes in Entities

Embeddable classes are used to represent the state of an entity but don't have a persistent identity of their own, unlike entity classes. Instances of an embeddable class share the identity of the entity that owns it. Embeddable classes exist only as the state of another entity. An entity may have single-valued or collection-valued embeddable class attributes.

Embeddable classes have the same rules as entity classes but are annotated with the javax.persistence.Embeddable annotation instead of @Entity.

The following embeddable class, ZipCode, has the fields zip and plusFour:

```
@Embeddable
public class ZipCode {
    String zip;
    String plusFour;
    ...
}
```

This embeddable class is used by the Address entity:

```
@Entity
public class Address {
    @Id
    protected long id;
    String street1;
    String street2;
```

```
        String city;
        String province;
        @Embedded
        ZipCode zipCode;
        String country;
        ...
}
```

Entities that own embeddable classes as part of their persistent state may annotate the field or property with the `javax.persistence.Embedded` annotation but are not required to do so.

Embeddable classes may themselves use other embeddable classes to represent their state. They may also contain collections of basic Java programming language types or other embeddable classes. Embeddable classes may also contain relationships to other entities or collections of entities. If the embeddable class has such a relationship, the relationship is from the target entity or collection of entities to the entity that owns the embeddable class.

8.2 Entity Inheritance

Entities support class inheritance, polymorphic associations, and polymorphic queries. Entity classes can extend non-entity classes, and non-entity classes can extend entity classes. Entity classes can be both abstract and concrete.

The `roster` example application demonstrates entity inheritance, as described in Section 9.2.2, "Entity Inheritance in the roster Application."

8.2.1 Abstract Entities

An abstract class may be declared an entity by decorating the class with `@Entity`. Abstract entities are like concrete entities but cannot be instantiated.

Abstract entities can be queried just like concrete entities. If an abstract entity is the target of a query, the query operates on all the concrete subclasses of the abstract entity:

```
@Entity
public abstract class Employee {
    @Id
    protected Integer employeeId;
    ...
}
```

```
@Entity
public class FullTimeEmployee extends Employee {
    protected Integer salary;
    ...
}
@Entity
public class PartTimeEmployee extends Employee {
    protected Float hourlyWage;
}
```

8.2.2 Mapped Superclasses

Entities may inherit from superclasses that contain persistent state and mapping information but are not entities. That is, the superclass is not decorated with the @Entity annotation and is not mapped as an entity by the Java Persistence provider. These superclasses are most often used when you have state and mapping information common to multiple entity classes.

Mapped superclasses are specified by decorating the class with the annotation javax.persistence.MappedSuperclass:

```
@MappedSuperclass
public class Employee {
    @Id
    protected Integer employeeId;
    ...
}
@Entity
public class FullTimeEmployee extends Employee {
    protected Integer salary;
    ...
}
@Entity
public class PartTimeEmployee extends Employee {
    protected Float hourlyWage;
    ...
}
```

Mapped superclasses cannot be queried and cannot be used in EntityManager or Query operations. You must use entity subclasses of the mapped superclass in EntityManager or Query operations. Mapped superclasses can't be targets of entity relationships. Mapped superclasses can be abstract or concrete.

Mapped superclasses do not have any corresponding tables in the underlying datastore. Entities that inherit from the mapped superclass define the table mappings. For instance, in the preceding code sample, the underlying tables would be FULLTIMEEMPLOYEE and PARTTIMEEMPLOYEE, but there is no EMPLOYEE table.

8.2.3 Non-Entity Superclasses

Entities may have non-entity superclasses, and these superclasses can be either abstract or concrete. The state of non-entity superclasses is nonpersistent, and any state inherited from the non-entity superclass by an entity class is nonpersistent. Non-entity superclasses may not be used in EntityManager or Query operations. Any mapping or relationship annotations in non-entity superclasses are ignored.

8.2.4 Entity Inheritance Mapping Strategies

You can configure how the Java Persistence provider maps inherited entities to the underlying datastore by decorating the root class of the hierarchy with the annotation javax.persistence.Inheritance. The following mapping strategies are used to map the entity data to the underlying database:

- A single table per class hierarchy
- A table per concrete entity class
- A "join" strategy, whereby fields or properties that are specific to a subclass are mapped to a different table than the fields or properties that are common to the parent class

The strategy is configured by setting the strategy element of @Inheritance to one of the options defined in the javax.persistence.InheritanceType enumerated type:

```
public enum InheritanceType {
    SINGLE_TABLE,
    JOINED,
    TABLE_PER_CLASS
};
```

The default strategy, InheritanceType.SINGLE_TABLE, is used if the @Inheritance annotation is not specified on the root class of the entity hierarchy.

8.2.4.1 The Single Table per Class Hierarchy Strategy

With this strategy, which corresponds to the default InheritanceType.SINGLE_TABLE, all classes in the hierarchy are mapped to a single table in the database. This table has a **discriminator column** containing a value that identifies the subclass to which the instance represented by the row belongs.

The discriminator column, whose elements are shown in Table 8–2, can be specified by using the javax.persistence.DiscriminatorColumn annotation on the root of the entity class hierarchy.

Table 8–2   *@DiscriminatorColumn Elements*

Type	Name	Description
String	name	The name of the column to be used as the discriminator column. The default is DTYPE. This element is optional.
DiscriminatorType	discriminatorType	The type of the column to be used as a discriminator column. The default is DiscriminatorType.STRING. This element is optional.
String	columnDefinition	The SQL fragment to use when creating the discriminator column. The default is generated by the Persistence provider and is implementation-specific. This element is optional.
String	length	The column length for String-based discriminator types. This element is ignored for non-String discriminator types. The default is 31. This element is optional.

The javax.persistence.DiscriminatorType enumerated type is used to set the type of the discriminator column in the database by setting the discriminatorType element of @DiscriminatorColumn to one of the defined types. DiscriminatorType is defined as follows:

```
public enum DiscriminatorType {
    STRING,
    CHAR,
    INTEGER
};
```

If @DiscriminatorColumn is not specified on the root of the entity hierarchy and a discriminator column is required, the Persistence provider assumes a default column name of DTYPE and column type of DiscriminatorType.STRING.

The javax.persistence.DiscriminatorValue annotation may be used to set the value entered into the discriminator column for each entity in a class hierarchy. You may decorate only concrete entity classes with @DiscriminatorValue.

If @DiscriminatorValue is not specified on an entity in a class hierarchy that uses a discriminator column, the Persistence provider will provide a default, implementation-specific value. If the discriminatorType element of @DiscriminatorColumn is DiscriminatorType.STRING, the default value is the name of the entity.

This strategy provides good support for polymorphic relationships between entities and queries that cover the entire entity class hierarchy. However, this strategy requires the columns that contain the state of subclasses to be nullable.

8.2.4.2 The Table per Concrete Class Strategy

In this strategy, which corresponds to InheritanceType.TABLE_PER_CLASS, each concrete class is mapped to a separate table in the database. All fields or properties in the class, including inherited fields or properties, are mapped to columns in the class's table in the database.

This strategy provides poor support for polymorphic relationships and usually requires either SQL UNION queries or separate SQL queries for each subclass for queries that cover the entire entity class hierarchy.

Support for this strategy is optional and may not be supported by all Java Persistence API providers. The default Java Persistence API provider in GlassFish Server does not support this strategy.

8.2.4.3 The Joined Subclass Strategy

In this strategy, which corresponds to InheritanceType.JOINED, the root of the class hierarchy is represented by a single table, and each subclass has a separate table that contains only those fields specific to that subclass. That is, the subclass table does not contain columns for inherited fields or properties. The subclass table also has a column or columns that represent its primary key, which is a foreign key to the primary key of the superclass table.

This strategy provides good support for polymorphic relationships but requires one or more join operations to be performed when instantiating entity subclasses. This may result in poor performance for extensive class hierarchies. Similarly, queries that cover the entire class hierarchy require join operations between the subclass tables, resulting in decreased performance.

Some Java Persistence API providers, including the default provider in GlassFish Server, require a discriminator column that corresponds to the root entity when using the joined subclass strategy. If you are not using automatic table creation in your application, make sure that the database table is set up correctly for the discriminator column defaults, or use the @DiscriminatorColumn annotation to match your database schema. For information on discriminator columns, see Section 8.2.4.1, "The Single Table per Class Hierarchy Strategy."

8.3 Managing Entities

Entities are managed by the entity manager, which is represented by
`javax.persistence.EntityManager` instances. Each `EntityManager` instance is
associated with a persistence context: a set of managed entity instances that exist
in a particular data store. A persistence context defines the scope under which
particular entity instances are created, persisted, and removed. The
`EntityManager` interface defines the methods that are used to interact with the
persistence context.

8.3.1 The EntityManager Interface

The `EntityManager` API creates and removes persistent entity instances, finds
entities by the entity's primary key, and allows queries to be run on entities.

8.3.1.1 Container-Managed Entity Managers

With a **container-managed entity manager**, an `EntityManager` instance's
persistence context is automatically propagated by the container to all application
components that use the `EntityManager` instance within a single Java Transaction
API (JTA) transaction.

JTA transactions usually involve calls across application components. To complete
a JTA transaction, these components usually need access to a single persistence
context. This occurs when an `EntityManager` is injected into the application
components by means of the `javax.persistence.PersistenceContext`
annotation. The persistence context is automatically propagated with the current
JTA transaction, and `EntityManager` references that are mapped to the same
persistence unit provide access to the persistence context within that transaction.
By automatically propagating the persistence context, application components
don't need to pass references to `EntityManager` instances to each other in order to
make changes within a single transaction. The Java EE container manages the
lifecycle of container-managed entity managers.

To obtain an `EntityManager` instance, inject the entity manager into the
application component:

```
@PersistenceContext
EntityManager em;
```

8.3.1.2 Application-Managed Entity Managers

With an **application-managed entity manager**, on the other hand, the persistence
context is not propagated to application components, and the lifecycle of
`EntityManager` instances is managed by the application.

Application-managed entity managers are used when applications need to access a persistence context that is not propagated with the JTA transaction across `EntityManager` instances in a particular persistence unit. In this case, each `EntityManager` creates a new, isolated persistence context. The `EntityManager` and its associated persistence context are created and destroyed explicitly by the application. They are also used when directly injecting `EntityManager` instances can't be done because `EntityManager` instances are not thread-safe. `EntityManagerFactory` instances are thread-safe.

Applications create `EntityManager` instances in this case by using the `createEntityManager` method of `javax.persistence.EntityManagerFactory`.

To obtain an `EntityManager` instance, you first must obtain an `EntityManagerFactory` instance by injecting it into the application component by means of the `javax.persistence.PersistenceUnit` annotation:

```
@PersistenceUnit
EntityManagerFactory emf;
```

Then obtain an `EntityManager` from the `EntityManagerFactory` instance:

```
EntityManager em = emf.createEntityManager();
```

Application-managed entity managers don't automatically propagate the JTA transaction context. Such applications need to manually gain access to the JTA transaction manager and add transaction demarcation information when performing entity operations. The `javax.transaction.UserTransaction` interface defines methods to begin, commit, and roll back transactions. Inject an instance of `UserTransaction` by creating an instance variable annotated with `@Resource`:

```
@Resource
UserTransaction utx;
```

To begin a transaction, call the `UserTransaction.begin` method. When all the entity operations are complete, call the `UserTransaction.commit` method to commit the transaction. The `UserTransaction.rollback` method is used to roll back the current transaction.

The following example shows how to manage transactions in an application that uses an application-managed entity manager:

```
@PersistenceUnit
EntityManagerFactory emf;
EntityManager em;
@Resource
UserTransaction utx;
```

```
...
em = emf.createEntityManager();
try {
    utx.begin();
    em.persist(SomeEntity);
    em.merge(AnotherEntity);
    em.remove(ThirdEntity);
    utx.commit();
} catch (Exception e) {
    utx.rollback();
}
```

8.3.1.3 Finding Entities Using the EntityManager

The `EntityManager.find` method is used to look up entities in the data store by the entity's primary key:

```
@PersistenceContext
EntityManager em;
public void enterOrder(int custID, CustomerOrder newOrder) {
    Customer cust = em.find(Customer.class, custID);
    cust.getOrders().add(newOrder);
    newOrder.setCustomer(cust);
}
```

8.3.1.4 Managing an Entity Instance's Lifecycle

You manage entity instances by invoking operations on the entity by means of an `EntityManager` instance. Entity instances are in one of four states: new, managed, detached, or removed.

- New entity instances have no persistent identity and are not yet associated with a persistence context.

- Managed entity instances have a persistent identity and are associated with a persistence context.

- Detached entity instances have a persistent identity and are not currently associated with a persistence context.

- Removed entity instances have a persistent identity, are associated with a persistent context, and are scheduled for removal from the data store.

8.3.1.5 Persisting Entity Instances

New entity instances become managed and persistent either by invoking the `persist` method or by a cascading `persist` operation invoked from related entities that have the `cascade=PERSIST` or `cascade=ALL` elements set in the relationship annotation. This means that the entity's data is stored to the database when the transaction associated with the persist operation is completed. If the entity is already managed, the persist operation is ignored, although the persist operation will cascade to related entities that have the cascade element set to PERSIST or ALL in the relationship annotation. If persist is called on a removed entity instance, the entity becomes managed. If the entity is detached, either persist will throw an IllegalArgumentException, or the transaction commit will fail. The following method performs a persist operation:

```
@PersistenceContext
EntityManager em;
...
public LineItem createLineItem(CustomerOrder order, Product product,
        int quantity) {
    LineItem li = new LineItem(order, product, quantity);
    order.getLineItems().add(li);
    em.persist(li);
    return li;
}
```

The persist operation is propagated to all entities related to the calling entity that have the cascade element set to ALL or PERSIST in the relationship annotation:

```
@OneToMany(cascade=ALL, mappedBy="order")
public Collection<LineItem> getLineItems() {
    return lineItems;
}
```

8.3.1.6 Removing Entity Instances

Managed entity instances are removed by invoking the remove method or by a cascading remove operation invoked from related entities that have the cascade=REMOVE or cascade=ALL elements set in the relationship annotation. If the remove method is invoked on a new entity, the remove operation is ignored, although remove will cascade to related entities that have the cascade element set to REMOVE or ALL in the relationship annotation. If remove is invoked on a detached entity, either remove will throw an IllegalArgumentException, or the transaction commit will fail. If invoked on an already removed entity, remove will be ignored. The entity's data will be removed from the data store when the transaction is completed or as a result of the flush operation.

In the following example, all LineItem entities associated with the order are also removed, as CustomerOrder.getLineItems has cascade=ALL set in the relationship annotation.

```
public void removeOrder(Integer orderId) {
    try {
        CustomerOrder order = em.find(CustomerOrder.class, orderId);
        em.remove(order);
    }
    ...
}
```

8.3.1.7 Synchronizing Entity Data to the Database

The state of persistent entities is synchronized to the database when the transaction with which the entity is associated commits. If a managed entity is in a bidirectional relationship with another managed entity, the data will be persisted, based on the owning side of the relationship.

To force synchronization of the managed entity to the data store, invoke the `flush` method of the `EntityManager` instance. If the entity is related to another entity and the relationship annotation has the `cascade` element set to `PERSIST` or `ALL`, the related entity's data will be synchronized with the data store when `flush` is called.

If the entity is removed, calling `flush` will remove the entity data from the data store.

8.3.2 Persistence Units

A persistence unit defines a set of all entity classes that are managed by `EntityManager` instances in an application. This set of entity classes represents the data contained within a single data store.

Persistence units are defined by the `persistence.xml` configuration file. The following is an example `persistence.xml` file:

```
<persistence>
    <persistence-unit name="OrderManagement">
        <description>This unit manages orders and customers.
            It does not rely on any vendor-specific features and can
            therefore be deployed to any persistence provider.
        </description>
        <jta-data-source>jdbc/MyOrderDB</jta-data-source>
        <jar-file>MyOrderApp.jar</jar-file>
        <class>com.widgets.CustomerOrder</class>
        <class>com.widgets.Customer</class>
    </persistence-unit>
</persistence>
```

This file defines a persistence unit named `OrderManagement`, which uses a JTA-aware data source, `jdbc/MyOrderDB`. The `jar-file` and `class` elements specify managed persistence classes: entity classes, embeddable classes, and mapped superclasses. The `jar-file` element specifies JAR files that are visible to the packaged persistence unit that contain managed persistence classes, whereas the `class` element explicitly names managed persistence classes.

The `jta-data-source` (for JTA-aware data sources) and `non-jta-data-source` (for non-JTA-aware data sources) elements specify the global JNDI name of the data source to be used by the container.

The JAR file or directory whose `META-INF` directory contains `persistence.xml` is called the root of the persistence unit. The scope of the persistence unit is determined by the persistence unit's root. Each persistence unit must be identified with a name that is unique to the persistence unit's scope.

Persistent units can be packaged as part of a WAR or EJB JAR file or can be packaged as a JAR file that can then be included in an WAR or EAR file.

- If you package the persistent unit as a set of classes in an EJB JAR file, `persistence.xml` should be put in the EJB JAR's `META-INF` directory.

- If you package the persistence unit as a set of classes in a WAR file, `persistence.xml` should be located in the WAR file's `WEB-INF/classes/META-INF` directory.

- If you package the persistence unit in a JAR file that will be included in a WAR or EAR file, the JAR file should be located in either

  – The `WEB-INF/lib` directory of a WAR

  – Or the EAR file's library directory

Note: In the Java Persistence API 1.0, JAR files could be located at the root of an EAR file as the root of the persistence unit. This is no longer supported. Portable applications should use the EAR file's library directory as the root of the persistence unit.

8.4 Querying Entities

The Java Persistence API provides the following methods for querying entities.

- The Java Persistence query language (JPQL) is a simple, string-based language similar to SQL used to query entities and their relationships. See Chapter 10, "The Java Persistence Query Language," for more information.

- The Criteria API is used to create typesafe queries using Java programming language APIs to query for entities and their relationships. See Chapter 11, "Using the Criteria API to Create Queries," for more information.

Both JPQL and the Criteria API have advantages and disadvantages.

Just a few lines long, JPQL queries are typically more concise and more readable than Criteria queries. Developers familiar with SQL will find it easy to learn the syntax of JPQL. JPQL named queries can be defined in the entity class using a Java programming language annotation or in the application's deployment descriptor. JPQL queries are not typesafe, however, and require a cast when retrieving the query result from the entity manager. This means that type-casting errors may not be caught at compile time. JPQL queries don't support open-ended parameters.

Criteria queries allow you to define the query in the business tier of the application. Although this is also possible using JPQL dynamic queries, Criteria queries provide better performance because JPQL dynamic queries must be parsed each time they are called. Criteria queries are typesafe and therefore don't require casting, as JPQL queries do. The Criteria API is just another Java programming language API and doesn't require developers to learn the syntax of another query language. Criteria queries are typically more verbose than JPQL queries and require the developer to create several objects and perform operations on those objects before submitting the query to the entity manager.

8.5 Database Schema Creation

The persistence provider can be configured to automatically create the database tables, load data into the tables, and remove the tables during application deployment using standard properties in the application's deployment descriptor. These tasks are typically used during the development phase of a release, not against a production database.

The following is an example of a `persistence.xml` deployment descriptor that specifies that the provider should drop all database artifacts using a provided script, create the artifacts with a provided script, and load data from a provided script when the application is deployed:

```xml
<?xml version="1.0" encoding="UTF-8"?>
<persistence version="2.1" xmlns="http://xmlns.jcp.org/xml/ns/persistence"
 xmlns:xsi="http://www.w3.org/2001/XMLSchema-instance"
 xsi:schemaLocation="http://xmlns.jcp.org/xml/ns/persistence
 http://xmlns.jcp.org/xml/ns/persistence/persistence_2_1.xsd">
  <persistence-unit name="examplePU" transaction-type="JTA">
    <jta-data-source>java:global/ExampleDataSource</jta-data-source>
    <properties>
        <property name="javax.persistence.schema-generation.database.action"
                value="drop-and-create"/>
```

```
        <property name="javax.persistence.schema-generation.create-source"
                value="script"/>
        <property
            name="javax.persistence.schema-generation.create-script-source"
            value="META-INF/sql/create.sql" />
        <property name="javax.persistence.sql-load-script-source"
                value="META-INF/sql/data.sql" />
        <property name="javax.persistence.schema-generation.drop-source"
                value="script" />
        <property
            name="javax.persistence.schema-generation.drop-script-source"
            value="META-INF/sql/drop.sql" />
    </properties>
  </persistence-unit>
</persistence>
```

8.5.1 Configuring an Application to Create or Drop Database Tables

The `javax.persistence.schema-generation.database.action` property is used to specify the action taken by the persistence provider when an application is deployed. If the property is not set, the persistence provider will not create or drop any database artifacts.

Table 8–3   Schema Creation Actions

Setting	Description
none	No schema creation or deletion will take place.
create	The provider will create the database artifacts on application deployment. The artifacts will remain unchanged after application redeployment.
drop-and-create	Any artifacts in the database will be deleted, and the provider will create the database artifacts on deployment.
drop	Any artifacts in the database will be deleted on application deployment.

In this example, the persistence provider will delete any remaining database artifacts and then create the artifacts when the application is deployed:

```
<property name="javax.persistence.schema-generation.database.action"
        value="drop-and-create"/>
```

By default, the object/relational metadata in the persistence unit is used to create the database artifacts. You may also supply scripts used by the provider to create and delete the database artifacts.

The `javax.persistence.schema-generation.create-source` and `javax.persistence.schema-generation.drop-source` properties control how the provider will create or delete the database artifacts.

Table 8–4   Settings for Create and Delete Source Properties

Setting	Description
metadata	Use the object/relational metadata in the application to create or delete the database artifacts.
script	Use a provided script for creating or deleting the database artifacts.
metadata-then-script	Use a combination of object/relational metadata, then a user-provided script to create or delete the database artifacts.
script-then-metadata	Use a combination of a user-provided script, then the object/relational metadata to create and delete the database artifacts.

In this example, the persistence provider will use a script packaged within the application to create the database artifacts:

```
<property name="javax.persistence.schema-generation.create-source"
        value="script"/>
```

If you specify a script in `create-source` or `drop-source`, specify the location of the script using the `javax.persistence.schema-generation.create-script-source` or `javax.persistence.schema-generation.drop-script-source` property. The location of the script is relative to the root of the persistence unit:

```
<property name="javax.persistence.schema-generation.create-script-source"
        value="META-INF/sql/create.sql" />
```

In the above example, the `create-script-source` is set to a SQL file called `create.sql` in the `META-INF/sql` directory relative to root of the persistence unit.

8.5.2 Loading Data Using SQL Scripts

If you want to populate the database tables with data before the application loads, specify the location of a load script in the `javax.persistence.sql-load-script-source` property. The location specified in this property is relative to the root of the persistence unit.

In this example, the load script is a file called `data.sql` in the `META-INF/sql` directory relative to the root of the persistence unit:

```
<property name="javax.persistence.sql-load-script-source"
          value="META-INF/sql/data.sql" />
```

8.6 Further Information about Persistence

For more information about the Java Persistence API, see

- Java Persistence 2.1 API specification:

  `http://jcp.org/en/jsr/detail?id=338`

- EclipseLink, the Java Persistence API implementation in GlassFish Server:

  `http://www.eclipse.org/eclipselink/jpa.php`

- EclipseLink team blog:

  `http://eclipselink.blogspot.com/`

- EclipseLink wiki documentation:

  `http://wiki.eclipse.org/EclipseLink`

9

Running the Persistence Examples

This chapter explains how to use the Java Persistence API. The material here focuses on the source code and settings of three examples. The first example, `order`, is an application that uses a stateful session bean to manage entities related to an ordering system. The second example, `roster`, is an application that manages a community sports system. The third example, `address-book`, is a web application that stores contact data. This chapter assumes that you are familiar with the concepts detailed in Chapter 8, "Introduction to the Java Persistence API."

The following topics are addressed here:

- The order Application
- The roster Application
- The address-book Application

9.1 The order Application

The `order` application is a simple inventory and ordering application for maintaining a catalog of parts and placing an itemized order of those parts. The application has entities that represent parts, vendors, orders, and line items. These entities are accessed using a stateful session bean that holds the business logic of the application. A simple singleton session bean creates the initial entities on application deployment. A Facelets web application manipulates the data and displays data from the catalog.

The information contained in an order can be divided into elements. What is the order number? What parts are included in the order? What parts make up that part? Who makes the part? What are the specifications for the part? Are there any schematics for the part? The order application is a simplified version of an ordering system that has all these elements.

The order application consists of a single WAR module that includes the enterprise bean classes, the entities, the support classes, and the Facelets XHTML and class files.

The database schema in the Java DB database for order is shown in Figure 9–1.

Note: In this diagram, for simplicity, the PERSISTENCE_ORDER_ prefix is omitted from the table names.

9.1.1 Entity Relationships in the order Application

The order application demonstrates several types of entity relationships: self-referential, one-to-one, one-to-many, many-to-one, and unidirectional relationships.

9.1.1.1 Self-Referential Relationships

A **self-referential** relationship occurs between relationship fields in the same entity. Part has a field, bomPart, which has a one-to-many relationship with the field parts, which is also in Part. That is, a part can be made up of many parts, and each of those parts has exactly one bill-of-material part.

The primary key for Part is a compound primary key, a combination of the partNumber and revision fields. This key is mapped to the PARTNUMBER and REVISION columns in the PERSISTENCE_ORDER_PART table:

```
...
@ManyToOne
@JoinColumns({
    @JoinColumn(name="BOMPARTNUMBER", referencedColumnName="PARTNUMBER"),
    @JoinColumn(name="BOMREVISION", referencedColumnName="REVISION")
})
public Part getBomPart() {
    return bomPart;
}
...
@OneToMany(mappedBy="bomPart")
public Collection<Part> getParts() {
    return parts;
}
...
```

Figure 9–1   Database Schema for the order Application

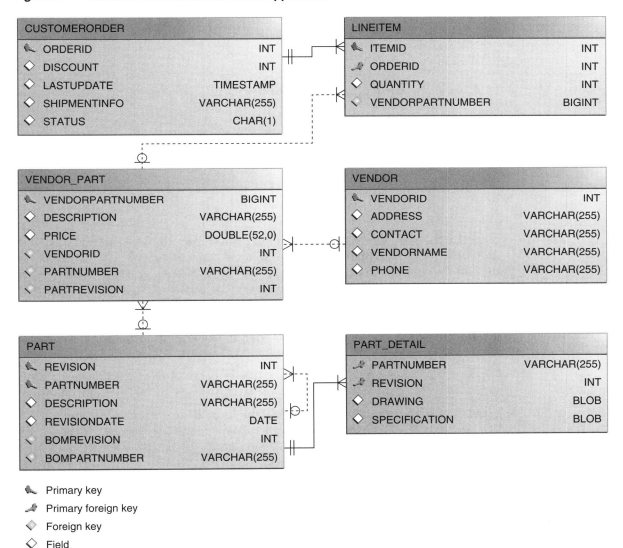

- Primary key
- Primary foreign key
- Foreign key
- Field

9.1.1.2 One-to-One Relationships

Part has a field, vendorPart, that has a one-to-one relationship with VendorPart's part field. That is, each part has exactly one vendor part, and vice versa.

Here is the relationship mapping in `Part`:

```
@OneToOne(mappedBy="part")
public VendorPart getVendorPart() {
    return vendorPart;
}
```

Here is the relationship mapping in `VendorPart`:

```
@OneToOne
@JoinColumns({
    @JoinColumn(name="PARTNUMBER", referencedColumnName="PARTNUMBER"),
    @JoinColumn(name="PARTREVISION", referencedColumnName="REVISION")
})
public Part getPart() {
    return part;
}
```

Note that, because `Part` uses a compound primary key, the `@JoinColumns` annotation is used to map the columns in the `PERSISTENCE_ORDER_VENDOR_PART` table to the columns in `PERSISTENCE_ORDER_PART`. The `PERSISTENCE_ORDER_VENDOR_PART` table's `PARTREVISION` column refers to `PERSISTENCE_ORDER_PART`'s `REVISION` column.

9.1.1.3 One-to-Many Relationship Mapped to Overlapping Primary and Foreign Keys

`CustomerOrder` has a field, `lineItems`, that has a one-to-many relationship with `LineItem`'s field `customerOrder`. That is, each order has one or more line item.

`LineItem` uses a compound primary key that is made up of the `orderId` and `itemId` fields. This compound primary key maps to the `ORDERID` and `ITEMID` columns in the `PERSISTENCE_ORDER_LINEITEM` table. `ORDERID` is a foreign key to the `ORDERID` column in the `PERSISTENCE_ORDER_CUSTOMERORDER` table. This means that the `ORDERID` column is mapped twice: once as a primary key field, `orderId`; and again as a relationship field, `order`.

Here is the relationship mapping in `CustomerOrder`:

```
@OneToMany(cascade=ALL, mappedBy="customerOrder")
public Collection<LineItem> getLineItems() {
    return lineItems;
}
```

Here is the relationship mapping in `LineItem`:

```
@Id
@ManyToOne
```

```
@JoinColumn(name="ORDERID")
public CustomerOrder getCustomerOrder() {
    return customerOrder;
}
```

9.1.1.4 Unidirectional Relationships

LineItem has a field, vendorPart, that has a unidirectional many-to-one relationship with VendorPart. That is, there is no field in the target entity in this relationship:

```
@JoinColumn(name="VENDORPARTNUMBER")
@ManyToOne
public VendorPart getVendorPart() {
    return vendorPart;
}
```

9.1.2 Primary Keys in the order Application

The order application uses several types of primary keys: single-valued primary keys, generated primary keys, and compound primary keys.

9.1.2.1 Generated Primary Keys

VendorPart uses a generated primary key value. That is, the application does not assign primary key values for the entities but instead relies on the persistence provider to generate the primary key values. The @GeneratedValue annotation is used to specify that an entity will use a generated primary key.

In VendorPart, the following code specifies the settings for generating primary key values:

```
@TableGenerator(
    name="vendorPartGen",
    table="PERSISTENCE_ORDER_SEQUENCE_GENERATOR",
    pkColumnName="GEN_KEY",
    valueColumnName="GEN_VALUE",
    pkColumnValue="VENDOR_PART_ID",
    allocationSize=10)
@Id
@GeneratedValue(strategy=GenerationType.TABLE, generator="vendorPartGen")
public Long getVendorPartNumber() {
    return vendorPartNumber;
}
```

The @TableGenerator annotation is used in conjunction with @GeneratedValue's strategy=TABLE element. That is, the strategy used to generate the primary keys is to use a table in the database. The @TableGenerator annotation is used to configure the settings for the generator table. The name element sets the name of the generator, which is vendorPartGen in VendorPart.

The PERSISTENCE_ORDER_SEQUENCE_GENERATOR table, whose two columns are GEN_KEY and GEN_VALUE, will store the generated primary key values. This table could be used to generate other entities' primary keys, so the pkColumnValue element is set to VENDOR_PART_ID to distinguish this entity's generated primary keys from other entities' generated primary keys. The allocationSize element specifies the amount to increment when allocating primary key values. In this case, each VendorPart's primary key will increment by 10.

The primary key field vendorPartNumber is of type Long, as the generated primary key's field must be an integral type.

9.1.2.2 Compound Primary Keys

A compound primary key is made up of multiple fields and follows the requirements described in Section 8.1.3, "Primary Keys in Entities." To use a compound primary key, you must create a wrapper class.

In order, two entities use compound primary keys: Part and LineItem.

- Part uses the PartKey wrapper class. Part's primary key is a combination of the part number and the revision number. PartKey encapsulates this primary key.

- LineItem uses the LineItemKey class. LineItem's primary key is a combination of the order number and the item number. LineItemKey encapsulates this primary key.

This is the LineItemKey compound primary key wrapper class:

```
package javaeetutorial.order.entity;

import java.io.Serializable;

public final class LineItemKey implements Serializable {

    private Integer customerOrder;
    private int itemId;

    public LineItemKey() {}

    public LineItemKey(Integer order, int itemId) {
        this.setCustomerOrder(order);
        this.setItemId(itemId);
    }
```

```java
@Override
public int hashCode() {
    return ((this.getCustomerOrder() == null
            ? 0 : this.getCustomerOrder().hashCode())
            ^ ((int) this.getItemId()));
}

@Override
public boolean equals(Object otherOb) {
    if (this == otherOb) {
        return true;
    }
    if (!(otherOb instanceof LineItemKey)) {
        return false;
    }
    LineItemKey other = (LineItemKey) otherOb;
    return ((this.getCustomerOrder() == null
            ? other.getCustomerOrder == null : this.getOrderId()
            .equals(other.getCustomerOrder()))
            && (this.getItemId == oother.getItemId()));
}

@Override
public String toString() {
    return "" + getCustomerOrder() + "-" + getItemId();
}

public Integer getCustomerOrder() {
    return customerOrder;
}

public void setCustomerOrder(Integer order) {
    this.customerOrder = order;
}

public int getItemId() {
    return itemId;
}

public void setItemId(int itemId) {
    this.itemId = itemId;
}
}
```

The @IdClass annotation is used to specify the primary key class in the entity class. In LineItem, @IdClass is used as follows:

```
@IdClass(LineItemKey.class)
@Entity
...
public class LineItem implements Serializable { ... }
```

The two fields in LineItem are tagged with the @Id annotation to mark those fields as part of the compound primary key:

```
@Id
public int getItemId() {
    return itemId;
}
...
@Id
@ManyToOne
@JoinColumn(name="ORDERID")
public CustomerOrder getCustomerOrder() {
    return customerOrder;
}
```

For customerOrder, you also use the @JoinColumn annotation to specify the column name in the table and that this column is an overlapping foreign key pointing at the PERSISTENCE_ORDER_CUSTOMERORDER table's ORDERID column (see Section 9.1.1.3, "One-to-Many Relationship Mapped to Overlapping Primary and Foreign Keys"). That is, customerOrder will be set by the CustomerOrder entity.

In LineItem's constructor, the line item number (LineItem.itemId) is set using the CustomerOrder.getNextId method:

```
public LineItem(CustomerOrder order, int quantity, VendorPart vendorPart) {
    this.customerOrder = order;
    this.itemId = order.getNextId();
    this.quantity = quantity;
    this.vendorPart = vendorPart;
}
```

CustomerOrder.getNextId counts the number of current line items, adds 1, and returns that number:

```
@Transient
public int getNextId() {
    return this.lineItems.size() + 1;
}
```

Part requires the @Column annotation on the two fields that comprise Part's compound primary key, because Part's compound primary key is an overlapping primary key/foreign key:

```
@IdClass(PartKey.class)
@Entity
...
public class Part implements Serializable {
    ...
    @Id
    @Column(nullable=false)
    public String getPartNumber() {
        return partNumber;
    }
    ...
    @Id
    @Column(nullable=false)
    public int getRevision() {
        return revision;
    }
    ...
}
```

9.1.3 Entity Mapped to More Than One Database Table

Part's fields map to more than one database table: PERSISTENCE_ORDER_PART and PERSISTENCE_ORDER_PART_DETAIL. The PERSISTENCE_ORDER_PART_DETAIL table holds the specification and schematics for the part. The @SecondaryTable annotation is used to specify the secondary table:

```
...
@Entity
@Table(name="PERSISTENCE_ORDER_PART")
@SecondaryTable(name="PERSISTENCE_ORDER_PART_DETAIL", pkJoinColumns={
    @PrimaryKeyJoinColumn(name="PARTNUMBER",
        referencedColumnName="PARTNUMBER"),
    @PrimaryKeyJoinColumn(name="REVISION",
        referencedColumnName="REVISION")
})
public class Part implements Serializable { ... }
```

PERSISTENCE_ORDER_PART_DETAIL and PERSISTENCE_ORDER_PART share the same primary key values. The pkJoinColumns element of @SecondaryTable is used to specify that PERSISTENCE_ORDER_PART_DETAIL's primary key columns are foreign keys to PERSISTENCE_ORDER_PART. The @PrimaryKeyJoinColumn annotation sets the primary key column names and specifies which column in the primary table the column refers to. In this case, the primary key column names for both PERSISTENCE_ORDER_PART_DETAIL and PERSISTENCE_ORDER_PART are the same: PARTNUMBER and REVISION, respectively.

9.1.4 Cascade Operations in the order Application

Entities that have relationships to other entities often have dependencies on the existence of the other entity in the relationship. For example, a line item is part of an order; if the order is deleted, then the line item also should be deleted. This is called a cascade delete relationship.

In order, there are two cascade delete dependencies in the entity relationships. If the CustomerOrder to which a LineItem is related is deleted, the LineItem also should be deleted. If the Vendor to which a VendorPart is related is deleted, the VendorPart also should be deleted.

You specify the cascade operations for entity relationships by setting the cascade element in the inverse (nonowning) side of the relationship. The cascade element is set to ALL in the case of CustomerOrder.lineItems. This means that all persistence operations (deletes, updates, and so on) are cascaded from orders to line items.

Here is the relationship mapping in CustomerOrder:

```
@OneToMany(cascade=ALL, mappedBy="customerOrder")
public Collection<LineItem> getLineItems() {
    return lineItems;
}
```

Here is the relationship mapping in LineItem:

```
@Id
@ManyToOne
@JoinColumn(name="ORDERID")
public CustomerOrder getCustomerOrder() {
    return customerOrder;
}
```

9.1.5 BLOB and CLOB Database Types in the order Application

The PARTDETAIL table in the database has a column, DRAWING, of type BLOB. BLOB stands for binary large objects, which are used for storing binary data, such as an image. The DRAWING column is mapped to the field Part.drawing of type java.io.Serializable. The @Lob annotation is used to denote that the field is a large object.

```
@Column(table="PERSISTENCE_ORDER_PART_DETAIL")
@Lob
public Serializable getDrawing() {
    return drawing;
}
```

PERSISTENCE_ORDER_PART_DETAIL also has a column, SPECIFICATION, of type CLOB. CLOB stands for character large objects, which are used to store string data too large to be stored in a VARCHAR column. SPECIFICATION is mapped to the field Part.specification of type java.lang.String. The @Lob annotation is also used here to denote that the field is a large object:

```
@Column(table="PERSISTENCE_ORDER_PART_DETAIL")
@Lob
public String getSpecification() {
    return specification;
}
```

Both of these fields use the @Column annotation and set the table element to the secondary table.

9.1.6 Temporal Types in the order Application

The CustomerOrder.lastUpdate persistent property, which is of type java.util.Date, is mapped to the PERSISTENCE_ORDER_CUSTOMERORDER.LASTUPDATE database field, which is of the SQL type TIMESTAMP. To ensure the proper mapping between these types, you must use the @Temporal annotation with the proper temporal type specified in @Temporal's element. @Temporal's elements are of type javax.persistence.TemporalType. The possible values are

- DATE, which maps to java.sql.Date

- TIME, which maps to java.sql.Time

- TIMESTAMP, which maps to java.sql.Timestamp

Here is the relevant section of CustomerOrder:

```
@Temporal(TIMESTAMP)
public Date getLastUpdate() {
    return lastUpdate;
}
```

9.1.7 Managing the order Application's Entities

The `RequestBean` stateful session bean contains the business logic and manages the entities of `order`. `RequestBean` uses the `@PersistenceContext` annotation to retrieve an entity manager instance, which is used to manage `order`'s entities in `RequestBean`'s business methods:

```
@PersistenceContext
private EntityManager em;
```

This `EntityManager` instance is a container-managed entity manager, so the container takes care of all the transactions involved in managing `order`'s entities.

9.1.7.1 Creating Entities

The `RequestBean.createPart` business method creates a new `Part` entity. The `EntityManager.persist` method is used to persist the newly created entity to the database:

```
Part part = new Part(partNumber,
        revision,
        description,
        revisionDate,
        specification,
        drawing);
em.persist(part);
```

The `ConfigBean` singleton session bean is used to initialize the data in `order`. `ConfigBean` is annotated with `@Startup`, which indicates that the EJB container should create `ConfigBean` when `order` is deployed. The `createData` method is annotated with `@PostConstruct` and creates the initial entities used by `order` by calling `RequestBean`'s business methods.

9.1.7.2 Finding Entities

The `RequestBean.getOrderPrice` business method returns the price of a given order based on the `orderId`. The `EntityManager.find` method is used to retrieve the entity from the database:

```
CustomerOrder order = em.find(CustomerOrder.class, orderId);
```

The first argument of `EntityManager.find` is the entity class, and the second is the primary key.

9.1.7.3 Setting Entity Relationships

The `RequestBean.createVendorPart` business method creates a `VendorPart` associated with a particular `Vendor`. The `EntityManager.persist` method is used to persist the newly created `VendorPart` entity to the database, and the `VendorPart.setVendor` and `Vendor.setVendorPart` methods are used to associate the `VendorPart` with the `Vendor`:

```
PartKey pkey = new PartKey();
pkey.setPartNumber(partNumber);
pkey.setRevision(revision);

Part part = em.find(Part.class, pkey);

VendorPart vendorPart = new VendorPart(description, price, part);
em.persist(vendorPart);

Vendor vendor = em.find(Vendor.class, vendorId);
vendor.addVendorPart(vendorPart);
vendorPart.setVendor(vendor);
```

9.1.7.4 Using Queries

The `RequestBean.adjustOrderDiscount` business method updates the discount applied to all orders. This method uses the `findAllOrders` named query, defined in `CustomerOrder`:

```
@NamedQuery(
    name="findAllOrders",
    query="SELECT co FROM CustomerOrder co " +
        "ORDER BY co.orderId"
)
```

The `EntityManager.createNamedQuery` method is used to run the query. Because the query returns a `List` of all the orders, the `Query.getResultList` method is used:

```
List orders = em.createNamedQuery(
        "findAllOrders")
        .getResultList();
```

The `RequestBean.getTotalPricePerVendor` business method returns the total price of all the parts for a particular vendor. This method uses a named parameter, `id`, defined in the named query `findTotalVendorPartPricePerVendor` defined in `VendorPart`:

```
@NamedQuery(
    name="findTotalVendorPartPricePerVendor",
```

```
query="SELECT SUM(vp.price) " +
"FROM VendorPart vp " +
"WHERE vp.vendor.vendorId = :id"
)
```

When running the query, the Query.setParameter method is used to set the named parameter id to the value of vendorId, the parameter to RequestBean.getTotalPricePerVendor:

```
return (Double) em.createNamedQuery(
        "findTotalVendorPartPricePerVendor")
        .setParameter("id", vendorId)
        .getSingleResult();
```

The Query.getSingleResult method is used for this query because the query returns a single value.

9.1.7.5 Removing Entities

The RequestBean.removeOrder business method deletes a given order from the database. This method uses the EntityManager.remove method to delete the entity from the database:

```
CustomerOrder order = em.find(CustomerOrder.class, orderId);
em.remove(order);
```

9.1.8 Running the order Example

You can use either NetBeans IDE or Maven to build, package, deploy, and run the order application. First, you will create the database tables in the Java DB server.

9.1.8.1 To Run the order Example Using NetBeans IDE

1. Make sure that GlassFish Server has been started (see Section 2.2, "Starting and Stopping GlassFish Server").

2. If the database server is not already running, start it by following the instructions in Section 2.4, "Starting and Stopping the Java DB Server."

3. From the **File** menu, choose **Open Project**.

4. In the Open Project dialog box, navigate to:

    tut-install/examples/persistence

5. Select the order folder.

6. Click **Open Project**.

7. In the **Projects** tab, right-click the order project and select **Run**.

   NetBeans IDE opens a web browser to the following URL:

   ```
   http://localhost:8080/order/
   ```

9.1.8.2 To Run the order Example Using Maven

1. Make sure that GlassFish Server has been started (see Section 2.2, "Starting and Stopping GlassFish Server").

2. If the database server is not already running, start it by following the instructions in Section 2.4, "Starting and Stopping the Java DB Server."

3. In a terminal window, go to:

   ```
   tut-install/examples/persistence/order/
   ```

4. Enter the following command:

   ```
   mvn install
   ```

   This compiles the source files and packages the application into a WAR file located at *tut-install*/examples/persistence/order/target/order.war. Then the WAR file is deployed to your GlassFish Server instance.

5. To create and update the order data, open a web browser to the following URL:

   ```
   http://localhost:8080/order/
   ```

9.2 The roster Application

The roster application maintains the team rosters for players in recreational sports leagues. The application has four components: Java Persistence API entities (Player, Team, and League), a stateful session bean (RequestBean), an application client (RosterClient), and three helper classes (PlayerDetails, TeamDetails, and LeagueDetails).

Functionally, roster is similar to the order application, with three new features that order does not have: many-to-many relationships, entity inheritance, and automatic table creation at deployment time.

The database schema in the Java DB database for the roster application is shown in Figure 9–2.

Figure 9–2 Database Schema for the roster Application

TEAM_PLAYER	
◇ PLAYER_ID	VARCHAR(255)
◇ TEAM_ID	VARCHAR(255)

PLAYER	
⚷ ID	VARCHAR(255)
◇ NAME	VARCHAR(255)
◇ POSITION	VARCHAR(255)
◇ SALARY	DOUBLE(52,0)

TEAM	
⚷ ID	VARCHAR(255)
◇ CITY	VARCHAR(255)
◇ NAME	VARCHAR(255)
◇ LEAGUE_ID	VARCHAR(255)

LEAGUE	
⚷ ID	VARCHAR(255)
◇ DTYPE	VARCHAR(31)
◇ NAME	VARCHAR(255)
◇ SPORT	VARCHAR(255)

⚷ Primary key
◇ Foreign key
◇ Field

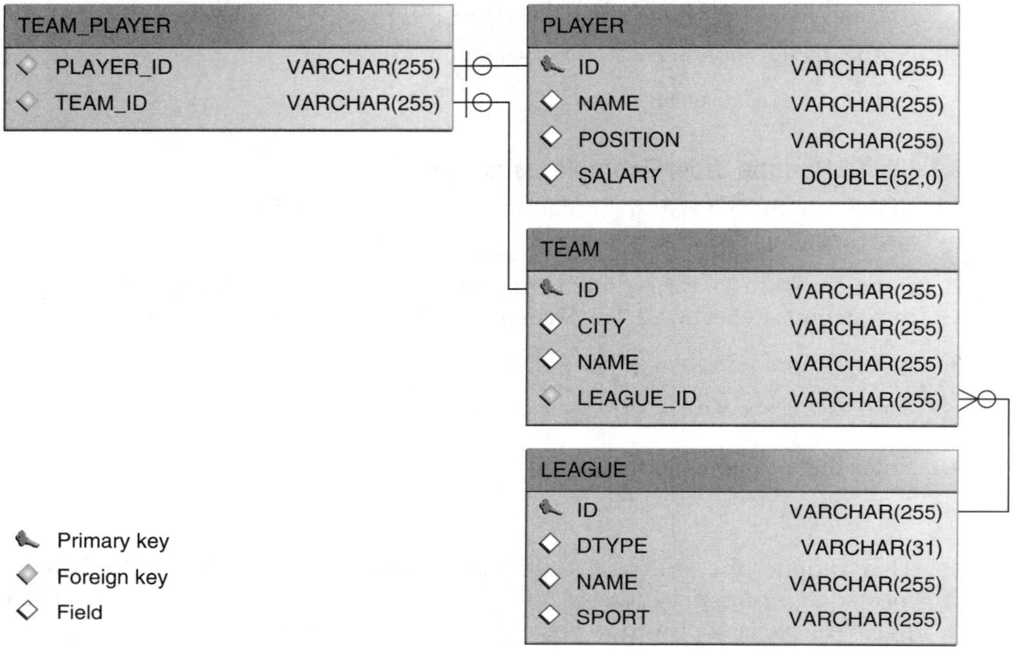

Note: In this diagram, for simplicity, the PERSISTENCE_ROSTER_ prefix is omitted from the table names.

9.2.1 Relationships in the roster Application

A recreational sports system has the following relationships.

- A player can be on many teams.
- A team can have many players.
- A team is in exactly one league.
- A league has many teams.

In roster this system is reflected by the following relationships between the Player, Team, and League entities.

- There is a many-to-many relationship between Player and Team.
- There is a many-to-one relationship between Team and League.

9.2.1.1 The Many-To-Many Relationship in roster

The many-to-many relationship between `Player` and `Team` is specified by using the `@ManyToMany` annotation. In `Team.java`, the `@ManyToMany` annotation decorates the `getPlayers` method:

```
@ManyToMany
@JoinTable(
    name="PERSISTENCE_ROSTER_TEAM_PLAYER",
    joinColumns=
        @JoinColumn(name="TEAM_ID", referencedColumnName="ID"),
    inverseJoinColumns=
        @JoinColumn(name="PLAYER_ID", referencedColumnName="ID")
)
public Collection<Player> getPlayers() {
    return players;
}
```

The `@JoinTable` annotation is used to specify a database table that will associate player IDs with team IDs. The entity that specifies the `@JoinTable` is the owner of the relationship, so the `Team` entity is the owner of the relationship with the `Player` entity. Because `roster` uses automatic table creation at deployment time, the container will create a join table named `PERSISTENCE_ROSTER_TEAM_PLAYER`.

`Player` is the inverse, or nonowning, side of the relationship with `Team`. As one-to-one and many-to-one relationships, the nonowning side is marked by the `mappedBy` element in the relationship annotation. Because the relationship between `Player` and `Team` is bidirectional, the choice of which entity is the owner of the relationship is arbitrary.

In `Player.java`, the `@ManyToMany` annotation decorates the `getTeams` method:

```
@ManyToMany(mappedBy="players")
public Collection<Team> getTeams() {
    return teams;
}
```

9.2.2 Entity Inheritance in the roster Application

The `roster` application shows how to use entity inheritance, as described in Section 8.2, "Entity Inheritance."

The League entity in roster is an abstract entity with two concrete subclasses: SummerLeague and WinterLeague. Because League is an abstract class, it cannot be instantiated:

```
@Entity
@Table(name = "PERSISTENCE_ROSTER_LEAGUE")
public abstract class League implements Serializable { ... }
```

Instead, when creating a league, clients use SummerLeague or WinterLeague. SummerLeague and WinterLeague inherit the persistent properties defined in League and add only a constructor that verifies that the sport parameter matches the type of sport allowed in that seasonal league. For example, here is the SummerLeague entity:

```
@Entity
public class SummerLeague extends League implements Serializable {

    /** Creates a new instance of SummerLeague */
    public SummerLeague() {
    }

    public SummerLeague(String id, String name, String sport)
            throws IncorrectSportException {
        this.id = id;
        this.name = name;
        if (sport.equalsIgnoreCase("swimming") ||
                sport.equalsIgnoreCase("soccer") ||
                sport.equalsIgnoreCase("basketball") ||
                sport.equalsIgnoreCase("baseball")) {
            this.sport = sport;
        } else {
            throw new IncorrectSportException("Sport is not a summer sport.");
        }
    }
}
```

The roster application uses the default mapping strategy of InheritanceType.SINGLE_TABLE, so the @Inheritance annotation is not required. If you want to use a different mapping strategy, decorate League with @Inheritance and specify the mapping strategy in the strategy element:

```
@Entity
@Inheritance(strategy=JOINED)
@Table(name="PERSISTENCE_ROSTER_LEAGUE")
public abstract class League implements Serializable { ... }
```

The `roster` application uses the default discriminator column name, so the `@DiscriminatorColumn` annotation is not required. Because you are using automatic table generation in `roster`, the Persistence provider will create a discriminator column called `DTYPE` in the `PERSISTENCE_ROSTER_LEAGUE` table, which will store the name of the inherited entity used to create the league. If you want to use a different name for the discriminator column, decorate `League` with `@DiscriminatorColumn` and set the `name` element:

```
@Entity
@DiscriminatorColumn(name="DISCRIMINATOR")
@Table(name="PERSISTENCE_ROSTER_LEAGUE")
public abstract class League implements Serializable { ... }
```

9.2.3 Criteria Queries in the roster Application

The `roster` application uses Criteria API queries, as opposed to the JPQL queries used in `order`. Criteria queries are Java programming language, typesafe queries defined in the business tier of `roster`, in the `RequestBean` stateful session bean.

9.2.3.1 Metamodel Classes in the roster Application

Metamodel classes model an entity's attributes and are used by Criteria queries to navigate to an entity's attributes. Each entity class in `roster` has a corresponding metamodel class, generated at compile time, with the same package name as the entity and appended with an underscore character (_). For example, the `roster.entity.Player` entity has a corresponding metamodel class, `roster.entity.Player_`.

Each persistent field or property in the entity class has a corresponding attribute in the entity's metamodel class. For the `Player` entity, the corresponding metamodel class is as follows:

```
@StaticMetamodel(Player.class)
public class Player_ {
    public static volatile SingularAttribute<Player, String> id;
    public static volatile SingularAttribute<Player, String> name;
    public static volatile SingularAttribute<Player, String> position;
    public static volatile SingularAttribute<Player, Double> salary;
    public static volatile CollectionAttribute<Player, Team> teams;
}
```

9.2.3.2 Obtaining a CriteriaBuilder Instance in RequestBean

The CriteriaBuilder interface defines methods to create criteria query objects
and create expressions for modifying those query objects. RequestBean creates an
instance of CriteriaBuilder by using a @PostConstruct method, init:

```
@PersistenceContext
private EntityManager em;
private CriteriaBuilder cb;

@PostConstruct
private void init() {
    cb = em.getCriteriaBuilder();
}
```

The EntityManager instance is injected at runtime, and then that EntityManager
object is used to create the CriteriaBuilder instance by calling
getCriteriaBuilder. The CriteriaBuilder instance is created in a
@PostConstruct method to ensure that the EntityManager instance has been
injected by the enterprise bean container.

9.2.3.3 Creating Criteria Queries in RequestBean's Business Methods

Many of the business methods in RequestBean define Criteria queries. One
business method, getPlayersByPosition, returns a list of players who play a
particular position on a team:

```
public List<PlayerDetails> getPlayersByPosition(String position) {
    logger.info("getPlayersByPosition");
    List<Player> players = null;

    try {
        CriteriaQuery<Player> cq = cb.createQuery(Player.class);
        if (cq != null) {
            Root<Player> player = cq.from(Player.class);

            // set the where clause
            cq.where(cb.equal(player.get(Player_.position), position));
            cq.select(player);
            TypedQuery<Player> q = em.createQuery(cq);
            players = q.getResultList();
        }
        return copyPlayersToDetails(players);
    } catch (Exception ex) {
        throw new EJBException(ex);
    }
}
```

A query object is created by calling the `CriteriaBuilder` object's `createQuery` method, with the type set to `Player` because the query will return a list of players.

The query root, the base entity from which the query will navigate to find the entity's attributes and related entities, is created by calling the `from` method of the query object. This sets the `FROM` clause of the query.

The `WHERE` clause, set by calling the `where` method on the query object, restricts the results of the query according to the conditions of an expression. The `CriteriaBuilder.equal` method compares the two expressions. In `getPlayersByPosition`, the `position` attribute of the `Player_` metamodel class, accessed by calling the `get` method of the query root, is compared to the `position` parameter passed to `getPlayersByPosition`.

The `SELECT` clause of the query is set by calling the `select` method of the query object. The query will return `Player` entities, so the query root object is passed as a parameter to `select`.

The query object is prepared for execution by calling `EntityManager.createQuery`, which returns a `TypedQuery<T>` object with the type of the query, in this case `Player`. This typed query object is used to execute the query, which occurs when the `getResultList` method is called, and a `List<Player>` collection is returned.

9.2.4 Automatic Table Generation in the roster Application

At deployment time, GlassFish Server will automatically drop and create the database tables used by `roster`. This is done by setting the `javax.persistence.schema-generation.database.action` property to `drop-and-create` in `persistence.xml`:

```
<persistence version="2.1"
    xmlns="http://xmlns.jcp.org/xml/ns/persistence"
    xmlns:xsi="http://www.w3.org/2001/XMLSchema-instance"
    xsi:schemaLocation="http://xmlns.jcp.org/xml/ns/persistence
        http://xmlns.jcp.org/xml/ns/persistence/persistence_2_1.xsd">
  <persistence-unit name="em" transaction-type="JTA">
    <jta-data-source>java:comp/DefaultDataSource</jta-data-source>
    <properties>
      <property name="javax.persistence.schema-generation.database.action"
                value="drop-and-create"/>
    </properties>
  </persistence-unit>
</persistence>
```

9.2.5 Running the roster Example

You can use either NetBeans IDE or Maven to build, package, deploy, and run the roster application.

9.2.5.1 To Run the roster Example Using NetBeans IDE

1. Make sure that GlassFish Server has been started (see Section 2.2, "Starting and Stopping GlassFish Server").

2. If the database server is not already running, start it by following the instructions in Section 2.4, "Starting and Stopping the Java DB Server."

3. From the **File** menu, choose **Open Project**.

4. In the Open Project dialog box, navigate to:

   `tut-install/examples/persistence`

5. Select the roster folder.

6. Select the **Open Required Projects** check box.

7. Click **Open Project**.

8. In the **Projects** tab, right-click the roster project and select **Build**.

   This will compile, package, and deploy the EAR to GlassFish Server.

   You will see the following partial output from the application client in the **Output** tab:

```
List all players in team T2:
P6 Ian Carlyle goalkeeper 555.0
P7 Rebecca Struthers midfielder 777.0
P8 Anne Anderson forward 65.0
P9 Jan Wesley defender 100.0
P10 Terry Smithson midfielder 100.0

List all teams in league L1:
T1 Honey Bees Visalia
T2 Gophers Manteca
T5 Crows Orland

List all defenders:
P2 Alice Smith defender 505.0
P5 Barney Bold defender 100.0
P9 Jan Wesley defender 100.0
P22 Janice Walker defender 857.0
P25 Frank Fletcher defender 399.0
```

9.2.5.2 To Run the roster Example Using Maven

1. Make sure that GlassFish Server has been started (see Section 2.2, "Starting and Stopping GlassFish Server").

2. If the database server is not already running, start it by following the instructions in Section 2.4, "Starting and Stopping the Java DB Server."

3. In a terminal window, go to:

   tut-install/examples/persistence/roster/roster-ear/

4. Enter the following command:

   ```
   mvn install
   ```

   This compiles the source files and packages the application into an EAR file located at *tut-install*/examples/persistence/roster/target/roster.ear. The EAR file is then deployed to GlassFish Server. GlassFish Server will then drop and create the database tables during deployment, as specified in persistence.xml.

   After successfully deploying the EAR, the client stubs are retrieved and the application client is run using the appclient application included with GlassFish Server.

   You will see the output, which begins as follows:

   ```
   [echo] running application client container.
   [exec] List all players in team T2:
   [exec] P6 Ian Carlyle goalkeeper 555.0
   [exec] P7 Rebecca Struthers midfielder 777.0
   [exec] P8 Anne Anderson forward 65.0
   [exec] P9 Jan Wesley defender 100.0
   [exec] P10 Terry Smithson midfielder 100.0

   [exec] List all teams in league L1:
   [exec] T1 Honey Bees Visalia
   [exec] T2 Gophers Manteca
   [exec] T5 Crows Orland

   [exec] List all defenders:
   [exec] P2 Alice Smith defender 505.0
   [exec] P5 Barney Bold defender 100.0
   [exec] P9 Jan Wesley defender 100.0
   [exec] P22 Janice Walker defender 857.0
   [exec] P25 Frank Fletcher defender 399.0
   ```

9.3 The address-book Application

The `address-book` example application is a simple web application that stores contact data. It uses a single entity class, `Contact`, that uses the Java API for JavaBeans Validation (Bean Validation) to validate the data stored in the persistent attributes of the entity, as described in Section 8.1.2.4, "Validating Persistent Fields and Properties."

9.3.1 Bean Validation Constraints in address-book

The `Contact` entity uses the `@NotNull`, `@Pattern`, and `@Past` constraints on the persistent attributes.

The `@NotNull` constraint marks the attribute as a required field. The attribute must be set to a non-null value before the entity can be persisted or modified. Bean Validation will throw a validation error if the attribute is null when the entity is persisted or modified.

The `@Pattern` constraint defines a regular expression that the value of the attribute must match before the entity can be persisted or modified. This constraint has two different uses in `address-book`.

- The regular expression declared in the `@Pattern` annotation on the `email` field matches email addresses of the form *name@domain name.top level domain*, allowing only valid characters for email addresses. For example, `username@example.com` will pass validation, as will `firstname.lastname@mail.example.com`. However, `firstname,lastname@example.com`, which contains an illegal comma character in the local name, will fail validation.

- The `mobilePhone` and `homePhone` fields are annotated with a `@Pattern` constraint that defines a regular expression to match phone numbers of the form *(xxx) xxx-xxxx*.

The `@Past` constraint is applied to the birthday field, which must be a `java.util.Date` in the past.

Here are the relevant parts of the `Contact` entity class:

```
@Entity
public class Contact implements Serializable {
    @Id
    @GeneratedValue(strategy = GenerationType.AUTO)
    private Long id;
    @NotNull
    protected String firstName;
```

```
@NotNull
protected String lastName;
@Pattern(regexp = "[a-z0-9!#$%&'*+/=?^_`{|}~-]+(?:\\."
        + "[a-z0-9!#$%&'*+/=?^_`{|}~-]+)*@"
        + "(?:[a-z0-9](?:[a-z0-9-]*[a-z0-9])?\\.)+[a-z0-9]"
        + "(?:[a-z0-9-]*[a-z0-9])?",
        message = "{invalid.email}")
protected String email;
@Pattern(regexp = "^\\(?(\\d{3})\\)?[- ]?(\\d{3})[- ]?(\\d{4})$",
        message = "{invalid.phonenumber}")
protected String mobilePhone;
@Pattern(regexp = "^\\(?(\\d{3})\\)?[- ]?(\\d{3})[- ]?(\\d{4})$",
        message = "{invalid.phonenumber}")
protected String homePhone;
@Temporal(javax.persistence.TemporalType.DATE)
@Past
protected Date birthday;
...
}
```

9.3.2 Specifying Error Messages for Constraints in address-book

Some of the constraints in the `Contact` entity specify an optional message:

```
@Pattern(regexp = "^\\(?(\\d{3})\\)?[- ]?(\\d{3})[- ]?(\\d{4})$',
        message = "{invalid.phonenumber}")
protected String homePhone;
```

The optional message element in the `@Pattern` constraint overrides the default validation message. The message can be specified directly:

```
@Pattern(regexp = "^\\(?(\\d{3})\\)?[- ]?(\\d{3})[- ]?(\\d{4})$",
        message = "Invalid phone number!")
protected String homePhone;
```

The constraints in `Contact`, however, are strings in the resource bundle `ValidationMessages.properties`, under *tut-install*/examples/persistence/ address-book/src/java/. This allows the validation messages to be located in one single properties file and the messages to be easily localized. Overridden Bean Validation messages must be placed in a resource bundle properties file named `ValidationMessages.properties` in the default package, with localized resource bundles taking the form `ValidationMessages_`*locale-prefix*`.properties`. For example, `ValidationMessages_es.properties` is the resource bundle used in Spanish-speaking locales.

9.3.3 Validating Contact Input from a JavaServer Faces Application

The `address-book` application uses a JavaServer Faces web front end to allow users to enter contacts. While JavaServer Faces has a form input validation mechanism using tags in Facelets XHTML files, `address-book` doesn't use these validation tags. Bean Validation constraints in JavaServer Faces managed beans, in this case in the `Contact` entity, automatically trigger validation when the forms are submitted.

The following code snippet from the `Create.xhtml` Facelets file shows some of the input form for creating new `Contact` instances:

```
<h:form>
    <table columns="3" role="presentation">
        <tr>
            <td><h:outputLabel value="#{bundle.CreateContactLabel_firstName}"
                            for="firstName" /></td>
            <td><h:inputText id="firstName"
                            value="#{contactController.selected.firstName}"
                            title="#{bundle.CreateContactTitle_firstName}"/>
            </td>
            <td><h:message for="firstName" /></td>
        </tr>
        <tr>
            <td><h:outputLabel value="#{bundle.CreateContactLabel_lastName}"
                            for="lastName" /></td>
            <td><h:inputText id="lastName"
                            value="#{contactController.selected.lastName}"
                            title="#{bundle.CreateContactTitle_lastName}" />
            </td>
            <td><h:message for="lastName" /></td>
        </tr>
        ...
    </table>
</h:form>
```

The `<h:inputText>` tags `firstName` and `lastName` are bound to the attributes in the `Contact` entity instance `selected` in the `ContactController` stateless session bean. Each `<h:inputText>` tag has an associated `<h:message>` tag that will display validation error messages. The form doesn't require any JavaServer Faces validation tags, however.

9.3.4 Running the address-book Example

You can use either NetBeans IDE or Maven to build, package, deploy, and run the `address-book` application.

9.3.4.1 To Run the address-book Example Using NetBeans IDE

1. Make sure that GlassFish Server has been started (see Section 2.2, "Starting and Stopping GlassFish Server").

2. If the database server is not already running, start it by following the instructions in Section 2.4, "Starting and Stopping the Java DB Server."

3. From the **File** menu, choose **Open Project**.

4. In the Open Project dialog box, navigate to:

   `tut-install/examples/persistence`

5. Select the `address-book` folder.

6. Click **Open Project**.

7. In the **Projects** tab, right-click the `address-book` project and select **Run**.

   After the application has been deployed, a web browser window appears at the following URL:

   `http://localhost:8080/address-book/`

8. Click **Show All Contact Items**, then **Create New Contact**. Enter values in the fields; then click **Save**.

   If any of the values entered violate the constraints in `Contact`, an error message will appear in red beside the field with the incorrect values.

9.3.4.2 To Run the address-book Example Using Maven

1. Make sure that GlassFish Server has been started (see Section 2.2, "Starting and Stopping GlassFish Server").

2. If the database server is not already running, start it by following the instructions in Section 2.4, "Starting and Stopping the Java DB Server."

3. In a terminal window, go to:

   `tut-install/examples/persistence/address-book/`

4. Enter the following command:

   `mvn install`

   This will compile and assemble the `address-book` application into a WAR. The WAR file is then deployed to GlassFish Server.

5. Open a web browser window and enter the following URL:

   `http://localhost:8080/address-book/`

6. Click **Show All Contact Items**, then **Create New Contact**. Enter values in the fields; then click **Save**.

   If any of the values entered violate the constraints in `Contact`, an error message will appear in red beside the field with the incorrect values.

10

The Java Persistence Query Language

The Java Persistence query language defines queries for entities and their persistent state. The query language allows you to write portable queries that work regardless of the underlying data store.

The query language uses the abstract persistence schemas of entities, including their relationships, for its data model and defines operators and expressions based on this data model. The scope of a query spans the abstract schemas of related entities that are packaged in the same persistence unit. The query language uses an SQL-like syntax to select objects or values based on entity abstract schema types and relationships among them.

This chapter relies on the material presented in earlier chapters. For conceptual information, see Chapter 8, "Introduction to the Java Persistence API." For code examples, see Chapter 9, "Running the Persistence Examples."

The following topics are addressed here:

- Query Language Terminology
- Creating Queries Using the Java Persistence Query Language
- Simplified Query Language Syntax
- Example Queries
- Full Query Language Syntax

10.1 Query Language Terminology

The following list defines some of the terms referred to in this chapter.

- **Abstract schema**: The persistent schema abstraction (persistent entities, their state, and their relationships) over which queries operate. The query language translates queries over this persistent schema abstraction into queries that are executed over the database schema to which entities are mapped.

- **Abstract schema type**: The type to which the persistent property of an entity evaluates in the abstract schema. That is, each persistent field or property in an entity has a corresponding state field of the same type in the abstract schema. The abstract schema type of an entity is derived from the entity class and the metadata information provided by Java language annotations.

- **Backus-Naur Form (BNF)**: A notation that describes the syntax of high-level languages. The syntax diagrams in this chapter are in BNF notation.

- **Navigation**: The traversal of relationships in a query language expression. The navigation operator is a period.

- **Path expression**: An expression that navigates to an entity's state or relationship field.

- **State field**: A persistent field of an entity.

- **Relationship field**: A persistent field of an entity whose type is the abstract schema type of the related entity.

10.2 Creating Queries Using the Java Persistence Query Language

The `EntityManager.createQuery` and `EntityManager.createNamedQuery` methods are used to query the datastore by using Java Persistence query language queries.

The `createQuery` method is used to create **dynamic queries**, which are queries defined directly within an application's business logic:

```
public List findWithName(String name) {
return em.createQuery(
    "SELECT c FROM Customer c WHERE c.name LIKE :custName")
    .setParameter("custName", name)
    .setMaxResults(10)
    .getResultList();
}
```

The `createNamedQuery` method is used to create **static queries**, or queries that are defined in metadata by using the `javax.persistence.NamedQuery` annotation.

The name element of @NamedQuery specifies the name of the query that will be used with the createNamedQuery method. The query element of @NamedQuery is the query:

```
@NamedQuery(
    name="findAllCustomersWithName",
    query="SELECT c FROM Customer c WHERE c.name LIKE :custName'
)
```

Here's an example of createNamedQuery, which uses the @NamedQuery:

```
@PersistenceContext
public EntityManager em;
...
customers = em.createNamedQuery("findAllCustomersWithName")
    .setParameter("custName", "Smith")
    .getResultList();
```

10.2.1 Named Parameters in Queries

Named parameters are query parameters that are prefixed with a colon (:). Named parameters in a query are bound to an argument by the following method:

```
javax.persistence.Query.setParameter(String name, Object value)
```

In the following example, the name argument to the findWithName business method is bound to the :custName named parameter in the query by calling Query.setParameter:

```
public List findWithName(String name) {
    return em.createQuery(
        "SELECT c FROM Customer c WHERE c.name LIKE :custName")
        .setParameter("custName", name)
        .getResultList();
}
```

Named parameters are case-sensitive and may be used by both dynamic and static queries.

10.2.2 Positional Parameters in Queries

You may use positional parameters instead of named parameters in queries. Positional parameters are prefixed with a question mark (?) followed by the numeric position of the parameter in the query. The method

Query.setParameter(integer position, Object value) is used to set the parameter values.

In the following example, the findWithName business method is rewritten to use input parameters:

```
public List findWithName(String name) {
    return em.createQuery(
        "SELECT c FROM Customer c WHERE c.name LIKE ?1")
        .setParameter(1, name)
        .getResultList();
}
```

Input parameters are numbered starting from 1. Input parameters are case-sensitive, and may be used by both dynamic and static queries.

10.3 Simplified Query Language Syntax

This section briefly describes the syntax of the query language so that you can quickly move on to Section 10.4, "Example Queries." When you are ready to learn about the syntax in more detail, read Section 10.5, "Full Query Language Syntax."

10.3.1 Select Statements

A select query has six clauses: SELECT, FROM, WHERE, GROUP BY, HAVING, and ORDER BY. The SELECT and FROM clauses are required, but the WHERE, GROUP BY, HAVING, and ORDER BY clauses are optional. Here is the high-level BNF syntax of a query language select query:

```
QL_statement ::= select_clause from_clause
  [where_clause][groupby_clause][having_clause][orderby_clause]
```

The BNF syntax defines the following clauses.

- The SELECT clause defines the types of the objects or values returned by the query.

- The FROM clause defines the scope of the query by declaring one or more **identification variables**, which can be referenced in the SELECT and WHERE clauses. An identification variable represents one of the following elements:

  - The abstract schema name of an entity

  - An element of a collection relationship

– An element of a single-valued relationship

– A member of a collection that is the multiple side of a one-to-many relationship

■ The WHERE clause is a conditional expression that restricts the objects or values retrieved by the query. Although the clause is optional, most queries have a WHERE clause.

■ The GROUP BY clause groups query results according to a set of properties.

■ The HAVING clause is used with the GROUP BY clause to further restrict the query results according to a conditional expression.

■ The ORDER BY clause sorts the objects or values returned by the query into a specified order.

10.3.2 Update and Delete Statements

Update and delete statements provide bulk operations over sets of entities. These statements have the following syntax:

```
update_statement :: = update_clause [where_clause]
delete_statement :: = delete_clause [where_clause]
```

The update and delete clauses determine the type of the entities to be updated or deleted. The WHERE clause may be used to restrict the scope of the update or delete operation.

10.4 Example Queries

The following queries are from the Player entity of the roster application, which is documented in Section 9.2, "The roster Application."

10.4.1 Simple Queries

If you are unfamiliar with the query language, these simple queries are a good place to start.

10.4.1.1 A Basic Select Query

```
SELECT p
FROM Player p
```

■ **Data retrieved**: All players.

- **Description**: The FROM clause declares an identification variable named p, omitting the optional keyword AS. If the AS keyword were included, the clause would be written as follows:

```
FROM Player AS p
```

The Player element is the abstract schema name of the Player entity.

- **See also**: Section 10.5.3.2, "Identification Variables."

10.4.1.2 Eliminating Duplicate Values

```
SELECT DISTINCT p
FROM Player p
WHERE p.position = ?1
```

- **Data retrieved**: The players with the position specified by the query's parameter.

- **Description**: The DISTINCT keyword eliminates duplicate values.

  The WHERE clause restricts the players retrieved by checking their position, a persistent field of the Player entity. The ?1 element denotes the input parameter of the query.

- **See also**: Section 10.5.5.2, "Input Parameters," and Section 10.5.6.2, "The DISTINCT Keyword."

10.4.1.3 Using Named Parameters

```
SELECT DISTINCT p
FROM Player p
WHERE p.position = :position AND p.name = :name
```

- **Data retrieved**: The players having the specified positions and names.

- **Description**: The position and name elements are persistent fields of the Player entity. The WHERE clause compares the values of these fields with the named parameters of the query, set using the Query.setNamedParameter method. The query language denotes a named input parameter using a colon (:) followed by an identifier. The first input parameter is :position, the second is :name.

10.4.2 Queries That Navigate to Related Entities

In the query language, an expression can traverse, or navigate, to related entities. These expressions are the primary difference between the Java Persistence query language and SQL. Queries navigates to related entities, whereas SQL joins tables.

10.4.2.1 A Simple Query with Relationships

```
SELECT DISTINCT p
FROM Player p, IN (p.teams) t
```

- **Data retrieved**: All players who belong to a team.

- **Description**: The FROM clause declares two identification variables: p and t. The p variable represents the Player entity, and the t variable represents the related Team entity. The declaration for t references the previously declared p variable. The IN keyword signifies that teams is a collection of related entities. The p.teams expression navigates from a Player to its related Team. The period in the p.teams expression is the navigation operator.

  You may also use the JOIN statement to write the same query:

```
SELECT DISTINCT p
FROM Player p JOIN p.teams t
```

  This query could also be rewritten as:

```
SELECT DISTINCT p
FROM Player p
WHERE p.team IS NOT EMPTY
```

10.4.2.2 Navigating to Single-Valued Relationship Fields

Use the JOIN clause statement to navigate to a single-valued relationship field:

```
SELECT t
FROM Team t JOIN t.league l
WHERE l.sport = 'soccer' OR l.sport ='football'
```

In this example, the query will return all teams that are in either soccer or football leagues.

10.4.2.3 Traversing Relationships with an Input Parameter

```
SELECT DISTINCT p
FROM Player p, IN (p.teams) AS t
WHERE t.city = :city
```

- **Data retrieved**: The players whose teams belong to the specified city.

- **Description**: This query is similar to the previous example but adds an input parameter. The AS keyword in the FROM clause is optional. In the WHERE clause, the period preceding the persistent variable city is a delimiter, not a navigation operator. Strictly speaking, expressions can navigate to relationship fields (related entities) but not to persistent fields. To access a persistent field, an expression uses the period as a delimiter.

  Expressions cannot navigate beyond (or further qualify) relationship fields that are collections. In the syntax of an expression, a collection-valued field is a terminal symbol. Because the teams field is a collection, the WHERE clause cannot specify p.teams.city (an illegal expression).

- **See also**: Part 10.5.4, "Path Expressions."

10.4.2.4 Traversing Multiple Relationships

```
SELECT DISTINCT p
FROM Player p, IN (p.teams) t
WHERE t.league = :league
```

- **Data retrieved**: The players who belong to the specified league.

- **Description**: The expressions in this query navigate over two relationships. The p.teams expression navigates the Player-Team relationship, and the t.league expression navigates the Team-League relationship.

In the other examples, the input parameters are String objects; in this example, the parameter is an object whose type is a League. This type matches the league relationship field in the comparison expression of the WHERE clause.

10.4.2.5 Navigating According to Related Fields

```
SELECT DISTINCT p
FROM Player p, IN (p.teams) t
WHERE t.league.sport = :sport
```

- **Data retrieved**: The players who participate in the specified sport.

- **Description**: The sport persistent field belongs to the League entity. To reach the sport field, the query must first navigate from the Player entity to Team (p.teams) and then from Team to the League entity (t.league). Because it is not a collection, the league relationship field can be followed by the sport persistent field.

10.4.3 Queries with Other Conditional Expressions

Every WHERE clause must specify a conditional expression, of which there are several kinds. In the previous examples, the conditional expressions are comparison expressions that test for equality. The following examples demonstrate some of the other kinds of conditional expressions. For descriptions of all conditional expressions, see Section 10.5.5, "WHERE Clause."

10.4.3.1 The LIKE Expression

```
SELECT p
FROM Player p
WHERE p.name LIKE 'Mich%'
```

- **Data retrieved**: All players whose names begin with "Mich."

- **Description**: The LIKE expression uses wildcard characters to search for strings that match the wildcard pattern. In this case, the query uses the LIKE expression and the % wildcard to find all players whose names begin with the string "Mich." For example, "Michael" and "Michelle" both match the wildcard pattern.

- **See also**: Section 10.5.5.7, "LIKE Expressions."

10.4.3.2 The IS NULL Expression

```
SELECT t
FROM Team t
WHERE t.league IS NULL
```

- **Data retrieved**: All teams not associated with a league.

- **Description**: The IS NULL expression can be used to check whether a relationship has been set between two entities. In this case, the query checks whether the teams are associated with any leagues and returns the teams that do not have a league.

- **See also**: Section 10.5.5.8, "NULL Comparison Expressions," and Section 10.5.5.14, "NULL Values."

10.4.3.3 The IS EMPTY Expression

```
SELECT p
FROM Player p
WHERE p.teams IS EMPTY
```

- **Data retrieved**: All players who do not belong to a team.

- **Description**: The teams relationship field of the Player entity is a collection. If a player does not belong to a team, the teams collection is empty, and the conditional expression is TRUE.

- **See also**: Section 10.5.5.9, "Empty Collection Comparison Expressions."

10.4.3.4 The BETWEEN Expression

```
SELECT DISTINCT p
FROM Player p
WHERE p.salary BETWEEN :lowerSalary AND :higherSalary
```

- **Data retrieved**: The players whose salaries fall within the range of the specified salaries.

- **Description**: This BETWEEN expression has three arithmetic expressions: a persistent field (p.salary) and the two input parameters (:lowerSalary and :higherSalary). The following expression is equivalent to the BETWEEN expression:

```
p.salary >= :lowerSalary AND p.salary <= :higherSalary
```

- **See also**: Section 10.5.5.5, "BETWEEN Expressions."

10.4.3.5 Comparison Operators

```
SELECT DISTINCT p1
FROM Player p1, Player p2
WHERE p1.salary > p2.salary AND p2.name = :name
```

- **Data retrieved**: All players whose salaries are higher than the salary of the player with the specified name.

- **Description**: The FROM clause declares two identification variables (p1 and p2) of the same type (Player). Two identification variables are needed because the WHERE clause compares the salary of one player (p2) with that of the other players (p1).

- **See also**: Section 10.5.3.2, "Identification Variables."

10.4.4 Bulk Updates and Deletes

The following examples show how to use the UPDATE and DELETE expressions in queries. UPDATE and DELETE operate on multiple entities according to the condition or conditions set in the WHERE clause. The WHERE clause in UPDATE and DELETE queries follows the same rules as SELECT queries.

10.4.4.1 Update Queries

```
UPDATE Player p
SET p.status = 'inactive'
WHERE p.lastPlayed < :inactiveThresholdDate
```

- **Description**: This query sets the status of a set of players to `inactive` if the player's last game was longer ago than the date specified in `inactiveThresholdDate`.

10.4.4.2 Delete Queries

```
DELETE
FROM Player p
WHERE p.status = 'inactive'
AND p.teams IS EMPTY
```

- **Description**: This query deletes all inactive players who are not on a team.

10.5 Full Query Language Syntax

This section discusses the query language syntax, as defined in the Java Persistence API 2.0 specification available at `http://jcp.org/en/jsr/detail?id=317`. Much of the following material paraphrases or directly quotes the specification.

10.5.1 BNF Symbols

Table 10–1 describes the BNF symbols used in this chapter.

Table 10–1   BNF Symbol Summary

Symbol	Description
`::=`	The element to the left of the symbol is defined by the constructs on the right.
`*`	The preceding construct may occur zero or more times.
`{...}`	The constructs within the braces are grouped together.
`[...]`	The constructs within the brackets are optional.
`|`	An exclusive OR.
`BOLDFACE`	A keyword; although capitalized in the BNF diagram, keywords are not case-sensitive.
White space	A whitespace character can be a space, a horizontal tab, or a line feed.

10.5.2 BNF Grammar of the Java Persistence Query Language

Here is the entire BNF diagram for the query language:

```
QL_statement ::= select_statement | update_statement | delete_statement
select_statement ::= select_clause from_clause [where_clause] [groupby_clause]
    [having_clause] [orderby_clause]
update_statement ::= update_clause [where_clause]
delete_statement ::= delete_clause [where_clause]
from_clause ::=
    FROM identification_variable_declaration
        {, {identification_variable_declaration |
            collection_member_declaration}}*
identification_variable_declaration ::=
        range_variable_declaration { join | fetch_join }*
range_variable_declaration ::= abstract_schema_name [AS]
        identification_variable
join ::= join_spec join_association_path_expression [AS]
        identification_variable
fetch_join ::= join_specFETCH join_association_path_expression
association_path_expression ::=
        collection_valued_path_expression |
        single_valued_association_path_expression
join_spec::= [LEFT [OUTER] |INNER] JOIN
join_association_path_expression ::=
        join_collection_valued_path_expression |
        join_single_valued_association_path_expression
join_collection_valued_path_expression::=
    identification_variable.collection_valued_association_field
join_single_valued_association_path_expression::=
        identification_variable.single_valued_association_field
collection_member_declaration ::=
        IN (collection_valued_path_expression) [AS]
        identification_variable
single_valued_path_expression ::=
        state_field_path_expression |
        single_valued_association_path_expression
state_field_path_expression ::=
    {identification_variable |
    single_valued_association_path_expression}.state_field
single_valued_association_path_expression ::=
    identification_variable.{single_valued_association_field.}*
    single_valued_association_field
collection_valued_path_expression ::=
    identification_variable.{single_valued_association_field.}*
    collection_valued_association_field
state_field ::=
```

```
    {embedded_class_state_field.}*simple_state_field
update_clause ::=UPDATE abstract_schema_name [[AS]
    identification_variable] SET update_item {, update_item}*
update_item ::= [identification_variable.]{state_field |
    single_valued_association_field} = new_value
new_value ::=
     simple_arithmetic_expression |
    string_primary |
    datetime_primary |
    boolean_primary |
    enum_primary simple_entity_expression |
    NULL
delete_clause ::= DELETE FROM abstract_schema_name [[AS]
    identification_variable]
select_clause ::= SELECT [DISTINCT] select_expression {,
    select_expression}*
select_expression ::=
    single_valued_path_expression |
    aggregate_expression |
    identification_variable |
    OBJECT(identification_variable) |
    constructor_expression
constructor_expression ::=
    NEW constructor_name(constructor_item {,
    constructor_item}*)
constructor_item ::= single_valued_path_expression |
    aggregate_expression
aggregate_expression ::=
    {AVG |MAX |MIN |SUM} ([DISTINCT]
        state_field_path_expression) |
    COUNT ([DISTINCT] identification_variable |
        state_field_path_expression |
        single_valued_association_path_expression)
where_clause ::= WHERE conditional_expression
groupby_clause ::= GROUP BY groupby_item {, groupby_item}*
groupby_item ::= single_valued_path_expression
having_clause ::= HAVING conditional_expression
orderby_clause ::= ORDER BY orderby_item {, orderby_item}*
orderby_item ::= state_field_path_expression [ASC |DESC]
subquery ::= simple_select_clause subquery_from_clause
    [where_clause] [groupby_clause] [having_clause]
subquery_from_clause ::=
    FROM subselect_identification_variable_declaration
        {, subselect_identification_variable_declaration}*
subselect_identification_variable_declaration ::=
    identification_variable_declaration |
    association_path_expression [AS] identification_variable |
```

```
        collection_member_declaration
simple_select_clause ::= SELECT [DISTINCT]
    simple_select_expression
simple_select_expression::=
    single_valued_path_expression |
    aggregate_expression |
    identification_variable
conditional_expression ::= conditional_term |
    conditional_expression OR conditional_term
conditional_term ::= conditional_factor | conditional_term AND
    conditional_factor
conditional_factor ::= [NOT] conditional_primary
conditional_primary ::= simple_cond_expression |(
    conditional_expression)
simple_cond_expression ::=
    comparison_expression |
    between_expression |
    like_expression |
    in_expression |
    null_comparison_expression |
    empty_collection_comparison_expression |
    collection_member_expression |
    exists_expression
between_expression ::=
    arithmetic_expression [NOT] BETWEEN
        arithmetic_expressionAND arithmetic_expression |
    string_expression [NOT] BETWEEN string_expression AND
        string_expression |
    datetime_expression [NOT] BETWEEN
        datetime_expression AND datetime_expression
in_expression ::=
    state_field_path_expression [NOT] IN (in_item {, in_item}*
    | subquery)
in_item ::= literal | input_parameter
like_expression ::=
    string_expression [NOT] LIKE pattern_value [ESCAPE
        escape_character]
null_comparison_expression ::=
    {single_valued_path_expression | input_parameter} IS [NOT]
        NULL
empty_collection_comparison_expression ::=
    collection_valued_path_expression IS [NOT] EMPTY
collection_member_expression ::= entity_expression
    [NOT] MEMBER [OF] collection_valued_path_expression
exists_expression::= [NOT] EXISTS (subquery)
all_or_any_expression ::= {ALL |ANY |SOME} (subquery)
comparison_expression ::=
```

```
        string_expression comparison_operator {string_expression |
        all_or_any_expression} |
        boolean_expression {= |<> } {boolean_expression |
        all_or_any_expression} |
        enum_expression {= |<> } {enum_expression |
        all_or_any_expression} |
        datetime_expression comparison_operator
            {datetime_expression | all_or_any_expression} |
        entity_expression {= |<> } {entity_expression |
        all_or_any_expression} |
        arithmetic_expression comparison_operator
            {arithmetic_expression | all_or_any_expression}
comparison_operator ::= = |> |>= |< |<= |<>
arithmetic_expression ::= simple_arithmetic_expression |
    (subquery)
simple_arithmetic_expression ::=
    arithmetic_term | simple_arithmetic_expression {+ |- }
        arithmetic_term
arithmetic_term ::= arithmetic_factor | arithmetic_term {* |/ }
    arithmetic_factor
arithmetic_factor ::= [{+ |- }] arithmetic_primary
arithmetic_primary ::=
    state_field_path_expression |
    numeric_literal |
    (simple_arithmetic_expression) |
    input_parameter |
    functions_returning_numerics |
    aggregate_expression
string_expression ::= string_primary | (subquery)
string_primary ::=
    state_field_path_expression |
    string_literal |
    input_parameter |
    functions_returning_strings |
    aggregate_expression
datetime_expression ::= datetime_primary | (subquery)
datetime_primary ::=
    state_field_path_expression |
    input_parameter |
    functions_returning_datetime |
    aggregate_expression
boolean_expression ::= boolean_primary | (subquery)
boolean_primary ::=
    state_field_path_expression |
    boolean_literal |
    input_parameter
enum_expression ::= enum_primary | (subquery)
```

```
enum_primary ::=
    state_field_path_expression |
    enum_literal |
    input_parameter
entity_expression ::=
    single_valued_association_path_expression |
        simple_entity_expression
simple_entity_expression ::=
    identification_variable |
    input_parameter
functions_returning_numerics::=
    LENGTH(string_primary) |
    LOCATE(string_primary, string_primary[,
        simple_arithmetic_expression]) |
    ABS(simple_arithmetic_expression) |
    SQRT(simple_arithmetic_expression) |
    MOD(simple_arithmetic_expression,
        simple_arithmetic_expression) |
    SIZE(collection_valued_path_expression)
functions_returning_datetime ::=
    CURRENT_DATE |
    CURRENT_TIME |
    CURRENT_TIMESTAMP
functions_returning_strings ::=
    CONCAT(string_primary, string_primary) |
    SUBSTRING(string_primary,
        simple_arithmetic_expression,
        simple_arithmetic_expression)|
    TRIM([[trim_specification] [trim_character] FROM]
        string_primary) |
    LOWER(string_primary) |
    UPPER(string_primary)
trim_specification ::= LEADING | TRAILING | BOTH
```

10.5.3 FROM Clause

The FROM clause defines the domain of the query by declaring identification variables.

10.5.3.1 Identifiers

An identifier is a sequence of one or more characters. The first character must be a valid first character (letter, $, _) in an identifier of the Java programming language, hereafter in this chapter called simply "Java." Each subsequent character in the sequence must be a valid nonfirst character (letter, digit, $, _) in a Java identifier. (For details, see the Java SE API documentation of the isJavaIdentifierStart and isJavaIdentifierPart methods of the Character class.) The question mark (?) is a reserved character in the query language and cannot be used in an identifier.

A query language identifier is case-sensitive, with two exceptions:

- Keywords
- Identification variables

An identifier cannot be the same as a query language keyword. Here is a list of query language keywords:

```
ABS
ALL
AND
ANY
AS
ASC
AVG
BETWEEN
BIT_LENGTH
BOTH
BY
CASE
CHAR_LENGTH
CHARACTER_LENGTH
CLASS
COALESCE
CONCAT
COUNT
CURRENT_DATE
CURRENT_TIMESTAMP
DELETE
DESC
DISTINCT
ELSE
EMPTY
END
ENTRY
ESCAPE
EXISTS
FALSE
FETCH
FROM
```

```
GROUP
HAVING
IN
INDEX
INNER
IS
JOIN
KEY
LEADING
LEFT
LENGTH
LIKE
LOCATE
LOWER
MAX
MEMBER
MIN
MOD
NEW
NOT
NULL
NULLIF
OBJECT
OF
OR
ORDER
OUTER
POSITION
SELECT
SET
SIZE
SOME
SQRT
SUBSTRING
SUM
THEN
TRAILING
TRIM
TRUE
TYPE
UNKNOWN
UPDATE
UPPER
```

```
VALUE
WHEN
WHERE
```

It is not recommended that you use an SQL keyword as an identifier, because the list of keywords may expand to include other reserved SQL words in the future.

10.5.3.2 Identification Variables

An identification variable is an identifier declared in the FROM clause. Although they can reference identification variables, the SELECT and WHERE clauses cannot declare them. All identification variables must be declared in the FROM clause.

Because it is an identifier, an identification variable has the same naming conventions and restrictions as an identifier, with the exception that an identification variable is case-insensitive. For example, an identification variable cannot be the same as a query language keyword. (See Section 10.5.3.1, "Identifiers," for more naming rules.) Also, within a given persistence unit, an identification variable name must not match the name of any entity or abstract schema.

The FROM clause can contain multiple declarations, separated by commas. A declaration can reference another identification variable that has been previously declared (to the left). In the following FROM clause, the variable t references the previously declared variable p:

```
FROM Player p, IN (p.teams) AS t
```

Even if it is not used in the WHERE clause, an identification variable's declaration can affect the results of the query. For example, compare the next two queries. The following query returns all players, whether or not they belong to a team:

```
SELECT p
FROM Player p
```

In contrast, because it declares the t identification variable, the next query fetches all players who belong to a team:

```
SELECT p
FROM Player p, IN (p.teams) AS t
```

The following query returns the same results as the preceding query, but the WHERE clause makes it easier to read:

```
SELECT p
FROM Player p
WHERE p.teams IS NOT EMPTY
```

An identification variable always designates a reference to a single value whose type is that of the expression used in the declaration. There are two kinds of declarations: range variable and collection member.

10.5.3.3 Range Variable Declarations

To declare an identification variable as an abstract schema type, you specify a range variable declaration. In other words, an identification variable can range over the abstract schema type of an entity. In the following example, an identification variable named p represents the abstract schema named `Player`:

```
FROM Player p
```

A range variable declaration can include the optional `AS` operator:

```
FROM Player AS p
```

To obtain objects, a query usually uses path expressions to navigate through the relationships. But for those objects that cannot be obtained by navigation, you can use a range variable declaration to designate a starting point, or query root.

If the query compares multiple values of the same abstract schema type, the `FROM` clause must declare multiple identification variables for the abstract schema:

```
FROM Player p1, Player p2
```

For an example of such a query, see Section 10.4.3.5, "Comparison Operators."

10.5.3.4 Collection Member Declarations

In a one-to-many relationship, the multiple side consists of a collection of entities. An identification variable can represent a member of this collection. To access a collection member, the path expression in the variable's declaration navigates through the relationships in the abstract schema. (For more information on path expressions, see Section 10.5.4, "Path Expressions.") Because a path expression can be based on another path expression, the navigation can traverse several relationships. See Section 10.4.2.4, "Traversing Multiple Relationships."

A collection member declaration must include the `IN` operator but can omit the optional `AS` operator.

In the following example, the entity represented by the abstract schema named `Player` has a relationship field called `teams`. The identification variable called t represents a single member of the `teams` collection:

```
FROM Player p, IN (p.teams) t
```

10.5.3.5 Joins

The `JOIN` operator is used to traverse over relationships between entities and is functionally similar to the `IN` operator.

In the following example, the query joins over the relationship between customers and orders:

```
SELECT c
FROM Customer c JOIN c.orders o
WHERE c.status = 1 AND o.totalPrice > 10000
```

The `INNER` keyword is optional:

```
SELECT c
FROM Customer c INNER JOIN c.orders o
WHERE c.status = 1 AND o.totalPrice > 10000
```

These examples are equivalent to the following query, which uses the `IN` operator:

```
SELECT c
FROM Customer c, IN (c.orders) o
WHERE c.status = 1 AND o.totalPrice > 10000
```

You can also join a single-valued relationship:

```
SELECT t
FROM Team t JOIN t.league l
WHERE l.sport = :sport
```

A `LEFT JOIN` or `LEFT OUTER JOIN` retrieves a set of entities where matching values in the join condition may be absent. The `OUTER` keyword is optional:

```
SELECT c.name, o.totalPrice
FROM CustomerOrder o LEFT JOIN o.customer c
```

A `FETCH JOIN` is a join operation that returns associated entities as a side effect of running the query. In the following example, the query returns a set of departments and, as a side effect, the associated employees of the departments, even though the employees were not explicitly retrieved by the `SELECT` clause:

```
SELECT d
FROM Department d LEFT JOIN FETCH d.employees
WHERE d.deptno = 1
```

10.5.4 Path Expressions

Path expressions are important constructs in the syntax of the query language for several reasons. First, path expressions define navigation paths through the relationships in the abstract schema. These path definitions affect both the scope and the results of a query. Second, path expressions can appear in any of the main clauses of a query (SELECT, DELETE, HAVING, UPDATE, WHERE, FROM, GROUP BY, ORDER BY). Finally, although much of the query language is a subset of SQL, path expressions are extensions not found in SQL.

10.5.4.1 Examples of Path Expressions

Here, the WHERE clause contains a single_valued_path_expression; the p is an identification variable, and salary is a persistent field of Player:

```
SELECT DISTINCT p
FROM Player p
WHERE p.salary BETWEEN :lowerSalary AND :higherSalary
```

Here, the WHERE clause also contains a single_valued_path_expression; t is an identification variable, league is a single-valued relationship field, and sport is a persistent field of league:

```
SELECT DISTINCT p
FROM Player p, IN (p.teams) t
WHERE t.league.sport = :sport
```

Here, the WHERE clause contains a collection_valued_path_expression; p is an identification variable, and teams designates a collection-valued relationship field:

```
SELECT DISTINCT p
FROM Player p
WHERE p.teams IS EMPTY
```

10.5.4.2 Expression Types

The type of a path expression is the type of the object represented by the ending element, which can be one of the following:

- Persistent field
- Single-valued relationship field
- Collection-valued relationship field

For example, the type of the expression p.salary is double because the terminating persistent field (salary) is a double.

In the expression p.teams, the terminating element is a collection-valued relationship field (teams). This expression's type is a collection of the abstract schema type named Team. Because Team is the abstract schema name for the Team entity, this type maps to the entity. For more information on the type mapping of abstract schemas, see Section 10.5.6.1, "Return Types."

10.5.4.3 Navigation

A path expression enables the query to navigate to related entities. The terminating elements of an expression determine whether navigation is allowed. If an expression contains a single-valued relationship field, the navigation can continue to an object that is related to the field. However, an expression cannot navigate beyond a persistent field or a collection-valued relationship field. For example, the expression `p.teams.league.sport` is illegal because `teams` is a collection-valued relationship field. To reach the `sport` field, the `FROM` clause could define an identification variable named `t` for the `teams` field:

```
FROM Player AS p, IN (p.teams) t
WHERE t.league.sport = 'soccer'
```

10.5.5 WHERE Clause

The `WHERE` clause specifies a conditional expression that limits the values returned by the query. The query returns all corresponding values in the data store for which the conditional expression is `TRUE`. Although usually specified, the `WHERE` clause is optional. If the `WHERE` clause is omitted, the query returns all values. The high-level syntax for the `WHERE` clause is as follows:

```
where_clause ::= WHERE conditional_expression
```

10.5.5.1 Literals

There are four kinds of literals: string, numeric, Boolean, and enum.

- **String literals**: A string literal is enclosed in single quotes:

  ```
  'Duke'
  ```

  If a string literal contains a single quote, you indicate the quote by using two single quotes:

  ```
  'Duke''s'
  ```

  Like a Java `String`, a string literal in the query language uses the Unicode character encoding.

- **Numeric literals**: There are two types of numeric literals: exact and approximate.

- An exact numeric literal is a numeric value without a decimal point, such as 65, –233, and +12. Using the Java integer syntax, exact numeric literals support numbers in the range of a Java `long`.

- An approximate numeric literal is a numeric value in scientific notation, such as 57., –85.7, and +2.1. Using the syntax of the Java floating-point literal, approximate numeric literals support numbers in the range of a Java `double`.

- **Boolean literals**: A Boolean literal is either `TRUE` or `FALSE`. These keywords are not case-sensitive.

- **Enum literals**: The Java Persistence query language supports the use of enum literals using the Java enum literal syntax. The enum class name must be specified as a fully qualified class name:

```
SELECT e
FROM Employee e
WHERE e.status = com.example.EmployeeStatus.FULL_TIME
```

10.5.5.2 Input Parameters

An input parameter can be either a named parameter or a positional parameter.

- A named input parameter is designated by a colon (`:`) followed by a string; for example, `:name`.

- A positional input parameter is designated by a question mark (`?`) followed by an integer. For example, the first input parameter is `?1`, the second is `?2`, and so forth.

The following rules apply to input parameters.

- They can be used only in a `WHERE` or `HAVING` clause.

- Positional parameters must be numbered, starting with the integer 1.

- Named parameters and positional parameters may not be mixed in a single query.

- Named parameters are case-sensitive.

10.5.5.3 Conditional Expressions

A `WHERE` clause consists of a conditional expression, which is evaluated from left to right within a precedence level. You can change the order of evaluation by using parentheses.

10.5.5.4 Operators and Their Precedence

Table 10–2 lists the query language operators in order of decreasing precedence.

Table 10–2   Query Language Order Precedence

Type	Precedence Order
Navigation	. (a period)
Arithmetic	+ – (unary)
	* / (multiplication and division)
	+ – (addition and subtraction)
Comparison	=
	>
	>=
	<
	<=
	<> (not equal)
	[NOT] BETWEEN
	[NOT] LIKE
	[NOT] IN
	IS [NOT] NULL
	IS [NOT] EMPTY
	[NOT] MEMBER OF
Logical	NOT
	AND
	OR

10.5.5.5 BETWEEN Expressions

A BETWEEN expression determines whether an arithmetic expression falls within a range of values.

These two expressions are equivalent:

```
p.age BETWEEN 15 AND 19
p.age >= 15 AND p.age <= 19
```

The following two expressions also are equivalent:

```
p.age NOT BETWEEN 15 AND 19
p.age < 15 OR p.age > 19
```

If an arithmetic expression has a NULL value, the value of the BETWEEN expression is unknown.

10.5.5.6 IN Expressions

An IN expression determines whether a string belongs to a set of string literals or whether a number belongs to a set of number values.

The path expression must have a string or numeric value. If the path expression has a NULL value, the value of the IN expression is unknown.

In the following example, the expression is TRUE if the country is UK , but FALSE if the country is Peru:

```
o.country IN ('UK', 'US', 'France')
```

You may also use input parameters:

```
o.country IN ('UK', 'US', 'France', :country)
```

10.5.5.7 LIKE Expressions

A LIKE expression determines whether a wildcard pattern matches a string.

The path expression must have a string or numeric value. If this value is NULL, the value of the LIKE expression is unknown. The pattern value is a string literal that can contain wildcard characters. The underscore (_) wildcard character represents any single character. The percent (%) wildcard character represents zero or more characters. The ESCAPE clause specifies an escape character for the wildcard characters in the pattern value. Table 10–3 shows some sample LIKE expressions.

Table 10–3   LIKE Expression Examples

Expression	TRUE	FALSE
address.phone LIKE '12%3'	'123' '12993'	'1234'
asentence.word LIKE 'l_se'	'lose'	'loose'
aword.underscored LIKE '_%' ESCAPE '\'	'_foo'	'bar'
address.phone NOT LIKE '12%3'	'1234'	'123' '12993'

10.5.5.8 NULL Comparison Expressions

A NULL comparison expression tests whether a single-valued path expression or an input parameter has a NULL value. Usually, the NULL comparison expression is used to test whether a single-valued relationship has been set:

```
SELECT t
FROM Team t
WHERE t.league IS NULL
```

This query selects all teams where the league relationship is not set. Note that the following query is *not* equivalent:

```
SELECT t
FROM Team t
WHERE t.league = NULL
```

The comparison with NULL using the equals operator (=) always returns an unknown value, even if the relationship is not set. The second query will always return an empty result.

10.5.5.9 Empty Collection Comparison Expressions

The IS [NOT] EMPTY comparison expression tests whether a collection-valued path expression has no elements. In other words, it tests whether a collection-valued relationship has been set.

If the collection-valued path expression is NULL, the empty collection comparison expression has a NULL value.

Here is an example that finds all orders that do not have any line items:

```
SELECT o
FROM CustomerOrder o
WHERE o.lineItems IS EMPTY
```

10.5.5.10 Collection Member Expressions

The [NOT] MEMBER [OF] collection member expression determines whether a value is a member of a collection. The value and the collection members must have the same type.

If either the collection-valued or single-valued path expression is unknown, the collection member expression is unknown. If the collection-valued path expression designates an empty collection, the collection member expression is FALSE.

The OF keyword is optional.

The following example tests whether a line item is part of an order:

```
SELECT o
FROM CustomerOrder o
WHERE :lineItem MEMBER OF o.lineItems
```

10.5.5.11 Subqueries

Subqueries may be used in the WHERE or HAVING clause of a query. Subqueries must be surrounded by parentheses.

The following example finds all customers who have placed more than ten orders:

```
SELECT c
FROM Customer c
WHERE (SELECT COUNT(o) FROM c.orders o) > 10
```

Subqueries may contain EXISTS, ALL, and ANY expressions.

- **EXISTS expressions**: The [NOT] EXISTS expression is used with a subquery and is true only if the result of the subquery consists of one or more values; otherwise, it is false.

  The following example finds all employees whose spouses are also employees:

  ```
  SELECT DISTINCT emp
  FROM Employee emp
  WHERE EXISTS (
       SELECT spouseEmp
       FROM Employee spouseEmp
       WHERE spouseEmp = emp.spouse)
  ```

- **ALL and ANY expressions**: The ALL expression is used with a subquery and is true if all the values returned by the subquery are true or if the subquery is empty.

  The ANY expression is used with a subquery and is true if some of the values returned by the subquery are true. An ANY expression is false if the subquery result is empty or if all the values returned are false. The SOME keyword is synonymous with ANY.

  The ALL and ANY expressions are used with the =, <, <=, >, >=, and <> comparison operators.

The following example finds all employees whose salaries are higher than the salaries of the managers in the employee's department:

```
SELECT emp
FROM Employee emp
WHERE emp.salary > ALL (
    SELECT m.salary
    FROM Manager m
    WHERE m.department = emp.department)
```

10.5.5.12 Functional Expressions

The query language includes several string, arithmetic, and date/time functions that may be used in the SELECT, WHERE, or HAVING clause of a query. The functions are listed in Table 10–4, Table 10–5, and Table 10–6.

In Table 10–4, the start and length arguments are of type int and designate positions in the String argument. The first position in a string is designated by 1.

Table 10–4   String Expressions

Function Syntax	Return Type
CONCAT(String, String)	String
LENGTH(String)	int
LOCATE(String, String [, start])	int
SUBSTRING(String, start, length)	String
TRIM([[LEADING|TRAILING|BOTH] char) FROM] (String)	String
LOWER(String)	String
UPPER(String)	String

The CONCAT function concatenates two strings into one string.

The LENGTH function returns the length of a string in characters as an integer.

The LOCATE function returns the position of a given string within a string. This function returns the first position at which the string was found as an integer. The first argument is the string to be located. The second argument is the string to be searched. The optional third argument is an integer that represents the starting string position. By default, LOCATE starts at the beginning of the string. The starting position of a string is 1. If the string cannot be located, LOCATE returns 0.

The SUBSTRING function returns a string that is a substring of the first argument based on the starting position and length.

The TRIM function trims the specified character from the beginning and/or end of a string. If no character is specified, TRIM removes spaces or blanks from the string. If the optional LEADING specification is used, TRIM removes only the leading characters from the string. If the optional TRAILING specification is used, TRIM removes only the trailing characters from the string. The default is BOTH, which removes the leading and trailing characters from the string.

The LOWER and UPPER functions convert a string to lowercase or uppercase, respectively.

In Table 10–5, the number argument can be an int, a float, or a double.

Table 10–5   Arithmetic Expressions

Function Syntax	Return Type
ABS(number)	int, float, or double
MOD(int, int)	int
SQRT(double)	double
SIZE(Collection)	int

The ABS function takes a numeric expression and returns a number of the same type as the argument.

The MOD function returns the remainder of the first argument divided by the second.

The SQRT function returns the square root of a number.

The SIZE function returns an integer of the number of elements in the given collection.

In Table 10–6, the date/time functions return the date, time, or timestamp on the database server.

Table 10–6   Date/Time Expressions

Function Syntax	Return Type
CURRENT_DATE	java.sql.Date
CURRENT_TIME	java.sql.Time
CURRENT_TIMESTAMP	java.sql.Timestamp

10.5.5.13 Case Expressions

Case expressions change based on a condition, similar to the `case` keyword of the Java programming language. The `CASE` keyword indicates the start of a case expression, and the expression is terminated by the `END` keyword. The `WHEN` and `THEN` keywords define individual conditions, and the `ELSE` keyword defines the default condition should none of the other conditions be satisfied.

The following query selects the name of a person and a conditional string, depending on the subtype of the `Person` entity. If the subtype is `Student`, the string `kid` is returned . If the subtype is `Guardian` or `Staff`, the string `adult` is returned. If the entity is some other subtype of `Person`, the string `unknown` is returned:

```
SELECT p.name
CASE TYPE(p)
    WHEN Student THEN 'kid'
    WHEN Guardian THEN 'adult'
    WHEN Staff THEN 'adult'
    ELSE 'unknown'
END
FROM Person p
```

The following query sets a discount for various types of customers. Gold-level customers get a 20% discount, silver-level customers get a 15% discount, bronze-level customers get a 10% discount, and everyone else gets a 5% discount:

```
UPDATE Customer c
SET c.discount =
    CASE c.level
        WHEN 'Gold' THEN 20
        WHEN 'SILVER' THEN 15
        WHEN 'Bronze' THEN 10
        ELSE 5
    END
```

10.5.5.14 NULL Values

If the target of a reference is not in the persistent store, the target is `NULL`. For conditional expressions containing `NULL`, the query language uses the semantics defined by SQL92. Briefly, these semantics are as follows.

- If a comparison or arithmetic operation has an unknown value, it yields a `NULL` value.

- Two `NULL` values are not equal. Comparing two `NULL` values yields an unknown value.

- The IS NULL test converts a NULL persistent field or a single-valued relationship field to TRUE. The IS NOT NULL test converts them to FALSE.

- Boolean operators and conditional tests use the three-valued logic defined by Table 10–7 and Table 10–8. (In these tables, T stands for TRUE, F for FALSE, and U for unknown.)

Table 10–7   AND Operator Logic

AND	T	F	U
T	T	F	U
F	F	F	F
U	U	F	U

Table 10–8   OR Operator Logic

OR	T	F	U
T	T	T	T
F	T	F	U
U	T	U	U

10.5.5.15 Equality Semantics

In the query language, only values of the same type can be compared. However, this rule has one exception: Exact and approximate numeric values can be compared. In such a comparison, the required type conversion adheres to the rules of Java numeric promotion.

The query language treats compared values as if they were Java types and not as if they represented types in the underlying data store. For example, a persistent field that could be either an integer or a NULL must be designated as an Integer object and not as an int primitive. This designation is required because a Java object can be NULL, but a primitive cannot.

Two strings are equal only if they contain the same sequence of characters. Trailing blanks are significant; for example, the strings 'abc' and 'abc ' are not equal.

Two entities of the same abstract schema type are equal only if their primary keys have the same value. Table 10–9 shows the operator logic of a negation, and Table 10–10 shows the truth values of conditional tests.

Table 10–9   NOT Operator Logic

NOT Value	Value
T	F
F	T
U	U

Table 10–10   Conditional Test

Conditional Test	T	F	U
Expression IS TRUE	T	F	F
Expression IS FALSE	F	T	F
Expression is unknown	F	F	T

10.5.6 SELECT Clause

The SELECT clause defines the types of the objects or values returned by the query.

10.5.6.1 Return Types

The return type of the SELECT clause is defined by the result types of the select expressions contained within it. If multiple expressions are used, the result of the query is an Object[], and the elements in the array correspond to the order of the expressions in the SELECT clause and in type to the result types of each expression.

A SELECT clause cannot specify a collection-valued expression. For example, the SELECT clause p.teams is invalid because teams is a collection. However, the clause in the following query is valid because t is a single element of the teams collection:

```
SELECT t
FROM Player p, IN (p.teams) t
```

The following query is an example of a query with multiple expressions in the SELECT clause:

```
SELECT c.name, c.country.name
FROM customer c
WHERE c.lastname = 'Coss' AND c.firstname = 'Roxane'
```

This query returns a list of Object[] elements; the first array element is a string denoting the customer name, and the second array element is a string denoting the name of the customer's country.

The result of a query may be the result of an aggregate function, listed in Table 10–11.

*Table 10–11 **Aggregate Functions in Select Statements***

Name	Return Type	Description
AVG	Double	Returns the mean average of the fields
COUNT	Long	Returns the total number of results
MAX	The type of the field	Returns the highest value in the result set
MIN	The type of the field	Returns the lowest value in the result set
SUM	Long (for integral fields) Double (for floating-point fields) BigInteger (for BigInteger fields) BigDecimal (for BigDecimal fields)	Returns the sum of all the values in the result set

For select method queries with an aggregate function (AVG, COUNT, MAX, MIN, or SUM) in the SELECT clause, the following rules apply.

- The AVG, MAX, MIN, and SUM functions return null if there are no values to which the function can be applied.

- The COUNT function returns 0 if there are no values to which the function can be applied.

The following example returns the average order quantity:

```
SELECT AVG(o.quantity)
FROM CustomerOrder o
```

The following example returns the total cost of the items ordered by Roxane Coss:

```
SELECT SUM(l.price)
FROM CustomerOrder o JOIN o.lineItems l JOIN o.customer c
WHERE c.lastname = 'Coss' AND c.firstname = 'Roxane'
```

The following example returns the total number of orders:

```
SELECT COUNT(o)
FROM CustomerOrder o
```

The following example returns the total number of items that have prices in Hal Incandenza's order:

```
SELECT COUNT(l.price)
FROM CustomerOrder o JOIN o.lineItems l JOIN o.customer c
WHERE c.lastname = 'Incandenza' AND c.firstname = 'Hal'
```

10.5.6.2 The DISTINCT Keyword

The DISTINCT keyword eliminates duplicate return values. If a query returns a java.util.Collection, which allows duplicates, you must specify the DISTINCT keyword to eliminate duplicates.

10.5.6.3 Constructor Expressions

Constructor expressions allow you to return Java instances that store a query result element instead of an Object[].

The following query creates a CustomerDetail instance per Customer matching the WHERE clause. A CustomerDetail stores the customer name and customer's country name. So the query returns a List of CustomerDetail instances:

```
SELECT NEW com.example.CustomerDetail(c.name, c.country.name)
FROM customer c
WHERE c.lastname = 'Coss' AND c.firstname = 'Roxane'
```

10.5.7 ORDER BY Clause

As its name suggests, the ORDER BY clause orders the values or objects returned by the query.

If the ORDER BY clause contains multiple elements, the left-to-right sequence of the elements determines the high-to-low precedence.

The ASC keyword specifies ascending order, the default, and the DESC keyword indicates descending order.

When using the ORDER BY clause, the SELECT clause must return an orderable set of objects or values. You cannot order the values or objects for values or objects not returned by the SELECT clause. For example, the following query is valid because the ORDER BY clause uses the objects returned by the SELECT clause:

```
SELECT o
FROM Customer c JOIN c.orders o JOIN c.address a
WHERE a.state = 'CA'
ORDER BY o.quantity, o.totalcost
```

The following example is *not* valid, because the ORDER BY clause uses a value not returned by the SELECT clause:

```
SELECT p.product_name
FROM CustomerOrder o, IN(o.lineItems) l JOIN o.customer c
WHERE c.lastname = 'Faehmel' AND c.firstname = 'Robert'
ORDER BY o.quantity
```

10.5.8 GROUP BY and HAVING Clauses

The GROUP BY clause allows you to group values according to a set of properties.

The following query groups the customers by their country and returns the number of customers per country:

```
SELECT c.country, COUNT(c)
FROM Customer c GROUP BY c.country
```

The HAVING clause is used with the GROUP BY clause to further restrict the returned result of a query.

The following query groups orders by the status of their customer and returns the customer status plus the average totalPrice for all orders where the corresponding customers have the same status. In addition, it considers only customers with status 1, 2, or 3, so orders of other customers are not taken into account:

```
SELECT c.status, AVG(o.totalPrice)
FROM CustomerOrder o JOIN o.customer c
GROUP BY c.status HAVING c.status IN (1, 2, 3)
```

11

Using the Criteria API to Create Queries

The Criteria API is used to define queries for entities and their persistent state by creating query-defining objects. Criteria queries are written using Java programming language APIs, are typesafe, and are portable. Such queries work regardless of the underlying data store.

The following topics are addressed here:

- Overview of the Criteria and Metamodel APIs
- Using the Metamodel API to Model Entity Classes
- Using the Criteria API and Metamodel API to Create Basic Typesafe Queries

11.1 Overview of the Criteria and Metamodel APIs

Similar to JPQL, the Criteria API is based on the abstract schema of persistent entities, their relationships, and embedded objects. The Criteria API operates on this abstract schema to allow developers to find, modify, and delete persistent entities by invoking Java Persistence API entity operations. The Metamodel API works in concert with the Criteria API to model persistent entity classes for Criteria queries.

The Criteria API and JPQL are closely related and are designed to allow similar operations in their queries. Developers familiar with JPQL syntax will find equivalent object-level operations in the Criteria API.

The following simple Criteria query returns all instances of the Pet entity in the data source:

```
EntityManager em = ...;
CriteriaBuilder cb = em.getCriteriaBuilder();
```

```
CriteriaQuery<Pet> cq = cb.createQuery(Pet.class);
Root<Pet> pet = cq.from(Pet.class);
cq.select(pet);
TypedQuery<Pet> q = em.createQuery(cq);
List<Pet> allPets = q.getResultList();
```

The equivalent JPQL query is

```
SELECT p
FROM Pet p
```

This query demonstrates the basic steps to create a Criteria query.

1. Use an `EntityManager` instance to create a `CriteriaBuilder` object.

2. Create a query object by creating an instance of the `CriteriaQuery` interface. This query object's attributes will be modified with the details of the query.

3. Set the query root by calling the `from` method on the `CriteriaQuery` object.

4. Specify what the type of the query result will be by calling the `select` method of the `CriteriaQuery` object.

5. Prepare the query for execution by creating a `TypedQuery<T>` instance, specifying the type of the query result.

6. Execute the query by calling the `getResultList` method on the `TypedQuery<T>` object. Because this query returns a collection of entities, the result is stored in a `List`.

The tasks associated with each step are discussed in detail in this chapter.

To create a `CriteriaBuilder` instance, call the `getCriteriaBuilder` method on the `EntityManager` instance:

```
CriteriaBuilder cb = em.getCriteriaBuilder();
```

Use the `CriteriaBuilder` instance to create a query object:

```
CriteriaQuery<Pet> cq = cb.createQuery(Pet.class);
```

The query will return instances of the `Pet` entity, so the type of the query is specified when the `CriteriaQuery` object is created to create a typesafe query.

Call the `from` method of the query object to set the FROM clause of the query and to specify the root of the query:

```
Root<Pet> pet = cq.from(Pet.class);
```

Call the `select` method of the query object, passing in the query root, to set the `SELECT` clause of the query:

```
cq.select(pet);
```

Now, use the query object to create a `TypedQuery<T>` object that can be executed against the data source. The modifications to the query object are captured to create a ready-to-execute query:

```
TypedQuery<Pet> q = em.createQuery(cq);
```

Execute this typed query object by calling its `getResultList` method, because this query will return multiple entity instances. The following statement stores the results in a `List<Pet>` collection-valued object:

```
List<Pet> allPets = q.getResultList();
```

11.2 Using the Metamodel API to Model Entity Classes

Use the Metamodel API to create a metamodel of the managed entities in a particular persistence unit. For each entity class in a particular package, a metamodel class is created with a trailing underscore and with attributes that correspond to the persistent fields or properties of the entity class.

The following entity class, `com.example.Pet`, has four persistent fields: `id`, `name`, `color`, and `owners`:

```
package com.example;
...
@Entity
public class Pet {
    @Id
    protected Long id;
    protected String name;
    protected String color;
    @ManyToOne
    protected Set<Person> owners;
    ...
}
```

The corresponding Metamodel class is as follows:

```
package com.example;
...
@StaticMetamodel(Pet.class)
public class Pet_ {
```

```
        public static volatile SingularAttribute<Pet, Long> id;
        public static volatile SingularAttribute<Pet, String> name;
        public static volatile SingularAttribute<Pet, String> color;
        public static volatile SetAttribute<Pet, Person> owners;
}
```

Criteria queries use the metamodel class and its attributes to refer to the managed entity classes and their persistent state and relationships.

11.2.1 Using Metamodel Classes

Metamodel classes that correspond to entity classes are of the following type:

```
javax.persistence.metamodel.EntityType<T>
```

Annotation processors typically generate metamodel classes either at development time or at runtime. Developers of applications that use Criteria queries may do either of the following:

- Generate static metamodel classes by using the persistence provider's annotation processor
- Obtain the metamodel class by doing one of the following:
    - Call the getModel method on the query root object
    - Obtain an instance of the Metamodel interface and then pass the entity type to the instance's entity method

The following code snippet shows how to obtain the Pet entity's metamodel class by calling Root<T>.getModel:

```
EntityManager em = ...;
CriteriaBuilder cb = em.getCriteriaBuilder();
CriteriaQuery cq = cb.createQuery(Pet.class);
Root<Pet> pet = cq.from(Pet.class);
EntityType<Pet> Pet_ = pet.getModel();
```

The following code snippet shows how to obtain the Pet entity's metamodel class by first obtaining a metamodel instance by using EntityManager.getMetamodel and then calling entity on the metamodel instance:

```
EntityManager em = ...;
Metamodel m = em.getMetamodel();
EntityType<Pet> Pet_ = m.entity(Pet.class);
```

> **Note:** The most common use case is to generate typesafe static metamodel classes at development time. Obtaining the metamodel classes dynamically, by calling `Root<T>.getModel` or `EntityManager.getMetamodel` and then the `entity` method, doesn't allow for type safety and doesn't allow the application to call persistent field or property names on the metamodel class.

11.3 Using the Criteria API and Metamodel API to Create Basic Typesafe Queries

The basic semantics of a Criteria query consists of a `SELECT` clause, a `FROM` clause, and an optional `WHERE` clause, similar to a JPQL query. Criteria queries set these clauses by using Java programming language objects, so the query can be created in a typesafe manner.

11.3.1 Creating a Criteria Query

The `javax.persistence.criteria.CriteriaBuilder` interface is used to construct

- Criteria queries
- Selections
- Expressions
- Predicates
- Ordering

To obtain an instance of the `CriteriaBuilder` interface, call the `getCriteriaBuilder` method on either an `EntityManager` or an `EntityManagerFactory` instance.

The following code shows how to obtain a `CriteriaBuilder` instance by using the `EntityManager.getCriteriaBuilder` method:

```
EntityManager em = ...;
CriteriaBuilder cb = em.getCriteriaBuilder();
```

Criteria queries are constructed by obtaining an instance of the following interface:

```
javax.persistence.criteria.CriteriaQuery
```

CriteriaQuery objects define a particular query that will navigate over one or more entities. Obtain CriteriaQuery instances by calling one of the CriteriaBuilder.createQuery methods. To create typesafe queries, call the CriteriaBuilder.createQuery method as follows:

```
CriteriaQuery<Pet> cq = cb.createQuery(Pet.class);
```

The CriteriaQuery object's type should be set to the expected result type of the query. In the preceding code, the object's type is set to CriteriaQuery<Pet> for a query that will find instances of the Pet entity.

The following code snippet creates a CriteriaQuery object for a query that returns a String:

```
CriteriaQuery<String> cq = cb.createQuery(String.class);
```

11.3.2 Query Roots

For a particular CriteriaQuery object, the root entity of the query, from which all navigation originates, is called the **query root**. It is similar to the FROM clause in a JPQL query.

Create the query root by calling the from method on the CriteriaQuery instance. The argument to the from method is either the entity class or an EntityType<T> instance for the entity.

The following code sets the query root to the Pet entity:

```
CriteriaQuery<Pet> cq = cb.createQuery(Pet.class);
Root<Pet> pet = cq.from(Pet.class);
```

The following code sets the query root to the Pet class by using an EntityType<T> instance:

```
EntityManager em = ...;
Metamodel m = em.getMetamodel();
EntityType<Pet> Pet_ = m.entity(Pet.class);
Root<Pet> pet = cq.from(Pet_);
```

Criteria queries may have more than one query root. This usually occurs when the query navigates from several entities.

The following code has two Root instances:

```
CriteriaQuery<Pet> cq = cb.createQuery(Pet.class);
Root<Pet> pet1 = cq.from(Pet.class);
Root<Pet> pet2 = cq.from(Pet.class);
```

11.3.3 Querying Relationships Using Joins

For queries that navigate to related entity classes, the query must define a join to the related entity by calling one of the From.join methods on the query root object or another join object. The join methods are similar to the JOIN keyword in JPQL.

The target of the join uses the Metamodel class of type EntityType<T> to specify the persistent field or property of the joined entity.

The join methods return an object of type Join<X, Y>, where X is the source entity and Y is the target of the join. In the following code snippet, Pet is the source entity, Owner is the target, and Pet_ is a statically generated metamodel class:

```
CriteriaQuery<Pet> cq = cb.createQuery(Pet.class);

Root<Pet> pet = cq.from(Pet.class);
Join<Pet, Owner> owner = pet.join(Pet_.owners);
```

You can chain joins together to navigate to related entities of the target entity without having to create a Join<X, Y> instance for each join:

```
CriteriaQuery<Pet> cq = cb.createQuery(Pet.class);

Root<Pet> pet = cq.from(Pet.class);
Join<Owner, Address> address = pet.join(Pet_.owners).join(Owner_.addresses);
```

11.3.4 Path Navigation in Criteria Queries

Path objects, which are used in the SELECT and WHERE clauses of a Criteria query, can be query root entities, join entities, or other Path objects. Use the Path.get method to navigate to attributes of the entities of a query.

The argument to the get method is the corresponding attribute of the entity's Metamodel class. The attribute can be either a single-valued attribute, specified by @SingularAttribute in the Metamodel class, or a collection-valued attribute, specified by one of @CollectionAttribute, @SetAttribute, @ListAttribute, or @MapAttribute.

The following query returns the names of all the pets in the data store. The get method is called on the query root, pet, with the name attribute of the Pet entity's Metamodel class, Pet_, as the argument:

```
CriteriaQuery<String> cq = cb.createQuery(String.class);

Root<Pet> pet = cq.from(Pet.class);
cq.select(pet.get(Pet_.name));
```

11.3.5 Restricting Criteria Query Results

Conditions that are set by calling the `CriteriaQuery.where` method can restrict the results of a query on the `CriteriaQuery` object. Calling the `where` method is analogous to setting the `WHERE` clause in a JPQL query.

The `where` method evaluates instances of the `Expression` interface to restrict the results according to the conditions of the expressions. To create `Expression` instances, use methods defined in the `Expression` and `CriteriaBuilder` interfaces.

11.3.5.1 The Expression Interface Methods

An `Expression` object is used in a query's `SELECT`, `WHERE`, or `HAVING` clause. Table 11–1 shows conditional methods you can use with `Expression` objects.

Table 11–1   Conditional Methods in the Expression Interface

Method	Description
isNull	Tests whether an expression is null
isNotNull	Tests whether an expression is not null
in	Tests whether an expression is within a list of values

The following query uses the `Expression.isNull` method to find all pets where the `color` attribute is null:

```
CriteriaQuery<Pet> cq = cb.createQuery(Pet.class);
Root<Pet> pet = cq.from(Pet.class);
cq.where(pet.get(Pet_.color).isNull());
```

The following query uses the `Expression.in` method to find all brown and black pets:

```
CriteriaQuery<Pet> cq = cb.createQuery(Pet.class);
Root<Pet> pet = cq.from(Pet.class);
cq.where(pet.get(Pet_.color).in("brown", "black"));
```

The `in` method can also check whether an attribute is a member of a collection.

11.3.5.2 Expression Methods in the CriteriaBuilder Interface

The `CriteriaBuilder` interface defines additional methods for creating expressions. These methods correspond to the arithmetic, string, date, time, and case operators and functions of JPQL. Table 11–2 shows conditional methods you can use with `CriteriaBuilder` objects.

Table 11–2   Conditional Methods in the CriteriaBuilder Interface

Conditional Method	Description
equal	Tests whether two expressions are equal
notEqual	Tests whether two expressions are not equal
gt	Tests whether the first numeric expression is greater than the second numeric expression
ge	Tests whether the first numeric expression is greater than or equal to the second numeric expression
lt	Tests whether the first numeric expression is less than the second numeric expression
le	Tests whether the first numeric expression is less than or equal to the second numeric expression
between	Tests whether the first expression is between the second and third expression in value
like	Tests whether the expression matches a given pattern

The following code uses the `CriteriaBuilder.equal` method:

```
CriteriaQuery<Pet> cq = cb.createQuery(Pet.class);
Root<Pet> pet = cq.from(Pet.class);
cq.where(cb.equal(pet.get(Pet_.name), "Fido"));
```

The following code uses the `CriteriaBuilder.gt` method:

```
CriteriaQuery<Pet> cq = cb.createQuery(Pet.class);
Root<Pet> pet = cq.from(Pet.class);
Date someDate = new Date(...);
cq.where(cb.gt(pet.get(Pet_.birthday), date));
```

The following code uses the `CriteriaBuilder.between` method:

```
CriteriaQuery<Pet> cq = cb.createQuery(Pet.class);
Root<Pet> pet = cq.from(Pet.class);
Date firstDate = new Date(...);
Date secondDate = new Date(...);
cq.where(cb.between(pet.get(Pet_.birthday), firstDate, secondDate));
```

The following code uses the `CriteriaBuilder.like` method:

```
CriteriaQuery<Pet> cq = cb.createQuery(Pet.class);
Root<Pet> pet = cq.from(Pet.class);
cq.where(cb.like(pet.get(Pet_.name), "*do"));
```

To specify multiple conditional predicates, use the compound predicate methods of the CriteriaBuilder interface, as shown in Table 11–3.

Table 11–3   Compound Predicate Methods in the CriteriaBuilder Interface

Method	Description
and	A logical conjunction of two Boolean expressions
or	A logical disjunction of two Boolean expressions
not	A logical negation of the given Boolean expression

The following code shows the use of compound predicates in queries:

```
CriteriaQuery<Pet> cq = cb.createQuery(Pet.class);
Root<Pet> pet = cq.from(Pet.class);
cq.where(cb.equal(pet.get(Pet_.name), "Fido")
        .and(cb.equal(pet.get(Pet_.color), "brown")));
```

11.3.6 Managing Criteria Query Results

For queries that return more than one result, it is often helpful to organize those results. The CriteriaQuery interface defines the following ordering and grouping methods:

- The orderBy method orders query results according to attributes of an entity

- The groupBy method groups the results of a query together according to attributes of an entity, and the having method restricts those groups according to a condition

11.3.6.1 Ordering Results

To order the results of a query, call the CriteriaQuery.orderBy method, passing in an Order object. To create an Order object, call either the CriteriaBuilder.asc or the CriteriaBuilder.desc method. The asc method is used to order the results by ascending value of the passed expression parameter. The desc method is used to order the results by descending value of the passed expression parameter. The following query shows the use of the desc method:

```
CriteriaQuery<Pet> cq = cb.createQuery(Pet.class);
Root<Pet> pet = cq.from(Pet.class);
cq.select(pet);
cq.orderBy(cb.desc(pet.get(Pet_.birthday)));
```

In this query, the results will be ordered by the pet's birthday from highest to lowest. That is, pets born in December will appear before pets born in May.

The following query shows the use of the asc method:

```
CriteriaQuery<Pet> cq = cb.createQuery(Pet.class);
Root<Pet> pet = cq.from(Pet.class);
Join<Owner, Address> address = pet.join(Pet_.owners).join(Owner_.address);
cq.select(pet);
cq.orderBy(cb.asc(address.get(Address_.postalCode)));
```

In this query, the results will be ordered by the pet owner's postal code from lowest to highest. That is, pets whose owner lives in the 10001 zip code will appear before pets whose owner lives in the 91000 zip code.

If more than one Order object is passed to orderBy, the precedence is determined by the order in which they appear in the argument list of orderBy. The first Order object has precedence.

The following code orders results by multiple criteria:

```
CriteriaQuery<Pet> cq = cb.createQuery(Pet.class);
Root<Pet> pet = cq.from(Pet.class);
Join<Pet, Owner> owner = pet.join(Pet_.owners);
cq.select(pet);
cq.orderBy(cb.asc(owner.get(Owner_.lastName)), owner.get(Owner_.firstName)));
```

The results of this query will be ordered alphabetically by the pet owner's last name, then first name.

11.3.6.2 Grouping Results

The CriteriaQuery.groupBy method partitions the query results into groups. To set these groups, pass an expression to groupBy:

```
CriteriaQuery<Pet> cq = cb.createQuery(Pet.class);
Root<Pet> pet = cq.from(Pet.class);
cq.groupBy(pet.get(Pet_.color));
```

This query returns all Pet entities and groups the results by the pet's color.

Use the CriteriaQuery.having method in conjunction with groupBy to filter over the groups. The having method, which takes a conditional expression as a parameter, restricts the query result according to the conditional expression:

```
CriteriaQuery<Pet> cq = cb.createQuery(Pet.class);
Root<Pet> pet = cq.from(Pet.class);
cq.groupBy(pet.get(Pet_.color));
cq.having(cb.in(pet.get(Pet_.color)).value("brown").value("blonde"));
```

In this example, the query groups the returned `Pet` entities by color, as in the preceding example. However, the only returned groups will be `Pet` entities where the `color` attribute is set to `brown` or `blonde`. That is, no gray-colored pets will be returned in this query.

11.3.7 Executing Queries

To prepare a query for execution, create a `TypedQuery<T>` object with the type of the query result, passing the `CriteriaQuery` object to `EntityManager.createQuery`.

To execute queries, call either `getSingleResult` or `getResultList` on the `TypedQuery<T>` object.

11.3.7.1 Single-Valued Query Results

Use the `TypedQuery<T>.getSingleResult` method to execute queries that return a single result:

```
CriteriaQuery<Pet> cq = cb.createQuery(Pet.class);
...
TypedQuery<Pet> q = em.createQuery(cq);
Pet result = q.getSingleResult();
```

11.3.7.2 Collection-Valued Query Results

Use the `TypedQuery<T>.getResultList` method to execute queries that return a collection of objects:

```
CriteriaQuery<Pet> cq = cb.createQuery(Pet.class);
...
TypedQuery<Pet> q = em.createQuery(cq);
List<Pet> results = q.getResultList();
```

12

Creating and Using String-Based Criteria Queries

This chapter describes how to create weakly typed string-based Criteria API queries.

The following topics are addressed here:

- Overview of String-Based Criteria API Queries
- Creating String-Based Queries
- Executing String-Based Queries

12.1 Overview of String-Based Criteria API Queries

String-based Criteria API queries ("string-based queries") are Java programming language queries that use strings rather than strongly typed metamodel objects to specify entity attributes when traversing a data hierarchy. String-based queries are constructed similarly to metamodel queries, can be static or dynamic, and can express the same kind of queries and operations as strongly typed metamodel queries.

Strongly typed metamodel queries are the preferred method of constructing Criteria API queries.

The main advantage of string-based queries over metamodel queries is the ability to construct Criteria queries at development time without the need to generate static metamodel classes or otherwise access dynamically generated metamodel classes.

The main disadvantage to string-based queries is their lack of type safety, which may lead to runtime errors due to type mismatches that would be caught at development time if you used strongly typed metamodel queries.

For information on constructing criteria queries, see Chapter 11, "Using the Criteria API to Create Queries."

12.2 Creating String-Based Queries

To create a string-based query, specify the attribute names of entity classes directly as strings, instead of specifying the attributes of the metamodel class. For example, this query finds all Pet entities where the value of the name attribute is Fido:

```
CriteriaQuery<Pet> cq = cb.createQuery(Pet.class);
Root<Pet> pet = cq.from(Pet.class);
cq.where(cb.equal(pet.get("name"), "Fido"));
```

The name of the attribute is specified as a string. This query is the equivalent of the following metamodel query:

```
CriteriaQuery<Pet> cq = cb.createQuery(Pet.class);
Metamodel m = em.getMetamodel();
EntityType<Pet> Pet_ = m.entity(Pet.class);
Root<Pet> pet = cq.from(Pet.class);
cq.where(cb.equal(pet.get(Pet_.name), "Fido"));
```

> **Note:** Type mismatch errors in string-based queries will not appear until the code is executed at runtime, unlike in the above metamodel query, where type mismatches will be caught at compile time.

Joins are specified in the same way:

```
CriteriaQuery<Pet> cq = cb.createQuery(Pet.class);
Root<Pet> pet = cq.from(Pet.class);
Join<Owner, Address> address = pet.join("owners").join("addresses");
```

All the conditional expressions, method expressions, path navigation methods, and result restriction methods used in metamodel queries can also be used in string-based queries. In each case, the attributes are specified using strings. For example, here is a string-based query that uses the in expression:

```
CriteriaQuery<Pet> cq = cb.createQuery(Pet.class);
Root<Pet> pet = cq.from(Pet.class);
cq.where(pet.get("color").in("brown", "black"));
```

Here is a string-based query that orders the results in descending order by date:

```
CriteriaQuery<Pet> cq = cb.createQuery(Pet.class);
Root<Pet> pet = cq.from(Pet.class);
cq.select(pet);
cq.orderBy(cb.desc(pet.get("birthday")));
```

12.3 Executing String-Based Queries

String-based queries are executed similarly to strongly typed Criteria queries. First create a javax.persistence.TypedQuery object by passing the criteria query object to the EntityManager.createQuery method, then call either getSingleResult or getResultList on the query object to execute the query:

```
CriteriaQuery<Pet> cq = cb.createQuery(Pet.class);
Root<Pet> pet = cq.from(Pet.class);
cq.where(cb.equal(pet.get("name"), "Fido"));
TypedQuery<Pet> q = em.createQuery(cq);
List<Pet> results = q.getResultList();
```

13

Controlling Concurrent Access to Entity Data with Locking

This chapter details how to handle concurrent access to entity data, and the locking strategies available to Java Persistence API application developers.

The following topics are addressed here:

- Overview of Entity Locking and Concurrency
- Lock Modes

13.1 Overview of Entity Locking and Concurrency

Entity data is **concurrently accessed** if the data in a data source is accessed at the same time by multiple applications. Ensure that the underlying data's integrity is preserved when it is accessed concurrently.

When data is updated in the database tables in a transaction, the persistence provider assumes the database management system will hold short-term read locks and long-term write locks to maintain data integrity. Most persistence providers will delay database writes until the end of the transaction, except when the application explicitly calls for a flush (that is, the application calls the `EntityManager.flush` method or executes queries with the flush mode set to `AUTO`).

By default, persistence providers use **optimistic locking**, where, before committing changes to the data, the persistence provider checks that no other transaction has modified or deleted the data since the data was read. This is accomplished by a version column in the database table, with a corresponding version attribute in the entity class. When a row is modified, the version value is incremented. The original transaction checks the version attribute, and if the data has been modified by another transaction, a `javax.persistence.OptimisticLockException` will be thrown, and the original transaction will be rolled back. When the application specifies optimistic lock modes, the persistence provider verifies that a particular entity has not changed since it was read from the database even if the entity data was not modified.

Pessimistic locking goes further than optimistic locking. With pessimistic locking, the persistence provider creates a transaction that obtains a long-term lock on the data until the transaction is completed, which prevents other transactions from modifying or deleting the data until the lock has ended. Pessimistic locking is a better strategy than optimistic locking when the underlying data is frequently accessed and modified by many transactions.

> **Note:** Using pessimistic locks on entities that are not subject to frequent modification may result in decreased application performance.

13.1.1 Using Optimistic Locking

Use the `javax.persistence.Version` annotation to mark a persistent field or property as a version attribute of an entity. The version attribute enables the entity for optimistic concurrency control. The persistence provider reads and updates the version attribute when an entity instance is modified during a transaction. The application may read the version attribute, but *must not* modify the value.

> **Note:** Although some persistence providers may support optimistic locking for entities that do not have version attributes, portable applications should always use entities with version attributes when using optimistic locking. If the application attempts to lock an entity that does not have a version attribute, and the persistence provider does not support optimistic locking for non-versioned entities, a `PersistenceException` will be thrown.

The `@Version` annotation has the following requirements.

- Only a single `@Version` attribute may be defined per entity.

- The `@Version` attribute must be in the primary table for an entity mapped to multiple tables.

- The type of the `@Version` attribute must be one of the following: `int`, `Integer`, `long`, `Long`, `short`, `Short`, or `java.sql.Timestamp`.

The following code snippet shows how to define a version attribute in an entity with persistent fields:

```
@Version
protected int version;
```

The following code snippet shows how to define a version attribute in an entity with persistent properties:

```
@Version
protected Short getVersion() { ... }
```

13.2 Lock Modes

The application may increase the level of locking for an entity by specifying the use of lock modes. Lock modes may be specified to increase the level of optimistic locking or to request the use of pessimistic locks.

The use of optimistic lock modes causes the persistence provider to check the version attributes for entities that were read (but not modified) during a transaction as well as for entities that were updated.

The use of pessimistic lock modes specifies that the persistence provider is to immediately acquire long-term read or write locks for the database data corresponding to entity state.

You can set the lock mode for an entity operation by specifying one of the lock modes defined in the `javax.persistence.LockModeType` enumerated type, listed in Table 13–1.

Table 13–1   Lock Modes for Concurrent Entity Access

Lock Mode	Description
OPTIMISTIC	Obtain an optimistic read lock for all entities with version attributes.
OPTIMISTIC_FORCE_INCREMENT	Obtain an optimistic read lock for all entities with version attributes, and increment the version attribute value.
PESSIMISTIC_READ	Immediately obtain a long-term read lock on the data to prevent the data from being modified or deleted. Other transactions may read the data while the lock is maintained, but may not modify or delete the data. The persistence provider is permitted to obtain a database write lock when a read lock was requested, but not vice versa.

Table 13–1   (Cont.) Lock Modes for Concurrent Entity Access

Lock Mode	Description
PESSIMISTIC_WRITE	Immediately obtain a long-term write lock on the data to prevent the data from being read, modified, or deleted.
PESSIMISTIC_FORCE_INCREMENT	Immediately obtain a long-term lock on the data to prevent the data from being modified or deleted, and increment the version attribute of versioned entities.
READ	A synonym for OPTIMISTIC. Use of LockModeType.OPTIMISTIC is to be preferred for new applications.
WRITE	A synonym for OPTIMISTIC_FORCE_INCREMENT. Use of LockModeType.OPTIMISTIC_FORCE_INCREMENT is to be preferred for new applications.
NONE	No additional locking will occur on the data in the database.

13.2.1 Setting the Lock Mode

To specify the lock mode, use one of the following techniques.

- Call the EntityManager.lock method, passing in one of the lock modes:

```
EntityManager em = ...;
Person person = ...;
em.lock(person, LockModeType.OPTIMISTIC);
```

- Call one of the EntityManager.find methods that take the lock mode as a parameter:

```
EntityManager em = ...;
String personPK = ...;
Person person = em.find(Person.class, personPK,
    LockModeType.PESSIMISTIC_WRITE);
```

- Call one of the EntityManager.refresh methods that take the lock mode as a parameter:

```
EntityManager em = ...;
String personPK = ...;
Person person = em.find(Person.class, personPK);
...
em.refresh(person, LockModeType.OPTIMISTIC_FORCE_INCREMENT);
```

- Call the `Query.setLockMode` or `TypedQuery.setLockMode` method, passing the lock mode as the parameter:

```
Query q = em.createQuery(...);
q.setLockMode(LockModeType.PESSIMISTIC_FORCE_INCREMENT);
```

- Add a `lockMode` element to the `@NamedQuery` annotation:

```
@NamedQuery(name="lockPersonQuery",
    query="SELECT p FROM Person p WHERE p.name LIKE :name",
    lockMode=PESSIMISTIC_READ)
```

13.2.2 Using Pessimistic Locking

Versioned entities, as well as entities that do not have version attributes, can be locked pessimistically.

To lock entities pessimistically, set the lock mode to `PESSIMISTIC_READ`, `PESSIMISTIC_WRITE`, or `PESSIMISTIC_FORCE_INCREMENT`.

If a pessimistic lock cannot be obtained on the database rows, and the failure to lock the data results in a transaction rollback, a `PessimisticLockException` is thrown. If a pessimistic lock cannot be obtained, but the locking failure doesn't result in a transaction rollback, a `LockTimeoutException` is thrown.

Pessimistically locking a versioned entity with `PESSIMISTIC_FORCE_INCREMENT` results in the version attribute being incremented even if the entity data is unmodified. When pessimistically locking a versioned entity, the persistence provider will perform the version checks that occur during optimistic locking, and if the version check fails, an `OptimisticLockException` will be thrown. An attempt to lock a non-versioned entity with `PESSIMISTIC_FORCE_INCREMENT` is not portable and may result in a `PersistenceException` if the persistence provider does not support optimistic locks for non-versioned entities. Locking a versioned entity with `PESSIMISTIC_WRITE` results in the version attribute being incremented if the transaction was successfully committed.

13.2.2.1 Pessimistic Locking Timeouts

Use the `javax.persistence.lock.timeout` property to specify the length of time in milliseconds the persistence provider should wait to obtain a lock on the database tables. If the time it takes to obtain a lock exceeds the value of this property, a `LockTimeoutException` will be thrown, but the current transaction will not be marked for rollback. If you set this property to `0`, the persistence provider should throw a `LockTimeoutException` if it cannot immediately obtain a lock.

> **Note:** Portable applications should not rely on the setting of
> javax.persistence.lock.timeout, because the locking strategy
> and underlying database may mean that the timeout value cannot
> be used. The value of javax.persistence.lock.timeout is a hint,
> not a contract.

This property may be set programmatically by passing it to the EntityManager
methods that allow lock modes to be specified, the Query.setLockMode and
TypedQuery.setLockMode methods, the @NamedQuery annotation, and the
Persistence.createEntityManagerFactory method. It may also be set as a
property in the persistence.xml deployment descriptor.

If javax.persistence.lock.timeout is set in multiple places, the value will be
determined in the following order:

1. The argument to one of the EntityManager or Query methods

2. The setting in the @NamedQuery annotation

3. The argument to the Persistence.createEntityManagerFactory method

4. The value in the persistence.xml deployment descriptor

14

Creating Fetch Plans with Entity Graphs

This chapter explains how to use entity graphs to create fetch plans for Java Persistence API operations and queries.

Entity graphs are templates for a particular Persistence query or operation. They are used when creating **fetch plans**, or groups of persistent fields that are retrieved at the same time. Application developers use fetch plans to group together related persistent fields to improve runtime performance.

By default, entity fields or properties are fetched lazily. Developers specify fields or properties as part of a fetch plan, and the persistence provider will fetch them eagerly.

For example, an email application that stores messages as `EmailMessage` entities prioritizes fetching some fields over others. The sender, subject, and date will be viewed the most often, in mailbox views and when the message is displayed. The `EmailMessage` entity has a collection of related `EmailAttachment` entities. For performance reasons the attachments should not be fetched until they are needed, but the file names of the attachment are important. A developer working on this application might make a fetch plan that eagerly fetches the important fields from `EmailMessage` and `EmailAttachment` while fetching the lower priority data lazily.

The following topics are addressed here:

- Entity Graph Basics

- Using Named Entity Graphs

- Using Entity Graphs in Query Operations

14.1 Entity Graph Basics

You can create entity graphs statically by using annotations or a deployment descriptor, or dynamically by using standard interfaces.

You can use an entity graph with the `EntityManager.find` method or as part of a JPQL or Criteria API query by specifying the entity graph as a hint to the operation or query.

Entity graphs have attributes that correspond to the fields that will be eagerly fetched during a `find` or query operation. The primary key and version fields of the entity class are always fetched and do not need to be explicitly added to an entity graph.

14.1.1 The Default Entity Graph

By default, all fields in an entity are fetched lazily unless the `fetch` attribute of the entity metadata is set to `javax.persistence.FetchType.EAGER`. The default entity graph consists of all the fields of an entity whose fields are set to be eagerly fetched.

For example, the following `EmailMessage` entity specifies that some fields will be fetched eagerly:

```
@Entity
public class EmailMessage implements Serializable {
    @Id
    String messageId;
    @Basic(fetch=EAGER)
    String subject;
    String body;
    @Basic(fetch=EAGER)
    String sender;
    @OneToMany(mappedBy="message", fetch=LAZY)
    Set<EmailAttachment> attachments;
    ...
}
```

The default entity graph for this entity would contain the `messageId`, `subject`, and `sender` fields, but not the `body` or `attachments` fields.

14.1.2 Using Entity Graphs in Persistence Operations

Entity graphs are used by creating an instance of the `javax.persistence.EntityGraph` interface by calling either

`EntityManager.getEntityGraph` for named entity graphs or
`EntityManager.createEntityGraph` for creating dynamic entity graphs.

A **named entity graph** is an entity graph specified by the `@NamedEntityGraph`
annotation applied to entity classes, or the `named-entity-graph` element in the
application's deployment descriptors. Named entity graphs defined within the
deployment descriptor override any annotation-based entity graphs with the
same name.

The created entity graph can be either a **fetch graph** or a **load graph**.

14.1.2.1 Fetch Graphs

To specify a fetch graph, set the `javax.persistence.fetchgraph` property when
you execute an `EntityManager.find` or query operation. A fetch graph consists of
only the fields explicitly specified in the `EntityGraph` instance, and ignores the
default entity graph settings:

In the following example, the default entity graph is ignored, and only the `body`
field is included in the dynamically created fetch graph:

```
EntityGraph<EmailMessage> eg = em.createEntityGraph(EmailMessage.class);
eg.addAttributeNodes("body");
...
Properties props = new Properties();
props.put("javax.persistence.fetchgraph", eg);
EmailMessage message = em.find(EmailMessage.class, id, props);
```

14.1.2.2 Load Graphs

To specify a load graph, set the `javax.persistence.loadgraph` property when
you execute an `EntityManager.find` or query operation. A load graph consists of
the fields explicitly specified in the `EntityGraph` instance plus any fields in the
default entity graph.

In the following example, the dynamically created load graph contains all the
fields in the default entity graph plus the `body` field:

```
EntityGraph<EmailMessage> eg = em.createEntityGraph(EmailMessage.class);
eg.addAttributeNodes("body");
...
Properties props = new Properties();
props.put("javax.persistence.loadgraph", eg);
EmailMessage message = em.find(EmailMessage.class, id, props);
```

14.2 Using Named Entity Graphs

Named entity graphs are created using annotations applied to entity classes or the `named-entity-graph` element and its sub-elements in the application's deployment descriptor. The persistence provider will scan for all named entity graphs, defined in both annotations and in XML, within an application. A named entity graph set using an annotation may be overridden using `named-entity-graph`.

14.2.1 Applying Named Entity Graph Annotations to Entity Classes

The `javax.persistence.NamedEntityGraph` annotation defines a single named entity graph and is applied at the class level. Multiple `@NamedEntityGraph` annotations may be defined for a class by adding them within a `javax.persistence.NamedEntityGraphs` class-level annotation.

The `@NamedEntityGraph` annotation must be applied on the root of the graph of entities. That is, if the `EntityManager.find` or query operation has as its root entity the `EmailMessage` class, the named entity graph used in the operation must be defined in the `EmailMessage` class:

```
@NamedEntityGraph
@Entity
public class EmailMessage {
    @Id
    String messageId;
    String subject;
    String body;
    String sender;
}
```

In this example, the `EmailMessage` class has a `@NamedEntityGraph` annotation to define a named entity graph that defaults to the name of the class, `EmailMessage`. No fields are included in the `@NamedEntityGraph` annotation as attribute nodes, and the fields are not annotated with metadata to set the fetch type, so the only field that will be eagerly fetched in either a load graph or fetch graph is `messageId`.

The attributes of a named entity graph are the fields of the entity that should be included in the entity graph. Add the fields to the entity graph by specifying them in the `attributeNodes` element of `@NamedEntityGraph` with a `javax.persistence.NamedAttributeNode` annotation:

```
@NamedEntityGraph(name="emailEntityGraph", attributeNodes={
    @NamedAttributeNode("subject"),
    @NamedAttributeNode("sender")
```

```
})
@Entity
public class EmailMessage { ... }
```

In this example, the name of the named entity graph is `emailEntityGraph` and includes the `subject` and `sender` fields.

Multiple `@NamedEntityGraph` definitions may be applied to a class by grouping them within a `@NamedEntityGraphs` annotation.

In the following example, two entity graphs are defined on the `EmailMessage` class. One is for a preview pane, which fetches only the sender, subject, and body of the message. The other is for a full view of the message, including any message attachments:

```
@NamedEntityGraphs({
    @NamedEntityGraph(name="previewEmailEntityGraph", attributeNodes={
        @NamedAttributeNode("subject"),
        @NamedAttributeNode("sender"),
        @NamedAttributeNode("body")
    }),
    @NamedEntityGraph(name="fullEmailEntityGraph", attributeNodes={
        @NamedAttributeNode("sender"),
        @NamedAttributeNode("subject"),
        @NamedAttributeNode("body"),
        @NamedAttributeNode("attachments")
    })
})
@Entity
public class EmailMessage { ... }
```

14.2.2 Obtaining EntityGraph Instances from Named Entity Graphs

Use the `EntityManager.getEntityGraph` method, passing in the named entity graph name, to obtain `EntityGraph` instances for a named entity graph:

```
EntityGraph<EmailMessage> eg = em.getEntityGraph("emailEntityGraph");
```

14.3 Using Entity Graphs in Query Operations

To specify entity graphs for both typed and untyped queries, call the `setHint` method on the query object and specify either `javax.persistence.loadgraph` or `javax.persistence.fetchgraph` as the property name and an `EntityGraph` instance as the value:

```
EntityGraph<EmailMessage> eg = em.getEntityGraph("previewEmailEntityGraph");
List<EmailMessage> messages = em.createNamedQuery("findAllEmailMessages")
        .setParameter("mailbox", "inbox")
        .setHint("javax.persistence.loadgraph", eg)
        .getResultList();
```

In this example, the `previewEmailEntityGraph` is used for the `findAllEmailMessages` named query.

Typed queries use the same technique:

```
EntityGraph<EmailMessage> eg = em.getEntityGraph("previewEmailEntityGraph");

CriteriaQuery<EmailMessage> cq = cb.createQuery(EmailMessage.class);
Root<EmailMessage> message = cq.from(EmailMessage.class);
TypedQuery<EmailMessage> q = em.createQuery(cq);
q.setHint("javax.persistence.loadgraph", eg);
List<EmailMessage> messages = q.getResultList();
```

15

Using a Second-Level Cache with Java Persistence API Applications

This chapter explains how to modify the second-level cache mode settings to improve the performance of applications that use the Java Persistence API.

The following topics are addressed here:

- Overview of the Second-Level Cache
- Specifying the Cache Mode Settings to Improve Performance

15.1 Overview of the Second-Level Cache

A **second-level cache** is a local store of entity data managed by the persistence provider to improve application performance. A second-level cache helps improve performance by avoiding expensive database calls, keeping the entity data local to the application. A second-level cache is typically transparent to the application, as it is managed by the persistence provider and underlies the persistence context of an application. That is, the application reads and commits data through the normal entity manager operations without knowing about the cache.

> **Note:** Persistence providers are not required to support a second-level cache. Portable applications should not rely on support by persistence providers for a second-level cache.

The second-level cache for a persistence unit may be configured to one of several second-level cache modes. The following cache mode settings are defined by the Java Persistence API.

Table 15–1   Cache Mode Settings for the Second-Level Cache

Cache Mode Setting	Description
ALL	All entity data is stored in the second-level cache for this persistence unit.
NONE	No data is cached in the persistence unit. The persistence provider must not cache any data.
ENABLE_SELECTIVE	Enable caching for entities that have been explicitly set with the @Cacheable annotation.
DISABLE_SELECTIVE	Enable caching for all entities except those that have been explicitly set with the @Cacheable(false) annotation.
UNSPECIFIED	The caching behavior for the persistence unit is undefined. The persistence provider's default caching behavior will be used.

One consequence of using a second-level cache in an application is that the underlying data may have changed in the database tables, while the value in the cache has not, a circumstance called a **stale read**. To avoid stale reads, use any of these strategies.

- Change the second-level cache to one of the cache mode settings.

- Control which entities may be cached (see Section 15.1.1, "Controlling whether Entities May Be Cached").

- Change the cache's retrieval or store modes (see Section 15.2.1, "Setting the Cache Retrieval and Store Modes").

Which of these strategies works best to avoid stale reads depends upon the application.

15.1.1 Controlling whether Entities May Be Cached

Use the javax.persistence.Cacheable annotation to specify that an entity class, and any subclasses, may be cached when using the ENABLE_SELECTIVE or DISABLE_SELECTIVE cache modes. Subclasses may override the @Cacheable setting by adding a @Cacheable annotation and changing the value.

To specify that an entity may be cached, add a @Cacheable annotation at the class level:

```
@Cacheable
@Entity
public class Person { ... }
```

By default, the @Cacheable annotation is true. The following example is equivalent:

```
@Cacheable(true)
@Entity
public class Person{ ... }
```

To specify that an entity must not be cached, add a @Cacheable annotation and set it to false:

```
@Cacheable(false)
@Entity
public class OrderStatus { ... }
```

When the ENABLE_SELECTIVE cache mode is set, the persistence provider will cache any entities that have the @Cacheable(true) annotation and any subclasses of that entity that have not been overridden. The persistence provider will not cache entities that have @Cacheable(false) or have no @Cacheable annotation. That is, the ENABLE_SELECTIVE mode will cache only entities that have been explicitly marked for the cache using the @Cacheable annotation.

When the DISABLE_SELECTIVE cache mode is set, the persistence provider will cache any entities that *do not* have the @Cacheable(false) annotation. Entities that do not have @Cacheable annotations, and entities with the @Cacheable(true) annotation, will be cached. That is, the DISABLE_SELECTIVE mode will cache all entities that have not been explicitly prevented from being cached.

If the cache mode is set to UNDEFINED, or is left unset, the behavior of entities annotated with @Cacheable is undefined. If the cache mode is set to ALL or NONE, the value of the @Cacheable annotation is ignored by the persistence provider.

15.2 Specifying the Cache Mode Settings to Improve Performance

To adjust the cache mode settings for a persistence unit, specify one of the cache modes as the value of the shared-cache-mode element in the persistence.xml deployment descriptor (shown in **bold**):

```
<persistence-unit name="examplePU" transaction-type="JTA">
    <provider>org.eclipse.persistence.jpa.PersistenceProvider</provider>
    <jta-data-source>java:comp/DefaultDataSource</jta-data-source>
```

```
<shared-cache-mode>DISABLE_SELECTIVE</shared-cache-mode>
</persistence-unit>
```

Note: Because support for a second-level cache is not required by the Java Persistence API specification, setting the second-level cache mode in `persistence.xml` will have no effect when you use a persistence provider that does not implement a second-level cache.

Alternatively, you can specify the shared cache mode by setting the `javax.persistence.sharedCache.mode` property to one of the shared cache mode settings:

```
EntityManagerFactory emf =
    Persistence.createEntityManagerFactory(
        "myExamplePU", new Properties().add(
            "javax.persistence.sharedCache.mode", "ENABLE_SELECTIVE"));
```

15.2.1 Setting the Cache Retrieval and Store Modes

If you have enabled the second-level cache for a persistence unit by setting the shared cache mode, you can further modify the behavior of the second-level cache by setting the `javax.persistence.cache.retrieveMode` and `javax.persistence.cache.storeMode` properties. You can set these properties at the persistence context level by passing the property name and value to the `EntityManager.setProperty` method, or you can set them on a per-EntityManager operation (`EntityManager.find` or `EntityManager.refresh`) or on a per-query level.

15.2.1.1 Cache Retrieval Mode

The cache retrieval mode, set by the `javax.persistence.retrieveMode` property, controls how data is read from the cache for calls to the `EntityManager.find` method and from queries.

You can set the `retrieveMode` property to one of the constants defined by the `javax.persistence.CacheRetrieveMode` enumerated type, either `USE` (the default) or `BYPASS`.

When the property is set to `USE`, data is retrieved from the second-level cache, if available. If the data is not in the cache, the persistence provider will read it from the database.

When the property is set to `BYPASS`, the second-level cache is bypassed and a call to the database is made to retrieve the data.

15.2.1.2 Cache Store Mode

The cache store mode, set by the `javax.persistence.storeMode` property, controls how data is stored in the cache.

You can set the `storeMode` property to one of the constants defined by the `javax.persistence.CacheStoreMode` enumerated type: either `USE` (the default), `BYPASS`, or `REFRESH`.

When the property is set to `USE`, the cache data is created or updated when data is read from or committed to the database. If data is already in the cache, setting the store mode to `USE` will not force a refresh when data is read from the database.

When the property is set to `BYPASS`, data read from or committed to the database is *not* inserted or updated in the cache. That is, the cache is unchanged.

When the property is set to `REFRESH`, the cache data is created or updated when data is read from or committed to the database, and a refresh is forced on data in the cache upon database reads.

15.2.1.3 Setting the Cache Retrieval or Store Mode

To set the cache retrieval or store mode for the persistence context, call the `EntityManager.setProperty` method with the property name and value pair:

```
EntityManager em = ...;
em.setProperty("javax.persistence.cache.storeMode", "BYPASS");
```

To set the cache retrieval or store mode when calling the `EntityManager.find` or `EntityManager.refresh` methods, first create a `Map<String, Object>` instance and add a name/value pair as follows:

```
EntityManager em = ...;
Map<String, Object> props = new HashMap<String, Object>();
props.put("javax.persistence.cache.retrieveMode", "BYPASS");
String personPK = ...;
Person person = em.find(Person.class, personPK, props);
```

> **Note:** The cache retrieve mode is ignored when calling the `EntityManager.refresh` method, as calls to `refresh` always result in data being read from the database, not the cache.

To set the retrieval or store mode when using queries, call the `Query.setHint` or `TypedQuery.setHint` methods, depending on the type of query:

```
EntityManager em = ...;
CriteriaQuery<Person> cq = ...;
```

```
TypedQuery<Person> q = em.createQuery(cq);
q.setHint("javax.persistence.cache.storeMode", "REFRESH");
...
```

Setting the store or retrieve mode in a query or when calling the
EntityManager.find or EntityManager.refresh method overrides the setting of
the entity manager.

15.2.2 Controlling the Second-Level Cache Programmatically

The javax.persistence.Cache interface defines methods for interacting with the
second-level cache programmatically. The Cache interface defines methods to do
the following:

- Check whether a particular entity has cached data

- Remove a particular entity from the cache

- Remove all instances (and instances of subclasses) of an entity class from the
  cache

- Clear the cache of all entity data

Note: If the second-level cache has been disabled, calls to the
Cache interface's methods have no effect, except for contains,
which will always return false.

15.2.2.1 Checking whether an Entity's Data Is Cached

Call the Cache.contains method to find out whether a given entity is currently in
the second-level cache. The contains method returns true if the entity's data is
cached, and false if the data is not in the cache:

```
EntityManager em = ...;
Cache cache = em.getEntityManagerFactory().getCache();
String personPK = ...;
if (cache.contains(Person.class, personPK)) {
    // the data is cached
} else {
    // the data is NOT cached
}
```

15.2.2.2 Removing an Entity from the Cache

Call one of the Cache.evict methods to remove a particular entity or all entities
of a given type from the second-level cache. To remove a particular entity from

the cache, call the `evict` method and pass in the entity class and the primary key of the entity:

```
EntityManager em = ...;
Cache cache = em.getEntityManagerFactory().getCache();
String personPK = ...;
cache.evict(Person.class, personPK);
```

To remove all instances of a particular entity class, including subclasses, call the `evict` method and specify the entity class:

```
EntityManager em = ...;
Cache cache = em.getEntityManagerFactory().getCache();
cache.evict(Person.class);
```

All instances of the `Person` entity class will be removed from the cache. If the `Person` entity has a subclass, `Student`, calls to the above method will remove all instances of `Student` from the cache as well.

15.2.2.3 Removing All Data from the Cache

Call the `Cache.evictAll` method to completely clear the second-level cache:

```
EntityManager em = ...;
Cache cache = em.getEntityManagerFactory().getCache();
cache.evictAll();
```

Part IV

Messaging

Part IV introduces messaging. This part contains the following chapters:

- Chapter 16, "Java Message Service Concepts"
- Chapter 17, "Java Message Service Examples"

16

Java Message Service Concepts

This chapter provides an introduction to the Java Message Service (JMS) API, a Java API that allows applications to create, send, receive, and read messages using reliable, asynchronous, loosely coupled communication. It covers the following topics:

- Overview of the JMS API
- Basic JMS API Concepts
- The JMS API Programming Model
- Using Advanced JMS Features
- Using the JMS API in Java EE Applications
- Further Information about JMS

16.1 Overview of the JMS API

This overview defines the concept of messaging, describes the JMS API and where it can be used, and explains how the JMS API works within the Java EE platform.

16.1.1 What Is Messaging?

Messaging is a method of communication between software components or applications. A messaging system is a peer-to-peer facility: A messaging client can send messages to, and receive messages from, any other client. Each client connects to a messaging agent that provides facilities for creating, sending, receiving, and reading messages.

Messaging enables distributed communication that is **loosely coupled**. A component sends a message to a destination, and the recipient can retrieve the message from the destination. What makes the communication loosely coupled is that the destination is all that the sender and receiver have in common. The sender and the receiver do not have to be available at the same time in order to communicate. In fact, the sender does not need to know anything about the receiver; nor does the receiver need to know anything about the sender. The sender and the receiver need to know only which message format and which destination to use. In this respect, messaging differs from tightly coupled technologies, such as Remote Method Invocation (RMI), which require an application to know a remote application's methods.

Messaging also differs from electronic mail (email), which is a method of communication between people or between software applications and people. Messaging is used for communication between software applications or software components.

16.1.2 What Is the JMS API?

The Java Message Service is a Java API that allows applications to create, send, receive, and read messages. The JMS API defines a common set of interfaces and associated semantics that allow programs written in the Java programming language to communicate with other messaging implementations.

The JMS API minimizes the set of concepts a programmer must learn in order to use messaging products but provides enough features to support sophisticated messaging applications. It also strives to maximize the portability of JMS applications across JMS providers.

JMS enables communication that is not only loosely coupled but also

- **Asynchronous**: A receiving client does not have to receive messages at the same time the sending client sends them. The sending client can send them and go on to other tasks; the receiving client can receive them much later.

- **Reliable**: A messaging provider that implements the JMS API can ensure that a message is delivered once and only once. Lower levels of reliability are available for applications that can afford to miss messages or to receive duplicate messages.

The current version of the JMS specification is Version 2.0. You can download a copy of the specification from the Java Community Process website: http://www.jcp.org/en/jsr/detail?id=343.

16.1.3 When Can You Use the JMS API?

An enterprise application provider is likely to choose a messaging API over a tightly coupled API, such as a remote procedure call (RPC), under the following circumstances.

- The provider wants the components not to depend on information about other components' interfaces, so components can be easily replaced.

- The provider wants the application to run whether or not all components are up and running simultaneously.

- The application business model allows a component to send information to another and to continue to operate without receiving an immediate response.

For example, components of an enterprise application for an automobile manufacturer can use the JMS API in situations like the following.

- The inventory component can send a message to the factory component when the inventory level for a product goes below a certain level so the factory can make more cars.

- The factory component can send a message to the parts components so the factory can assemble the parts it needs.

- The parts components in turn can send messages to their own inventory and order components to update their inventories and to order new parts from suppliers.

- Both the factory and the parts components can send messages to the accounting component to update budget numbers.

- The business can publish updated catalog items to its sales force.

Using messaging for these tasks allows the various components to interact with one another efficiently, without tying up network or other resources. Figure 16–1 illustrates how this simple example might work.

Figure 16–1 Messaging in an Enterprise Application

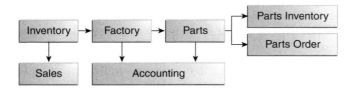

Manufacturing is only one example of how an enterprise can use the JMS API. Retail applications, financial services applications, health services applications, and many others can make use of messaging.

16.1.4 How Does the JMS API Work with the Java EE Platform?

When the JMS API was first introduced, its most important purpose was to allow Java applications to access existing messaging-oriented middleware (MOM) systems. Since that time, many vendors have adopted and implemented the JMS API, so a JMS product can now provide a complete messaging capability for an enterprise.

The JMS API is an integral part of the Java EE platform, and application developers can use messaging with Java EE components. JMS 2.0 is part of the Java EE 7 release.

The JMS API in the Java EE platform has the following features.

- Application clients, Enterprise JavaBeans (EJB) components, and web components can send or synchronously receive a JMS message. Application clients can in addition set a message listener that allows JMS messages to be delivered to it asynchronously by being notified when a message is available.

- Message-driven beans, which are a kind of enterprise bean, enable the asynchronous consumption of messages in the EJB container. An application server typically pools message-driven beans to implement concurrent processing of messages.

- Message send and receive operations can participate in Java Transaction API (JTA) transactions, which allow JMS operations and database accesses to take place within a single transaction.

The JMS API enhances the other parts of the Java EE platform by simplifying enterprise development, allowing loosely coupled, reliable, asynchronous interactions among Java EE components and legacy systems capable of messaging. A developer can easily add new behavior to a Java EE application that has existing business events by adding a new message-driven bean to operate on specific business events. The Java EE platform, moreover, enhances the JMS API by providing support for JTA transactions and allowing for the concurrent consumption of messages. For more information, see the Enterprise JavaBeans specification, v3.2.

The JMS provider can be integrated with the application server using the Java EE Connector architecture. You access the JMS provider through a resource adapter.

This capability allows vendors to create JMS providers that can be plugged in to multiple application servers, and it allows application servers to support multiple JMS providers. For more information, see theS Java EE Connector architecture specification, v1.7.S

16.2 Basic JMS API Concepts

This section introduces the most basic JMS API concepts, the ones you must know to get started writing simple application clients that use the JMS API.

The next section introduces the JMS API programming model. Later sections cover more advanced concepts, including the ones you need in order to write applications that use message-driven beans.

16.2.1 JMS API Architecture

A JMS application is composed of the following parts.

- A **JMS provider** is a messaging system that implements the JMS interfaces and provides administrative and control features. An implementation of the Java EE platform that supports the full profile includes a JMS provider.

- **JMS clients** are the programs or components, written in the Java programming language, that produce and consume messages. Any Java EE application component can act as a JMS client.

  Java SE applications can also act as JMS clients; the *Message Queue Developer's Guide for Java Clients* in the GlassFish Server documentation (https://glassfish.java.net/docs/) explains how to make this work.

- **Messages** are the objects that communicate information between JMS clients.

- **Administered objects** are JMS objects configured for the use of clients. The two kinds of JMS administered objects are destinations and connection factories, described in Section 16.3.1, "JMS Administered Objects." An administrator can create objects that are available to all applications that use a particular installation of GlassFish Server; alternatively, a developer can use annotations to create objects that are specific to a particular application.

Figure 16–2 illustrates the way these parts interact. Administrative tools or annotations allow you to bind destinations and connection factories into a JNDI namespace. A JMS client can then use resource injection to access the administered objects in the namespace and then establish a logical connection to the same objects through the JMS provider.

Figure 16–2   JMS API Architecture

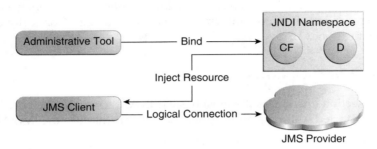

16.2.2 Messaging Styles

Before the JMS API existed, most messaging products supported either the point-to-point or the publish/subscribe style of messaging. The JMS specification defines compliance for each style. A JMS provider must implement both styles, and the JMS API provides interfaces that are specific to each. The following subsections describe these messaging styles.

The JMS API, however, makes it unnecessary to use only one of the two styles. It allows you to use the same code to send and receive messages using either the PTP or the pub/sub style. The destinations you use remain specific to one style, and the behavior of the application will depend in part on whether you are using a queue or a topic. However, the code itself can be common to both styles, making your applications flexible and reusable. This tutorial describes and illustrates this coding approach, using the greatly simplified API provided by JMS 2.0.

16.2.2.1 Point-to-Point Messaging Style

A **point-to-point** (PTP) product or application is built on the concept of message **queues**, senders, and receivers. Each message is addressed to a specific queue, and receiving clients extract messages from the queues established to hold their messages. Queues retain all messages sent to them until the messages are consumed or expire.

PTP messaging, illustrated in Figure 16–3, has the following characteristics.

- Each message has only one consumer.

- The receiver can fetch the message whether or not it was running when the client sent the message.

Figure 16–3   Point-to-Point Messaging

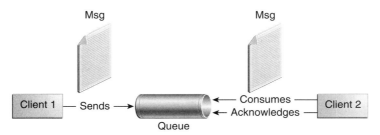

Use PTP messaging when every message you send must be processed successfully by one consumer.

16.2.2.2   Publish/Subscribe Messaging Style

In a **publish/subscribe** (pub/sub) product or application, clients address messages to a **topic**, which functions somewhat like a bulletin board. Publishers and subscribers can dynamically publish or subscribe to the topic. The system takes care of distributing the messages arriving from a topic's multiple publishers to its multiple subscribers. Topics retain messages only as long as it takes to distribute them to subscribers.

With pub/sub messaging, it is important to distinguish between the consumer that subscribes to a topic (the subscriber) and the subscription that is created. The consumer is a JMS object within an application, while the subscription is an entity within the JMS provider. Normally, a topic can have many consumers, but a subscription has only one subscriber. It is possible, however, to create shared subscriptions; see Section 16.3.6.5, "Creating Shared Subscriptions," for details. See Section 16.3.6.3, "Consuming Messages from Topics," for details on the semantics of pub/sub messaging.

Pub/sub messaging has the following characteristics.

- Each message can have multiple consumers.

- A client that subscribes to a topic can consume only messages sent *after* the client has created a subscription, and the consumer must continue to be active in order for it to consume messages.

  The JMS API relaxes this requirement to some extent by allowing applications to create **durable subscriptions**, which receive messages sent while the consumers are not active. Durable subscriptions provide the flexibility and reliability of queues but still allow clients to send messages to many recipients. For more information about durable subscriptions, see Section 16.3.6.4, "Creating Durable Subscriptions."

Use pub/sub messaging when each message can be processed by any number of consumers (or none). Figure 16–4 illustrates pub/sub messaging.

Figure 16–4   Publish/Subscribe Messaging

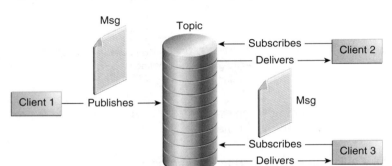

16.2.3 Message Consumption

Messaging products are inherently asynchronous: There is no fundamental timing dependency between the production and the consumption of a message. However, the JMS specification uses this term in a more precise sense. Messages can be consumed in either of two ways.

- **Synchronously**: A consumer explicitly fetches the message from the destination by calling the `receive` method. The `receive` method can block until a message arrives or can time out if a message does not arrive within a specified time limit.

- **Asynchronously**: An application client or a Java SE client can register a **message listener** with a consumer. A message listener is similar to an event listener. Whenever a message arrives at the destination, the JMS provider delivers the message by calling the listener's `onMessage` method, which acts on the contents of the message. In a Java EE application, a message-driven bean serves as a message listener (it too has an `onMessage` method), but a client does not need to register it with a consumer.

16.3 The JMS API Programming Model

The basic building blocks of a JMS application are

- Administered objects: connection factories and destinations
- Connections

- Sessions
- JMSContext objects, which combine a connection and a session in one object
- Message producers
- Message consumers
- Messages

Figure 16–5 shows how all these objects fit together in a JMS client application.

Figure 16–5 The JMS API Programming Model

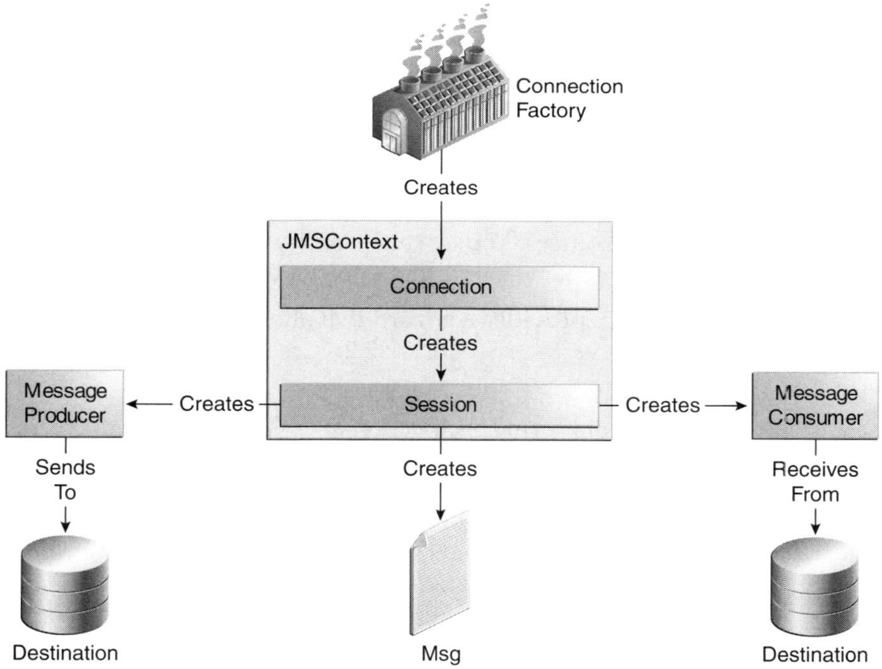

JMS also provides queue browsers, objects that allow an application to browse messages on a queue.

This section describes all these objects briefly and provides sample commands and code snippets that show how to create and use the objects. The last subsection briefly describes JMS API exception handling.

Examples that show how to combine all these objects in applications appear in Chapter 17, "Java Message Service Examples," beginning with Section 17.2,

"Writing Simple JMS Applications." For more detail, see the JMS API documentation, part of the Java EE API documentation.

16.3.1 JMS Administered Objects

Two parts of a JMS application, destinations and connection factories, are commonly maintained administratively rather than programmatically. The technology underlying these objects is likely to be very different from one implementation of the JMS API to another. Therefore, the management of these objects belongs with other administrative tasks that vary from provider to provider.

JMS clients access administered objects through interfaces that are portable, so a client application can run with little or no change on more than one implementation of the JMS API. Ordinarily, an administrator configures administered objects in a JNDI namespace, and JMS clients then access them by using resource injection.

With GlassFish Server, you can use the `asadmin create-jms-resource` command or the Administration Console to create JMS administered objects in the form of connector resources. You can also specify the resources in a file named `glassfish-resources.xml` that you can bundle with an application.

NetBeans IDE provides a wizard that allows you to create JMS resources for GlassFish Server. See Section 17.2.2, "Creating JMS Administered Objects," for details.

The Java EE platform specification allows a developer to create administered objects using annotations or deployment descriptor elements. Objects created in this way are specific to the application for which they are created. See Section 16.5.1, "Creating Resources for Java EE Applications," for details. Definitions in a deployment descriptor override those specified by annotations.

16.3.1.1 JMS Connection Factories

A **connection factory** is the object a client uses to create a connection to a provider. A connection factory encapsulates a set of connection configuration parameters that has been defined by an administrator. Each connection factory is an instance of the `ConnectionFactory`, `QueueConnectionFactory`, or `TopicConnectionFactory` interface. To learn how to create connection factories, see Section 17.2.2, "Creating JMS Administered Objects."

At the beginning of a JMS client program, you usually inject a connection factory resource into a `ConnectionFactory` object. A Java EE server must provide a JMS connection factory with the logical JNDI name `java:comp/DefaultJMSConnectionFactory`. The actual JNDI name will be implementation-specific.

For example, the following code fragment looks up the default JMS connection factory and assigns it to a `ConnectionFactory` object:

```
@Resource(lookup = "java:comp/DefaultJMSConnectionFactory")
private static ConnectionFactory connectionFactory;
```

16.3.1.2 JMS Destinations

A **destination** is the object a client uses to specify the target of messages it produces and the source of messages it consumes. In the PTP messaging style, destinations are called queues. In the pub/sub messaging style, destinations are called topics. A JMS application can use multiple queues or topics (or both). To learn how to create destination resources, see Section 17.2.2, "Creating JMS Administered Objects."

To create a destination using GlassFish Server, you create a JMS destination resource that specifies a JNDI name for the destination.

In the GlassFish Server implementation of JMS, each destination resource refers to a physical destination. You can create a physical destination explicitly, but if you do not, the Application Server creates it when it is needed and deletes it when you delete the destination resource.

In addition to injecting a connection factory resource into a client program, you usually inject a destination resource. Unlike connection factories, destinations are specific to either the PTP or pub/sub messaging style. To create an application that allows you to use the same code for both topics and queues, you assign the destination to a `Destination` object.

The following code specifies two resources, a queue and a topic. The resource names are mapped to destination resources created in the JNDI namespace:

```
@Resource(lookup = "jms/MyQueue")
private static Queue queue;

@Resource(lookup = "jms/MyTopic")
private static Topic topic;
```

In a Java EE application, JMS administered objects are normally placed in the `jms` naming subcontext.

With the common interfaces, you can mix or match connection factories and destinations. That is, in addition to using the `ConnectionFactory` interface, you can inject a `QueueConnectionFactory` resource and use it with a `Topic`, and you can inject a `TopicConnectionFactory` resource and use it with a `Queue`. The behavior of the application will depend on the kind of destination you use and not on the kind of connection factory you use.

16.3.2 Connections

A **connection** encapsulates a virtual connection with a JMS provider. For example, a connection could represent an open TCP/IP socket between a client and a provider service daemon. You use a connection to create one or more sessions.

Note: In the Java EE platform, the ability to create multiple sessions from a single connection is limited to application clients. In web and enterprise bean components, a connection can create no more than one session.

You normally create a connection by creating a JMSContext object. See Section 16.3.4, "JMSContext Objects," for details.

16.3.3 Sessions

A **session** is a single-threaded context for producing and consuming messages.

You normally create a session (as well as a connection) by creating a JMSContext object. See Section 16.3.4, "JMSContext Objects," for details. You use sessions to create message producers, message consumers, messages, queue browsers, and temporary destinations.

Sessions serialize the execution of message listeners; for details, see Section 16.3.6.1, "JMS Message Listeners."

A session provides a transactional context with which to group a set of sends and receives into an atomic unit of work. For details, see Section 16.4.4, "Using JMS Local Transactions."

16.3.4 JMSContext Objects

A JMSContext object combines a connection and a session in a single object. That is, it provides both an active connection to a JMS provider and a single-threaded context for sending and receiving messages.

You use the JMSContext to create the following objects:

- Message producers
- Message consumers

- Messages
- Queue browsers
- Temporary queues and topics (see Section 16.4.3, "Creating Temporary Destinations")

You can create a JMSContext in a try-with-resources block.

To create a JMSContext, call the createContext method on the connection factory:

```
JMSContext context = connectionFactory.createContext();
```

When called with no arguments from an application client or a Java SE client, or from the Java EE web or EJB container when there is no active JTA transaction in progress, the createContext method creates a non-transacted session with an acknowledgment mode of JMSContext.AUTO_ACKNOWLEDGE. When called with no arguments from the web or EJB container when there is an active JTA transaction in progress, the createContext method creates a transacted session. For information about the way JMS transactions work in Java EE applications, see Section 16.5, "Using the JMS API in Java EE Applications."

From an application client or a Java SE client, you can also call the createContext method with the argument JMSContext.SESSION_TRANSACTED to create a transacted session:

```
JMSContext context =
        connectionFactory.createContext(JMSContext.SESSION_TRANSACTED);
```

The session uses local transactions; see Section 16.4.4, "Using JMS Local Transactions," for details.

Alternatively, you can specify a non-default acknowledgment mode; see Section 16.4.1, "Controlling Message Acknowledgment," for more information.

When you use a JMSContext, message delivery normally begins as soon as you create a consumer. See Section 16.3.6, "JMS Message Consumers," for more information.

If you create a JMSContext in a try-with-resources block, you do not need to close it explicitly. It will be closed when the try block comes to an end. Make sure that your application completes all its JMS activity within the try-with-resources block. If you do not use a try-with-resources block, you must call the close method on the JMSContext to close the connection when the application has finished its work.

16.3.5 JMS Message Producers

A **message producer** is an object that is created by a JMSContext or a session and used for sending messages to a destination. A message producer created by a JMSContext implements the JMSProducer interface. You could create it this way:

```
try (JMSContext context = connectionFactory.createContext();) {
    JMSProducer producer = context.createProducer();
    ...
```

However, a JMSProducer is a lightweight object that does not consume significant resources. For this reason, you do not need to save the JMSProducer in a variable; you can create a new one each time you send a message. You send messages to a specific destination by using the send method. For example:

```
context.createProducer().send(dest, message);
```

You can create the message in a variable before sending it, as shown here, or you can create it within the send call. See Section 16.3.7, "JMS Messages," for more information.

16.3.6 JMS Message Consumers

A **message consumer** is an object that is created by a JMSContext or a session and used for receiving messages sent to a destination. A message producer created by a JMSContext implements the JMSConsumer interface. The simplest way to create a message consumer is to use the JMSContext.createConsumer method:

```
try (JMSContext context = connectionFactory.createContext();) {
    JMSConsumer consumer = context.createConsumer(dest);
    ...
```

A message consumer allows a JMS client to register interest in a destination with a JMS provider. The JMS provider manages the delivery of messages from a destination to the registered consumers of the destination.

When you use a JMSContext to create a message consumer, message delivery begins as soon as you have created the consumer. You can disable this behavior by calling setAutoStart(false) when you create the JMSContext and then calling the start method explicitly to start message delivery. If you want to stop message delivery temporarily without closing the connection, you can call the stop method; to restart message delivery, call start.

You use the receive method to consume a message synchronously. You can use this method at any time after you create the consumer.

If you specify no arguments or an argument of 0, the method blocks indefinitely until a message arrives:

```
Message m = consumer.receive();
Message m = consumer.receive(0);
```

For a simple client, this may not matter. But if it is possible that a message might not be available, use a synchronous receive with a timeout: Call the `receive` method with a timeout argument greater than 0. One second is a recommended timeout value:

```
Message m = consumer.receive(1000); // time out after a second
```

To enable asynchronous message delivery from an application client or a Java SE client, you use a message listener, as described in the next section.

You can use the `JMSContext.createDurableConsumer` method to create a durable topic subscription. This method is valid only if you are using a topic. For details, see Section 16.3.6.4, "Creating Durable Subscriptions." For topics, you can also create shared consumers; see Section 16.3.6.5, "Creating Shared Subscriptions."

16.3.6.1 JMS Message Listeners

A message listener is an object that acts as an asynchronous event handler for messages. This object implements the `MessageListener` interface, which contains one method, `onMessage`. In the `onMessage` method, you define the actions to be taken when a message arrives.

From an application client or a Java SE client, you register the message listener with a specific message consumer by using the `setMessageListener` method. For example, if you define a class named `Listener` that implements the `MessageListener` interface, you can register the message listener as follows:

```
Listener myListener = new Listener();
consumer.setMessageListener(myListener);
```

When message delivery begins, the JMS provider automatically calls the message listener's `onMessage` method whenever a message is delivered. The `onMessage` method takes one argument of type `Message`, which your implementation of the method can cast to another message subtype as needed (see Section 16.3.7.3, "Message Bodies").

In the Java EE web or EJB container, you use message-driven beans for asynchronous message delivery. A message-driven bean also implements the `MessageListener` interface and contains an `onMessage` method. For details, see Section 16.5.4, "Using Message-Driven Beans to Receive Messages Asynchronously."

Your `onMessage` method should handle all exceptions. Throwing a `RuntimeException` is considered a programming error.

For a simple example of the use of a message listener, see Section 17.2.6, "Using a Message Listener for Asynchronous Message Delivery." Chapter 17, "Java Message Service Examples," contains several more examples of message listeners and message-driven beans.

16.3.6.2 JMS Message Selectors

If your messaging application needs to filter the messages it receives, you can use a JMS message selector, which allows a message consumer for a destination to specify the messages that interest it. Message selectors assign the work of filtering messages to the JMS provider rather than to the application. For an example of an application that uses a message selector, see Section 17.7, "Sending Messages from a Session Bean to an MDB."

A message selector is a `String` that contains an expression. The syntax of the expression is based on a subset of the SQL92 conditional expression syntax. The message selector in the example selects any message that has a `NewsType` property that is set to the value `'Sports'` or `'Opinion'`:

```
NewsType = 'Sports' OR NewsType = 'Opinion'
```

The `createConsumer` and `createDurableConsumer` methods, as well as the methods for creating shared consumers, allow you to specify a message selector as an argument when you create a message consumer.

The message consumer then receives only messages whose headers and properties match the selector. (See Section 16.3.7.1, "Message Headers," and Section 16.3.7.2, "Message Properties.") A message selector cannot select messages on the basis of the content of the message body.

16.3.6.3 Consuming Messages from Topics

The semantics of consuming messages from topics are more complex than the semantics of consuming messages from queues.

An application consumes messages from a topic by creating a subscription on that topic and creating a consumer on that subscription. Subscriptions may be durable or nondurable, and they may be shared or unshared.

A subscription may be thought of as an entity within the JMS provider itself, whereas a consumer is a JMS object within the application.

A subscription will receive a copy of every message that is sent to the topic after the subscription is created, unless a message selector is specified. If a message selector is specified, only those messages whose properties match the message selector will be added to the subscription.

Unshared subscriptions are restricted to a single consumer. In this case, all the messages in the subscription are delivered to that consumer. Shared subscriptions allow multiple consumers. In this case, each message in the subscription is delivered to only one consumer. JMS does not define how messages are distributed between multiple consumers on the same subscription.

Subscriptions may be durable or nondurable.

A nondurable subscription exists only as long as there is an active consumer on the subscription. This means that any messages sent to the topic will be added to the subscription only while a consumer exists and is not closed.

A nondurable subscription may be either unshared or shared.

- An unshared nondurable subscription does not have a name and may have only a single consumer object associated with it. It is created automatically when the consumer object is created. It is not persisted and is deleted automatically when the consumer object is closed.

  The `JMSContext.createConsumer` method creates a consumer on an unshared nondurable subscription if a topic is specified as the destination.

- A shared nondurable subscription is identified by name and an optional client identifier, and may have several consumer objects consuming messages from it. It is created automatically when the first consumer object is created. It is not persisted and is deleted automatically when the last consumer object is closed. See Section 16.3.6.5, "Creating Shared Subscriptions," for more information.

At the cost of higher overhead, a subscription may be durable. A durable subscription is persisted and continues to accumulate messages until explicitly deleted, even if there are no consumer objects consuming messages from it. See Section 16.3.6.4, "Creating Durable Subscriptions," for details.

16.3.6.4 Creating Durable Subscriptions

To ensure that a pub/sub application receives all sent messages, use durable subscriptions for the consumers on the topic.

Like a nondurable subscription, a durable subscription may be either unshared or shared.

- An unshared durable subscription is identified by name and client identifier (which must be set) and may have only a single consumer object associated with it.

- A shared durable subscription is identified by name and an optional client identifier, and may have several consumer objects consuming messages from it.

A durable subscription that exists but that does not currently have a non-closed consumer object associated with it is described as being inactive.

You can use the `JMSContext.createDurableConsumer` method to create a consumer on an unshared durable subscription. An unshared durable subscription can have only one active consumer at a time.

A consumer identifies the durable subscription from which it consumes messages by specifying a unique identity that is retained by the JMS provider. Subsequent consumer objects that have the same identity resume the subscription in the state in which it was left by the preceding consumer. If a durable subscription has no active consumer, the JMS provider retains the subscription's messages until they are received by the subscription or until they expire.

You establish the unique identity of an unshared durable subscription by setting the following:

- A client ID for the connection
- A topic and a subscription name for the subscription

You can set the client ID administratively for a client-specific connection factory using either the command line or the Administration Console. (In an application client or a Java SE client, you can instead call `JMSContext.setClientID`.)

After using this connection factory to create the `JMSContext`, you call the `createDurableConsumer` method with two arguments: the topic and a string that specifies the name of the subscription:

```
String subName = "MySub";
JMSConsumer consumer = context.createDurableConsumer(myTopic, subName);
```

The subscription becomes active after you create the consumer. Later, you might close the consumer:

```
consumer.close();
```

The JMS provider stores the messages sent to the topic, as it would store messages sent to a queue. If the program or another application calls `createDurableConsumer` using the same connection factory and its client ID, the same topic, and the same subscription name, then the subscription is reactivated and the JMS provider delivers the messages that were sent while the subscription was inactive.

To delete a durable subscription, first close the consumer, then call the unsubscribe method with the subscription name as the argument:

```
consumer.close();
context.unsubscribe(subName);
```

The unsubscribe method deletes the state the provider maintains for the subscription.

Figure 16–6 and Figure 16–7 show the difference between a nondurable and a durable subscription. With an ordinary, nondurable subscription, the consumer and the subscription begin and end at the same point and are, in effect, identical. When the consumer is closed, the subscription also ends. Here, create stands for a call to JMSContext.createConsumer with a Topic argument, and close stands for a call to JMSConsumer.close. Any messages sent to the topic between the time of the first close and the time of the second create are not added to either subscription. In Figure 16–6, the consumers receive messages M1, M2, M5, and M6, but they do not receive messages M3 and M4.

Figure 16–6   Nondurable Subscriptions and Consumers

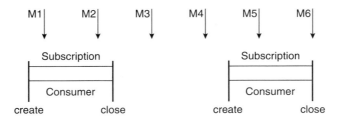

With a durable subscription, the consumer can be closed and re-created, but the subscription continues to exist and to hold messages until the application calls the unsubscribe method. In Figure 16–7, create stands for a call to JMSContext.createDurableConsumer, close stands for a call to JMSConsumer.close, and unsubscribe stands for a call to JMSContext.unsubscribe. Messages sent after the first consumer is closed are received when the second consumer is created (on the same durable subscription), so even though messages M2, M4, and M5 arrive while there is no consumer, they are not lost.

Figure 16–7 Consumers on a Durable Subscription

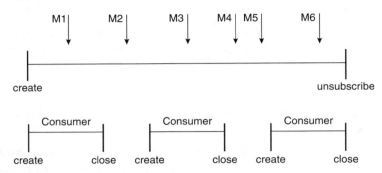

A shared durable subscription allows you to use multiple consumers to receive messages from a durable subscription. If you use a shared durable subscription, the connection factory you use does not need to have a client identifier. To create a shared durable subscription, call the `JMSContext.createSharedDurableConsumer` method, specifying the topic and subscription name:

```
JMSConsumer consumer =
        context.createSharedDurableConsumer(topic, "MakeItLast");
```

For examples of Java EE applications that use durable subscriptions, see the following sections:

- Section 17.2.9, "Acknowledging Messages"
- Section 17.3.1, "Using Durable Subscriptions"
- Section 17.4.2, "Using Shared Durable Subscriptions"
- Section 17.7, "Sending Messages from a Session Bean to an MDB"

16.3.6.5 Creating Shared Subscriptions

A topic subscription created by the `createConsumer` or `createDurableConsumer` method can have only one consumer (although a topic can have many). Multiple clients consuming from the same topic have, by definition, multiple subscriptions to the topic, and all the clients receive all the messages sent to the topic (unless they filter them with message selectors).

It is, however, possible to create a nondurable shared subscription to a topic by using the `createSharedConsumer` method and specifying not only a destination but a subscription name:

```
consumer = context.createSharedConsumer(topicName, "SubName");
```

With a shared subscription, messages will be distributed among multiple clients that use the same topic and subscription name. Each message sent to the topic will be added to every subscription (subject to any message selectors), but each message added to a subscription will be delivered to only one of the consumers on that subscription, so it will be received by only one of the clients. A shared subscription can be useful if you want to share the message load among several consumers on the subscription rather than having just one consumer on the subscription receive each message. This feature can improve the scalability of Java EE application client applications and Java SE applications. (Message-driven beans share the work of processing messages from a topic among multiple threads.)

See Section 17.4.1, "Using Shared Nondurable Subscriptions," for a simple example of using shared nondurable consumers.

You can also create shared durable subscriptions by using the `JMSContext.createSharedDurableConsumer` method. For details, see Section 16.3.6.4, "Creating Durable Subscriptions."

16.3.7 JMS Messages

The ultimate purpose of a JMS application is to produce and consume messages that can then be used by other software applications. JMS messages have a basic format that is simple but highly flexible, allowing you to create messages that match formats used by non-JMS applications on heterogeneous platforms.

A JMS message can have three parts: a header, properties, and a body. Only the header is required. The following sections describe these parts.

For complete documentation of message headers, properties, and bodies, see the documentation of the `Message` interface in the API documentation. For a list of possible message types, see Section 16.3.7.3, "Message Bodies."

16.3.7.1 Message Headers

A JMS message header contains a number of predefined fields that contain values used by both clients and providers to identify and route messages. Table 16–1 lists and describes the JMS message header fields and indicates how their values are set. For example, every message has a unique identifier, which is represented in the header field `JMSMessageID`. The value of another header field, `JMSDestination`, represents the queue or the topic to which the message is sent. Other fields include a timestamp and a priority level.

Each header field has associated setter and getter methods, which are documented in the description of the `Message` interface. Some header fields are intended to be set by a client, but many are set automatically by the send method, which overrides any client-set values.

Table 16–1 How JMS Message Header Field Values Are Set

Header Field	Description	Set By
JMSDestination	Destination to which the message is being sent	JMS provider send method
JMSDeliveryMode	Delivery mode specified when the message was sent (see Section 16.4.2.1, "Specifying Message Persistence")	JMS provider send method
JMSDeliveryTime	The time the message was sent plus the delivery delay specified when the message was sent (see Section 16.4.2.4, "Specifying a Delivery Delay")	JMS provider send method
JMSExpiration	Expiration time of the message (see Section 16.4.2.3, "Allowing Messages to Expire")	JMS provider send method
JMSPriority	The priority of the message (see Section 16.4.2.2, "Setting Message Priority Levels")	JMS provider send method
JMSMessageID	Value that uniquely identifies each message sent by a provider	JMS provider send method
JMSTimestamp	The time the message was handed off to a provider to be sent	JMS provider send method
JMSCorrelationID	Value that links one message to another; commonly the JMSMessageID value is used	Client application
JMSReplyTo	Destination where replies to the message should be sent	Client application
JMSType	Type identifier supplied by client application	Client application
JMSRedelivered	Whether the message is being redelivered	JMS provider prior to delivery

16.3.7.2 Message Properties

You can create and set properties for messages if you need values in addition to those provided by the header fields. You can use properties to provide compatibility with other messaging systems, or you can use them to create message selectors (see Section 16.3.6.2, "JMS Message Selectors"). For an example of setting a property to be used as a message selector, see Section 17.7, "Sending Messages from a Session Bean to an MDB."

The JMS API provides some predefined property names that begin with JMSX. A JMS provider is required to implement only one of these, JMSXDeliveryCount (which specifies the number of times a message has been delivered); the rest are optional. The use of these predefined properties or of user-defined properties in applications is optional.

16.3.7.3 Message Bodies

The JMS API defines six different types of messages. Each message type corresponds to a different message body. These message types allow you to send and receive data in many different forms. Table 16–2 describes these message types.

Table 16–2   JMS Message Types

Message Type	Body Contains
TextMessage	A java.lang.String object (for example, the contents of an XML file).
MapMessage	A set of name-value pairs, with names as String objects and values as primitive types in the Java programming language. The entries can be accessed sequentially by enumerator or randomly by name. The order of the entries is undefined.
BytesMessage	A stream of uninterpreted bytes. This message type is for literally encoding a body to match an existing message format.
StreamMessage	A stream of primitive values in the Java programming language, filled and read sequentially.
ObjectMessage	A Serializable object in the Java programming language.
Message	Nothing. Composed of header fields and properties only. This message type is useful when a message body is not required.

The JMS API provides methods for creating messages of each type and for filling in their contents. For example, to create and send a TextMessage, you might use the following statements:

```
TextMessage message = context.createTextMessage();
message.setText(msg_text);     // msg_text is a String
context.createProducer().send(message);
```

At the consuming end, a message arrives as a generic Message object. You can then cast the object to the appropriate message type and use more specific methods to access the body and extract the message contents (and its headers and properties if needed). For example, you might use the stream-oriented read methods of BytesMessage. You must always cast to the appropriate message type to retrieve the body of a StreamMessage.

Instead of casting the message to a message type, you can call the getBody method on the Message, specifying the type of the message as an argument. For example, you can retrieve a TextMessage as a String. The following code fragment uses the getBody method:

```
Message m = consumer.receive();
if (m instanceof TextMessage) {
    String message = m.getBody(String.class);
    System.out.println("Reading message: " + message);
} else {
    // Handle error or process another message type
}
```

The JMS API provides shortcuts for creating and receiving a TextMessage, BytesMessage, MapMessage, or ObjectMessage. For example, you do not have to wrap a string in a TextMessage; instead, you can send and receive the string directly. For example, you can send a string as follows:

```
String message = "This is a message";
context.createProducer().send(dest, message);
```

You can receive the message by using the receiveBody method:

```
String message = receiver.receiveBody(String.class);
```

You can use the receiveBody method to receive any type of message except StreamMessage and Message, as long as the body of the message can be assigned to a particular type.

An empty Message can be useful if you want to send a message that is simply a signal to the application. Some of the examples in Chapter 17, "Java Message Service Examples," send an empty message after sending a series of text messages. For example:

```
context.createProducer().send(dest, context.createMessage());
```

The consumer code can then interpret a non-text message as a signal that all the messages sent have now been received.

The examples in Chapter 17, "Java Message Service Examples," use messages of type TextMessage, MapMessage, and Message.

16.3.8 JMS Queue Browsers

Messages sent to a queue remain in the queue until the message consumer for that queue consumes them. The JMS API provides a `QueueBrowser` object that allows you to browse the messages in the queue and display the header values for each message. To create a `QueueBrowser` object, use the `JMSContext.createBrowser` method. For example:

```
QueueBrowser browser = context.createBrowser(queue);
```

See Section 17.2.7, "Browsing Messages on a Queue," for an example of using a `QueueBrowser` object.

The `createBrowser` method allows you to specify a message selector as a second argument when you create a `QueueBrowser`. For information on message selectors, see Section 16.3.6.2, "JMS Message Selectors."

The JMS API provides no mechanism for browsing a topic. Messages usually disappear from a topic as soon as they appear: If there are no message consumers to consume them, the JMS provider removes them. Although durable subscriptions allow messages to remain on a topic while the message consumer is not active, JMS does not define any facility for examining them.

16.3.9 JMS Exception Handling

The root class for all checked exceptions in the JMS API is `JMSException`. The root cause for all unchecked exceptions in the JMS API is `JMSRuntimeException`.

Catching `JMSException` and `JMSRuntimeException` provides a generic way of handling all exceptions related to the JMS API.

The `JMSException` and `JMSRuntimeException` classes include the following subclasses, described in the API documentation:

- `IllegalStateException, IllegalStateRuntimeException`
- `InvalidClientIDException, InvalidClientIDRuntimeException`
- `InvalidDestinationException, InvalidDestinationRuntimeException`
- `InvalidSelectorException, InvalidSelectorRuntimeException`
- `JMSSecurityException, JMSSecurityRuntimeException`
- `MessageEOFException`
- `MessageFormatException, MessageFormatRuntimeException`
- `MessageNotReadableException`

- `MessageNotWriteableException`, `MessageNotWriteableRuntimeException`

- `ResourceAllocationException`, `ResourceAllocationRuntimeException`

- `TransactionInProgressException`,
  `TransactionInProgressRuntimeException`

- `TransactionRolledBackException`,
  `TransactionRolledBackRuntimeException`

All the examples in the tutorial catch and handle `JMSException` or `JMSRuntimeException` when it is appropriate to do so.

16.4 Using Advanced JMS Features

This section explains how to use features of the JMS API to achieve the level of reliability and performance your application requires. Many people use JMS in their applications because they cannot tolerate dropped or duplicate messages and because they require that every message be received once and only once. The JMS API provides this functionality.

The most reliable way to produce a message is to send a `PERSISTENT` message, and to do so within a transaction.

JMS messages are `PERSISTENT` by default; `PERSISTENT` messages will not be lost in the event of JMS provider failure. For details, see Section 16.4.2.1, "Specifying Message Persistence."

Transactions allow multiple messages to be sent or received in an atomic operation. In the Java EE platform they also allow message sends and receives to be combined with database reads and writes in an atomic transaction. A **transaction** is a unit of work into which you can group a series of operations, such as message sends and receives, so that the operations either all succeed or all fail. For details, see Section 16.4.4, "Using JMS Local Transactions."

The most reliable way to consume a message is to do so within a transaction, either from a queue or from a durable subscription to a topic. For details, see the following sections:

- Section 16.3.6.4, "Creating Durable Subscriptions"

- Section 16.4.3, "Creating Temporary Destinations"

- Section 16.4.4, "Using JMS Local Transactions"

Some features primarily allow an application to improve performance. For example, you can set messages to expire after a certain length of time (see Section 16.4.2.3, "Allowing Messages to Expire"), so that consumers do not receive unnecessary outdated information. You can send messages asynchronously; see Section 16.4.5, "Sending Messages Asynchronously."

You can also specify various levels of control over message acknowledgment; see Section 16.4.1, "Controlling Message Acknowledgment."

Other features can provide useful capabilities unrelated to reliability. For example, you can create temporary destinations that last only for the duration of the connection in which they are created. See Section 16.4.3, "Creating Temporary Destinations," for details.

The following sections describe these features as they apply to application clients or Java SE clients. Some of the features work differently in the Java EE web or EJB container; in these cases, the differences are noted here and are explained in detail in Section 16.5, "Using the JMS API in Java EE Applications."

16.4.1 Controlling Message Acknowledgment

Until a JMS message has been acknowledged, it is not considered to be successfully consumed. The successful consumption of a message ordinarily takes place in three stages.

1. The client receives the message.

2. The client processes the message.

3. The message is acknowledged. Acknowledgment is initiated either by the JMS provider or by the client, depending on the session acknowledgment mode.

In locally transacted sessions (see Section 16.4.4, "Using JMS Local Transactions"), a message is acknowledged when the session is committed. If a transaction is rolled back, all consumed messages are redelivered.

In a JTA transaction (in the Java EE web or EJB container) a message is acknowledged when the transaction is committed.

In nontransacted sessions, when and how a message is acknowledged depend on a value that may be specified as an argument of the createContext method. The possible argument values are as follows.

- JMSContext.AUTO_ACKNOWLEDGE: This setting is the default for application clients and Java SE clients. The JMSContext automatically acknowledges a client's receipt of a message either when the client has successfully returned from a call to receive or when the MessageListener it has called to process the message returns successfully.

A synchronous receive in a `JMSContext` that is configured to use auto-acknowledgment is the one exception to the rule that message consumption is a three-stage process as described earlier. In this case, the receipt and acknowledgment take place in one step, followed by the processing of the message.

- `JMSContext.CLIENT_ACKNOWLEDGE`: A client acknowledges a message by calling the message's `acknowledge` method. In this mode, acknowledgment takes place on the session level: Acknowledging a consumed message automatically acknowledges the receipt of *all* messages that have been consumed by its session. For example, if a message consumer consumes ten messages and then acknowledges the fifth message delivered, all ten messages are acknowledged.

> **Note:** In the Java EE platform, the `JMSContext.CLIENT_ACKNOWLEDGE` setting can be used only in an application client, not in a web component or enterprise bean.

- `JMSContext.DUPS_OK_ACKNOWLEDGE`: This option instructs the `JMSContext` to lazily acknowledge the delivery of messages. This is likely to result in the delivery of some duplicate messages if the JMS provider fails, so it should be used only by consumers that can tolerate duplicate messages. (If the JMS provider redelivers a message, it must set the value of the `JMSRedelivered` message header to `true`.) This option can reduce session overhead by minimizing the work the session does to prevent duplicates.

If messages have been received from a queue but not acknowledged when a `JMSContext` is closed, the JMS provider retains them and redelivers them when a consumer next accesses the queue. The provider also retains unacknowledged messages if an application closes a `JMSContext` that has been consuming messages from a durable subscription. (See Section 16.3.6.4, "Creating Durable Subscriptions.") Unacknowledged messages that have been received from a nondurable subscription will be dropped when the `JMSContext` is closed.

If you use a queue or a durable subscription, you can use the `JMSContext.recover` method to stop a nontransacted `JMSContext` and restart it with its first unacknowledged message. In effect, the `JMSContext`'s series of delivered messages is reset to the point after its last acknowledged message. The messages it now delivers may be different from those that were originally delivered, if messages have expired or if higher-priority messages have arrived. For a consumer on a nondurable subscription, the provider may drop unacknowledged messages when the `JMSContext.recover` method is called.

The sample program in Section 17.2.9, "Acknowledging Messages," demonstrates two ways to ensure that a message will not be acknowledged until processing of the message is complete.

16.4.2 Specifying Options for Sending Messages

You can set a number of options when you send a message. These options enable you to perform the following tasks:

- Specify that messages are persistent, meaning they must not be lost in the event of a provider failure (Section 16.4.2.1, "Specifying Message Persistence")

- Set priority levels for messages, which can affect the order in which the messages are delivered (Section 16.4.2.2, "Setting Message Priority Levels")

- Specify an expiration time for messages so they will not be delivered if they are obsolete (Section 16.4.2.3, "Allowing Messages to Expire")

- Specify a delivery delay for messages so that they will not be delivered until a specified amount of time has expired (Section 16.4.2.4, "Specifying a Delivery Delay")

Method chaining allows you to specify more than one of these options when you create a producer and call the `send` method; see Section 16.4.2.5, "Using JMSProducer Method Chaining."

16.4.2.1 Specifying Message Persistence

The JMS API supports two delivery modes specifying whether messages are lost if the JMS provider fails. These delivery modes are fields of the `DeliveryMode` interface.

- The default delivery mode, `PERSISTENT`, instructs the JMS provider to take extra care to ensure that a message is not lost in transit in case of a JMS provider failure. A message sent with this delivery mode is logged to stable storage when it is sent.

- The `NON_PERSISTENT` delivery mode does not require the JMS provider to store the message or otherwise guarantee that it is not lost if the provider fails.

To specify the delivery mode, use the `setDeliveryMode` method of the `JMSProducer` interface to set the delivery mode for all messages sent by that producer.

You can use method chaining to set the delivery mode when you create a producer and send a message. The following call creates a producer with a NON_ PERSISTENT delivery mode and uses it to send a message:

```
context.createProducer()
        .setDeliveryMode(DeliveryMode.NON_PERSISTENT).send(dest, msg);
```

If you do not specify a delivery mode, the default is PERSISTENT. Using the NON_ PERSISTENT delivery mode may improve performance and reduce storage overhead, but you should use it only if your application can afford to miss messages.

16.4.2.2 Setting Message Priority Levels

You can use message priority levels to instruct the JMS provider to deliver urgent messages first. Use the setPriority method of the JMSProducer interface to set the priority level for all messages sent by that producer.

You can use method chaining to set the priority level when you create a producer and send a message. For example, the following call sets a priority level of 7 for a producer and then sends a message:

```
context.createProducer().setPriority(7).send(dest, msg);
```

The ten levels of priority range from 0 (lowest) to 9 (highest). If you do not specify a priority level, the default level is 4. A JMS provider tries to deliver higher-priority messages before lower-priority ones, but does not have to deliver messages in exact order of priority.

16.4.2.3 Allowing Messages to Expire

By default, a message never expires. If a message will become obsolete after a certain period, however, you may want to set an expiration time. Use the setTimeToLive method of the JMSProducer interface to set a default expiration time for all messages sent by that producer.

For example, a message that contains rapidly changing data such as a stock price will become obsolete after a few minutes, so you might configure messages to expire after that time.

You can use method chaining to set the time to live when you create a producer and send a message. For example, the following call sets a time to live of five minutes for a producer and then sends a message:

```
context.createProducer().setTimeToLive(300000).send(dest, msg);
```

If the specified timeToLive value is 0, the message never expires.

When the message is sent, the specified timeToLive is added to the current time to give the expiration time. Any message not delivered before the specified expiration time is destroyed. The destruction of obsolete messages conserves storage and computing resources.

16.4.2.4 Specifying a Delivery Delay

You can specify a length of time that must elapse after a message is sent before the JMS provider delivers the message. Use the setDeliveryDelay method of the JMSProducer interface to set a delivery delay for all messages sent by that producer.

You can use method chaining to set the delivery delay when you create a producer and send a message. For example, the following call sets a delivery delay of 3 seconds for a producer and then sends a message:

```
context.createProducer().setDeliveryDelay(3000).send(dest, msg);
```

16.4.2.5 Using JMSProducer Method Chaining

The setter methods on the JMSProducer interface return JMSProducer objects, so you can use method chaining to create a producer, set multiple properties, and send a message. For example, the following chained method calls create a producer, set a user-defined property, set the expiration, delivery mode, and priority for the message, and then send a message to a queue:

```
context.createProducer()
       .setProperty("MyProperty", "MyValue")
       .setTimeToLive(10000)
       .setDeliveryMode(NON_PERSISTENT)
       .setPriority(2)
       .send(queue, body);
```

You can also call the JMSProducer methods to set properties on a message and then send the message in a separate send method call. You can also set message properties directly on a message.

16.4.3 Creating Temporary Destinations

Normally, you create JMS destinations (queues and topics) administratively rather than programmatically. Your JMS provider includes a tool to create and remove destinations, and it is common for destinations to be long-lasting.

The JMS API also enables you to create destinations (TemporaryQueue and TemporaryTopic objects) that last only for the duration of the connection in which they are created. You create these destinations dynamically using the

JMSContext.createTemporaryQueue and the JMSContext.createTemporaryTopic methods, as in the following example:

```
TemporaryTopic replyTopic = context.createTemporaryTopic();
```

The only message consumers that can consume from a temporary destination are those created by the same connection that created the destination. Any message producer can send to the temporary destination. If you close the connection to which a temporary destination belongs, the destination is closed and its contents are lost.

You can use temporary destinations to implement a simple request/reply mechanism. If you create a temporary destination and specify it as the value of the JMSReplyTo message header field when you send a message, then the consumer of the message can use the value of the JMSReplyTo field as the destination to which it sends a reply. The consumer can also reference the original request by setting the JMSCorrelationID header field of the reply message to the value of the JMSMessageID header field of the request. For example, an onMessage method can create a JMSContext so that it can send a reply to the message it receives. It can use code such as the following:

```
replyMsg = context.createTextMessage("Consumer processed message: "
        + msg.getText());
replyMsg.setJMSCorrelationID(msg.getJMSMessageID());
context.createProducer().send((Topic) msg.getJMSReplyTo(), replyMsg);
```

For an example, see Section 17.8, "Using an Entity to Join Messages from Two MDBs."

16.4.4 Using JMS Local Transactions

A **transaction** groups a series of operations into an atomic unit of work. If any one of the operations fails, the transaction can be rolled back, and the operations can be attempted again from the beginning. If all the operations succeed, the transaction can be committed.

In an application client or a Java SE client, you can use local transactions to group message sends and receives. You use the JMSContext.commit method to commit a transaction. You can send multiple messages in a transaction, and the messages will not be added to the queue or topic until the transaction is committed. If you receive multiple messages in a transaction, they will not be acknowledged until the transaction is committed.

You can use the JMSContext.rollback method to roll back a transaction. A transaction rollback means that all produced messages are destroyed and all consumed messages are recovered and redelivered unless they have expired (see Section 16.4.2.3, "Allowing Messages to Expire").

A transacted session is always involved in a transaction. To create a transacted session, call the createContext method as follows:

```
JMSContext context =
        connectionFactory.createContext(JMSContext.SESSION_TRANSACTED);
```

As soon as the commit or the rollback method is called, one transaction ends and another transaction begins. Closing a transacted session rolls back its transaction in progress, including any pending sends and receives.

In an application running in the Java EE web or EJB container, you cannot use local transactions. Instead, you use JTA transactions, described in Section 16.5, "Using the JMS API in Java EE Applications."

You can combine several sends and receives in a single JMS local transaction, so long as they are all performed using the same JMSContext.

Do not use a single transaction if you use a request/reply mechanism, in which you send a message and then receive a reply to that message. If you try to use a single transaction, the program will hang, because the send cannot take place until the transaction is committed. The following code fragment illustrates the problem:

```
// Don't do this!
outMsg.setJMSReplyTo(replyQueue);
context.createProducer().send(outQueue, outMsg);
consumer = context.createConsumer(replyQueue);
inMsg = consumer.receive();
context.commit();
```

Because a message sent during a transaction is not actually sent until the transaction is committed, the transaction cannot contain any receives that depend on that message's having been sent.

The production and the consumption of a message cannot both be part of the same transaction. The reason is that the transactions take place between the clients and the JMS provider, which intervenes between the production and the consumption of the message. Figure 16–8 illustrates this interaction.

Figure 16–8 Using JMS Local Transactions

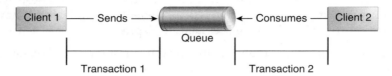

The sending of one or more messages to one or more destinations by Client 1 can form a single transaction, because it forms a single set of interactions with the JMS provider using a single JMSContext. Similarly, the receiving of one or more messages from one or more destinations by Client 2 also forms a single transaction using a single JMSContext. But because the two clients have no direct interaction and are using two different JMSContext objects, no transactions can take place between them.

Another way of putting this is that a transaction is a contract between a client and a JMS provider that defines whether a message is sent to a destination or whether a message is received from the destination. It is not a contract between the sending client and the receiving client.

This is the fundamental difference between messaging and synchronized processing. Instead of tightly coupling the sender and the receiver of a message, JMS couples the sender of a message with the destination, and it separately couples the destination with the receiver of the message. Therefore, while the sends and receives each have a tight coupling with the JMS provider, they do not have any coupling with each other.

When you create a JMSContext, you can specify whether it is transacted by using the JMSContext.SESSION_TRANSACTED argument to the createContext method. For example:

```
try (JMSContext context = connectionFactory.createContext(
        JMSContext.SESSION_TRANSACTED);) {
    ...
```

The commit and the rollback methods for local transactions are associated with the session that underlies the JMSContext. You can combine operations on more than one queue or topic, or on a combination of queues and topics, in a single transaction if you use the same session to perform the operations. For example, you can use the same JMSContext to receive a message from a queue and send a message to a topic in the same transaction.

The example in Section 17.3.2, "Using Local Transactions," shows how to use JMS local transactions.

16.4.5 Sending Messages Asynchronously

Normally, when you send a persistent message, the send method blocks until the JMS provider confirms that the message was sent successfully. The asynchronous send mechanism allows your application to send a message and continue work while waiting to learn whether the send completed.

This feature is currently available only in application clients and Java SE clients.

Sending a message asynchronously involves supplying a callback object. You specify a CompletionListener with an onCompletion method. For example, the following code instantiates a CompletionListener named SendListener. It then calls the setAsync method to specify that sends from this producer should be asynchronous and should use the specified listener:

```
CompletionListener listener = new SendListener();
context.createProducer().setAsync(listener).send(dest, message);
```

The CompletionListener class must implement two methods, onCompletion and onException. The onCompletion method is called if the send succeeds, and the onException method is called if it fails. A simple implementation of these methods might look like this:

```
@Override
public void onCompletion(Message message) {
    System.out.println("onCompletion method: Send has completed.");
}

@Override
public void onException(Message message, Exception e) {
    System.out.println("onException method: send failed: " + e.toString());
    System.out.println("Unsent message is: \n" + message);
}
```

16.5 Using the JMS API in Java EE Applications

This section describes how using the JMS API in enterprise bean applications or web applications differs from using it in application clients.

A general rule in the Java EE platform specification applies to all Java EE components that use the JMS API within EJB or web containers: Application components in the web and EJB containers must not attempt to create more than one active (not closed) Session object per connection. Multiple JMSContext objects are permitted, however, since they combine a single connection and a single session.

This rule does not apply to application clients. The application client container supports the creation of multiple sessions for each connection.

16.5.1 Creating Resources for Java EE Applications

You can use annotations to create application-specific connection factories and destinations for Java EE enterprise bean or web components. The resources you create in this way are visible only to the application for which you create them.

You can also use deployment descriptor elements to create these resources. Elements specified in the deployment descriptor override elements specified in annotations. See Section 5.1, "Packaging Applications," in *The Java EE 7 Tutorial, Volume 1*, for basic information about deployment descriptors. You must use a deployment descriptor to create application-specific resources for application clients.

To create a destination, use a @JMSDestinationDefinition annotation like the following on a class:

```
@JMSDestinationDefinition(
    name = "java:app/jms/myappTopic",
    interfaceName = "javax.jms.Topic",
    destinationName = "MyPhysicalAppTopic"
)
```

The name, interfaceName, and destinationName elements are required. You can optionally specify a description element. To create multiple destinations, enclose them in a @JMSDestinationDefinitions annotation, separated by commas.

To create a connection factory, use a @JMSConnectionFactoryDefinition annotation like the following on a class:

```
@JMSConnectionFactoryDefinition(
    name="java:app/jms/MyConnectionFactory"
)
```

The name element is required. You can optionally specify a number of other elements, such as clientId if you want to use the connection factory for durable subscriptions, or description. If you do not specify the interfaceName element, the default interface is javax.jms.ConnectionFactory. To create multiple connection factories, enclose them in a @JMSConnectionFactoryDefinitions annotation, separated by commas.

You need to specify the annotation only once for a given application, in any of the components.

> **Note:** If your application contains one or more message-driven beans, you may want to place the annotation on one of the message-driven beans. If you place the annotation on a sending component such as an application client, you need to specify the `mappedName` element to look up the topic, instead of using the `destinationLookup` property of the activation configuration specification.

When you inject the resource into a component, use the value of the `name` element in the definition annotation as the value of the `lookup` element in the `@Resource` annotation:

```
@Resource(lookup = "java:app/jms/myappTopic")
private Topic topic;
```

The following portable JNDI namespaces are available. Which ones you can use depends on how your application is packaged:

- `java:global`: Makes the resource available to all deployed applications

- `java:app`: Makes the resource available to all components in all modules in a single application

- `java:module`: Makes the resource available to all components within a given module (for example, all enterprise beans within an EJB module)

- `java:comp`: Makes the resource available to a single component only (except in a web application, where it is equivalent to `java:module`)

See the API documentation for details on these annotations. The examples in Section 17.5, "Sending and Receiving Messages Using a Simple Web Application," Section 17.7, "Sending Messages from a Session Bean to an MDB," and Section 17.8, "Using an Entity to Join Messages from Two MDBs," all use the `@JMSDestinationDefinition` annotation. The other JMS examples do not use these annotations. The examples that consist only of application clients are not deployed in the application server and must therefore communicate with each other using administratively created resources that exist outside of individual applications.

16.5.2 Using Resource Injection in Enterprise Bean or Web Components

You may use resource injection to inject both administered objects and `JMSContext` objects in Java EE applications.

16.5.2.1 Injecting a ConnectionFactory, Queue, or Topic

Normally, you use the @Resource annotation to inject a ConnectionFactory, Queue, or Topic into your Java EE application. These objects must be created administratively before you deploy your application. You may want to use the default connection factory, whose JNDI name is java:comp/DefaultJMSConnectionFactory.

When you use resource injection in an application client component, you normally declare the JMS resource static:

```
@Resource(lookup = "java:comp/DefaultJMSConnectionFactory")
private static ConnectionFactory connectionFactory;

@Resource(lookup = "jms/MyQueue")
private static Queue queue;
```

However, when you use this annotation in a session bean, a message-driven bean, or a web component, do *not* declare the resource static:

```
@Resource(lookup = "java:comp/DefaultJMSConnectionFactory")
private ConnectionFactory connectionFactory;

@Resource(lookup = "jms/MyTopic")
private Topic topic;
```

If you declare the resource static in these components, runtime errors will result.

16.5.2.2 Injecting a JMSContext Object

To access a JMSContext object in an enterprise bean or web component, instead of injecting the ConnectionFactory resource and then creating a JMSContext, you can use the @Inject and @JMSConnectionFactory annotations to inject a JMSContext. To use the default connection factory, use code like the following:

```
@Inject
private JMSContext context1;
```

To use your own connection factory, use code like the following:

```
@Inject
@JMSConnectionFactory("jms/MyConnectionFactory")
private JMSContext context2;
```

16.5.3 Using Java EE Components to Produce and to Synchronously Receive Messages

An application that produces messages or synchronously receives them can use a Java EE web or EJB component, such as a managed bean, a servlet, or a session bean, to perform these operations. The example in Section 17.7, "Sending Messages from a Session Bean to an MDB," uses a stateless session bean to send messages to a topic. The example in Section 17.5, "Sending and Receiving Messages Using a Simple Web Application," uses managed beans to produce and to consume messages.

Because a synchronous receive with no specified timeout ties up server resources, this mechanism usually is not the best application design for a web or EJB component. Instead, use a synchronous receive that specifies a timeout value, or use a message-driven bean to receive messages asynchronously. For details about synchronous receives, see Section 16.3.6, "JMS Message Consumers."

Using the JMS API in a Java EE component is in many ways similar to using it in an application client. The main differences are the areas of resource management and transactions.

16.5.3.1 Managing JMS Resources in Web and EJB Components

The JMS resources are a connection and a session, usually combined in a `JMSContext` object. In general, it is important to release JMS resources when they are no longer being used. Here are some useful practices to follow.

- If you wish to maintain a JMS resource only for the life span of a business method, use a `try`-with-resources statement to create the `JMSContext` so that it will be closed automatically at the end of the `try` block.

- To maintain a JMS resource for the duration of a transaction or request, inject the `JMSContext` as described in Section 16.5.2.2, "Injecting a JMSContext Object." This will also cause the resource to be released when it is no longer needed.

- If you would like to maintain a JMS resource for the life span of an enterprise bean instance, you can use a `@PostConstruct` callback method to create the resource and a `@PreDestroy` callback method to close the resource. However, there is normally no need to do this, since application servers usually maintain a pool of connections. If you use a stateful session bean and you wish to maintain the JMS resource in a cached state, you must close the resource in a `@PrePassivate` callback method and set its value to `null`, and you must create it again in a `@PostActivate` callback method.

16.5.3.2 Managing Transactions in Session Beans

Instead of using local transactions, you use JTA transactions. You can use either container-managed transactions or bean-managed transactions. Normally, you use container-managed transactions for bean methods that perform sends or receives, allowing the EJB container to handle transaction demarcation. Because container-managed transactions are the default, you do not have to specify them.

You can use bean-managed transactions and the `javax.transaction.UserTransaction` interface's transaction demarcation methods, but you should do so only if your application has special requirements and you are an expert in using transactions. Usually, container-managed transactions produce the most efficient and correct behavior. This tutorial does not provide any examples of bean-managed transactions.

16.5.4 Using Message-Driven Beans to Receive Messages Asynchronously

Section 3.3, "What Is a Message-Driven Bean?," and Section 16.1.4, "How Does the JMS API Work with the Java EE Platform?," describe how the Java EE platform supports a special kind of enterprise bean, the message-driven bean, which allows Java EE applications to process JMS messages asynchronously. Other Java EE web and EJB components allow you to send messages and to receive them synchronously but not asynchronously.

A message-driven bean is a message listener to which messages can be delivered from either a queue or a topic. The messages can be sent by any Java EE component (from an application client, another enterprise bean, or a web component) or from an application or a system that does not use Java EE technology.

A message-driven bean class has the following requirements.

- It must be annotated with the `@MessageDriven` annotation if it does not use a deployment descriptor.

- The class must be defined as `public`, but not as `abstract` or `final`.

- It must contain a public constructor with no arguments.

It is recommended, but not required, that a message-driven bean class implement the message listener interface for the message type it supports. A bean that supports the JMS API implements the `javax.jms.MessageListener` interface, which means that it must provide an `onMessage` method with the following signature:

```
void onMessage(Message inMessage)
```

The onMessage method is called by the bean's container when a message has arrived for the bean to service. This method contains the business logic that handles the processing of the message. It is the message-driven bean's responsibility to parse the message and perform the necessary business logic.

A message-driven bean differs from an application client's message listener in the following ways.

- In an application client, you must create a JMSContext, then create a JMSConsumer, then call setMessageListener to activate the listener. For a message-driven bean, you need only define the class and annotate it, and the EJB container creates it for you.

- The bean class uses the @MessageDriven annotation, which typically contains an activationConfig element containing @ActivationConfigProperty annotations that specify properties used by the bean or the connection factory. These properties can include the connection factory, a destination type, a durable subscription, a message selector, or an acknowledgment mode. Some of the examples in Chapter 17, "Java Message Service Examples," set these properties. You can also set the properties in the deployment descriptor.

- The application client container has only one instance of a MessageListener, which is called on a single thread at a time. A message-driven bean, however, may have multiple instances, configured by the container, which may be called concurrently by multiple threads (although each instance is called by only one thread at a time). Message-driven beans may therefore allow much faster processing of messages than message listeners.

- You do not need to specify a message acknowledgment mode unless you use bean-managed transactions. The message is consumed in the transaction in which the onMessage method is invoked.

Table 16–3 lists the activation configuration properties defined by the JMS specification.

Table 16–3   @ActivationConfigProperty Settings for Message-Driven Beans

Property Name	Description
acknowledgeMode	Acknowledgment mode, used only for bean-managed transactions; the default is Auto-acknowledge (Dups-ok-acknowledge is also permitted)
destinationLookup	The lookup name of the queue or topic from which the bean will receive messages
destinationType	Either javax.jms.Queue or javax.jms.Topic

Table 16–3   (Cont.) @ActivationConfigProperty Settings for Message-Driven Beans

Property Name	Description
subscriptionDurability	For durable subscriptions, set the value to Durable; see Section 16.3.6.4, "Creating Durable Subscriptions," for more information
clientId	For durable subscriptions, the client ID for the connection (optional)
subscriptionName	For durable subscriptions, the name of the subscription
messageSelector	A string that filters messages; see Section 16.3.6.2, "JMS Message Selectors," for information
connectionFactoryLookup	The lookup name of the connection factory to be used to connect to the JMS provider from which the bean will receive messages

For example, here is the message-driven bean used in Section 17.6, "Receiving Messages Asynchronously Using a Message-Driven Bean":

```
@MessageDriven(activationConfig = {
    @ActivationConfigProperty(propertyName = "destinationLookup",
            propertyValue = "jms/MyQueue"),
    @ActivationConfigProperty(propertyName = "destinationType",
            propertyValue = "javax.jms.Queue")
})
public class SimpleMessageBean implements MessageListener {

    @Resource
    private MessageDrivenContext mdc;
    static final Logger logger = Logger.getLogger("SimpleMessageBean");

    public SimpleMessageBean() {
    }

    @Override
    public void onMessage(Message inMessage) {

        try {
            if (inMessage instanceof TextMessage) {
                logger.log(Level.INFO,
                        "MESSAGE BEAN: Message received: {0}",
                        inMessage.getBody(String.class));
            } else {
```

```
            logger.log(Level.WARNING,
                    "Message of wrong type: {0}",
                    inMessage.getClass().getName());
        }
    } catch (JMSException e) {
        logger.log(Level.SEVERE,
                "SimpleMessageBean.onMessage: JMSException: {0}",
                e.toString());
        mdc.setRollbackOnly();
    }
    }
}
```

If JMS is integrated with the application server using a resource adapter, the JMS resource adapter handles these tasks for the EJB container.

The bean class commonly injects a `MessageDrivenContext` resource, which provides some additional methods you can use for transaction management (`setRollbackOnly`, for example):

```
@Resource
private MessageDrivenContext mdc;
```

A message-driven bean never has a local or remote interface. Instead, it has only a bean class.

A message-driven bean is similar in some ways to a stateless session bean: Its instances are relatively short-lived and retain no state for a specific client. The instance variables of the message-driven bean instance can contain some state across the handling of client messages: for example, an open database connection, or an object reference to an enterprise bean object.

Like a stateless session bean, a message-driven bean can have many interchangeable instances running at the same time. The container can pool these instances to allow streams of messages to be processed concurrently. The container attempts to deliver messages in chronological order when that would not impair the concurrency of message processing, but no guarantees are made as to the exact order in which messages are delivered to the instances of the message-driven bean class. If message order is essential to your application, you may want to configure your application server to use just one instance of the message-driven bean.

For details on the lifecycle of a message-driven bean, see Section 3.7.4, "The Lifecycle of a Message-Driven Bean."

16.5.5 Managing JTA Transactions

Java EE application clients and Java SE clients use JMS local transactions (described in Section 16.4.4, "Using JMS Local Transactions"), which allow the grouping of sends and receives within a specific JMS session. Java EE applications that run in the web or EJB container commonly use JTA transactions to ensure the integrity of accesses to external resources. The key difference between a JTA transaction and a JMS local transaction is that a JTA transaction is controlled by the application server's transaction managers. JTA transactions may be **distributed**, which means that they can encompass multiple resources in the same transaction, such as a JMS provider and a database.

For example, distributed transactions allow multiple applications to perform atomic updates on the same database, and they allow a single application to perform atomic updates on multiple databases.

In a Java EE application that uses the JMS API, you can use transactions to combine message sends or receives with database updates and other resource manager operations. You can access resources from multiple application components within a single transaction. For example, a servlet can start a transaction, access multiple databases, invoke an enterprise bean that sends a JMS message, invoke another enterprise bean that modifies an EIS system using the Connector Architecture, and finally commit the transaction. Your application cannot, however, both send a JMS message and receive a reply to it within the same transaction.

JTA transactions within the EJB and web containers can be either of two kinds.

- **Container-managed transactions**: The container controls the integrity of your transactions without your having to call `commit` or `rollback`. Container-managed transactions are easier to use than bean-managed transactions. You can specify appropriate transaction attributes for your enterprise bean methods.

  Use the `Required` transaction attribute (the default) to ensure that a method is always part of a transaction. If a transaction is in progress when the method is called, the method will be part of that transaction; if not, a new transaction will be started before the method is called and will be committed when the method returns. See Section 22.3.1, "Transaction Attributes," for more information.

- **Bean-managed transactions**: You can use these in conjunction with the `javax.transaction.UserTransaction` interface, which provides its own `commit` and `rollback` methods you can use to delimit transaction boundaries. Bean-managed transactions are recommended only for those who are experienced in programming transactions.

You can use either container-managed transactions or bean-managed transactions with message-driven beans. To ensure that all messages are received and handled within the context of a transaction, use container-managed transactions and use the Required transaction attribute (the default) for the onMessage method.

When you use container-managed transactions, you can call the following MessageDrivenContext methods.

- setRollbackOnly: Use this method for error handling. If an exception occurs, setRollbackOnly marks the current transaction so that the only possible outcome of the transaction is a rollback.

- getRollbackOnly: Use this method to test whether the current transaction has been marked for rollback.

If you use bean-managed transactions, the delivery of a message to the onMessage method takes place outside the JTA transaction context. The transaction begins when you call the UserTransaction.begin method within the onMessage method, and it ends when you call UserTransaction.commit or UserTransaction.rollback. Any call to the Connection.createSession method must take place within the transaction.

Using bean-managed transactions allows you to process the message by using more than one transaction or to have some parts of the message processing take place outside a transaction context. However, if you use container-managed transactions, the message is received by the MDB and processed by the onMessage method within the same transaction. It is not possible to achieve this behavior with bean-managed transactions.

When you create a JMSContext in a JTA transaction (in the web or EJB container), the container ignores any arguments you specify, because it manages all transactional properties. When you create a JMSContext in the web or EJB container and there is no JTA transaction, the value (if any) passed to the createContext method should be JMSContext.AUTO_ACKNOWLEDGE or JMSContext.DUPS_OK_ACKNOWLEDGE.

When you use container-managed transactions, you normally use the Required transaction attribute (the default) for your enterprise bean's business methods.

You do not specify the activation configuration property acknowledgeMode when you create a message-driven bean that uses container-managed transactions. The container acknowledges the message automatically when it commits the transaction.

If a message-driven bean uses bean-managed transactions, the message receipt cannot be part of the bean-managed transaction. You can set the activation configuration property acknowledgeMode to Auto-acknowledge or

Dups-ok-acknowledge to specify how you want the message received by the message-driven bean to be acknowledged.

If the onMessage method throws a RuntimeException, the container does not acknowledge processing the message. In that case, the JMS provider will redeliver the unacknowledged message in the future.

16.6 Further Information about JMS

For more information about JMS, see

- Java Message Service website:

  http://www.oracle.com/technetwork/java/
  index-jsp-142945.html

- Java Message Service specification, version 2.0, available from:

  http://jcp.org/en/jsr/detail?id=343

17

Java Message Service Examples

This chapter provides examples that show how to use the JMS API in various kinds of Java EE applications. The following topics are addressed here:

- Overview of the JMS Examples
- Writing Simple JMS Applications
- Writing More Advanced JMS Applications
- Writing High Performance and Scalable JMS Applications
- Sending and Receiving Messages Using a Simple Web Application
- Receiving Messages Asynchronously Using a Message-Driven Bean
- Sending Messages from a Session Bean to an MDB
- Using an Entity to Join Messages from Two MDBs
- Using NetBeans IDE to Create JMS Resources

The examples are in the *tut-install*/examples/jms/ directory.

The steps to build and run each example are as follows.

1. Use NetBeans IDE or Maven to compile, package, and in some cases deploy the example.

2. Use NetBeans IDE, Maven, or the appclient command to run the application client, or use the browser to run the web application examples.

Before you deploy or run the examples, you need to create resources for them. Some examples have a glassfish-resources.xml file that is used to create resources for that example and others. You can use the asadmin command to create the resources.

To use the `asadmin` and `appclient` commands, you need to put the GlassFish Server `bin` directories in your command path, as described in Section 2.1.1.1, "SDK Installation Tips."

17.1 Overview of the JMS Examples

Table 17–1 and Table 17–2 list the examples used in this chapter, describe what they do, and refer to the section that describes them fully. The example directory for each example is relative to the *tut-install*/`examples`/`jms`/ directory.

Table 17–1   JMS Examples That Show the Use of Java EE Application Clients

Example Directory	Description
simple/producer	Using an application client to send messages; see Section 17.2.4, "Sending Messages"
simple/synchconsumer	Using an application client to receive messages synchronously; see Section 17.2.5, "Receiving Messages Synchronously"
simple/asynchconsumer	Using an application client to receive messages asynchronously; see Section 17.2.6, "Using a Message Listener for Asynchronous Message Delivery"
simple/messagebrowser	Using an application client to use a `QueueBrowser` to browse a queue; see Section 17.2.7, "Browsing Messages on a Queue"
simple/clientackconsumer	Using an application client to acknowledge messages received synchronously; see Section 17.2.9, "Acknowledging Messages"
durablesubscriptionexample	Using an application client to create a durable subscription on a topic; see Section 17.3.1, "Using Durable Subscriptions"
transactedexample	Using an application client to send and receive messages in local transactions (also uses request-reply messaging); see Section 17.3.2, "Using Local Transactions"
shared/sharedconsumer	Using an application client to create shared nondurable topic subscriptions; see Section 17.4.1, "Using Shared Nondurable Subscriptions"
shared/shareddurableconsumer	Using an application client to create shared durable topic subscriptions; see Section 17.4.2, "Using Shared Durable Subscriptions"

Table 17–2   JMS Examples That Show the Use of Java EE Web and EJB Components

Example Directory	Description
websimplemessage	Using managed beans to send messages and to receive messages synchronously; see Section 17.5, "Sending and Receiving Messages Using a Simple Web Application"
simplemessage	Using an application client to send messages, and using a message-driven bean to receive messages asynchronously; see Section 17.6, "Receiving Messages Asynchronously Using a Message-Driven Bean"
clientsessionmdb	Using a session bean to send messages, and using a message-driven bean to receive messages; see Section 17.7, "Sending Messages from a Session Bean to an MDB"
clientmdbentity	Using an application client, two message-driven beans, and JPA persistence to create a simple HR application; see Section 17.8, "Using an Entity to Join Messages from Two MDBs"

17.2 Writing Simple JMS Applications

This section shows how to create, package, and run simple JMS clients that are packaged as application clients. The clients demonstrate the basic tasks a JMS application must perform:

- Creating a JMSContext
- Creating message producers and consumers
- Sending and receiving messages

Each example uses two clients: one that sends messages and one that receives them. You can run the clients in two terminal windows.

When you write a JMS client to run in an enterprise bean application, you use many of the same methods in much the same sequence as for an application client. However, there are some significant differences. Section 16.5, "Using the JMS API in Java EE Applications," describes these differences, and this chapter provides examples that illustrate them.

The examples for this section are in the *tut-install*/examples/jms/simple/ directory, under the following subdirectories:

producer/
synchconsumer/
asynchconsumer/

```
messagebrowser/
clientackconsumer/
```

Before running the examples, you need to start GlassFish Server and create administered objects.

17.2.1 Starting the JMS Provider

When you use GlassFish Server, your JMS provider is GlassFish Server. Start the server as described in Section 2.2, "Starting and Stopping GlassFish Server."

17.2.2 Creating JMS Administered Objects

This example uses the following JMS administered objects:

- A connection factory
- Two destination resources: a topic and a queue

Before you run the applications, you can use the `asadmin add-resources` command to create needed JMS resources, specifying as the argument a file named `glassfish-resources.xml`. This file can be created in any project using NetBeans IDE, although you can also create it by hand. A file for the needed resources is present in the `jms/simple/producer/src/main/setup/` directory.

The JMS examples use a connection factory with the logical JNDI lookup name `java:comp/DefaultJMSConnectionFactory`, which is preconfigured on GlassFish Server.

You can also use the `asadmin create-jms-resource` command to create resources, the `asadmin list-jms-resources` command to display their names, and the `asadmin delete-jms-resource` command to remove them.

17.2.2.1 To Create Resources for the Simple Examples

A `glassfish-resources.xml` file in one of the Maven projects can create all the resources needed for the simple examples.

1. Make sure that GlassFish Server has been started (see Section 2.2, "Starting and Stopping GlassFish Server").

2. In a command window, go to the `Producer` example:

    ```
    cd tut-install/jms/simple/producer
    ```

3. Create the resources using the `asadmin add-resources` command:

    ```
    asadmin add-resources src/main/setup/glassfish-resources.xml
    ```

4. Verify the creation of the resources:

```
asadmin list-jms-resources
```

The command lists the two destinations and connection factory specified in the `glassfish-resources.xml` file in addition to the platform default connection factory:

```
jms/MyQueue
jms/MyTopic
jms/__defaultConnectionFactory
Command list-jms-resources executed successfully.
```

In GlassFish Server, the Java EE `java:comp/DefaultJMSConnectionFactory` resource is mapped to a connection factory named `jms/__defaultConnectionFactory`.

17.2.3 Building All the Simple Examples

To run the simple examples using GlassFish Server, package each example in an application client JAR file. The application client JAR file requires a manifest file, located in the `src/main/java/META-INF/` directory for each example, along with the `.class` file.

The `pom.xml` file for each example specifies a plugin that creates an application client JAR file. You can build the examples using either NetBeans IDE or Maven.

17.2.3.1 To Build All the Simple Examples Using NetBeans IDE

1. From the **File** menu, choose **Open Project**.

2. In the Open Project dialog box, navigate to:

   tut-install/examples/jms

3. Expand the `jms` node and select the `simple` folder.

4. Click **Open Project** to open all the simple examples.

5. In the **Projects** tab, right-click the `simple` project and select **Build** to build all the examples.

   This command places the application client JAR files in the `target` directories for the examples.

17.2.3.2 To Build All the Simple Examples Using Maven

1. In a terminal window, go to:

```
cd tut-install/jms/simple
```

2. Enter the following command to build all the projects:

```
mvn install
```

This command places the application client JAR files in the `target` directories for the examples.

17.2.4 Sending Messages

This section describes how to use a client to send messages. The `Producer.java` client will send messages in all of these examples.

The general steps this example performs are as follows.

1. Inject resources for the administered objects used by the example.

2. Accept and verify command-line arguments. You can use this example to send any number of messages to either a queue or a topic, so you specify the destination type and the number of messages on the command line when you run the program.

3. Create a `JMSContext`, then send the specified number of text messages in the form of strings, as described in Section 16.3.7.3, "Message Bodies."

4. Send a final message of type `Message` to indicate that the consumer should expect no more messages.

5. Catch any exceptions.

17.2.4.1 The Producer.java Client

The sending client, `Producer.java`, performs the following steps.

1. Injects resources for a connection factory, queue, and topic:

```
@Resource(lookup = "java:comp/DefaultJMSConnectionFactory")
private static ConnectionFactory connectionFactory;
@Resource(lookup = "jms/MyQueue")
private static Queue queue;
@Resource(lookup = "jms/MyTopic")
private static Topic topic;
```

2. Retrieves and verifies command-line arguments that specify the destination type and the number of arguments:

```
final int NUM_MSGS;
String destType = args[0];
System.out.println("Destination type is " + destType);
if ( ! ( destType.equals("queue") || destType.equals("topic") ) ) {
    System.err.println("Argument must be \"queue\" or " + "\"topic\"");
    System.exit(1);
}
if (args.length == 2){
    NUM_MSGS = (new Integer(args[1])).intValue();
} else {
    NUM_MSGS = 1;
}
```

3. Assigns either the queue or the topic to a destination object, based on the specified destination type:

```
Destination dest = null;
try {
    if (destType.equals("queue")) {
        dest = (Destination) queue;
    } else {
        dest = (Destination) topic;
    }
} catch (Exception e) {
    System.err.println("Error setting destination: " + e.toString());
    System.exit(1);
}
```

4. Within a `try`-with-resources block, creates a `JMSContext`:

```
try (JMSContext context = connectionFactory.createContext();) {
```

5. Sets the message count to zero, then creates a `JMSProducer` and sends one or more messages to the destination and increments the count. Messages in the form of strings are of the `TextMessage` message type:

```
int count = 0;
for (int i = 0; i < NUM_MSGS; i++) {
    String message = "This is message " + (i + 1)
            + " from producer";
    // Comment out the following line to send many messages
    System.out.println("Sending message: " + message);
```

```
                    context.createProducer().send(dest, message);
                    count += 1;
                }
                System.out.println("Text messages sent: " + count);
```

6. Sends an empty control message to indicate the end of the message stream:

```
context.createProducer().send(dest, context.createMessage());
```

Sending an empty message of no specified type is a convenient way for an application to indicate to the consumer that the final message has arrived.

7. Catches and handles any exceptions. The end of the try-with-resources block automatically causes the JMSContext to be closed:

```
} catch (Exception e) {
    System.err.println("Exception occurred: " + e.toString());
    System.exit(1);
}
System.exit(0);
```

17.2.4.2 To Run the Producer Client

You can run the client using the appclient command. The Producer client takes one or two command-line arguments: a destination type and, optionally, a number of messages. If you do not specify a number of messages, the client sends one message.

You will use the client to send three messages to a queue.

1. Make sure that GlassFish Server has been started (see Section 2.2, "Starting and Stopping GlassFish Server") and that you have created resources and built the simple JMS examples (see Section 17.2.2, "Creating JMS Administered Objects," and Section 17.2.3, "Building All the Simple Examples").

2. In a terminal window, go to the producer directory:

```
cd producer
```

3. Run the Producer program, sending three messages to the queue:

```
appclient -client target/producer.jar queue 3
```

The output of the program looks like this (along with some additional output):

```
Destination type is queue
Sending message: This is message 1 from producer
```

```
Sending message: This is message 2 from producer
Sending message: This is message 3 from producer
Text messages sent: 3
```

The messages are now in the queue, waiting to be received.

> **Note:** When you run an application client, the command may take a long time to complete.

17.2.5 Receiving Messages Synchronously

This section describes the receiving client, which uses the `receive` method to consume messages synchronously. This section then explains how to run the clients using GlassFish Server.

17.2.5.1 The SynchConsumer.java Client

The receiving client, `SynchConsumer.java`, performs the following steps.

1. Injects resources for a connection factory, queue, and topic.

2. Assigns either the queue or the topic to a destination object, based on the specified destination type.

3. Within a `try-with-resources` block, creates a `JMSContext`.

4. Creates a `JMSConsumer`, starting message delivery:

```
consumer = context.createConsumer(dest);
```

5. Receives the messages sent to the destination until the end-of-message-stream control message is received:

```
int count = 0;
while (true) {
    Message m = consumer.receive(1000);
    if (m != null) {
        if (m instanceof TextMessage) {
            System.out.println(
                    "Reading message: " + m.getBody(String.class));
            count += 1;
        } else {
            break;
        }
    }
}
System.out.println("Messages received: " + count);
```

Because the control message is not a `TextMessage`, the receiving client terminates the `while` loop and stops receiving messages after the control message arrives.

6. Catches and handles any exceptions. The end of the `try-with-resources` block automatically causes the `JMSContext` to be closed.

The `SynchConsumer` client uses an indefinite `while` loop to receive messages, calling `receive` with a timeout argument.

17.2.5.2 To Run the SynchConsumer and Producer Clients

You can run the client using the `appclient` command. The `SynchConsumer` client takes one command-line argument, the destination type.

These steps show how to receive and send messages synchronously using both a queue and a topic. The steps assume you already ran the `Producer` client and have three messages waiting in the queue.

1. In the same terminal window where you ran `Producer`, go to the `synchconsumer` directory:

    ```
    cd ../synchconsumer
    ```

2. Run the `SynchConsumer` client, specifying the queue:

    ```
    appclient -client target/synchconsumer.jar queue
    ```

    The output of the client looks like this (along with some additional output):

    ```
    Destination type is queue
    Reading message: This is message 1 from producer
    Reading message: This is message 2 from producer
    Reading message: This is message 3 from producer
    Messages received: 3
    ```

3. Now try running the clients in the opposite order. Run the `SynchConsumer` client:

    ```
    appclient -client target/synchconsumer.jar queue
    ```

    The client displays the destination type and then waits for messages.

4. Open a new terminal window and run the `Producer` client:

    ```
    cd tut-install/jms/simple/producer
    appclient -client target/producer.jar queue 3
    ```

When the messages have been sent, the `SynchConsumer` client receives them and exits.

5. Now run the `Producer` client using a topic instead of a queue:

    ```
    appclient -client target/producer.jar topic 3
    ```

    The output of the client looks like this (along with some additional output):

    ```
    Destination type is topic
    Sending message: This is message 1 from producer
    Sending message: This is message 2 from producer
    Sending message: This is message 3 from producer
    Text messages sent: 3
    ```

6. Now, in the other terminal window, run the `SynchConsumer` client using the topic:

    ```
    appclient -client target/synchconsumer.jar topic
    ```

    The result, however, is different. Because you are using a subscription on a topic, messages that were sent before you created the subscription on the topic will not be added to the subscription and delivered to the consumer. (For details, see Section 16.2.2.2, "Publish/Subscribe Messaging Style," and Section 16.3.6.3, "Consuming Messages from Topics.") Instead of receiving the messages, the client waits for messages to arrive.

7. Leave the `SynchConsumer` client running and run the `Producer` client again:

    ```
    appclient -client target/producer.jar topic 3
    ```

    Now the `SynchConsumer` client receives the messages:

    ```
    Destination type is topic
    Reading message: This is message 1 from producer
    Reading message: This is message 2 from producer
    Reading message: This is message 3 from producer
    Messages received: 3
    ```

    Because these messages were sent after the consumer was started, the client receives them.

17.2.6 Using a Message Listener for Asynchronous Message Delivery

This section describes the receiving clients in an example that uses a message listener for asynchronous message delivery. This section then explains how to compile and run the clients using GlassFish Server.

> **Note:** In the Java EE platform, message listeners can be used only in application clients, as in this example. To allow asynchronous message delivery in a web or enterprise bean application, you use a message-driven bean, shown in later examples in this chapter.

17.2.6.1 Writing the AsynchConsumer.java and TextListener.java Clients

The sending client is `Producer.java`, the same client used in Section 17.2.4, "Sending Messages," and Section 17.2.5, "Receiving Messages Synchronously."

An asynchronous consumer normally runs indefinitely. This one runs until the user types the character q or Q to stop the client.

The client, `AsynchConsumer.java`, performs the following steps.

1. Injects resources for a connection factory, queue, and topic.

2. Assigns either the queue or the topic to a destination object, based on the specified destination type.

3. In a `try-with-resources` block, creates a `JMSContext`.

4. Creates a `JMSConsumer`.

5. Creates an instance of the `TextListener` class and registers it as the message listener for the `JMSConsumer`:

   ```
   listener = new TextListener();
   consumer.setMessageListener(listener);
   ```

6. Listens for the messages sent to the destination, stopping when the user types the character q or Q (it uses a `java.io.InputStreamReader` to do this).

7. Catches and handles any exceptions. The end of the `try-with-resources` block automatically causes the `JMSContext` to be closed, thus stopping delivery of messages to the message listener.

The message listener, `TextListener.java`, follows these steps.

1. When a message arrives, the `onMessage` method is called automatically.

2. If the message is a `TextMessage`, the `onMessage` method displays its content as a string value. If the message is not a text message, it reports this fact:

```
public void onMessage(Message m) {
    try {
        if (m instanceof TextMessage) {
            System.out.println(
                    "Reading message: " + m.getBody(String.class));
```

```
        } else {
            System.out.println("Message is not a TextMessage");
        }
    } catch (JMSException | JMSRuntimeException e) {
        System.err.println("JMSException in onMessage(): "
                + e.toString());
    }
}
```

For this example, you will use the same connection factory and destinations you created in Section 17.2.2.1, "To Create Resources for the Simple Examples."

The steps assume that you have already built and packaged all the examples using NetBeans IDE or Maven.

17.2.6.2 To Run the AsynchConsumer and Producer Clients

You will need two terminal windows, as you did in Section 17.2.5, "Receiving Messages Synchronously."

1. In the terminal window where you ran the SynchConsumer client, go to the asynchconsumer example directory:

    ```
    cd tut-install/jms/simple/asynchconsumer
    ```

2. Run the AsynchConsumer client, specifying the topic destination type:

    ```
    appclient -client target/asynchconsumer.jar topic
    ```

    The client displays the following lines (along with some additional output) and then waits for messages:

    ```
    Destination type is topic
    To end program, enter Q or q, then <return>
    ```

3. In the terminal window where you ran the Producer client previously, run the client again, sending three messages:

    ```
    appclient -client target/producer.jar topic 3
    ```

    The output of the client looks like this (along with some additional output):

    ```
    Destination type is topic
    Sending message: This is message 1 from producer
    Sending message: This is message 2 from producer
    Sending message: This is message 3 from producer
    Text messages sent: 3
    ```

In the other window, the `AsynchConsumer` client displays the following (along with some additional output):

```
Destination type is topic
To end program, enter Q or q, then <return>
Reading message: This is message 1 from producer
Reading message: This is message 2 from producer
Reading message: This is message 3 from producer
Message is not a TextMessage
```

The last line appears because the client has received the non-text control message sent by the `Producer` client.

4. Enter Q or q and press **Return** to stop the `AsynchConsumer` client.

5. Now run the clients using a queue.

   In this case, as with the synchronous example, you can run the `Producer` client first, because there is no timing dependency between the sender and receiver:

   ```
   appclient -client target/producer.jar queue 3
   ```

   The output of the client looks like this:

   ```
   Destination type is queue
   Sending message: This is message 1 from producer
   Sending message: This is message 2 from producer
   Sending message: This is message 3 from producer
   Text messages sent: 3
   ```

6. In the other window, run the `AsynchConsumer` client:

   ```
   appclient -client target/asynchconsumer.jar queue
   ```

   The output of the client looks like this (along with some additional output):

   ```
   Destination type is queue
   To end program, enter Q or q, then <return>
   Reading message: This is message 1 from producer
   Reading message: This is message 2 from producer
   Reading message: This is message 3 from producer
   Message is not a TextMessage
   ```

7. Enter Q or q and press **Return** to stop the client.

17.2.7 Browsing Messages on a Queue

This section describes an example that creates a QueueBrowser object to examine messages on a queue, as described in Section 16.3.8, "JMS Queue Browsers." This section then explains how to compile, package, and run the example using GlassFish Server.

17.2.7.1 The MessageBrowser.java Client

To create a QueueBrowser for a queue, you call the JMSContext.createBrowser method with the queue as the argument. You obtain the messages in the queue as an Enumeration object. You can then iterate through the Enumeration object and display the contents of each message.

The MessageBrowser.java client performs the following steps.

1. Injects resources for a connection factory and a queue.

2. In a try-with-resources block, creates a JMSContext.

3. Creates a QueueBrowser:

```
QueueBrowser browser = context.createBrowser(queue);
```

4. Retrieves the Enumeration that contains the messages:

```
Enumeration msgs = browser.getEnumeration();
```

5. Verifies that the Enumeration contains messages, then displays the contents of the messages:

```
if ( !msgs.hasMoreElements() ) {
    System.out.println("No messages in queue");
} else {
    while (msgs.hasMoreElements()) {
        Message tempMsg = (Message)msgs.nextElement();
        System.out.println("Message: " + tempMsg);
    }
}
```

6. Catches and handles any exceptions. The end of the try-with-resources block automatically causes the JMSContext to be closed.

Dumping the message contents to standard output retrieves the message body and properties in a format that depends on the implementation of the toString method. In GlassFish Server, the message format looks something like this:

```
Text:   This is message 3 from producer
Class:             com.sun.messaging.jmq.jmsclient.TextMessageImpl
```

```
getJMSMessageID():    ID:ID:8-10.152.23.26(bf:27:4:e:e7:ec)-55645-1363100335526
getJMSTimestamp():     1129061034355
getJMSCorrelationID(): null
JMSReplyTo:            null
JMSDestination:        PhysicalQueue
getJMSDeliveryMode():  PERSISTENT
getJMSRedelivered():   false
getJMSType():          null
getJMSExpiration():    0
getJMSPriority():      4
Properties:            {JMSXDeliveryCount=0}
```

Instead of displaying the message contents this way, you can call some of the `Message` interface's getter methods to retrieve the parts of the message you want to see.

For this example, you will use the connection factory and queue you created for Section 17.2.5, "Receiving Messages Synchronously." It is assumed that you have already built and packaged all the examples.

17.2.7.2 To Run the QueueBrowser Client

To run the `MessageBrowser` example using the `appclient` command, follow these steps.

You also need the `Producer` example to send the message to the queue, and one of the consumer clients to consume the messages after you inspect them.

To run the clients, you need two terminal windows.

1. In a terminal window, go to the `producer` directory:

    ```
    cd tut-install/examples/jms/simple/producer
    ```

2. Run the `Producer` client, sending one message to the queue, along with the non-text control message:

    ```
    appclient -client target/producer.jar queue
    ```

    The output of the client looks like this (along with some additional output):

    ```
    Destination type is queue
    Sending message: This is message 1 from producer
    Text messages sent: 1
    ```

3. In another terminal window, go to the `messagebrowser` directory:

    ```
    cd tut-install/jms/simple/messagebrowser
    ```

4. Run the `MessageBrowser` client using the following command:

```
appclient -client target/messagebrowser.jar
```

The output of the client looks something like this (along with some additional output):

```
Message:
Text:    This is message 1 from producer
Class:              com.sun.messaging.jmq.jmsclient.TextMessageImpl
getJMSMessageID():  ID:9-10.152.23.26(bf:27:4:e:e7:ec)-55645-1363100335526
getJMSTimestamp():      1363100335526
getJMSCorrelationID():  null
JMSReplyTo:             null
JMSDestination:         PhysicalQueue
getJMSDeliveryMode():   PERSISTENT
getJMSRedelivered():    false
getJMSType():           null
getJMSExpiration():     0
getJMSPriority():       4
Properties:             {JMSXDeliveryCount=0}

Message:
Class:              com.sun.messaging.jmq.jmsclient.MessageImpl
getJMSMessageID():  ID:10-10.152.23.26(bf:27:4:e:e7:ec)-55645-1363100335526
getJMSTimestamp():      1363100335526
getJMSCorrelationID():  null
JMSReplyTo:             null
JMSDestination:         PhysicalQueue
getJMSDeliveryMode():   PERSISTENT
getJMSRedelivered():    false
getJMSType():           null
getJMSExpiration():     0
getJMSPriority():       4
Properties:             {JMSXDeliveryCount=0}
```

The first message is the `TextMessage`, and the second is the non-text control message.

5. Go to the `synchconsumer` directory.

6. Run the `SynchConsumer` client to consume the messages:

```
appclient -client target/synchconsumer.jar queue
```

The output of the client looks like this (along with some additional output):

```
Destination type is queue
Reading message: This is message 1 from producer
Messages received: 1
```

17.2.8 Running Multiple Consumers on the Same Destination

To illustrate further the way point-to-point and publish/subscribe messaging works, you can use the `Producer` and `SynchConsumer` examples to send messages that are then consumed by two clients running simultaneously.

1. Open three command windows. In one, go to the `producer` directory. In the other two, go to the `synchconsumer` directory.

2. In each of the `synchconsumer` windows, start running the client, receiving messages from a queue:

   ```
   appclient -client target/synchconsumer.jar queue
   ```

   Wait until you see the "Destination type is queue" message in both windows.

3. In the `producer` window, run the client, sending 20 or so messages to the queue:

   ```
   appclient -client target/producer.jar queue 20
   ```

4. Look at the output in the `synchconsumer` windows. In point-to-point messaging, each message can have only one consumer. Therefore, each of the clients receives some of the messages. One of the clients receives the non-text control message, reports the number of messages received, and exits.

5. In the window of the client that did not receive the non-text control message, enter Control-C to exit the program.

6. Next, run the `synchconsumer` clients using a topic. In each window, run the following command:

   ```
   appclient -client target/synchconsumer.jar topic
   ```

   Wait until you see the "Destination type is topic" message in both windows.

7. In the `producer` window, run the client, sending 20 or so messages to the topic:

   ```
   appclient -client target/producer.jar topic 20
   ```

8. Again, look at the output in the `synchconsumer` windows. In publish/subscribe messaging, a copy of every message is sent to each

subscription on the topic. Therefore, each of the clients receives all 20 text messages as well as the non-text control message.

17.2.9 Acknowledging Messages

JMS provides two alternative ways for a consuming client to ensure that a message is not acknowledged until the application has finished processing the message:

- Using a synchronous consumer in a JMSContext that has been configured to use the CLIENT_ACKNOWLEDGE setting

- Using a message listener for asynchronous message delivery in a JMSContext that has been configured to use the default AUTO_ACKNOWLEDGE setting

> **Note:** In the Java EE platform, CLIENT_ACKNOWLEDGE sessions can be used only in application clients, as in this example.

The clientackconsumer example demonstrates the first alternative, in which a synchronous consumer uses client acknowledgment. The asynchconsumer example described in Section 17.2.6, "Using a Message Listener for Asynchronous Message Delivery," demonstrates the second alternative.

For information about message acknowledgment, see Section 16.4.1, "Controlling Message Acknowledgment."

Table 17–3 describes four possible interactions between types of consumers and types of acknowledgment.

Table 17–3   Message Acknowledgment with Synchronous and Asynchronous Consumers

Consumer Type	Acknowledgment Type	Behavior
Synchronous	Client	Client acknowledges message after processing is complete
Asynchronous	Client	Client acknowledges message after processing is complete
Synchronous	Auto	Acknowledgment happens immediately after receive call; message cannot be redelivered if any subsequent processing steps fail
Asynchronous	Auto	Message is automatically acknowledged when onMessage method returns

The example is under the *tut-install*/examples/jms/simple/clientackconsumer directory.

The example client, ClientAckConsumer.java, creates a JMSContext that specifies client acknowledgment:

```
try (JMSContext context =
     connectionFactory.createContext(JMSContext.CLIENT_ACKNOWLEDGE);) {
   ...
```

The client uses a while loop almost identical to that used by SynchConsumer.java, with the exception that after processing each message, it calls the acknowledge method on the JMSContext:

```
context.acknowledge();
```

The example uses the following objects:

- The jms/MyQueue resource that you created for Section 17.2.5, "Receiving Messages Synchronously"

- java:comp/DefaultJMSConnectionFactory, the platform default connection factory preconfigured with GlassFish Server

17.2.9.1 To Run the ClientAckConsumer Client

1. In a terminal window, go to the following directory:

   tut-install/examples/jms/simple/producer/

2. Run the Producer client, sending some messages to the queue:

   ```
   appclient -client target/producer.jar queue 3
   ```

3. In another terminal window, go to the following directory:

   tut-install/examples/jms/simple/clientackconsumer/

4. To run the client, use the following command:

   ```
   appclient -client target/clientackconsumer.jar
   ```

   The client output looks like this (along with some additional output):

   ```
   Created client-acknowledge JMSContext
   Reading message: This is message 1 from producer
   Acknowledging TextMessage
   Reading message: This is message 2 from producer
   Acknowledging TextMessage
   Reading message: This is message 3 from producer
   ```

```
Acknowledging TextMessage
Acknowledging non-text control message
```

The client acknowledges each message explicitly after processing it, just as a JMSContext configured to use AUTO_ACKNOWLEDGE does automatically after a MessageListener returns successfully from processing a message received asynchronously.

17.3 Writing More Advanced JMS Applications

The following examples show how to use some of the more advanced features of the JMS API: durable subscriptions and transactions.

17.3.1 Using Durable Subscriptions

The durablesubscriptionexample example shows how unshared durable subscriptions work. It demonstrates that a durable subscription continues to exist and accumulate messages even when there is no active consumer on it.

The example consists of two modules, a durableconsumer application that creates a durable subscription and consumes messages, and an unsubscriber application that enables you to unsubscribe from the durable subscription after you have finished running the durableconsumer application.

For information on durable subscriptions, see Section 16.3.6.4, "Creating Durable Subscriptions."

The main client, DurableConsumer.java, is under the *tut-install*/examples/jms/durablesubscriptionexample/durableconsumer/ directory.

The example uses a connection factory, jms/DurableConnectionFactory, that has a client ID.

The DurableConsumer client creates a JMSContext using the connection factory. It then stops the JMSContext, calls createDurableConsumer to create a durable subscription and a consumer on the topic by specifying a subscription name, registers a message listener, and starts the JMSContext again. The subscription is created only if it does not already exist, so the example can be run repeatedly:

```
try (JMSContext context = durableConnectionFactory.createContext();) {
    context.stop();
    consumer = context.createDurableConsumer(topic, "MakeItLast");
    listener = new TextListener();
    consumer.setMessageListener(listener);
    context.start();
    ...
```

To send messages to the topic, you run the `producer` client.

The `unsubscriber` example contains a very simple `Unsubscriber` client, which creates a `JMSContext` on the same connection factory and then calls the `unsubscribe` method, specifying the subscription name:

```
try (JMSContext context = durableConnectionFactory.createContext();) {
    System.out.println("Unsubscribing from durable subscription");
    context.unsubscribe("MakeItLast");
} ...
```

17.3.1.1 To Create Resources for the Durable Subscription Example

1. Make sure that GlassFish Server has been started (see Section 2.2, "Starting and Stopping GlassFish Server").

2. In a terminal window, go to the `durableconsumer` example:

   ```
   cd tut-install/jms/durablesubscriptionexample/durableconsumer/
   ```

3. Create the resources using the `asadmin add-resources` command:

   ```
   asadmin add-resources src/main/setup/glassfish-resources.xml
   ```

   The command output reports the creation of a connector connection pool and a connector resource.

4. Verify the creation of the resources:

   ```
   asadmin list-jms-resources
   ```

   In addition to the resources you created for the simple examples, the command lists the new connection factory:

   ```
   jms/MyQueue
   jms/MyTopic
   jms/__defaultConnectionFactory
   jms/DurableConnectionFactory
   Command list-jms-resources executed successfully.
   ```

17.3.1.2 To Run the Durable Subscription Example

1. In a terminal window, go to the following directory:

   ```
   tut-install/examples/jms/durablesubscriptionexample/
   ```

2. Build the `durableconsumer` and `unsubscriber` examples:

   ```
   mvn install
   ```

3. Go to the `durableconsumer` directory:

```
cd durableconsumer
```

4. To run the client, enter the following command:

```
appclient -client target/durableconsumer.jar
```

The client creates the durable consumer and then waits for messages:

```
Creating consumer for topic
Starting consumer
To end program, enter Q or q, then <return>
```

5. In another terminal window, run the `Producer` client, sending some messages to the topic:

```
cd tut-install/examples/jms/simple/producer
appclient -client target/producer.jar topic 3
```

6. After the `DurableConsumer` client receives the messages, enter q or Q to exit the program. At this point, the client has behaved like any other asynchronous consumer.

7. Now, while the `DurableConsumer` client is not running, use the `Producer` client to send more messages:

```
appclient -client target/producer.jar topic 2
```

If a durable subscription did not exist, these messages would be lost, because no consumer on the topic is currently running. However, the durable subscription is still active, and it retains the messages.

8. Run the `DurableConsumer` client again. It immediately receives the messages that were sent while it was inactive:

```
Creating consumer for topic
Starting consumer
To end program, enter Q or q, then <return>
Reading message: This is message 1 from producer
Reading message: This is message 2 from producer
Message is not a TextMessage
```

9. Enter q or Q to exit the program.

17.3.1.3 To Run the unsubscriber Example

After you have finished running the `DurableConsumer` client, run the `unsubscriber` example to unsubscribe from the durable subscription.

1. In a terminal window, go to the following directory:

   tut-install/examples/jms/durablesubscriptionexample/unsubscriber/

2. To run the Unsubscriber client, enter the following command:

   ```
   appclient -client target/unsubscriber.jar
   ```

   The client reports that it is unsubscribing from the durable subscription.

17.3.2 Using Local Transactions

The transactedexample example demonstrates the use of local transactions in a JMS client application. It also demonstrates the use of the request/reply messaging pattern described in Section 16.4.3, "Creating Temporary Destinations," although it uses permanent rather than temporary destinations. The example consists of three modules, genericsupplier, retailer, and vendor, which can be found under the *tut-install*/examples/jms/transactedexample/ directory. The source code can be found in the src/main/java/javaeetutorial trees for each module. The genericsupplier and retailer modules each contain a single class, genericsupplier/GenericSupplier.java and retailer/Retailer.java, respectively. The vendor module is more complex, containing four classes: vendor/Vendor.java, vendor/VendorMessageListener.java, vendor/Order.java, and vendor/SampleUtilities.java.

The example shows how to use a queue and a topic in a single transaction as well as how to pass a JMSContext to a message listener's constructor function. The example represents a highly simplified e-commerce application in which the following actions occur.

1. A retailer (retailer/src/main/java/javaeetutorial/retailer/ Retailer.java) sends a MapMessage to a vendor order queue, ordering a quantity of computers, and waits for the vendor's reply:

   ```
   outMessage = context.createMapMessage();
   outMessage.setString("Item", "Computer(s)");
   outMessage.setInt("Quantity", quantity);
   outMessage.setJMSReplyTo(retailerConfirmQueue);
   context.createProducer().send(vendorOrderQueue, outMessage);
   System.out.println("Retailer: ordered " + quantity + " computer(s)");
   orderConfirmReceiver = context.createConsumer(retailerConfirmQueue);
   ```

2. The vendor (vendor/src/main/java/javaeetutorial/retailer/ Vendor.java) receives the retailer's order message and sends an order message to the supplier order topic in one transaction. This JMS transaction uses a single session, so you can combine a receive from a queue with a send

to a topic. Here is the code that uses the same session to create a consumer for a queue:

```
vendorOrderReceiver = session.createConsumer(vendorOrderQueue);
```

The following code receives the incoming message, sends an outgoing message, and commits the JMSContext. The message processing has been removed to keep the sequence simple:

```
inMessage = vendorOrderReceiver.receive();
// Process the incoming message and format the outgoing
// message
...
context.createProducer().send(supplierOrderTopic, orderMessage);
...
context.commit();
```

For simplicity, there are only two suppliers, one for CPUs and one for hard drives.

3. Each supplier (genericsupplier/src/main/java/javaeetutorial/retailer/ GenericSupplier.java) receives the order from the order topic, checks its inventory, and then sends the items ordered to the queue named in the order message's JMSReplyTo field. If it does not have enough of the item in stock, the supplier sends what it has. The synchronous receive from the topic and the send to the queue take place in one JMS transaction:

```
receiver = context.createConsumer(SupplierOrderTopic);
...
inMessage = receiver.receive();
if (inMessage instanceof MapMessage) {
    orderMessage = (MapMessage) inMessage;
} ...
// Process message
outMessage = context.createMapMessage();
// Add content to message
context.createProducer().send(
        (Queue) orderMessage.getJMSReplyTo(),
        outMessage);
// Display message contents
context.commit();
```

4. The vendor receives the suppliers' replies from its confirmation queue and updates the state of the order. Messages are processed by an asynchronous message listener, VendorMessageListener; this step shows the use of JMS transactions with a message listener.

```
MapMessage component = (MapMessage) message;
...
int orderNumber = component.getInt("VendorOrderNumber");
Order order = Order.getOrder(orderNumber).processSubOrder(component);
context.commit();
```

5. When all outstanding replies are processed for a given order, the vendor message listener sends a message notifying the retailer whether it can fulfill the order:

```
Queue replyQueue = (Queue) order.order.getJMSReplyTo();
MapMessage retailerConfirmMessage = context.createMapMessage();
// Format the message
context.createProducer().send(replyQueue, retailerConfirmMessage);
context.commit();
```

6. The retailer receives the message from the vendor:

```
inMessage = (MapMessage) orderConfirmReceiver.receive();
```

The retailer then places a second order for twice as many computers as in the first order, so these steps are executed twice.

Figure 17–1 illustrates these steps.

Figure 17–1   Transactions: JMS Client Example

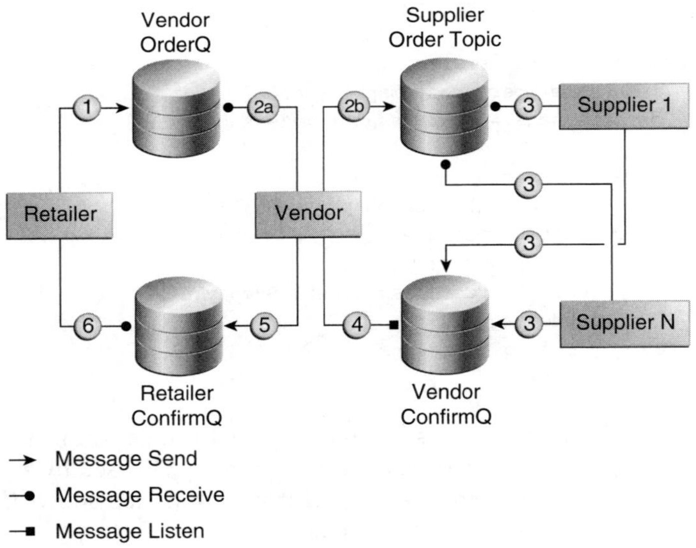

→ Message Send

• Message Receive

▪ Message Listen

All the messages use the MapMessage message type. Synchronous receives are used for all message reception except when the vendor processes the replies of the suppliers. These replies are processed asynchronously and demonstrate how to use transactions within a message listener.

At random intervals, the Vendor client throws an exception to simulate a database problem and cause a rollback.

All clients except Retailer use transacted contexts.

The example uses three queues named jms/AQueue, jms/BQueue, and jms/CQueue, and one topic named jms/OTopic.

17.3.2.1 To Create Resources for the transactedexample Example

1. Make sure that GlassFish Server has been started (see Section 2.2, "Starting and Stopping GlassFish Server").

2. In a command window, go to the genericsupplier example:

   ```
   cd tut-install/jms/transactedexample/genericsupplier
   ```

3. Create the resources using the asadmin add-resources command:

   ```
   asadmin add-resources src/main/setup/glassfish-resources.xml
   ```

4. Verify the creation of the resources:

   ```
   asadmin list-jms-resources
   ```

   In addition to the resources you created for the simple examples and the durable subscription example, the command lists the four new destinations:

   ```
   jms/MyQueue
   jms/MyTopic
   jms/AQueue
   jms/BQueue
   jms/CQueue
   jms/OTopic
   jms/__defaultConnectionFactory
   jms/DurableConnectionFactory
   Command list-jms-resources executed successfully.
   ```

17.3.2.2 To Run the transactedexample Clients

You will need four terminal windows to run the clients. Make sure that you start the clients in the correct order.

1. In a terminal window, go to the following directory:

    tut-install/examples/jms/transactedexample/

2. To build and package all the modules, enter the following command:

    ```
    mvn install
    ```

3. Go to the genericsupplier directory:

    ```
    cd genericsupplier
    ```

4. Use the following command to start the CPU supplier client:

    ```
    appclient -client target\genericsupplier.jar CPU
    ```

    After some initial output, the client reports the following:

    ```
    Starting CPU supplier
    ```

5. In a second terminal window, go to the genericsupplier directory:

    ```
    cd tut-install/examples/jms/transactedexample/genericsupplier
    ```

6. Use the following command to start the hard drive supplier client:

    ```
    appclient -client target\genericsupplier.jar HD
    ```

    After some initial output, the client reports the following:

    ```
    Starting Hard Drive supplier
    ```

7. In a third terminal window, go to the vendor directory:

    ```
    cd tut-install/examples/jms/transactedexample/vendor
    ```

8. Use the following command to start the Vendor client:

    ```
    appclient -client target\vendor.jar
    ```

    After some initial output, the client reports the following:

    ```
    Starting vendor
    ```

9. In another terminal window, go to the retailer directory:

    ```
    cd tut-install/examples/jms/transactedexample/retailer
    ```

10. Use a command like the following to run the `Retailer` client. The argument specifies the number of computers to order:

```
appclient -client target/retailer.jar 4
```

After some initial output, the `Retailer` client reports something like the following. In this case, the first order is filled, but the second is not:

```
Retailer: Quantity to be ordered is 4
Retailer: Ordered 4 computer(s)
Retailer: Order filled
Retailer: Placing another order
Retailer: Ordered 8 computer(s)
Retailer: Order not filled
```

The `Vendor` client reports something like the following, stating in this case that it is able to send all the computers in the first order, but not in the second:

```
Vendor: Retailer ordered 4 Computer(s)
Vendor: Ordered 4 CPU(s) and hard drive(s)
  Vendor: Committed transaction 1
Vendor: Completed processing for order 1
Vendor: Sent 4 computer(s)
  Vendor: committed transaction 2
Vendor: Retailer ordered 8 Computer(s)
Vendor: Ordered 8 CPU(s) and hard drive(s)
  Vendor: Committed transaction 1
Vendor: Completed processing for order 2
Vendor: Unable to send 8 computer(s)
  Vendor: Committed transaction 2
```

The CPU supplier reports something like the following. In this case, it is able to send all the CPUs for both orders:

```
CPU Supplier: Vendor ordered 4 CPU(s)
CPU Supplier: Sent 4 CPU(s)
  CPU Supplier: Committed transaction
CPU Supplier: Vendor ordered 8 CPU(s)
CPU Supplier: Sent 8 CPU(s)
  CPU Supplier: Committed transaction
```

The hard drive supplier reports something like the following. In this case, it has a shortage of hard drives for the second order:

```
Hard Drive Supplier: Vendor ordered 4 Hard Drive(s)
Hard Drive Supplier: Sent 4 Hard Drive(s)
  Hard Drive Supplier: Committed transaction
Hard Drive Supplier: Vendor ordered 8 Hard Drive(s)
```

```
Hard Drive Supplier: Sent 1 Hard Drive(s)
  Hard Drive Supplier: Committed transaction
```

11. Repeat steps 4 through 10 as many times as you wish. Occasionally, the vendor will report an exception that causes a rollback:

```
Vendor: JMSException occurred: javax.jms.JMSException: Simulated
database concurrent access exception
  Vendor: Rolled back transaction 1
```

12. After you finish running the clients, you can delete the destination resources by using the following commands:

```
asadmin delete-jms-resource jms/AQueue
asadmin delete-jms-resource jms/BQueue
asadmin delete-jms-resource jms/CQueue
asadmin delete-jms-resource jms/OTopic
```

17.4 Writing High Performance and Scalable JMS Applications

This section describes how to use the JMS API to write applications that can handle high volumes of messages robustly. These examples use both nondurable and durable shared consumers.

17.4.1 Using Shared Nondurable Subscriptions

This section describes the receiving clients in an example that shows how to use a shared consumer to distribute messages sent to a topic among different consumers. This section then explains how to compile and run the clients using GlassFish Server.

You may wish to compare this example to the results of Section 17.2.8, "Running Multiple Consumers on the Same Destination," using an unshared consumer. In that example, messages are distributed among the consumers on a queue, but each consumer on the topic receives all the messages because each consumer on the topic is using a separate topic subscription.

In this example, however, messages are distributed among multiple consumers on a topic, because all the consumers are sharing the same subscription. Each message added to the topic subscription is received by only one consumer, similarly to the way in which each message added to a queue is received by only one consumer.

A topic may have multiple subscriptions. Each message sent to the topic will be added to each topic subscription. However, if there are multiple consumers on a particular subscription, each message added to that subscription will be delivered to only one of those consumers.

17.4.1.1 Writing the Clients for the Shared Consumer Example

The sending client is `Producer.java`, the same client used in previous examples.

The receiving client is `SharedConsumer.java`. It is very similar to `AsynchConsumer.java`, except that it always uses a topic. It performs the following steps.

1. Injects resources for a connection factory and topic.

2. In a try-with-resources block, creates a `JMSContext`.

3. Creates a consumer on a shared nondurable subscription, specifying a subscription name:

   ```
   consumer = context.createSharedConsumer(topic, "SubName");
   ```

4. Creates an instance of the `TextListener` class and registers it as the message listener for the shared consumer.

5. Listens for the messages published to the destination, stopping when the user types the character q or Q.

6. Catches and handles any exceptions. The end of the try-with-resources block automatically causes the `JMSContext` to be closed.

The `TextListener.java` class is identical to the one for the `asynchconsumer` example.

For this example, you will use the default connection factory and the topic you created in Section 17.2.2.1, "To Create Resources for the Simple Examples."

17.4.1.2 To Run the SharedConsumer and Producer Clients

1. Make sure that GlassFish Server has been started (see Section 2.2, "Starting and Stopping GlassFish Server").

2. Open three command windows. In the first, go to the `simple/producer/` directory:

   ```
   cd tut-install/examples/jms/simple/producer
   ```

3. In the second and third command windows, go to the `shared/sharedconsumer/` directory:

   ```
   cd tut-install/examples/jms/shared/sharedconsumer/
   ```

4. In one of the `sharedconsumer` windows, build the example:

```
mvn install
```

5. In each of the two `sharedconsumer` windows, start running the client. You do not need to specify a `topic` argument:

```
appclient -client target/sharedconsumer.jar
```

Wait until you see the following output in both windows:

```
Waiting for messages on topic
To end program, enter Q or q, then <return>
```

6. In the `producer` window, run the client, specifying the topic and a number of messages:

```
appclient -client target/producer.jar topic 20
```

Each consumer client receives some of the messages. Only one of the clients receives the non-text message that signals the end of the message stream.

7. Enter Q or q and press **Return** to stop each client and see a report of the number of text messages received.

17.4.2 Using Shared Durable Subscriptions

The `shareddurableconsumer` client shows how to use shared durable subscriptions. It shows how shared durable subscriptions combine the advantages of durable subscriptions (the subscription remains active when the client is not) with those of shared consumers (the message load can be divided among multiple clients).

The example is much more similar to the `sharedconsumer` example than to the `DurableConsumer.java` client. It uses two classes, `SharedDurableConsumer.java` and `TextListener.java`, which can be found under the *tut-install*/examples/jms/ shared/shareddurableconsumer/ directory.

The client uses `java:comp/DefaultJMSConnectionFactory`, the connection factory that does not have a client identifier, as is recommended for shared durable subscriptions. It uses the `createSharedDurableConsumer` method with a subscription name to establish the subscription:

```
consumer = context.createSharedDurableConsumer(topic, "MakeItLast");
```

You run the example in combination with the `Producer.java` client.

17.4.2.1 To Run the SharedDurableConsumer and Producer Clients

1. Make sure that GlassFish Server has been started (see Section 2.2, "Starting and Stopping GlassFish Server").

2. In a terminal window, go to the following directory:

   tut-install/examples/jms/shared/shareddurableconsumer/

3. To compile and package the client, enter the following command:

   ```
   mvn install
   ```

4. Run the client first to establish the durable subscription:

   ```
   appclient -client target/shareddurableconsumer.jar
   ```

5. The client displays the following and pauses:

   ```
   Waiting for messages on topic
   To end program, enter Q or q, then <return>
   ```

6. In the shareddurableconsumer window, enter q or Q to exit the program. The subscription remains active, although the client is not running.

7. Open another terminal window and go to the producer example directory:

   ```
   cd tut-install/examples/jms/simple/producer
   ```

8. Run the producer example, sending a number of messages to the topic:

   ```
   appclient -client target/producer.jar topic 6
   ```

9. After the producer has sent the messages, open a third terminal window and go to the shareddurableconsumer directory.

10. Run the client in both the first and third terminal windows. Whichever client starts first will receive all the messages that were sent when there was no active subscriber:

    ```
    appclient -client target/shareddurableconsumer.jar
    ```

11. With both shareddurableconsumer clients still running, go to the producer window and send a larger number of messages to the topic:

    ```
    appclient -client target/producer.jar topic 25
    ```

    Now the messages will be shared by the two consumer clients. If you continue sending groups of messages to the topic, each client receives some of the messages. If you exit one of the clients and send more messages, the other client will receive all the messages.

17.5 Sending and Receiving Messages Using a Simple Web Application

Web applications can use the JMS API to send and receive messages, as noted in Section 16.5.3, "Using Java EE Components to Produce and to Synchronously Receive Messages." This section describes the components of a very simple web application that uses the JMS API.

This section assumes that you are familiar with the basics of JavaServer Faces technology, described in Part III, "The Web Tier," in *The Java EE 7 Tutorial, Volume 1.*

The example, websimplemessage, is under the *tut-install*/jms/examples/ directory. It uses sending and receiving Facelets pages as well as corresponding backing beans. When a user enters a message in the text field of the sending page and clicks a button, the backing bean for the page sends the message to a queue and displays it on the page. When the user goes to the receiving page and clicks another button, the backing bean for that page receives the message synchronously and displays it.

Figure 17–2   The websimplemessage Application

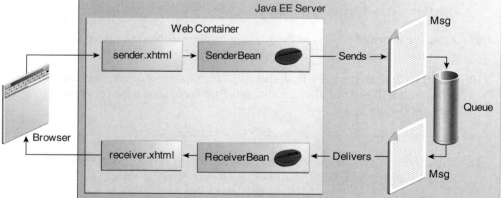

17.5.1 The websimplemessage Facelets Pages

The Facelets pages for the example are as follows.

- sender.xhtml, which provides a labeled h:InputText tag where the user enters the message, along with two command buttons. When the user clicks the Send Message button, the senderBean.sendMessage method is called to send the message to the queue and display its contents. When the user clicks the Go to Receive Page button, the receiver.xhtml page appears.

- receiver.xhtml, which also provides two command buttons. When the user clicks the Receive Message button, the receiverBean.getMessage method is called to fetch the message from the queue and display its contents. When the user clicks the Send Another Message button, the sender.xhtml page appears again.

17.5.2 The websimplemessage Managed Beans

The two managed beans for the example are as follows.

- SenderBean.java, a CDI managed bean with one property, messageText, and one business method, sendMessage. The class is annotated with @JMSDestinationDefinition to create a component-private queue:

```
@JMSDestinationDefinition(
        name = "java:comp/jms/webappQueue",
        interfaceName = "javax.jms.Queue",
        destinationName = "PhysicalWebappQueue")
@Named
@RequestScoped
public class SenderBean {
```

The sendMessage method injects a JMSContext (using the default connection factory) and the queue, creates a producer, sends the message the user typed on the Facelets page, and creates a FacesMessage to display on the Facelets page:

```
@Inject
private JMSContext context;
@Resource(lookup = "java:comp/jms/webappQueue")
private Queue queue;
private String messageText;
...
public void sendMessage() {
    try {
        String text = "Message from producer: " + messageText;
        context.createProducer().send(queue, text);
```

```
        FacesMessage facesMessage =
                new FacesMessage("Sent message: " + text);
        FacesContext.getCurrentInstance()
                .addMessage(null, facesMessage);
    } catch (Throwable t) {
        logger.log(Level.SEVERE,
                "SenderBean.sendMessage: Exception: {0}",
                t.toString());
    }
}
```

- `ReceiverBean.java`, a CDI managed bean with one business method, `getMessage`. The method injects a `JMSContext` (using the default connection factory) and the queue that was defined in `SenderBean`, creates a consumer, receives the message, and creates a `FacesMessage` to display on the Facelets page:

```
@Inject
private JMSContext context;
@Resource(lookup = "java:comp/jms/webappQueue")
private Queue queue;
...
public void getMessage() {
    try {
        JMSConsumer receiver = context.createConsumer(queue);
        String text = receiver.receiveBody(String.class);

        if (text != null) {
            FacesMessage facesMessage =
                    new FacesMessage("Reading message: " + text);
            FacesContext.getCurrentInstance().addMessage(null,
                    facesMessage);
        } else {
            FacesMessage facesMessage =
                    new FacesMessage("No message received after 1 second");
            FacesContext.getCurrentInstance().addMessage(null,
                    facesMessage);
        }
    } catch (Throwable t) {
        logger.log(Level.SEVERE,
                "ReceiverBean.getMessage: Exception: {0}",
                t.toString());
    }
}
```

17.5.3 Running the websimplemessage Example

You can use either NetBeans IDE or Maven to build, package, deploy, and run the websimplemessage application.

17.5.3.1 Creating Resources for the websimplemessage Example

This example uses an annotation-defined queue and the preconfigured default connection factory `java:comp/DefaultJMSConnectionFactory`.

17.5.3.2 To Package and Deploy websimplemessage Using NetBeans IDE

1. Make sure that GlassFish Server has been started (see Section 2.2, "Starting and Stopping GlassFish Server").

2. From the **File** menu, choose **Open Project**.

3. In the Open Project dialog box, navigate to:

   tut-install/examples/jms

4. Select the `websimplemessage` folder.

5. Click **Open Project**.

6. In the **Projects** tab, right-click the `websimplemessage` project and select **Build**.

   This command builds and deploys the project.

17.5.3.3 To Package and Deploy websimplemessage Using Maven

1. Make sure that GlassFish Server has been started (see Section 2.2, "Starting and Stopping GlassFish Server").

2. In a terminal window, go to:

   tut-install/examples/jms/websimplemessage/

3. To compile the source files and package and deploy the application, use the following command:

   ```
   mvn install
   ```

17.5.3.4 To Run the websimplemessage Example

1. In a web browser, enter the following URL:

   ```
   http://localhost:8080/websimplemessage
   ```

2. Enter a message in the text field and click **Send Message**.

If, for example, you enter "Hello, Duke", the following appears below the buttons:

```
Sent message: Message from producer: Hello, Duke
```

3. Click **Go to Receive Page**.

4. Click **Receive Message**.

The following appears below the buttons:

```
Reading message: Message from producer: Hello, Duke
```

5. Click **Send Another Message** to return to the sending page.

6. After you have finished running the application, undeploy it using either the **Services** tab of NetBeans IDE or the `mvn cargo:undeploy` command.

17.6 Receiving Messages Asynchronously Using a Message-Driven Bean

If you are writing an application to run in the Java EE application client container or on the Java SE platform, and you want to receive messages asynchronously, you need to define a class that implements the `MessageListener` interface, create a `JMSConsumer`, and call the method `setMessageListener`.

If you're writing an application to run in the Java EE web or EJB container and want it to receive messages asynchronously, you also need to need to define a class that implements the `MessageListener` interface. However, instead of creating a `JMSConsumer` and calling the method `setMessageListener`, you must configure your message listener class to be a message-driven bean. The application server will then take care of the rest.

Message-driven beans can implement any messaging type. Most commonly, however, they implement the Java Message Service (JMS) technology.

This section describes a simple message-driven bean example. Before proceeding, you should read the basic conceptual information in Section 3.3, "What Is a Message-Driven Bean?," as well as Section 16.5.4, "Using Message-Driven Beans to Receive Messages Asynchronously."

17.6.1 Overview of the simplemessage Example

The `simplemessage` application has the following components:

- `SimpleMessageClient`: An application client that sends several messages to a queue

■ `SimpleMessageBean`: A message-driven bean that asynchronously processes the messages that are sent to the queue

Figure 17–3 illustrates the structure of this application. The application client sends messages to the queue, which was created administratively using the Administration Console. The JMS provider (in this case, GlassFish Server) delivers the messages to the instances of the message-driven bean, which then processes the messages.

Figure 17–3   The simplemessage Application

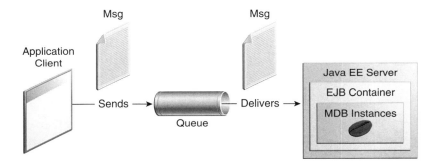

The source code for this application is in the *tut-install*/examples/jms/simplemessage/ directory.

17.6.2 The simplemessage Application Client

The `SimpleMessageClient` sends messages to the queue that the `SimpleMessageBean` listens to. The client starts by injecting the connection factory and queue resources:

```
@Resource(lookup = "java:comp/DefaultJMSConnectionFactory")
private static ConnectionFactory connectionFactory;

@Resource(lookup = "jms/MyQueue")
private static Queue queue;
```

Next, the client creates the `JMSContext` in a `try`-with-resources block:

```
String text;
final int NUM_MSGS = 3;

try (JMSContext context = connectionFactory.createContext();) {
```

Finally, the client sends several text messages to the queue:

```
for (int i = 0; i < NUM_MSGS; i++) {
    text = "This is message " + (i + 1);
    System.out.println("Sending message: " + text);
    context.createProducer().send(queue, text);
}
```

17.6.3 The simplemessage Message-Driven Bean Class

The code for the `SimpleMessageBean` class illustrates the requirements of a message-driven bean class described in Section 16.5.4, "Using Message-Driven Beans to Receive Messages Asynchronously."

The first few lines of the `SimpleMessageBean` class use the `@MessageDriven` annotation's `activationConfig` attribute to specify configuration properties:

```
@MessageDriven(activationConfig = {
    @ActivationConfigProperty(propertyName = "destinationLookup",
            propertyValue = "jms/MyQueue"),
    @ActivationConfigProperty(propertyName = "destinationType",
            propertyValue = "javax.jms.Queue")
})
```

See Table 16–3 on page 293 for a list of the available properties.

See Section 17.7, "Sending Messages from a Session Bean to an MDB," for examples of the `subscriptionDurability`, `clientId`, `subscriptionName`, and `messageSelector` properties.

17.6.3.1 The onMessage Method

When the queue receives a message, the EJB container invokes the message listener method or methods. For a bean that uses JMS, this is the `onMessage` method of the `MessageListener` interface.

In the `SimpleMessageBean` class, the `onMessage` method casts the incoming message to a `TextMessage` and displays the text:

```
public void onMessage(Message inMessage) {

    try {
        if (inMessage instanceof TextMessage) {
            logger.log(Level.INFO,
                    "MESSAGE BEAN: Message received: {0}",
                    inMessage.getBody(String.class));
        } else {
            logger.log(Level.WARNING,
```

```
                              "Message of wrong type: {0}",
                              inMessage.getClass().getName());
            }
        } catch (JMSException e) {
            logger.log(Level.SEVERE,
                    "SimpleMessageBean.onMessage: JMSException: {0}",
                    e.toString());
            mdc.setRollbackOnly();
        }
    }
}
```

17.6.4 Running the simplemessage Example

You can use either NetBeans IDE or Maven to build, deploy, and run the
simplemessage example.

17.6.4.1 Creating Resources for the simplemessage Example

This example uses the queue named jms/MyQueue and the preconfigured default
connection factory java:comp/DefaultJMSConnectionFactory.

If you have run the simple JMS examples in Section 17.2, "Writing Simple JMS
Applications," and have not deleted the resources, you already have the queue.
Otherwise, follow the instructions in Section 17.2.2.1, "To Create Resources for the
Simple Examples," to create it.

For more information on creating JMS resources, see Section 17.2.2, "Creating JMS
Administered Objects."

17.6.4.2 To Run the simplemessage Example Using NetBeans IDE

1. Make sure that GlassFish Server has been started (see Section 2.2, "Starting
   and Stopping GlassFish Server").

2. From the **File** menu, choose **Open Project**.

3. In the Open Project dialog box, navigate to:

   tut-install/examples/jms/simplemessage

4. Select the simplemessage folder.

5. Select the **Open Required Projects** check box and click **Open Project**.

6. In the **Projects** tab, right-click the simplemessage project and select **Build**. (If
   NetBeans IDE suggests that you run a priming build, click the box to do so.)

   This command packages the application client and the message-driven bean,
   then creates a file named simplemessage.ear in the

`simplemessage-ear/target/` directory. It then deploys the `simplemessage-ear` module, retrieves the client stubs, and runs the application client.

The output in the output window looks like this (preceded by application client container output):

```
Sending message: This is message 1
Sending message: This is message 2
Sending message: This is message 3
To see if the bean received the messages,
 check <install_dir>/domains/domain1/logs/server.log.
```

In the server log file, lines similar to the following appear:

```
MESSAGE BEAN: Message received: This is message 1
MESSAGE BEAN: Message received: This is message 2
MESSAGE BEAN: Message received: This is message 3
```

The received messages may appear in a different order from the order in which they were sent.

7. After you have finished running the application, undeploy it using the **Services** tab.

17.6.4.3 To Run the simplemessage Example Using Maven

1. Make sure that GlassFish Server has been started (see Section 2.2, "Starting and Stopping GlassFish Server").

2. In a terminal window, go to:

   `tut-install/examples/jms/simplemessage/`

3. To compile the source files and package the application, use the following command:

   ```
   mvn install
   ```

   This target packages the application client and the message-driven bean, then creates a file named `simplemessage.ear` in the `simplemessage-ear/target/` directory. It then deploys the `simplemessage-ear` module, retrieves the client stubs, and runs the application client.

   The output in the terminal window looks like this (preceded by application client container output):

   ```
   Sending message: This is message 1
   Sending message: This is message 2
   ```

```
Sending message: This is message 3
To see if the bean received the messages,
 check <install_dir>/domains/domain1/logs/server.log.
```

In the server log file, lines similar to the following appear:

```
MESSAGE BEAN: Message received: This is message 1
MESSAGE BEAN: Message received: This is message 2
MESSAGE BEAN: Message received: This is message 3
```

The received messages may appear in a different order from the order in which they were sent.

4. After you have finished running the application, undeploy it using the mvn cargo:undeploy command.

17.7 Sending Messages from a Session Bean to an MDB

This section explains how to write, compile, package, deploy, and run an application that uses the JMS API in conjunction with a session bean. The application contains the following components:

- An application client that invokes a session bean

- A session bean that publishes several messages to a topic

- A message-driven bean that receives and processes the messages using a durable topic subscription and a message selector

You will find the source files for this section in the *tut-install*/examples/jms/ clientsessionmdb/ directory. Path names in this section are relative to this directory.

17.7.1 Writing the Application Components for the clientsessionmdb Example

This application demonstrates how to send messages from an enterprise bean (in this case, a session bean) rather than from an application client, as in the example in Section 17.6, "Receiving Messages Asynchronously Using a Message-Driven Bean." Figure 17–4 illustrates the structure of this application. Sending messages from an enterprise bean is very similar to sending messages from a managed bean, which was shown in Section 17.5, "Sending and Receiving Messages Using a Simple Web Application."

Figure 17–4   An Enterprise Bean Application: Client to Session Bean to Message-Driven Bean

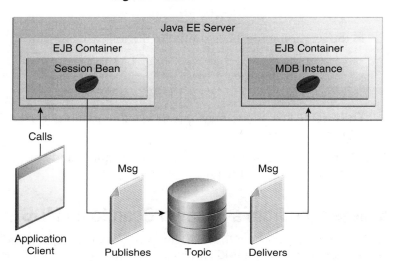

The Publisher enterprise bean in this example is the enterprise-application equivalent of a wire-service news feed that categorizes news events into six news categories. The message-driven bean could represent a newsroom, where the sports desk, for example, would set up a subscription for all news events pertaining to sports.

The application client in the example injects the Publisher enterprise bean's remote home interface and then calls the bean's business method. The enterprise bean creates 18 text messages. For each message, it sets a String property randomly to one of six values representing the news categories and then publishes the message to a topic. The message-driven bean uses a message selector for the property to limit which of the published messages will be delivered to it.

17.7.1.1 Coding the Application Client: MyAppClient.java

The application client, MyAppClient.java, found under clientsessionmdb-app-client, performs no JMS API operations and so is simpler than the client in Section 17.6, "Receiving Messages Asynchronously Using a Message-Driven Bean." The client uses dependency injection to obtain the Publisher enterprise bean's business interface:

```
@EJB(name="PublisherRemote")
private static PublisherRemote publisher;
```

The client then calls the bean's business method twice.

17.7.1.2 Coding the Publisher Session Bean

The Publisher bean is a stateless session bean that has one business method. The Publisher bean uses a remote interface rather than a local interface because it is accessed from the application client.

The remote interface, `PublisherRemote.java`, found under `clientsessionmdb-ejb`, declares a single business method, `publishNews`.

The bean class, `PublisherBean.java`, also found under `clientsessionmdb-ejb`, implements the `publishNews` method and its helper method `chooseType`. The bean class injects `SessionContext` and `Topic` resources (the topic is defined in the message-driven bean). It then injects a `JMSContext`, which uses the preconfigured default connection factory unless you specify otherwise. The bean class begins as follows:

```
@Stateless
@Remote({
    PublisherRemote.class
})
public class PublisherBean implements PublisherRemote {

    @Resource
    private SessionContext sc;
    @Resource(lookup = "java:module/jms/newsTopic")
    private Topic topic;
    @Inject
    private JMSContext context;
    ...
```

The business method `publishNews` creates a `JMSProducer` and publishes the messages.

17.7.1.3 Coding the Message-Driven Bean: MessageBean.java

The message-driven bean class, `MessageBean.java`, found under `clientsessionmdb-ejb`, is almost identical to the one in Section 17.6, "Receiving Messages Asynchronously Using a Message-Driven Bean." However, the `@MessageDriven` annotation is different, because instead of a queue, the bean is using a topic, a durable subscription, and a message selector. The bean defines a topic for the use of the application; the definition uses the `java:module` scope because both the session bean and the message-driven bean are in the same module. Because the destination is defined in the message-driven bean, the `@MessageDriven` annotation uses the `destinationLookup` activation config property. (See Section 16.5.1, "Creating Resources for Java EE Applications," for more information.) The annotation also sets the activation config properties `messageSelector`, `subscriptionDurability`, `clientId`, and `subscriptionName`, as follows:

```
@JMSDestinationDefinition(
        name = "java:module/jms/newsTopic",
        interfaceName = "javax.jms.Topic",
        destinationName = "PhysicalNewsTopic")
@MessageDriven(activationConfig = {
    @ActivationConfigProperty(propertyName = "destinationLookup",
            propertyValue = "java:module/jms/newsTopic"),
    @ActivationConfigProperty(propertyName = "destinationType",
            propertyValue = "javax.jms.Topic"),
    @ActivationConfigProperty(propertyName = "messageSelector",
            propertyValue = "NewsType = 'Sports' OR NewsType = 'Opinion'"),
    @ActivationConfigProperty(propertyName = "subscriptionDurability",
            propertyValue = "Durable"),
    @ActivationConfigProperty(propertyName = "clientId",
            propertyValue = "MyID"),
    @ActivationConfigProperty(propertyName = "subscriptionName",
            propertyValue = "MySub")
})
```

The topic is the one defined in the `PublisherBean`. The message selector in this case represents both the sports and opinion desks, just to demonstrate the syntax of message selectors.

The JMS resource adapter uses these properties to create a connection factory for the message-driven bean that allows the bean to use a durable subscription.

17.7.2 Running the clientsessionmdb Example

You can use either NetBeans IDE or Maven to build, deploy, and run the `simplemessage` example.

This example uses an annotation-defined topic and the preconfigured default connection factory `java:comp/DefaultJMSConnectionFactory`, so you do not have to create resources for it.

17.7.2.1 To Run clientsessionmdb Using NetBeans IDE

1. Make sure that GlassFish Server has been started (see Section 2.2, "Starting and Stopping GlassFish Server").

2. From the **File** menu, choose **Open Project**.

3. In the Open Project dialog box, navigate to:

   `tut-install/examples/jms/clientsessionmdb`

4. Select the `clientsessionmdb` folder.

5. Select the **Open Required Projects** check box and click **Open Project**.

6. In the **Projects** tab, right-click the `clientsessionmdb` project and select **Build**. (If NetBeans IDE suggests that you run a priming build, click the box to do so.)

   This command creates the following:

   ■ An application client JAR file that contains the client class file and the session bean's remote interface, along with a manifest file that specifies the main class and places the EJB JAR file in its classpath

   ■ An EJB JAR file that contains both the session bean and the message-driven bean

   ■ An application EAR file that contains the two JAR files

   The `clientsessionmdb.ear` file is created in the `clientsessionmdb-ear/target/` directory.

   The command then deploys the EAR file, retrieves the client stubs, and runs the client.

   The client displays these lines:

   ```
   To view the bean output,
    check <install_dir>/domains/domain1/logs/server.log.
   ```

   The output from the enterprise beans appears in the server log file. The Publisher session bean sends two sets of 18 messages numbered 0 through 17. Because of the message selector, the message-driven bean receives only the messages whose `NewsType` property is `Sports` or `Opinion`.

7. Use the **Services** tab to undeploy the application after you have finished running it.

17.7.2.2 To Run clientsessionmdb Using Maven

1. Make sure that GlassFish Server has been started (see Section 2.2, "Starting and Stopping GlassFish Server").

2. In a terminal window, go to:

   `tut-install/examples/jms/clientsessionmdb/`

3. To compile the source files and package, deploy, and run the application, enter the following command:

```
mvn install
```

This command creates the following:

- An application client JAR file that contains the client class file and the session bean's remote interface, along with a manifest file that specifies the main class and places the EJB JAR file in its classpath

- An EJB JAR file that contains both the session bean and the message-driven bean

- An application EAR file that contains the two JAR files

The clientsessionmdb.ear file is created in the clientsessionmdb-ear/ target/ directory.

The command then deploys the EAR file, retrieves the client stubs, and runs the client.

The client displays these lines:

```
To view the bean output,
 check <install_dir>/domains/domain1/logs/server.log.
```

The output from the enterprise beans appears in the server log file. The Publisher session bean sends two sets of 18 messages numbered 0 through 17. Because of the message selector, the message-driven bean receives only the messages whose NewsType property is Sports or Opinion.

4. Undeploy the application after you have finished running it:

```
mvn cargo:undeploy
```

17.8 Using an Entity to Join Messages from Two MDBs

This section explains how to write, compile, package, deploy, and run an application that uses the JMS API with an entity. The application uses the following components:

- An application client that both sends and receives messages

- Two message-driven beans

- An entity class

You will find the source files for this section in the *tut-install*/examples/jms/ clientmdbentity/ directory. Path names in this section are relative to this directory.

17.8.1 Overview of the clientmdbentity Example Application

This application simulates, in a simplified way, the work flow of a company's human resources (HR) department when it processes a new hire. This application also demonstrates how to use the Java EE platform to accomplish a task that many JMS applications need to perform.

A messaging client must often wait for several messages from various sources. It then uses the information in all these messages to assemble a message that it then sends to another destination. The common term for this design pattern (which is not specific to JMS) is **joining messages**. Such a task must be transactional, with all the receives and the send as a single transaction. If not all the messages are received successfully, the transaction can be rolled back. For an application client example that illustrates this task, see Section 17.3.2, "Using Local Transactions."

A message-driven bean can process only one message at a time in a transaction. To provide the ability to join messages, an application can have the message-driven bean store the interim information in a Java Persistence API entity. The entity can then determine whether all the information has been received; when it has, the entity can report this back to one of the message-driven beans, which then creates and sends the message to the other destination. After it has completed its task, the entity can be removed.

The basic steps of the application are as follows.

1. The HR department's application client generates an employee ID for each new hire and then publishes a message (M1) containing the new hire's name, employee ID, and position. It publishes the message to a topic because the message needs to be consumed by two message-driven beans. The client then creates a temporary queue, ReplyQueue, with a message listener that waits for a reply to the message. (See Section 16.4.3, "Creating Temporary Destinations," for more information.)

2. Two message-driven beans process each message: One bean, OfficeMDB, assigns the new hire's office number, and the other bean, EquipmentMDB, assigns the new hire's equipment. The first bean to process the message creates and persists an entity named SetupOffice, then calls a business method of the entity to store the information it has generated. The second bean locates the existing entity and calls another business method to add its information.

3. When both the office and the equipment have been assigned, the entity business method returns a value of true to the message-driven bean that called the method. The message-driven bean then sends to the reply queue a message (M2) describing the assignments. Then it removes the entity. The application client's message listener retrieves the information.

Figure 17–5 illustrates the structure of this application. Of course, an actual HR application would have more components; other beans could set up payroll and benefits records, schedule orientation, and so on.

Figure 17–5 assumes that OfficeMDB is the first message-driven bean to consume the message from the client. OfficeMDB then creates and persists the SetupOffice entity and stores the office information. EquipmentMDB then finds the entity, stores the equipment information, and learns that the entity has completed its work. EquipmentMDB then sends the message to the reply queue and removes the entity.

Figure 17–5   An Enterprise Bean Application: Client to Message-Driven Beans to Entity

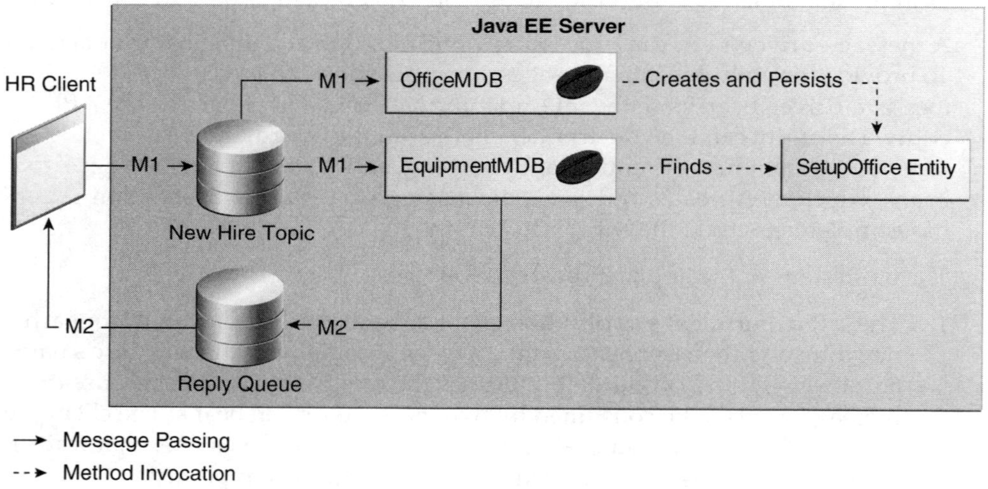

→ Message Passing
--▸ Method Invocation

17.8.2 Writing the Application Components for the clientmdbentity Example

Writing the components of the application involves coding the application client, the message-driven beans, and the entity class.

17.8.2.1 Coding the Application Client: HumanResourceClient.java

The application client, `HumanResourceClient.java`, found under `clientmdbentity-app-client`, performs the following steps:

1. Defines a topic for the application, using the `java:app` namespace because the topic is used in both the application client and the EJB module

2. Injects `ConnectionFactory` and `Topic` resources

3. Creates a `TemporaryQueue` to receive notification of processing that occurs, based on new-hire events it has published

4. Creates a `JMSConsumer` for the `TemporaryQueue`, sets the `JMSConsumer`'s message listener, and starts the connection

5. Creates a `MapMessage`

6. Creates five new employees with randomly generated names, positions, and ID numbers (in sequence) and publishes five messages containing this information

The message listener, `HRListener`, waits for messages that contain the assigned office and equipment for each employee. When a message arrives, the message listener displays the information received and determines whether all five messages have arrived. When they have, the message listener notifies the `main` method, which then exits.

17.8.2.2 Coding the Message-Driven Beans for the clientmdbentity Example

This example uses two message-driven beans, both under `clientmdbentity-ejb`:

- `EquipmentMDB.java`
- `OfficeMDB.java`

The beans take the following steps.

1. They inject a `MessageDrivenContext` resource, an `EntityManager`, and a `JMSContext`.

2. The `onMessage` method retrieves the information in the message. The `EquipmentMDB`'s `onMessage` method chooses equipment, based on the new hire's position; the `OfficeMDB`'s `onMessage` method randomly generates an office number.

3. After a slight delay to simulate real world processing hitches, the `onMessage` method calls a helper method, `compose`.

4. The `compose` method takes the following steps.

    a. It either creates and persists the `SetupOffice` entity or finds it by primary key.

    b. It uses the entity to store the equipment or the office information in the database, calling either the `doEquipmentList` or the `doOfficeNumber` business method.

    c. If the business method returns `true`, meaning that all of the information has been stored, it retrieves the reply destination information from the message, creates a `JMSProducer`, and sends a reply message that contains the information stored in the entity.

    d. It removes the entity.

17.8.2.3 Coding the Entity Class for the clientmdbentity Example

The `SetupOffice.java` class, also under `clientmdbentity-ejb`, is an entity class. The entity and the message-driven beans are packaged together in an EJB JAR file. The entity class is declared as follows:

```
@Entity
public class SetupOffice implements Serializable {
```

The class contains a no-argument constructor and a constructor that takes two arguments, the employee ID and name. It also contains getter and setter methods for the employee ID, name, office number, and equipment list. The getter method for the employee ID has the `@Id` annotation to indicate that this field is the primary key:

```
@Id
public String getEmployeeId() {
    return id;
}
```

The class also implements the two business methods, `doEquipmentList` and `doOfficeNumber`, and their helper method, `checkIfSetupComplete`.

The message-driven beans call the business methods and the getter methods.

The `persistence.xml` file for the entity specifies the most basic settings:

```
<?xml version="1.0" encoding="UTF-8"?>
<persistence version="2.1"
             xmlns="http://xmlns.jcp.org/xml/ns/persistence"
             xmlns:xsi="http://www.w3.org/2001/XMLSchema-instance"
             xsi:schemaLocation="http://xmlns.jcp.org/xml/ns/persistence
                http://xmlns.jcp.org/xml/ns/persistence/persistence_2_1.xsd">
```

```
<persistence-unit name="clientmdbentity-ejbPU" transaction-type="JTA">
  <provider>org.eclipse.persistence.jpa.PersistenceProvider</provider>
  <jta-data-source>java:comp/DefaultDataSource</jta-data-source>
  <properties>
    <property name="eclipselink.ddl-generation"
            value="drop-and-create-tables"/>
  </properties>
</persistence-unit>
</persistence>
```

17.8.3 Running the clientmdbentity Example

You can use either NetBeans IDE or Maven to build, deploy, and run the `clientmdbentity` example.

Because the example defines its own application-private topic and uses the preconfigured default connection factory `java:comp/DefaultJMSConnectionFactory` and the preconfigured default JDBC resource `java:comp/DefaultDataSource`, you do not need to create resources for it.

17.8.3.1 To Run clientmdbentity Using NetBeans IDE

1. Make sure that GlassFish Server has been started (see Section 2.2, "Starting and Stopping GlassFish Server"), as well as the database server (see Section 2.4, "Starting and Stopping the Java DB Server").

2. From the **File** menu, choose **Open Project**.

3. In the Open Project dialog box, navigate to:

   tut-install/examples/jms/clientmdbentity

4. Select the `clientmdbentity` folder.

5. Select the **Open Required Projects** check box and click **Open Project**.

6. In the **Projects** tab, right-click the `clientmdbentity` project and select **Build**.

   This command creates the following:

   - An application client JAR file that contains the client class and listener class files, along with a manifest file that specifies the main class

   - An EJB JAR file that contains the message-driven beans and the entity class, along with the `persistence.xml` file

   - An application EAR file that contains the two JAR files along with an `application.xml` file

The `clientmdbentity.ear` file is created in the `clientmdbentity-ear/target/` directory.

The command then deploys the EAR file, retrieves the client stubs, and runs the application client.

17.8.3.2 To Run clientmdbentity Using Maven

1. Make sure that GlassFish Server has been started (see Section 2.2, "Starting and Stopping GlassFish Server"), as well as the database server (see Section 2.4, "Starting and Stopping the Java DB Server").

2. In a terminal window, go to:

   tut-install/examples/jms/clientmdbentity/

3. To compile the source files and package, deploy, and run the application, enter the following command:

   ```
   mvn install
   ```

   This command creates the following:

   - An application client JAR file that contains the client class and listener class files, along with a manifest file that specifies the main class

   - An EJB JAR file that contains the message-driven beans and the entity class, along with the `persistence.xml` file

   - An application EAR file that contains the two JAR files along with an `application.xml` file

   The command then deploys the application, retrieves the client stubs, and runs the application client.

17.8.3.3 Viewing the Application Output

The output in the NetBeans IDE output window or in the terminal window looks something like this (preceded by application client container output and Maven output):

```
SENDER: Setting hire ID to 50, name Bill Tudor, position Programmer
SENDER: Setting hire ID to 51, name Carol Jones, position Senior Programmer
SENDER: Setting hire ID to 52, name Mark Wilson, position Manager
SENDER: Setting hire ID to 53, name Polly Wren, position Senior Programmer
SENDER: Setting hire ID to 54, name Joe Lawrence, position Director
Waiting for 5 message(s)
```

```
New hire event processed:
  Employee ID: 52
  Name: Mark Wilson
  Equipment: Tablet
  Office number: 294
Waiting for 4 message(s)
New hire event processed:
  Employee ID: 53
  Name: Polly Wren
  Equipment: Laptop
  Office number: 186
Waiting for 3 message(s)
New hire event processed:
  Employee ID: 54
  Name: Joe Lawrence
  Equipment: Mobile Phone
  Office number: 135
Waiting for 2 message(s)
New hire event processed:
  Employee ID: 50
  Name: Bill Tudor
  Equipment: Desktop System
  Office number: 200
Waiting for 1 message(s)
New hire event processed:
  Employee ID: 51
  Name: Carol Jones
  Equipment: Laptop
  Office number: 262
```

The output from the message-driven beans and the entity class appears in the server log.

For each employee, the application first creates the entity and then finds it. You may see runtime errors in the server log, and transaction rollbacks may occur. The errors occur if both of the message-driven beans discover at the same time that the entity does not yet exist, so they both try to create it. The first attempt succeeds, but the second fails because the bean already exists. After the rollback, the second message-driven bean tries again and succeeds in finding the entity. Container-managed transactions allow the application to run correctly, in spite of these errors, with no special programming.

To undeploy the application after you have finished running it, use the **Services** tab or issue the `mvn cargo:undeploy` command.

17.9 Using NetBeans IDE to Create JMS Resources

When you write your own JMS applications, you will need to create resources for them. This section explains how to use NetBeans IDE to create `src/main/setup/ glassfish-resources.xml` files similar to those used in the examples in this chapter. It also explains how to use NetBeans IDE to delete the resources.

You can also create, list, and delete JMS resources using the Administration Console or the `asadmin create-jms-resource`, `asadmin list-jms-resources`, and `asadmin delete-jms-resources` commands. For information, consult the GlassFish Server documentation or enter `asadmin help` *command-name*.

17.9.1 To Create JMS Resources Using NetBeans IDE

Follow these steps to create a JMS resource in GlassFish Server using NetBeans IDE. Repeat these steps for each resource you need.

1. Right-click the project for which you want to create resources and select **New**, then select **Other**.

2. In the New File wizard, under **Categories**, select **GlassFish**.

3. Under **File Types**, select **JMS Resource**.

4. On the General Attributes - JMS Resource page, in the **JNDI Name** field, enter the name of the resource.

   By convention, JMS resource names begin with `jms/`.

5. Select the option for the resource type.

   Normally, this is either `javax.jms.Queue`, `javax.jms.Topic`, or `javax.jms.ConnectionFactory`.

6. Click **Next**.

7. On the JMS Properties page, for a queue or topic, enter a name for a physical queue in the **Value** field for the **Name** property.

   You can enter any value for this required field.

   Connection factories have no required properties. In a few situations, you may need to specify a property.

8. Click **Finish**.

   A file named `glassfish-resources.xml` is created in your Maven project, in a directory named `src/main/setup/`. In the **Projects** tab, you can find it under the **Other Sources** node. You will need to run the `asadmin add-resources` command to create the resources in GlassFish Server.

17.9.2 To Delete JMS Resources Using NetBeans IDE

1. In the **Services** tab, expand the **Servers** node, then expand the GlassFish Server node.

2. Expand the **Resources** node, then expand the **Connector Resources** node.

3. Expand the **Admin Object Resources** node.

4. Right-click any destination you want to remove and select **Unregister**.

5. Expand the **Connector Connection Pools** node.

6. Right-click the connection pool that corresponds to the connection factory you removed and select **Unregister**.

   When you remove a connector connection pool, the associated connector resource is also deleted. This action removes the connection factory.

Part V
Security

Part V explores security concepts and examples. This part contains the following chapters:

- Chapter 18, "Introduction to Security in the Java EE Platform"
- Chapter 19, "Getting Started Securing Web Applications"
- Chapter 20, "Getting Started Securing Enterprise Applications"
- Chapter 21, "Java EE Security: Advanced Topics"

18

Introduction to Security in the Java EE Platform

This chapter introduces basic security concepts and security mechanisms. More information on these concepts and mechanisms can be found in the chapter on security in the Java EE 7 specification.

Other chapters in this Part discuss security requirements in web tier and enterprise tier applications.

- Chapter 19, "Getting Started Securing Web Applications," explains how to add security to web components, such as servlets.

- Chapter 20, "Getting Started Securing Enterprise Applications," explains how to add security to Java EE components, such as enterprise beans and application clients.

The following topics are addressed here:

- Overview of Java EE Security

- Security Mechanisms

- Securing Containers

- Securing GlassFish Server

- Working with Realms, Users, Groups, and Roles

- Establishing a Secure Connection Using SSL

- Further Information about Security

18.1 Overview of Java EE Security

Every enterprise that has either sensitive resources that can be accessed by many users or resources that traverse unprotected, open networks, such as the Internet, needs to be protected.

Enterprise tier and web tier applications are made up of components that are deployed into various containers. These components are combined to build a multitier enterprise application. Security for components is provided by their containers. A container provides two kinds of security: declarative and programmatic.

- **Declarative security** expresses an application component's security requirements by using either deployment descriptors or annotations.

  A deployment descriptor is an XML file that is external to the application and that expresses an application's security structure, including security roles, access control, and authentication requirements. For more information about deployment descriptors, read Section 18.3.2, "Using Deployment Descriptors for Declarative Security."

  Annotations, also called metadata, are used to specify information about security within a class file. When the application is deployed, this information can be either used by or overridden by the application deployment descriptor. Annotations save you from having to write declarative information inside XML descriptors. Instead, you simply put annotations on the code, and the required information gets generated. For this tutorial, annotations are used for securing applications wherever possible. For more information about annotations, see Section 18.3.1, "Using Annotations to Specify Security Information."

- **Programmatic security** is embedded in an application and is used to make security decisions. Programmatic security is useful when declarative security alone is not sufficient to express the security model of an application. For more information about programmatic security, read Section 18.3.3, "Using Programmatic Security."

18.1.1 A Simple Application Security Walkthrough

The security behavior of a Java EE environment may be better understood by examining what happens in a simple application with a web client, a user interface, and enterprise bean business logic.

In the following example, which is taken from the Java EE 7 Specification, the web client relies on the web server to act as its authentication proxy by collecting user authentication data from the client and using it to establish an authenticated session.

18.1.1.1 Step 1: Initial Request

In the first step of this example, the web client requests the main application URL. This action is shown in Figure 18–1.

Figure 18–1   Initial Request

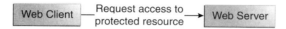

Since the client has not yet authenticated itself to the application environment, the server responsible for delivering the web portion of the application, hereafter referred to as the *web server*, detects this and invokes the appropriate authentication mechanism for this resource. For more information on these mechanisms, see Section 18.2, "Security Mechanisms."

18.1.1.2 Step 2: Initial Authentication

The web server returns a form that the web client uses to collect authentication data, such as user name and password, from the user. The web client forwards the authentication data to the web server, where it is validated by the web server, as shown in Figure 18–2. The validation mechanism may be local to a server or may leverage the underlying security services. On the basis of the validation, the web server sets a credential for the user.

Figure 18–2   Initial Authentication

18.1.1.3 Step 3: URL Authorization

The credential is used for future determinations of whether the user is authorized to access restricted resources it may request. The web server consults the security policy associated with the web resource to determine the security roles that are permitted access to the resource. The security policy is derived from annotations or from the deployment descriptor. The web container then tests the user's credential against each role to determine whether it can map the user to the role. Figure 18–3 shows this process.

Figure 18–3   URL Authorization

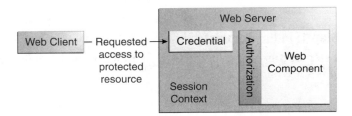

The web server's evaluation stops with an "is authorized" outcome when the web server is able to map the user to a role. A "not authorized" outcome is reached if the web server is unable to map the user to any of the permitted roles.

18.1.1.4 Step 4: Fulfilling the Original Request

If the user is authorized, the web server returns the result of the original URL request, as shown in Figure 18–4.

Figure 18–4   Fulfilling the Original Request

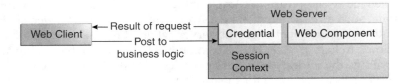

In our example, the response URL of a web page is returned, enabling the user to post form data that needs to be handled by the business-logic component of the application. See Chapter 19, "Getting Started Securing Web Applications," for more information on protecting web applications.

18.1.1.5 Step 5: Invoking Enterprise Bean Business Methods

The web page performs the remote method call to the enterprise bean, using the user's credential to establish a secure association between the web page and the enterprise bean, as shown in Figure 18–5. The association is implemented as two related security contexts: one in the web server and one in the EJB container.

Figure 18–5   Invoking an Enterprise Bean Business Method

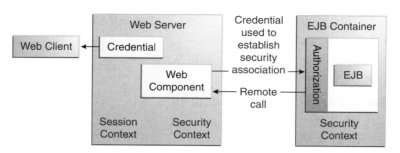

The EJB container is responsible for enforcing access control on the enterprise bean method. The container consults the security policy associated with the enterprise bean to determine the security roles that are permitted access to the method. The security policy is derived from annotations or from the deployment descriptor. For each role, the EJB container determines whether it can map the caller to the role by using the security context associated with the call.

The container's evaluation stops with an "is authorized" outcome when the container is able to map the caller's credential to a role. A "not authorized" outcome is reached if the container is unable to map the caller to any of the permitted roles. A "not authorized" result causes an exception to be thrown by the container and propagated back to the calling web page.

If the call is authorized, the container dispatches control to the enterprise bean method. The result of the bean's execution of the call is returned to the web page and ultimately to the user by the web server and the web client.

18.1.2 Features of a Security Mechanism

A properly implemented security mechanism will provide the following functionality:

- Prevent unauthorized access to application functions and business or personal data (authentication)

- Hold system users accountable for operations they perform (non-repudiation)

- Protect a system from service interruptions and other breaches that affect quality of service

Ideally, properly implemented security mechanisms will also be

- Easy to administer
- Transparent to system users
- Interoperable across application and enterprise boundaries

18.1.3 Characteristics of Application Security

Java EE applications consist of components that can contain both protected and unprotected resources. Often, you need to protect resources to ensure that only authorized users have access. Authorization provides controlled access to protected resources. Authorization is based on identification and authentication. **Identification** is a process that enables recognition of an entity by a system, and authentication is a process that verifies the identity of a user, device, or other entity in a computer system, usually as a prerequisite to allowing access to resources in a system.

Authorization and authentication are not required for an entity to access unprotected resources. Accessing a resource without authentication is referred to as unauthenticated, or anonymous, access.

The characteristics of application security that, when properly addressed, help to minimize the security threats faced by an enterprise include the following.

- **Authentication**: The means by which communicating entities, such as client and server, prove to each other that they are acting on behalf of specific identities that are authorized for access. This ensures that users are who they say they are.

- **Authorization**, or **access control**: The means by which interactions with resources are limited to collections of users or programs for the purpose of enforcing integrity, confidentiality, or availability constraints. This ensures that users have permission to perform operations or access data.

- **Data integrity**: The means used to prove that information has not been modified by a third party, an entity other than the source of the information. For example, a recipient of data sent over an open network must be able to detect and discard messages that were modified after they were sent. This ensures that only authorized users can modify data.

- **Confidentiality**, or **data privacy**: The means used to ensure that information is made available only to users who are authorized to access it. This ensures that only authorized users can view sensitive data.

- **Non-repudiation**: The means used to prove that a user who performed some action cannot reasonably deny having done so. This ensures that transactions can be proved to have happened.

- **Quality of Service**: The means used to provide better service to selected network traffic over various technologies.

- **Auditing**: The means used to capture a tamper-resistant record of security-related events for the purpose of being able to evaluate the effectiveness of security policies and mechanisms. To enable this, the system maintains a record of transactions and security information.

18.2 Security Mechanisms

The characteristics of an application should be considered when deciding the layer and type of security to be provided for applications. The following sections discuss the characteristics of the common mechanisms that can be used to secure Java EE applications. Each of these mechanisms can be used individually or with others to provide protection layers based on the specific needs of your implementation.

18.2.1 Java SE Security Mechanisms

Java SE provides support for a variety of security features and mechanisms.

- **Java Authentication and Authorization Service (JAAS)** is a set of APIs that enable services to authenticate and enforce access controls upon users. JAAS provides a pluggable and extensible framework for programmatic user authentication and authorization. JAAS is a core Java SE API and is an underlying technology for Java EE security mechanisms.

- **Java Generic Security Services (Java GSS-API)** is a token-based API used to securely exchange messages between communicating applications. The GSS-API offers application programmers uniform access to security services atop a variety of underlying security mechanisms, including Kerberos.

- **Java Cryptography Extension (JCE)** provides a framework and implementations for encryption, key generation and key agreement, and Message Authentication Code (MAC) algorithms. Support for encryption includes symmetric, asymmetric, block, and stream ciphers. Block ciphers operate on groups of bytes; stream ciphers operate on one byte at a time. The software also supports secure streams and sealed objects.

- **Java Secure Sockets Extension (JSSE)** provides a framework and an implementation for a Java version of the Secure Sockets Layer (SSL) and

Transport Layer Security (TLS) protocols and includes functionality for data encryption, server authentication, message integrity, and optional client authentication to enable secure Internet communications.

- **Simple Authentication and Security Layer (SASL)** is an Internet standard (RFC 2222) that specifies a protocol for authentication and optional establishment of a security layer between client and server applications. SASL defines how authentication data is to be exchanged but does not itself specify the contents of that data. SASL is a framework into which specific authentication mechanisms that specify the contents and semantics of the authentication data can fit.

Java SE also provides a set of tools for managing keystores, certificates, and policy files; generating and verifying JAR signatures; and obtaining, listing, and managing Kerberos tickets.

For more information on Java SE security, visit `http://docs.oracle.com/javase/7/docs/technotes/guides/security/`.

18.2.2 Java EE Security Mechanisms

Java EE security services are provided by the component container and can be implemented by using declarative or programmatic techniques (see Section 18.3, "Securing Containers"). Java EE security services provide a robust and easily configured security mechanism for authenticating users and authorizing access to application functions and associated data at many different layers. Java EE security services are separate from the security mechanisms of the operating system.

18.2.2.1 Application-Layer Security

In Java EE, component containers are responsible for providing application-layer security, security services for a specific application type tailored to the needs of the application. At the application layer, application firewalls can be used to enhance application protection by protecting the communication stream and all associated application resources from attacks.

Java EE security is easy to implement and configure and can offer fine-grained access control to application functions and data. However, as is inherent to security applied at the application layer, security properties are not transferable to applications running in other environments and protect data only while it is residing in the application environment. In the context of a traditional enterprise application, this is not necessarily a problem, but when applied to a web services application, in which data often travels across several intermediaries, you would need to use the Java EE security mechanisms along with transport-layer security and message-layer security for a complete security solution.

The advantages of using application-layer security include the following.

- Security is uniquely suited to the needs of the application.
- Security is fine grained, with application-specific settings.

The disadvantages of using application-layer security include the following.

- The application is dependent on security attributes that are not transferable between application types.
- Support for multiple protocols makes this type of security vulnerable.
- Data is close to or contained within the point of vulnerability.

For more information on providing security at the application layer, see Section 18.3, "Securing Containers."

18.2.2.2 Transport-Layer Security

Transport-layer security is provided by the transport mechanisms used to transmit information over the wire between clients and providers; thus, transport-layer security relies on secure HTTP transport (HTTPS) using Secure Sockets Layer (SSL). Transport security is a point-to-point security mechanism that can be used for authentication, message integrity, and confidentiality. When running over an SSL-protected session, the server and client can authenticate each other and negotiate an encryption algorithm and cryptographic keys before the application protocol transmits or receives its first byte of data. Security is active from the time the data leaves the client until it arrives at its destination, or vice versa, even across intermediaries. The problem is that the data is not protected once it gets to the destination. One solution is to encrypt the message before sending.

Transport-layer security is performed in a series of phases, as follows.

- The client and server agree on an appropriate algorithm.
- A key is exchanged using public-key encryption and certificate-based authentication.
- A symmetric cipher is used during the information exchange.

Digital certificates are necessary when running HTTPS using SSL. The HTTPS service of most web servers will not run unless a digital certificate has been installed. Digital certificates have already been created for GlassFish Server.

The advantages of using transport-layer security include the following.

- It is relatively simple, well-understood, standard technology.
- It applies to both a message body and its attachments.

The disadvantages of using transport-layer security include the following.

- It is tightly coupled with the transport-layer protocol.
- It represents an all-or-nothing approach to security. This implies that the security mechanism is unaware of message contents, so that you cannot selectively apply security to portions of the message as you can with message-layer security.
- Protection is transient. The message is protected only while in transit. Protection is removed automatically by the endpoint when it receives the message.
- It is not an end-to-end solution, simply point-to-point.

For more information on transport-layer security, see Section 18.6, "Establishing a Secure Connection Using SSL."

18.2.2.3 Message-Layer Security

In message-layer security, security information is contained within the SOAP message and/or SOAP message attachment, which allows security information to travel along with the message or attachment. For example, a portion of the message may be signed by a sender and encrypted for a particular receiver. When sent from the initial sender, the message may pass through intermediate nodes before reaching its intended receiver. In this scenario, the encrypted portions continue to be opaque to any intermediate nodes and can be decrypted only by the intended receiver. For this reason, message-layer security is also sometimes referred to as end-to-end security.

The advantages of message-layer security include the following.

- Security stays with the message over all hops and after the message arrives at its destination.
- Security can be selectively applied to different portions of a message and, if using XML Web Services Security, to attachments.
- Message security can be used with intermediaries over multiple hops.
- Message security is independent of the application environment or transport protocol.

The disadvantage of using message-layer security is that it is relatively complex and adds some overhead to processing.

GlassFish Server supports message security using Metro, a web services stack that uses Web Services Security (WSS) to secure messages. Because this message security is specific to Metro and is not a part of the Java EE platform, this tutorial does not discuss using WSS to secure messages. See the *Metro User's Guide* at `https://metro.java.net/guide/`.

18.3 Securing Containers

In Java EE, the component containers are responsible for providing application security. A container provides two types of security: declarative and programmatic.

18.3.1 Using Annotations to Specify Security Information

Annotations enable a declarative style of programming and so encompass both the declarative and programmatic security concepts. Users can specify information about security within a class file by using annotations. GlassFish Server uses this information when the application is deployed. Not all security information can be specified by using annotations, however. Some information must be specified in the application deployment descriptors.

Specific annotations that can be used to specify security information within an enterprise bean class file are described in Section 20.2.1, "Securing an Enterprise Bean Using Declarative Security." Chapter 19, "Getting Started Securing Web Applications," describes how to use annotations to secure web applications where possible. Deployment descriptors are described only where necessary.

For more information on annotations, see Section 18.7, "Further Information about Security."

18.3.2 Using Deployment Descriptors for Declarative Security

Declarative security can express an application component's security requirements by using deployment descriptors. Because deployment descriptor information is declarative, it can be changed without the need to modify the source code. At runtime, the Java EE server reads the deployment descriptor and acts upon the corresponding application, module, or component accordingly. Deployment descriptors must provide certain structural information for each component if this information has not been provided in annotations or is not to be defaulted.

This part of the tutorial does not document how to create deployment descriptors; it describes only the elements of the deployment descriptor relevant to security. NetBeans IDE provides tools for creating and modifying deployment descriptors.

Different types of components use different formats, or schemas, for their deployment descriptors. The security elements of deployment descriptors discussed in this tutorial include the following.

- Web components may use a web application deployment descriptor named web.xml.

  The schema for web component deployment descriptors is provided in Chapter 14 of the Java Servlet 3.1 specification (JSR 340), which can be downloaded from http://jcp.org/en/jsr/detail?id=340.

- Enterprise JavaBeans components may use an EJB deployment descriptor named META-INF/ejb-jar.xml, contained in the EJB JAR file.

  The schema for enterprise bean deployment descriptors is provided in Chapter 14 of the EJB 3.2 Core Contracts and Requirements Specification (JSR 345), which can be downloaded from http://jcp.org/en/jsr/detail?id=345.

18.3.3 Using Programmatic Security

Programmatic security is embedded in an application and is used to make security decisions. Programmatic security is useful when declarative security alone is not sufficient to express the security model of an application. The API for programmatic security consists of methods of the EJBContext interface and the HttpServletRequest interface. These methods allow components to make business-logic decisions based on the security role of the caller or remote user.

Programmatic security is discussed in more detail in the following sections:

- Section 19.3, "Using Programmatic Security with Web Applications"
- Section 20.2.2, "Securing an Enterprise Bean Programmatically"

18.4 Securing GlassFish Server

This tutorial describes deployment to GlassFish Server, which provides highly secure, interoperable, and distributed component computing based on the Java EE security model. GlassFish Server supports the Java EE 7 security model. You can configure GlassFish Server for the following purposes.

- Adding, deleting, or modifying authorized users. For more information on this topic, see Section 18.5, "Working with Realms, Users, Groups, and Roles."

- Configuring secure HTTP and Internet Inter-Orb Protocol (IIOP) listeners.

- Configuring secure Java Management Extensions (JMX) connectors.

- Adding, deleting, or modifying existing or custom realms.

- Defining an interface for pluggable authorization providers using Java Authorization Contract for Containers (JACC). JACC defines security contracts between GlassFish Server and authorization policy modules. These contracts specify how the authorization providers are installed, configured, and used in access decisions.

- Using pluggable audit modules.

- Customizing authentication mechanisms. All implementations of Java EE 7 compatible web containers are required to support the Servlet Profile of JSR 196, which offers an avenue for customizing the authentication mechanism applied by the web container on behalf of one or more applications.

- Setting and changing policy permissions for an application.

18.5 Working with Realms, Users, Groups, and Roles

You often need to protect resources to ensure that only authorized users have access. See Section 18.1.3, "Characteristics of Application Security," for an introduction to the concepts of authentication, identification, and authorization.

This section discusses setting up users so that they can be correctly identified and either given access to protected resources or denied access if they are not authorized to access the protected resources. To authenticate a user, you need to follow these basic steps.

1. The application developer writes code to prompt for a user name and password. The various methods of authentication are discussed in Section 19.2.2, "Specifying Authentication Mechanisms."

2. The application developer communicates how to set up security for the deployed application by use of a metadata annotation or deployment descriptor. This step is discussed in Section 18.5.3, "Setting Up Security Roles."

3. The server administrator sets up authorized users and groups in GlassFish Server. This is discussed in Section 18.5.2, "Managing Users and Groups in GlassFish Server."

4. The application deployer maps the application's security roles to users, groups, and principals defined in GlassFish Server. This topic is discussed in Section 18.5.4, "Mapping Roles to Users and Groups."

18.5.1 What Are Realms, Users, Groups, and Roles?

A **realm** is a security policy domain defined for a web or application server. A realm contains a collection of users, who may or may not be assigned to a group. Managing users in GlassFish Server is discussed in Section 18.5.2, "Managing Users and Groups in GlassFish Server."

An application will often prompt for a user name and password before allowing access to a protected resource. After the user name and password have been entered, that information is passed to the server, which either authenticates the user and sends the protected resource or does not authenticate the user, in which case access to the protected resource is denied. This type of user authentication is discussed in Section 19.2.3, "Specifying an Authentication Mechanism in the Deployment Descriptor."

In some applications, authorized users are assigned to roles. In this situation, the role assigned to the user in the application must be mapped to a principal or group defined on the application server. Figure 18–6 shows this. More information on mapping roles to users and groups can be found in Section 18.5.3, "Setting Up Security Roles."

Figure 18–6 Mapping Roles to Users and Groups

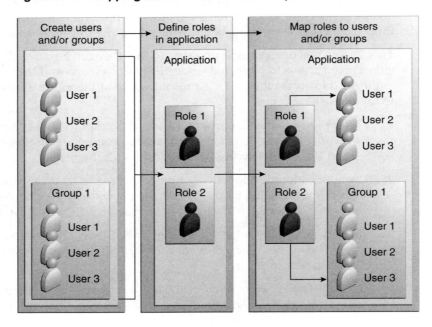

The following sections provide more information on realms, users, groups, and roles.

18.5.1.1 What Is a Realm?

The protected resources on a server can be partitioned into a set of protection spaces, each with its own authentication scheme and/or authorization database containing a collection of users and groups. A realm is a complete database of users and groups identified as valid users of one or more applications and controlled by the same authentication policy.

The Java EE server authentication service can govern users in multiple realms. The `file`, `admin-realm`, and `certificate` realms come preconfigured for GlassFish Server.

In the `file` realm, the server stores user credentials locally in a file named `keyfile`. You can use the Administration Console to manage users in the `file` realm. When using the `file` realm, the server authentication service verifies user identity by checking the `file` realm. This realm is used for the authentication of all clients except for web browser clients that use HTTPS and certificates.

In the `certificate` realm, the server stores user credentials in a certificate database. When using the `certificate` realm, the server uses certificates with HTTPS to authenticate web clients. To verify the identity of a user in the `certificate` realm, the authentication service verifies an X.509 certificate. For step-by-step instructions for creating this type of certificate, see Section 21.1, "Working with Digital Certificates." The common name field of the X.509 certificate is used as the principal name.

The `admin-realm` is also a `file` realm and stores administrator user credentials locally in a file named `admin-keyfile`. You can use the Administration Console to manage users in this realm in the same way you manage users in the `file` realm. For more information, see Section 18.5.2, "Managing Users and Groups in GlassFish Server."

18.5.1.2 What Is a User?

A **user** is an individual or application program identity that has been defined in GlassFish Server. In a web application, a user can have associated with that identity a set of roles that entitle the user to access all resources protected by those roles. Users can be associated with a group.

A Java EE user is similar to an operating system user. Typically, both types of users represent people. However, these two types of users are not the same. The Java EE server authentication service has no knowledge of the user name and password you provide when you log in to the operating system. The Java EE server authentication service is not connected to the security mechanism of the operating system. The two security services manage users that belong to different realms.

18.5.1.3 What Is a Group?

A **group** is a set of authenticated users, classified by common traits, defined in GlassFish Server. A Java EE user of the `file` realm can belong to a group in GlassFish Server. (A user in the `certificate` realm cannot.) A group in GlassFish Server is a category of users classified by common traits, such as job title or customer profile. For example, most customers of an e-commerce application might belong to the CUSTOMER group, but the big spenders would belong to the PREFERRED group. Categorizing users into groups makes it easier to control the access of large numbers of users.

A group in GlassFish Server has a different scope from a role. A group is designated for the entire GlassFish Server, whereas a role is associated only with a specific application in GlassFish Server.

18.5.1.4 What Is a Role?

A **role** is an abstract name for the permission to access a particular set of resources in an application. A role can be compared to a key that can open a lock. Many people might have a copy of the key. The lock doesn't care who you are, only that you have the right key.

18.5.1.5 Some Other Terminology

The following terminology is also used to describe the security requirements of the Java EE platform.

- A **principal** is an entity that can be authenticated by an authentication protocol in a security service that is deployed in an enterprise. A principal is identified by using a principal name and authenticated by using authentication data.

- A **security policy domain**, also known as a **security domain** or **realm**, is a scope over which a common security policy is defined and enforced by the security administrator of the security service.

- **Security attributes** are a set of attributes associated with every principal. The security attributes have many uses: for example, access to protected resources and auditing of users. Security attributes can be associated with a principal by an authentication protocol.

- A **credential** is an object that contains or references security attributes used to authenticate a principal for Java EE services. A principal acquires a credential upon authentication or from another principal that allows its credential to be used.

18.5.2 Managing Users and Groups in GlassFish Server

Follow these steps for managing users before you run the tutorial examples.

18.5.2.1 To Add Users to GlassFish Server

1. Start GlassFish Server, if you haven't already done so.

   Information on starting GlassFish Server is available in Section 2.2, "Starting and Stopping GlassFish Server."

2. Start the Administration Console, if you haven't already done so.

   To start the Administration Console, open a web browser and specify the URL `http://localhost:4848/`. If you changed the default Admin port during installation, enter the correct port number in place of `4848`.

3. In the navigation tree, expand the **Configurations** node, then expand the **server-config** node.

4. Expand the **Security** node.

5. Expand the **Realms** node.

6. Select the realm to which you are adding users.

   - Select the `file` realm to add users you want to access applications running in this realm.

     For the example security applications, select the `file` realm.

   - Select the `admin-realm` to add users you want to enable as system administrators of GlassFish Server.

   You cannot add users to the `certificate` realm by using the Administration Console. In the `certificate` realm, you can add only certificates. For information on adding (importing) certificates to the `certificate` realm, see Section 21.1.2, "Adding Users to the Certificate Realm."

7. On the Edit Realm page, click **Manage Users**.

8. On the File Users or Admin Users page, click **New** to add a new user to the realm.

9. On the New File Realm User page, enter values in the **User ID**, **Group List**, **New Password**, and **Confirm New Password** fields.

For the Admin Realm, the **Group List** field is read-only, and the group name is asadmin. Restart GlassFish Server and the Administration Console after you add a user to the Admin Realm.

For more information on these properties, see Section 18.5, "Working with Realms, Users, Groups, and Roles."

For the example security applications, specify a user with any name and password you like, but make sure that the user is assigned to the group TutorialUser. The user name and password are case-sensitive. Keep a record of the user name and password for working with the examples later in this tutorial.

10. Click **OK** to add this user to the realm, or click **Cancel** to quit without saving.

18.5.3 Setting Up Security Roles

When you design an enterprise bean or web component, you should always think about the kinds of users who will access the component. For example, a web application for a human resources department might have a different request URL for someone who has been assigned the role of DEPT_ADMIN than for someone who has been assigned the role of DIRECTOR. The DEPT_ADMIN role may let you view employee data, but the DIRECTOR role enables you to modify employee data, including salary data. Each of these security roles is an abstract logical grouping of users that is defined by the person who assembles the application. When an application is deployed, the deployer will map the roles to security identities in the operational environment, as shown in Figure 18–6 on page 372.

For Java EE components, you define security roles using the @DeclareRoles and @RolesAllowed metadata annotations.

The following is an example of an application in which the role of DEPT-ADMIN is authorized for methods that review employee payroll data, and the role of DIRECTOR is authorized for methods that change employee payroll data.

The enterprise bean would be annotated as shown in the following code:

```
import javax.annotation.security.DeclareRoles;
import javax.annotation.security.RolesAllowed;
...
@DeclareRoles({"DEPT-ADMIN", "DIRECTOR"})
@Stateless public class PayrollBean implements Payroll {
    @Resource SessionContext ctx;

    @RolesAllowed("DEPT-ADMIN")
    public void reviewEmployeeInfo(EmplInfo info) {
```

```
        oldInfo = ... read from database;

        // ...
    }

    @RolesAllowed("DIRECTOR")
    public void updateEmployeeInfo(EmplInfo info) {

        newInfo = ... update database;
        // ...
    }
    ...
}
```

For a servlet, you can use the `@HttpConstraint` annotation within the `@ServletSecurity` annotation to specify the roles that are allowed to access the servlet. For example, a servlet might be annotated as follows:

```
@WebServlet(name = "PayrollServlet", urlPatterns = {"/payroll"})
@ServletSecurity(
@HttpConstraint(transportGuarantee = TransportGuarantee.CONFIDENTIAL,
    rolesAllowed = {"DEPT-ADMIN", "DIRECTOR"}))
public class GreetingServlet extends HttpServlet {
```

These annotations are discussed in more detail in Section 19.4.2.1, "Specifying Security for Basic Authentication Using Annotations," and Section 20.2.1, "Securing an Enterprise Bean Using Declarative Security."

After users have provided their login information and the application has declared what roles are authorized to access protected parts of an application, the next step is to map the security role to the name of a user, or principal.

18.5.4 Mapping Roles to Users and Groups

When you are developing a Java EE application, you don't need to know what categories of users have been defined for the realm in which the application will be run. In the Java EE platform, the security architecture provides a mechanism for mapping the roles defined in the application to the users or groups defined in the runtime realm.

The role names used in the application are often the same as the group names defined in GlassFish Server. Under these circumstances, you can enable a default principal-to-role mapping in GlassFish Server by using the Administration Console. Section 19.4.1, "To Set Up Your System for Running the Security Examples," explains how to do this. All the tutorial security examples use default principal-to-role mapping. With that setting enabled, if the group name defined on GlassFish Server matches the role name defined in the application, there is no need to use the runtime deployment descriptor to provide a mapping. The application server will implicitly make this mapping, as long as the names of the groups and roles match.

If the role names used in an application are not the same as the group names defined on the server, use the runtime deployment descriptor to specify the mapping. The following example demonstrates how to do this mapping in the `glassfish-web.xml` file, which is the file used for web applications:

```
<glassfish-web-app>
    ...
    <security-role-mapping>
        <role-name>Mascot</role-name>
        <principal-name>Duke</principal-name>
    </security-role-mapping>

    <security-role-mapping>
        <role-name>Admin</role-name>
        <group-name>Director</group-name>
    </security-role-mapping>
    ...
</glassfish-web-app>
```

A role can be mapped to specific principals, specific groups, or both. The principal or group names must be valid principals or groups in the current default realm or in the realm specified in the `login-config` element. In this example, the role of `Mascot` used in the application is mapped to a principal, named `Duke`, that exists on the application server. Mapping a role to a specific principal is useful when the person occupying that role may change. For this application, you would need to modify only the runtime deployment descriptor rather than search and replace throughout the application for references to this principal.

Also in this example, the role of `Admin` is mapped to a group of users assigned the group name of `Director`. This is useful because the group of people authorized to access director-level administrative data has to be maintained only in GlassFish Server. The application developer does not need to know who these people are, but only needs to define the group of people who will be given access to the information.

The `role-name` must match the `role-name` in the `security-role` element of the corresponding deployment descriptor or the role name defined in a `@DeclareRoles` annotation.

18.6 Establishing a Secure Connection Using SSL

Secure Sockets Layer (SSL) technology is security that is implemented at the transport layer (see Section 18.2.2.2, "Transport-Layer Security," for more information about transport-layer security). SSL allows web browsers and web servers to communicate over a secure connection. In this secure connection, the data is encrypted before being sent and then is decrypted upon receipt and before processing. Both the browser and the server encrypt all traffic before sending any data.

SSL addresses the following important security considerations.

- **Authentication**: During your initial attempt to communicate with a web server over a secure connection, that server will present your web browser with a set of credentials in the form of a server certificate (also called a public key certificate). The purpose of the certificate is to verify that the site is who and what it claims to be. In some cases, the server may request a certificate proving that the client is who and what it claims to be; this mechanism is known as client authentication.

- **Confidentiality**: When data is being passed between the client and the server on a network, third parties can view and intercept this data. SSL responses are encrypted so that the data cannot be deciphered by the third party and the data remains confidential.

- **Integrity**: When data is being passed between the client and the server on a network, third parties can view and intercept this data. SSL helps guarantee that the data will not be modified in transit by that third party.

The SSL protocol is designed to be as efficient as securely possible. However, encryption and decryption are computationally expensive processes from a performance standpoint. It is not strictly necessary to run an entire web application over SSL, and it is customary for a developer to decide which pages require a secure connection and which do not. Pages that might require a secure connection include those for login, personal information, shopping cart checkouts, or credit card information transmittal. Any page within an application can be requested over a secure socket by simply prefixing the address with `https:` instead of `http:`. Any pages that absolutely require a secure connection should check the protocol type associated with the page request and take the appropriate action if `https:` is not specified.

Using name-based virtual hosts on a secured connection can be problematic. This is a design limitation of the SSL protocol itself. The **SSL handshake**, whereby the client browser accepts the server certificate, must occur before the HTTP request is accessed. As a result, the request information containing the virtual host name cannot be determined before authentication, and it is therefore not possible to assign multiple certificates to a single IP address. If all virtual hosts on a single IP address need to authenticate against the same certificate, the addition of multiple virtual hosts should not interfere with normal SSL operations on the server. Be aware, however, that most client browsers will compare the server's domain name against the domain name listed in the certificate, if any; this is applicable primarily to official certificates signed by a certificate authority (CA). If the domain names do not match, these browsers will display a warning to the client. In general, only address-based virtual hosts are commonly used with SSL in a production environment.

18.6.1 Verifying and Configuring SSL Support

As a general rule, you must address the following issues to enable SSL for a server.

- There must be a `Connector` element for an SSL connector in the server deployment descriptor.

- There must be valid keystore and certificate files.

- The location of the keystore file and its password must be specified in the server deployment descriptor.

An SSL HTTPS connector is already enabled in GlassFish Server.

For testing purposes and to verify that SSL support has been correctly installed, load the default introduction page with a URL that connects to the port defined in the server deployment descriptor:

```
https://localhost:8181/
```

The `https` in this URL indicates that the browser should be using the SSL protocol. The `localhost` in this example assumes that you are running the example on your local machine as part of the development process. The `8181` in this example is the secure port that was specified where the SSL connector was created. If you are using a different server or port, modify this value accordingly.

The first time that you load this application, the New Site Certificate or Security Alert dialog box appears. Click **Next** to move through the series of dialog boxes, and click **Finish** when you reach the last dialog box. The certificates will appear only the first time. When you accept the certificates, subsequent hits to this site assume that you still trust the content.

18.7 Further Information about Security

For more information about security in Java EE applications, see

- Java EE 7 specification:

  `http://jcp.org/en/jsr/detail?id=342`

- Enterprise JavaBeans 3.2 specification:

  `http://jcp.org/en/jsr/detail?id=345`

- Implementing Enterprise Web Services 1.3 specification:

  `http://jcp.org/en/jsr/detail?id=109`

- Java SE security information:

  `http://docs.oracle.com/javase/7/docs/technotes/guides/security/`

- Java Servlet 3.1 specification:

  `http://jcp.org/en/jsr/detail?id=340`

- Java Authorization Contract for Containers 1.5 specification:

  `http://jcp.org/en/jsr/detail?id=115`

19

Getting Started Securing Web Applications

The ways to implement security for Java EE web applications are discussed in a general way in Section 18.3, "Securing Containers." This chapter provides more detail and a few examples that explore these security services as they relate to web components.

A web application is accessed using a web browser over a network, such as the Internet or a company's intranet. As discussed in Section 1.3, "Distributed Multitiered Applications," the Java EE platform uses a distributed multitiered application model, and web applications run in the web tier.

Web applications contain resources that can be accessed by many users. These resources often traverse unprotected, open networks, such as the Internet. In such an environment, a substantial number of web applications will require some type of security.

Securing applications and their clients in the business tier and the EIS tier is discussed in Chapter 20, "Getting Started Securing Enterprise Applications."

The following topics are addressed here:

- Overview of Web Application Security
- Securing Web Applications
- Using Programmatic Security with Web Applications
- Examples: Securing Web Applications

19.1 Overview of Web Application Security

In the Java EE platform, web components provide the dynamic extension capabilities for a web server. Web components can be Java servlets or JavaServer Faces pages.

Certain aspects of web application security can be configured when the application is installed, or deployed, to the web container. Annotations and/or deployment descriptors are used to relay information to the deployer about security and other aspects of the application. Specifying this information in annotations or in the deployment descriptor helps the deployer set up the appropriate security policy for the web application. Any values explicitly specified in the deployment descriptor override any values specified in annotations.

Security for Java EE web applications can be implemented in the following ways.

- **Declarative security** can be implemented using either metadata annotations or an application's deployment descriptor. See Section 18.1, "Overview of Java EE Security," for more information.

    Declarative security for web applications is described in Section 19.2, "Securing Web Applications."

- **Programmatic security** is embedded in an application and can be used to make security decisions when declarative security alone is not sufficient to express the security model of an application. Declarative security alone may not be sufficient when conditional login in a particular work flow, instead of for all cases, is required in the middle of an application. See Section 18.1, "Overview of Java EE Security," for more information.

    Servlet 3.1 provides the `authenticate`, `login`, and `logout` methods of the `HttpServletRequest` interface. With the addition of the `authenticate`, `login`, and `logout` methods to the Servlet specification, an application deployment descriptor is no longer required for web applications but may still be used to further specify security requirements beyond the basic default values.

    Programmatic security is discussed in Section 19.3, "Using Programmatic Security with Web Applications."

- **Message security** works with web services and incorporates security features, such as digital signatures and encryption, into the header of a SOAP message, working in the application layer, ensuring end-to-end security. Message security is not a component of Java EE 7 and is mentioned here for informational purposes only.

Some of the material in this chapter builds on material presented earlier in this tutorial. In particular, this chapter assumes that you are familiar with the information in the following chapters:

- Chapter 6, "Getting Started with Web Applications," in *The Java EE 7 Tutorial, Volume 1*

- Chapter 7, "JavaServer Faces Technology," in *The Java EE 7 Tutorial, Volume 1*

- Chapter 17, "Java Servlet Technology," in *The Java EE 7 Tutorial, Volume 1*

- Chapter 18, "Introduction to Security in the Java EE Platform," in this book

19.2 Securing Web Applications

Web applications are created by application developers who give, sell, or otherwise transfer the application to an application deployer for installation into a runtime environment. Application developers communicate how to set up security for the deployed application by using annotations or deployment descriptors. This information is passed on to the deployer, who uses it to define method permissions for security roles, set up user authentication, and set up the appropriate transport mechanism. If the application developer doesn't define security requirements, the deployer will have to determine the security requirements independently.

Some elements necessary for security in a web application cannot be specified as annotations for all types of web applications. This chapter explains how to secure web applications using annotations wherever possible. It explains how to use deployment descriptors where annotations cannot be used.

19.2.1 Specifying Security Constraints

A **security constraint** is used to define the access privileges to a collection of resources using their URL mapping.

If your web application uses a servlet, you can express the security constraint information by using annotations. Specifically, you use the @HttpConstraint and, optionally, the @HttpMethodConstraint annotations within the @ServletSecurity annotation to specify a security constraint.

If your web application does not use a servlet, however, you must specify a security-constraint element in the deployment descriptor file. The authentication mechanism cannot be expressed using annotations, so if you use any authentication method other than BASIC (the default), a deployment descriptor is required.

The following subelements can be part of a `security-constraint`.

- **Web resource collection** (`web-resource-collection`): A list of URL patterns (the part of a URL *after* the host name and port you want to constrain) and HTTP operations (the methods within the files that match the URL pattern you want to constrain) that describe a set of resources to be protected. Web resource collections are discussed in Section 19.2.1.1, "Specifying a Web Resource Collection."

- **Authorization constraint** (`auth-constraint`): Specifies whether authentication is to be used and names the roles authorized to perform the constrained requests. For more information about authorization constraints, see Section 19.2.1.2, "Specifying an Authorization Constraint."

- **User data constraint** (`user-data-constraint`): Specifies how data is protected when transported between a client and a server. User data constraints are discussed in Section 19.2.1.3, "Specifying a Secure Connection."

19.2.1.1 Specifying a Web Resource Collection

A web resource collection consists of the following subelements.

- `web-resource-name` is the name you use for this resource. Its use is optional.

- `url-pattern` is used to list the request URI to be protected. Many applications have both unprotected and protected resources. To provide unrestricted access to a resource, do not configure a security constraint for that particular request URI.

  The request URI is the part of a URL *after* the host name and port. For example, let's say that you have an e-commerce site with a catalog that you would want anyone to be able to access and browse, and a shopping cart area for customers only. You could set up the paths for your web application so that the pattern `/cart/*` is protected but nothing else is protected. Assuming that the application is installed at context path `/myapp`, the following are true.

  - `http://localhost:8080/myapp/index.xhtml` is *not* protected.

  - `http://localhost:8080/myapp/cart/index.xhtml` *is* protected.

  A user will be prompted to log in the first time he or she accesses a resource in the `cart/` subdirectory.

- `http-method` or `http-method-omission` is used to specify which methods should be protected or which methods should be omitted from protection. An

HTTP method is protected by a `web-resource-collection` under any of the following circumstances:

– If no HTTP methods are named in the collection (which means that all are protected)

– If the collection specifically names the HTTP method in an `http-method` subelement

– If the collection contains one or more `http-method-omission` elements, none of which names the HTTP method

19.2.1.2 Specifying an Authorization Constraint

An authorization constraint (`auth-constraint`) contains the `role-name` element. You can use as many `role-name` elements as needed here.

An authorization constraint establishes a requirement for authentication and names the roles authorized to access the URL patterns and HTTP methods declared by this security constraint. If there is no authorization constraint, the container must accept the request without requiring user authentication. If there is an authorization constraint but no roles are specified within it, the container will not allow access to constrained requests under any circumstances. Each role name specified here must either correspond to the role name of one of the `security-role` elements defined for this web application or be the specially reserved role name *, which indicates all roles in the web application. Role names are case sensitive. The roles defined for the application must be mapped to users and groups defined on the server, except when default principal-to-role mapping is used.

For more information about security roles, see Section 19.2.4, "Declaring Security Roles." For information on mapping security roles, see Section 18.5.4, "Mapping Roles to Users and Groups."

For a servlet, the `@HttpConstraint` and `@HttpMethodConstraint` annotations accept a `rolesAllowed` element that specifies the authorized roles.

19.2.1.3 Specifying a Secure Connection

A user data constraint (`user-data-constraint` in the deployment descriptor) contains the `transport-guarantee` subelement. A user data constraint can be used to require that a protected transport-layer connection, such as HTTPS, be used for all constrained URL patterns and HTTP methods specified in the security constraint. The choices for transport guarantee are CONFIDENTIAL, INTEGRAL, or NONE. If you specify CONFIDENTIAL or INTEGRAL as a security constraint, it generally means that the use of SSL is required and applies to all requests that match the URL patterns in the web resource collection, not just to the login dialog box.

The strength of the required protection is defined by the value of the transport guarantee, as follows.

- Specify CONFIDENTIAL when the application requires that data be transmitted so as to prevent other entities from observing the contents of the transmission.

- Specify INTEGRAL when the application requires that the data be sent between client and server in such a way that it cannot be changed in transit.

- Specify NONE to indicate that the container must accept the constrained requests on any connection, including an unprotected one.

Note: In practice, Java EE servers treat the CONFIDENTIAL and INTEGRAL transport guarantee values identically.

The user data constraint is handy to use in conjunction with basic and form-based user authentication. When the login authentication method is set to BASIC or FORM, passwords are not protected, meaning that passwords sent between a client and a server on an unprotected session can be viewed and intercepted by third parties. Using a user data constraint with the user authentication mechanism can alleviate this concern. Configuring a user authentication mechanism is described in Section 19.2.3, "Specifying an Authentication Mechanism in the Deployment Descriptor."

To guarantee that data is transported over a secure connection, ensure that SSL support is configured for your server. SSL support is already configured for GlassFish Server.

Note: After you switch to SSL for a session, you should never accept any non-SSL requests for the rest of that session. For example, a shopping site might not use SSL until the checkout page, and then it might switch to using SSL to accept your card number. After switching to SSL, you should stop listening to non-SSL requests for this session. The reason for this practice is that the session ID itself was not encrypted on the earlier communications. This is not so bad when you're only doing your shopping, but after the credit card information is stored in the session, you don't want anyone to use that information to fake the purchase transaction against your credit card. This practice could be easily implemented by using a filter.

19.2.1.4 Specifying Security Constraints for Resources

You can create security constraints for resources within your application. For example, you could allow users with the role of PARTNER full access to all resources at the URL pattern /acme/wholesale/* and allow users with the role of CLIENT full access to all resources at the URL pattern /acme/retail/*. This is the recommended way to protect resources if you do not want to protect some HTTP methods while leaving other HTTP methods unprotected. An example of a deployment descriptor that would demonstrate this functionality is the following:

```
<!-- SECURITY CONSTRAINT #1 -->
<security-constraint>
    <web-resource-collection>
        <web-resource-name>wholesale</web-resource-name>
        <url-pattern>/acme/wholesale/*</url-pattern>
    </web-resource-collection>
    <auth-constraint>
        <role-name>PARTNER</role-name>
    </auth-constraint>
    <user-data-constraint>
        <transport-guarantee>CONFIDENTIAL</transport-guarantee>
    </user-data-constraint>
</security-constraint>

<!-- SECURITY CONSTRAINT #2 -->
<security-constraint>
    <web-resource-collection>
        <web-resource-name>retail</web-resource-name>
        <url-pattern>/acme/retail/*</url-pattern>
    </web-resource-collection>
    <auth-constraint>
        <role-name>CLIENT</role-name>
    </auth-constraint>
    <user-data-constraint>
        <transport-guarantee>CONFIDENTIAL</transport-guarantee>
    </user-data-constraint>
</security-constraint>
```

19.2.2 Specifying Authentication Mechanisms

A user authentication mechanism specifies

- The way a user gains access to web content
- With basic authentication, the realm in which the user will be authenticated
- With form-based authentication, additional attributes

When an authentication mechanism is specified, the user must be authenticated before access is granted to any resource that is constrained by a security constraint. There can be multiple security constraints applying to multiple resources, but the same authentication method will apply to all constrained resources in an application.

Before you can authenticate a user, you must have a database of user names, passwords, and roles configured on your web or application server. For information on setting up the user database, see Section 18.5.2, "Managing Users and Groups in GlassFish Server."

The Java EE platform supports the following authentication mechanisms:

- Basic authentication

- Form-based authentication

- Digest authentication

- Client authentication

- Mutual authentication

Basic, form-based, and digest authentication are discussed in this section. Client and mutual authentication are discussed in Chapter 21, "Java EE Security: Advanced Topics."

HTTP basic authentication and form-based authentication are not very secure authentication mechanisms. Basic authentication sends user names and passwords over the Internet as Base64-encoded text. Form-based authentication sends this data as plain text. In both cases, the target server is not authenticated. Therefore, these forms of authentication leave user data exposed and vulnerable. If someone can intercept the transmission, the user name and password information can easily be decoded.

However, when a secure transport mechanism, such as SSL, or security at the network level, such as the Internet Protocol Security (IPsec) protocol or virtual private network (VPN) strategies, is used in conjunction with basic or form-based authentication, some of these concerns can be alleviated. To specify a secure transport mechanism, use the elements described in Section 19.2.1.3, "Specifying a Secure Connection."

19.2.2.1 HTTP Basic Authentication

Specifying **HTTP basic authentication** requires that the server request a user name and password from the web client and verify that the user name and password are valid by comparing them against a database of authorized users in the specified or default realm.

Basic authentication is the default when you do not specify an authentication mechanism.

When basic authentication is used, the following actions occur.

1. A client requests access to a protected resource.

2. The web server returns a dialog box that requests the user name and password.

3. The client submits the user name and password to the server.

4. The server authenticates the user in the specified realm and, if successful, returns the requested resource.

Figure 19–1 shows what happens when you specify HTTP basic authentication.

Figure 19–1   HTTP Basic Authentication

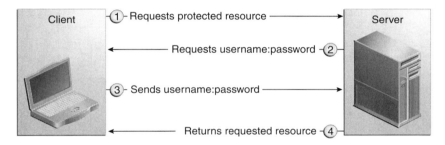

19.2.2.2 Form-Based Authentication

Form-based authentication allows the developer to control the look and feel of the login authentication screens by customizing the login screen and error pages that an HTTP browser presents to the end user. When form-based authentication is declared, the following actions occur.

1. A client requests access to a protected resource.

2. If the client is unauthenticated, the server redirects the client to a login page.

3. The client submits the login form to the server.

4. The server attempts to authenticate the user.

   ■ If authentication succeeds, the authenticated user's principal is checked to ensure that it is in a role that is authorized to access the resource. If the user is authorized, the server redirects the client to the resource by using the stored URL path.

- If authentication fails, the client is forwarded or redirected to an error page.

Figure 19–2 shows what happens when you specify form-based authentication.

Figure 19–2   Form-Based Authentication

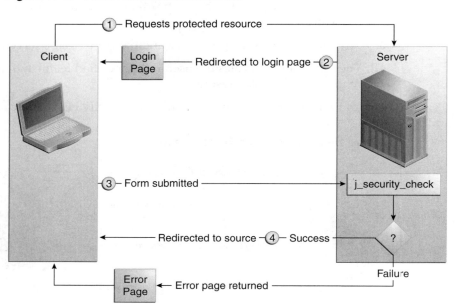

Section 19.4.3, "The hello1-formauth Example: Form-Based Authentication with a JavaServer Faces Application," shows an example application that uses form-based authentication.

When you create a form-based login, be sure to maintain sessions using cookies or SSL session information.

For authentication to proceed appropriately, the action of the login form must always be j_security_check. This restriction is made so that the login form will work no matter which resource it is for and to avoid requiring the server to specify the action field of the outbound form. The following code snippet shows how the form should be coded into the HTML page:

```
<form method="POST" action="j_security_check">
    <input type="text" name="j_username">
    <input type="password" name="j_password">
</form>
```

19.2.2.3 Digest Authentication

Like basic authentication, **digest authentication** authenticates a user based on a user name and a password. However, unlike basic authentication, digest authentication does not send user passwords over the network. Instead, the client sends a one-way cryptographic hash of the password and additional data. Although passwords are not sent on the wire, digest authentication requires that clear-text password equivalents be available to the authenticating container so that it can validate received authenticators by calculating the expected digest.

19.2.3 Specifying an Authentication Mechanism in the Deployment Descriptor

To specify an authentication mechanism, use the `login-config` element. It can contain the following subelements.

- The `auth-method` subelement configures the authentication mechanism for the web application. The element content must be either NONE, BASIC, DIGEST, FORM, or CLIENT-CERT.

- The `realm-name` subelement indicates the realm name to use when the basic authentication scheme is chosen for the web application.

- The `form-login-config` subelement specifies the login and error pages that should be used when form-based login is specified.

> **Note:** Another way to specify form-based authentication is to use the `authenticate`, `login`, and `logout` methods of `HttpServletRequest`, as discussed in Section 19.3.1, "Authenticating Users Programmatically."

When you try to access a web resource that is constrained by a `security-constraint` element, the web container activates the authentication mechanism that has been configured for that resource. The authentication mechanism specifies how the user will be prompted to log in. If the `login-config` element is present and the `auth-method` element contains a value other than NONE, the user must be authenticated to access the resource. If you do not specify an authentication mechanism, authentication of the user is not required.

The following example shows how to declare form-based authentication in your deployment descriptor:

```
<login-config>
    <auth-method>FORM</auth-method>
    <realm-name>file</realm-name>
    <form-login-config>
```

```
        <form-login-page>/login.xhtml</form-login-page>
        <form-error-page>/error.xhtml</form-error-page>
    </form-login-config>
</login-config>
```

The login and error page locations are specified relative to the location of the deployment descriptor. Examples of login and error pages are shown in Section 19.4.3.1, "Creating the Login Form and the Error Page."

The following example shows how to declare digest authentication in your deployment descriptor:

```
<login-config>
    <auth-method>DIGEST</auth-method>
</login-config>
```

19.2.4 Declaring Security Roles

You can declare security role names used in web applications by using the `security-role` element of the deployment descriptor. Use this element to list all the security roles that you have referenced in your application.

The following snippet of a deployment descriptor declares the roles that will be used in an application using the `security-role` element and specifies which of these roles is authorized to access protected resources using the `auth-constraint` element:

```
<security-constraint>
    <web-resource-collection>
        <web-resource-name>Protected Area</web-resource-name>
        <url-pattern>/security/protected/*</url-pattern>
        <http-method>PUT</http-method>
        <http-method>DELETE</http-method>
        <http-method>GET</http-method>
        <http-method>POST</http-method>
    </web-resource-collection>
    <auth-constraint>
        <role-name>manager</role-name>
    </auth-constraint>
</security-constraint>

 <!-- Security roles used by this web application -->
<security-role>
    <role-name>manager</role-name>
</security-role>
```

```
<security-role>
    <role-name>employee</role-name>
</security-role>
```

In this example, the `security-role` element lists all the security roles used in the application: `manager` and `employee`. This enables the deployer to map all the roles defined in the application to users and groups defined in GlassFish Server.

The `auth-constraint` element specifies the role, `manager`, that can access the HTTP methods PUT, DELETE, GET, and POST located in the directory specified by the `url-pattern` element (`/security/protected/*`).

The `@ServletSecurity` annotation cannot be used in this situation because its constraints apply to all URL patterns specified by the `@WebServlet` annotation.

19.3 Using Programmatic Security with Web Applications

Programmatic security is used by security-aware applications when declarative security alone is not sufficient to express the security model of the application.

19.3.1 Authenticating Users Programmatically

The following methods of the `HttpServletRequest` interface enable you to authenticate users for a web application programmatically.

- `authenticate` allows an application to instigate authentication of the request caller by the container from within an unconstrained request context. A login dialog box displays and collects the user name and password for authentication purposes.

- `login` allows an application to collect user name and password information as an alternative to specifying form-based authentication in an application deployment descriptor.

- `logout` allows an application to reset the caller identity of a request.

The following example code shows how to use the `login` and `logout` methods (the methods are in **bold**):

```
package test;

import java.io.IOException;
import java.io.PrintWriter;
import java.math.BigDecimal;
import javax.ejb.EJB;
import javax.servlet.ServletException;
import javax.servlet.annotation.WebServlet;
```

```java
import javax.servlet.http.HttpServlet;
import javax.servlet.http.HttpServletRequest;
import javax.servlet.http.HttpServletResponse;

@WebServlet(name="TutorialServlet", urlPatterns={"/TutorialServlet"})
public class TutorialServlet extends HttpServlet {
    @EJB
    private ConverterBean converterBean;

    /**
     * Processes requests for both HTTP <code>GET</code>
     *     and <code>POST</code> methods.
     * @param request servlet request
     * @param response servlet response
     * @throws ServletException if a servlet-specific error occurs
     * @throws IOException if an I/O error occurs
     */
    protected void processRequest(HttpServletRequest request,
            HttpServletResponse response)
    throws ServletException, IOException {
        response.setContentType("text/html;charset=UTF-8");
        PrintWriter out = response.getWriter();
        try {

            out.println("<html>");
            out.println("<head>");
            out.println("<title>Servlet TutorialServlet</title>");
            out.println("</head>");
            out.println("<body>");
            request.login("TutorialUser", "TutorialUser");
            BigDecimal result =
                converterBean.dollarToYen(new BigDecimal("1.0"));
          out.println("<h1>Servlet TutorialServlet result of dollarToYen= "
                + result + "</h1>");
            out.println("</body>");
            out.println("</html>");
        } catch (Exception e) {
            throw new ServletException(e);
        } finally {
            request.logout();
            out.close();
        }
    }
}
```

The following example code shows how to use the `authenticate` method (the method is in **bold**):

```
package com.example.test;

import java.io.*;
import javax.servlet.*;
import javax.servlet.http.*;
public class TestServlet extends HttpServlet {

    protected void processRequest(HttpServletRequest request,
            HttpServletResponse response)
            throws ServletException, IOException {
        response.setContentType("text/html;charset=UTF-8");
        PrintWriter out = response.getWriter();
        try {
            request.authenticate(response);
            out.println("Authenticate Successful");
        } finally {
            out.close();
        }
    }
}
```

19.3.2 Checking Caller Identity Programmatically

In general, security management should be enforced by the container in a manner that is transparent to the web component. The security API described in this section should be used only in the less frequent situations in which the web component methods need to access the security context information.

Servlet 3.1 specifies the following methods that enable you to access security information about the component's caller.

■ `getRemoteUser` determines the user name with which the client authenticated. The `getRemoteUser` method returns the name of the remote user (the caller) associated by the container with the request. If no user has been authenticated, this method returns `null`.

■ `isUserInRole` determines whether a remote user is in a specific security role. If no user has been authenticated, this method returns `false`. This method expects a `String` user `role-name` parameter.

The `security-role-ref` element should be declared in the deployment descriptor with a `role-name` subelement containing the role name to be passed to the method. Using security role references is discussed in Section 19.3.4, "Declaring and Linking Role References."

- `getUserPrincipal` determines the principal name of the current user and returns a `java.security.Principal` object. If no user has been authenticated, this method returns `null`. Calling the `getName` method on the `Principal` returned by `getUserPrincipal` returns the name of the remote user.

Your application can make business-logic decisions based on the information obtained using these APIs.

19.3.3 Example Code for Programmatic Security

The following code demonstrates the use of programmatic security for the purposes of programmatic login. This servlet does the following.

1. It displays information about the current user.

2. It prompts the user to log in.

3. It prints out the information again to demonstrate the effect of the `login` method.

4. It logs the user out.

5. It prints out the information again to demonstrate the effect of the `logout` method.

```
package enterprise.programmatic_login;

import java.io.*;
import java.net.*;
import javax.annotation.security.DeclareRoles;
import javax.servlet.*;
import javax.servlet.http.*;

@DeclareRoles("javaee7user")
public class LoginServlet extends HttpServlet {

    /**
     * Processes requests for both HTTP GET and POST methods.
     * @param request servlet request
     * @param response servlet response
     */
    protected void processRequest(HttpServletRequest request,
                HttpServletResponse response)
            throws ServletException, IOException {
        response.setContentType("text/html;charset=UTF-8");
        PrintWriter out = response.getWriter();
        try {
            String userName = request.getParameter("txtUserName");
```

```
                   String password = request.getParameter("txtPassword");

                   out.println("Before Login" + "<br><br>");
                   out.println("IsUserInRole?.."
                           + request.isUserInRole("javaee7user")+"<br>");
                   out.println("getRemoteUser?.."
                           + request.getRemoteUser()+"<br>");
                   out.println("getUserPrincipal?.."
                           + request.getUserPrincipal()+"<br>");
                   out.println("getAuthType?.."
                           + request.getAuthType()+"<br><br>");

                   try {
                       request.login(userName, password);
                   } catch(ServletException ex) {
                       out.println("Login Failed with a ServletException.."
                           + ex.getMessage());
                       return;
                   }
                   out.println("After Login..."+"<br><br>");
                   out.println("IsUserInRole?.."
                           + request.isUserInRole("javaee7user")+"<br>");
                   out.println("getRemoteUser?.."
                           + request.getRemoteUser()+"<br>");
                   out.println("getUserPrincipal?.."
                           + request.getUserPrincipal()+"<br>");
                   out.println("getAuthType?.."
                           + request.getAuthType()+"<br><br>");

                   request.logout();
                   out.println("After Logout..."+"<br><br>");
                   out.println("IsUserInRole?.."
                           + request.isUserInRole("javaee7user")+"<br>");
                   out.println("getRemoteUser?.."
                           + request.getRemoteUser()+"<br>");
                   out.println("getUserPrincipal?.."
                           + request.getUserPrincipal()+"<br>");
                   out.println("getAuthType?.." + request.getAuthType()+"<br>");
               } finally {
                   out.close();
               }
           }
       ...
   }
```

19.3.4 Declaring and Linking Role References

A **security role reference** is a mapping between the name of a role that is called from a web component using isUserInRole(String role) and the name of a security role that has been defined for the application. If no security-role-ref element is declared in a deployment descriptor and the isUserInRole method is called, the container defaults to checking the provided role name against the list of all security roles defined for the web application. Using the default method instead of using the security-role-ref element limits your flexibility to change role names in an application without also recompiling the servlet making the call.

The security-role-ref element is used when an application uses the HttpServletRequest.isUserInRole(String role). The value passed to the isUserInRole method is a String representing the role name of the user. The value of the role-name element must be the String used as the parameter to the HttpServletRequest.isUserInRole(String role). The role-link must contain the name of one of the security roles defined in the security-role elements. The container uses the mapping of security-role-ref to security-role when determining the return value of the call.

For example, to map the security role reference cust to the security role with role name bankCustomer, the elements would look like this:

```
<servlet>
...
    <security-role-ref>
        <role-name>cust</role-name>
        <role-link>bankCustomer</role-link>
    </security-role-ref>
...
</servlet>
```

If the servlet method is called by a user in the bankCustomer security role, isUserInRole("cust") returns true.

The role-link element in the security-role-ref element must match a role-name defined in the security-role element of the same web.xml deployment descriptor, as shown here:

```
<security-role>
    <role-name>bankCustomer</role-name>
</security-role>
```

A security role reference, including the name defined by the reference, is scoped to the component whose deployment descriptor contains the security-role-ref deployment descriptor element.

19.4 Examples: Securing Web Applications

Some basic setup is required before any of the example applications will run correctly. The examples use annotations, programmatic security, and/or declarative security to demonstrate adding security to existing web applications.

Here are some other locations where you will find examples of securing various types of applications:

- Section 20.3.1, "The cart-secure Example: Securing an Enterprise Bean with Declarative Security"
- Section 20.3.2, "The converter-secure Example: Securing an Enterprise Bean with Programmatic Security"
- GlassFish samples: `https://glassfish-samples.java.net/`

19.4.1 To Set Up Your System for Running the Security Examples

To set up your system for running the security examples, you need to configure a user database that the application can use for authenticating users. Before continuing, follow these steps.

1. Make sure that GlassFish Server has been started (see Section 2.2, "Starting and Stopping GlassFish Server").

2. Add an authorized user to GlassFish Server. For the examples in this chapter and in Chapter 20, "Getting Started Securing Enterprise Applications," add a user to the `file` realm of GlassFish Server, and assign the user to the group `TutorialUser`.

   a. From the Administration Console, expand the **Configurations** node, then expand the **server-config** node.

   b. Expand the **Security** node.

   c. Expand the **Realms** node.

   d. Select the **File** node.

   e. On the Edit Realm page, click **Manage Users**.

   f. On the File Users page, click **New**.

   g. In the **User ID** field, enter a user ID.

   h. In the **Group List** field, enter `TutorialUser`.

    i. In the **New Password** and **Confirm New Password** fields, enter a password.

    j. Click **OK**.

    Be sure to write down the user name and password for the user you create so that you can use it for testing the example applications. Authentication is case sensitive for both the user name and password, so write down the user name and password exactly. This topic is discussed more in Section 18.5.2, "Managing Users and Groups in GlassFish Server."

3. Set up Default Principal to Role Mapping in GlassFish Server.

    a. From the Administration Console, expand the **Configurations** node, then expand the **server-config** node.

    b. Select the **Security** node.

    c. Select the **Default Principal to Role Mapping Enabled** check box.

    d. Click **Save**.

19.4.2 The hello2-basicauth Example: Basic Authentication with a Servlet

This example explains how to use basic authentication with a servlet. With basic authentication of a servlet, the web browser presents a standard login dialog box that is not customizable. When a user submits his or her name and password, the server determines whether the user name and password are those of an authorized user and sends the requested web resource if the user is authorized to view it.

In general, the following steps are necessary for adding basic authentication to an unsecured servlet, such as the ones described in Chapter 6, "Getting Started with Web Applications," in *The Java EE 7 Tutorial, Volume 1*. In the example application included with this tutorial, many of these steps have been completed for you and are listed here simply to show what needs to be done should you wish to create a similar application. This application can be found in the *tut-install*/examples/security/hello2-basicauth/ directory.

1. Follow the steps in Section 19.4.1, "To Set Up Your System for Running the Security Examples."

2. Create a web module for the servlet example, hello2,as described in Chapter 6, "Getting Started with Web Applications," in *The Java EE 7 Tutorial, Volume 1*.

3. Add the appropriate security annotations to the servlet. The security annotations are described in Section 19.4.2.1, "Specifying Security for Basic Authentication Using Annotations."

4. Build, package, and deploy the web application by following the steps in Section 19.4.2.2, "To Build, Package, and Deploy the hello2-basicauth Example Using NetBeans IDE," or Section 19.4.2.3, "To Build, Package, and Deploy the hello2-basicauth Example Using Maven."

5. Run the web application by following the steps in Section 19.4.2.4, "To Run the hello2-basicauth Example."

19.4.2.1 Specifying Security for Basic Authentication Using Annotations

The default authentication mechanism used by GlassFish Server is basic authentication. With basic authentication, GlassFish Server spawns a standard login dialog box to collect user name and password data for a protected resource. Once the user is authenticated, access to the protected resource is permitted.

To specify security for a servlet, use the `@ServletSecurity` annotation. This annotation allows you to specify both specific constraints on HTTP methods and more general constraints that apply to all HTTP methods for which no specific constraint is specified. Within the `@ServletSecurity` annotation, you can specify the following annotations.

■ The `@HttpMethodConstraint` annotation applies to a specific HTTP method.

■ The more general `@HttpConstraint` annotation applies to all HTTP methods for which there is no corresponding `@HttpMethodConstraint` annotation.

Both the `@HttpMethodConstraint` and `@HttpConstraint` annotations within the `@ServletSecurity` annotation can specify the following.

■ A `transportGuarantee` element that specifies the data protection requirements (that is, whether or not SSL/TLS is required) that must be satisfied by the connections on which requests arrive. Valid values for this element are `NONE` and `CONFIDENTIAL`.

■ A `rolesAllowed` element that specifies the names of the authorized roles.

For the `hello2-basicauth` application, the `GreetingServlet` has the following annotations:

```
@WebServlet(name = "GreetingServlet", urlPatterns = {"/greeting"})
@ServletSecurity(
@HttpConstraint(transportGuarantee = TransportGuarantee.CONFIDENTIAL,
    rolesAllowed = {"TutorialUser"}))
```

These annotations specify that the request URI /greeting can be accessed only by users who have been authorized to access this URL because they have been verified to be in the role TutorialUser. The data will be sent over a protected transport in order to keep the user name and password data from being read in transit.

If you use the @ServletSecurity annotation, you do not need to specify security settings in the deployment descriptor. Use the deployment descriptor to specify settings for nondefault authentication mechanisms, for which you cannot use the @ServletSecurity annotation.

19.4.2.2 To Build, Package, and Deploy the hello2-basicauth Example Using NetBeans IDE

1. Follow the steps in Section 19.4.1, "To Set Up Your System for Running the Security Examples."

2. From the **File** menu, choose **Open Project**.

3. In the Open Project dialog box, navigate to:

   tut-install/examples/security

4. Select the hello2-basicauth folder.

5. Click **Open Project**.

6. In the **Projects** tab, right-click the hello2-basicauth project and select **Build**.

   This command builds the example application and deploys it to your GlassFish Server instance.

19.4.2.3 To Build, Package, and Deploy the hello2-basicauth Example Using Maven

1. Follow the steps in Section 19.4.1, "To Set Up Your System for Running the Security Examples."

2. In a terminal window, go to:

   tut-install/examples/security/hello2-basicauth/

3. Enter the following command:

   ```
   mvn install
   ```

   This command builds and packages the application into a WAR file, hello2-basicauth.war, that is located in the target directory, then deploys the WAR file.

19.4.2.4 To Run the hello2-basicauth Example

1. In a web browser, enter the following URL:

   ```
   https://localhost:8181/hello2-basicauth/greeting
   ```

   You may be prompted to accept the security certificate for the server. If so, accept the security certificate. If the browser warns that the certificate is invalid because it is self-signed, add a security exception for the application.

   An Authentication Required dialog box appears. Its appearance varies, depending on the browser you use.

2. Enter a user name and password combination that corresponds to a user who has already been created in the `file` realm of GlassFish Server and has been assigned to the group `TutorialUser`; then click **OK**.

   Basic authentication is case sensitive for both the user name and password, so enter the user name and password exactly as defined for GlassFish Server.

   The server returns the requested resource if all the following conditions are met.

   - A user with the user name you entered is defined for GlassFish Server.

   - The user with the user name you entered has the password you entered.

   - The user name and password combination you entered is assigned to the group `TutorialUser` in GlassFish Server.

   - The role of `TutorialUser`, as defined for the application, is mapped to the group `TutorialUser`, as defined for GlassFish Server.

3. Enter a name in the field and click **Submit**.

   Because you have already been authorized, the name you enter in this step does not have any limitations. You have unlimited access to the application now.

   The application responds by saying "Hello" to the name you entered.

19.4.3 The hello1-formauth Example: Form-Based Authentication with a JavaServer Faces Application

This example explains how to use form-based authentication with a JavaServer Faces application. With form-based authentication, you can customize the login screen and error pages that are presented to the web client for authentication of the user name and password. When a user submits his or her name and password, the server determines whether the user name and password are those of an authorized user and, if authorized, sends the requested web resource.

This example, `hello1-formauth`, adds security to the basic JavaServer Faces application shown in Section 6.3, "A Web Module That Uses JavaServer Faces Technology: The hello1 Example," in *The Java EE 7 Tutorial, Volume 1*.

In general, the steps necessary for adding form-based authentication to an unsecured JavaServer Faces application are similar to those described in Section 19.4.2, "The hello2-basicauth Example: Basic Authentication with a Servlet." The major difference is that you must use a deployment descriptor to specify the use of form-based authentication, as described in Section 19.4.3.2, "Specifying Security for the Form-Based Authentication Example." In addition, you must create a login form page and a login error page, as described in Section 19.4.3.1, "Creating the Login Form and the Error Page."

This application can be found in the *tut-install*/examples/security/ hello1-formauth/ directory.

19.4.3.1 Creating the Login Form and the Error Page

When using form-based login mechanisms, you must specify a page that contains the form you want to use to obtain the user name and password, as well as a page to display if login authentication fails. This section discusses the login form and the error page used in this example. Section 19.4.3.2, "Specifying Security for the Form-Based Authentication Example," shows how you specify these pages in the deployment descriptor.

The login page can be an HTML page or a servlet, and it must return an HTML page containing a form that conforms to specific naming conventions (see the Java Servlet 3.1 specification for more information on these requirements). To do this, include the elements that accept user name and password information between <form></form> tags in your login page. The content of an HTML page or servlet for a login page should be coded as follows:

```
<form method="post" action="j_security_check">
    <input type="text" name="j_username">
    <input type="password" name= "j_password">
</form>
```

The full code for the login page used in this example can be found at *tut-install*/examples/security/hello1-formauth/src/main/webapp/login.html. Here is the code for this page:

```
<html lang="en">
    <head>
        <title>Login Form</title>
```

```
    </head>
    <body>
        <h2>Hello, please log in:</h2>
        <form method="post" action="j_security_check">
            <table role="presentation">
                <tr>
                    <td>Please type your user name: </td>
                    <td><input type="text" name="j_username"
                                size="20"/></td>
                </tr>
                <tr>
                    <td>Please type your password: </td>
                    <td><input type="password" name="j_password"
                                size="20"/></td>
                </tr>
            </table>
            <p></p>
            <input type="submit" value="Submit"/>
             
            <input type="reset" value="Reset"/>
        </form>
    </body>
</html>
```

The login error page is displayed if the user enters a user name and password combination that is not authorized to access the protected URI. For this example, the login error page can be found at *tut-install*/examples/security/ hello1-formauth/src/main/webapp/error.html. For this example, the login error page explains the reason for receiving the error page and provides a link that will allow the user to try again. Here is the code for this page:

```
<html lang="en">
    <head>
        <title>Login Error</title>
    </head>
    <body>
        <h2>Invalid user name or password.</h2>

        <p>Please enter a user name or password that is authorized to access
            this application. For this application, this means a user that
            has been created in the <code>file</code> realm and has been
            assigned to the <em>group</em> of <code>TutorialUser</code>.</p>
        <p><a href="login.html">Return to login page</a></p>
    </body>
</html>
```

19.4.3.2 Specifying Security for the Form-Based Authentication Example

This example takes a very simple servlet-based web application and adds form-based security. To specify form-based instead of basic authentication for a JavaServer Faces example, you must use the deployment descriptor.

The following sample code shows the security elements added to the deployment descriptor for this example, which can be found in *tut-install*/examples/ security/hello1-formauth/src/main/webapp/WEB-INF/web.xml:

```
<security-constraint>
    <display-name>Constraint1</display-name>
    <web-resource-collection>
        <web-resource-name>wrcoll</web-resource-name>
        <description/>
        <url-pattern>/*</url-pattern>
    </web-resource-collection>
    <auth-constraint>
        <description/>
        <role-name>TutorialUser</role-name>
    </auth-constraint>
</security-constraint>

<login-config>
    <auth-method>FORM</auth-method>
    <realm-name>file</realm-name>
    <form-login-config>
        <form-login-page>/login.xhtml</form-login-page>
        <form-error-page>/error.xhtml</form-error-page>
    </form-login-config>
</login-config>

<security-role>
    <description/>
    <role-name>TutorialUser</role-name>
</security-role>
```

19.4.3.3 To Build, Package, and Deploy the hello1-formauth Example Using NetBeans IDE

1. Follow the steps in Section 19.4.1, "To Set Up Your System for Running the Security Examples."

2. From the **File** menu, choose **Open Project**.

3. In the Open Project dialog box, navigate to:

   tut-install/examples/security

4. Select the `hello1-formauth` folder.

5. Click **Open Project**.

6. In the **Projects** tab, right-click the `hello1-formauth` project and select **Build**.

This command builds the example application and deploys it to your GlassFish Server instance.

19.4.3.4 To Build, Package, and Deploy the hello1-formauth Example Using Maven

1. Follow the steps in Section 19.4.1, "To Set Up Your System for Running the Security Examples."

2. In a terminal window, go to:

`tut-install/examples/security/hello1-formauth/`

3. Enter the following command at the terminal window or command prompt:

`mvn install`

This command builds and packages the application into a WAR file, `hello1-formauth.war`, that is located in the `target` directory, then deploys the WAR file to GlassFish Server.

19.4.3.5 To Run the hello1-formauth Example

To run the web client for `hello1-formauth`, follow these steps.

1. Open a web browser to the following URL:

`http://localhost:8080/hello1-formauth/`

2. In the login form, enter a user name and password combination that corresponds to a user who has already been created in the `file` realm of GlassFish Server and has been assigned to the group `TutorialUser`.

Form-based authentication is case sensitive for both the user name and password, so enter the user name and password exactly as defined for GlassFish Server.

3. Click **Submit**.

If you entered My_Name as the name and My_Pwd for the password, the server returns the requested resource if all the following conditions are met.

- A user with the user name My_Name is defined for GlassFish Server.

- The user with the user name My_Name has a password My_Pwd defined for GlassFish Server.

- The user My_Name with the password My_Pwd is assigned to the group TutorialUser in GlassFish Server.

- The role TutorialUser, as defined for the application, is mapped to the group TutorialUser, as defined for GlassFish Server.

When these conditions are met and the server has authenticated the user, the application appears.

4. Enter your name and click **Submit**.

   Because you have already been authorized, the name you enter in this step does not have any limitations. You have unlimited access to the application now.

   The application responds by saying "Hello" to you.

Next Steps

For additional testing and to see the login error page generated, close and reopen your browser, enter the application URL, and enter a user name and password that are not authorized.

20

Getting Started Securing Enterprise Applications

This chapter describes how to administer security for enterprise applications.

The following topics are addressed here:

- Basic Security Tasks for Enterprise Applications
- Securing Enterprise Beans
- Examples: Securing Enterprise Beans

20.1 Basic Security Tasks for Enterprise Applications

System administrators, application developers, bean providers, and deployers are responsible for administering security for enterprise applications. The basic security tasks are as follows:

- Setting up a database of users and assigning them to the proper group
- Setting up identity propagation
- Setting GlassFish Server properties that enable the applications to run properly, such as setting default principal-to-role mapping
- Annotating the classes and methods of an enterprise application to provide information about which methods need to have restricted access

The sections on the security examples in this chapter and the previous chapter explain how to perform these tasks.

20.2 Securing Enterprise Beans

Enterprise beans are Java EE components that implement EJB technology. Enterprise beans run in the EJB container, a runtime environment within GlassFish Server. Although transparent to the application developer, the EJB container provides system-level services, such as transactions and security to its enterprise beans, which form the core of transactional Java EE applications.

Enterprise bean methods can be secured in either of the following ways.

- **Declarative security** (preferred): Expresses an application component's security requirements using either deployment descriptors or annotations. The presence of an annotation in the business method of an enterprise bean class that specifies method permissions is all that is needed for method protection and authentication in some situations. This section discusses this simple and efficient method of securing enterprise beans.

Because of some limitations to the simplified method of securing enterprise beans, you would want to continue to use the deployment descriptor to specify security information in some instances. An authentication mechanism must be configured on the server for the simple solution to work. Basic authentication is GlassFish Server's default authentication method.

This tutorial explains how to invoke user name/password authentication of authorized users by decorating the enterprise application's business methods with annotations that specify method permissions.

To make the deployer's task easier, the application developer can define security roles. A security role is a grouping of permissions that a given type of application users must have in order to successfully use the application. For example, in a payroll application, some users will want to view their own payroll information (employee), some will need to view others' payroll information (manager), and some will need to be able to change others' payroll information (payrollDept). The application developer would determine the potential users of the application and which methods would be accessible to which users. The application developer would then decorate classes or methods of the enterprise bean with annotations that specify the types of users authorized to access those methods. Using annotations to specify authorized users is described in Section 20.2.1.1, "Specifying Authorized Users by Declaring Security Roles."

When one of the annotations is used to define method permissions, the deployment system will automatically require user name/password authentication. In this type of authentication, a user is prompted to enter a user name and password, which will be compared against a database of known users. If the user is found and the password matches, the roles that the user is assigned will be compared against the roles that are authorized to access the method. If the user is authenticated and found to have a role that is authorized to access that method, the data will be returned to the user.

Using declarative security is discussed in Section 20.2.1, "Securing an Enterprise Bean Using Declarative Security."

- **Programmatic security**: For an enterprise bean, code embedded in a business method that is used to access a caller's identity programmatically and that uses this information to make security decisions. Programmatic security is useful when declarative security alone is not sufficient to express the security model of an application.

  In general, security management should be enforced by the container in a manner that is transparent to the enterprise beans' business methods. The programmatic security APIs described in this chapter should be used only in the less frequent situations in which the enterprise bean business methods need to access the security-context information, such as when you want to grant access based on the time of day or other nontrivial condition checks for a particular role.

  Programmatic security is discussed in Section 20.2.2, "Securing an Enterprise Bean Programmatically."

Some of the material in this chapter assumes that you have already read Chapter 3, "Enterprise Beans"; Chapter 4, "Getting Started with Enterprise Beans"; and Chapter 18, "Introduction to Security in the Java EE Platform."

This section discusses securing a Java EE application where one or more modules, such as EJB JAR files, are packaged into an EAR file, the archive file that holds the application. Security annotations will be used in the Java programming class files to specify authorized users and basic, or user name/password, authentication.

Enterprise beans often provide the business logic of a web application. In these cases, packaging the enterprise bean within the web application's WAR module simplifies deployment and application organization. Enterprise beans may be packaged within a WAR module as Java class files or within a JAR file that is bundled within the WAR module. When a servlet or JavaServer Faces page handles the web front end and the application is packaged into a WAR module as a Java class file, security for the application can be handled in the application's web.xml file. The EJB in the WAR file can have its own deployment descriptor, ejb-jar.xml, if required. Securing web applications using web.xml is discussed in Chapter 19, "Getting Started Securing Web Applications."

The following sections describe declarative and programmatic security mechanisms that can be used to protect enterprise bean resources. The protected resources include enterprise bean methods that are called from application clients, web components, or other enterprise beans.

For more information on this topic, read the Enterprise JavaBeans 3.2 specification. This document can be downloaded from http://jcp.org/en/ jsr/detail?id=345. Chapter 12 of this specification, "Security Management," discusses security management for enterprise beans.

20.2.1 Securing an Enterprise Bean Using Declarative Security

Declarative security enables the application developer to specify which users are authorized to access which methods of the enterprise beans and to authenticate these users with basic, or user name/password, authentication. Frequently, the person who is developing an enterprise application is not the same person who is responsible for deploying the application. An application developer who uses declarative security to define method permissions and authentication mechanisms is passing along to the deployer a security view of the enterprise beans contained in the EJB JAR. When a security view is passed on to the deployer, he or she uses this information to define method permissions for security roles. If you don't define a security view, the deployer will have to determine what each business method does to determine which users are authorized to call each method.

A security view consists of a set of security roles, a semantic grouping of permissions that a given type of users of an application must have to successfully access the application. Security roles are meant to be logical roles, representing a type of user. You can define method permissions for each security role. A method permission is a permission to invoke a specified group of methods of an enterprise bean's business interface, home interface, component interface, and/or web service endpoints. After method permissions are defined, user name/password authentication will be used to verify the identity of the user.

It is important to keep in mind that security roles are used to define the logical security view of an application. They should not be confused with the user groups, users, principals, and other concepts that exist in GlassFish Server. An additional step is required to map the roles defined in the application to users, groups, and principals that are the components of the user database in the file realm of GlassFish Server. These steps are outlined in Section 18.5.4, "Mapping Roles to Users and Groups."

The following sections show how an application developer uses declarative security to either secure an application or to create a security view to pass along to the deployer.

20.2.1.1 Specifying Authorized Users by Declaring Security Roles

This section discusses how to use annotations to specify the method permissions for the methods of a bean class. For more information on these annotations, refer to the Common Annotations for the Java Platform specification at http://jcp.org/en/jsr/detail?id=250.

Method permissions can be specified on the class, the business methods of the class, or both. Method permissions can be specified on a method of the bean class to override the method permissions value specified on the entire bean class. The following annotations are used to specify method permissions.

- @DeclareRoles: Specifies all the roles that the application will use, including roles not specifically named in a @RolesAllowed annotation. The set of security roles the application uses is the total of the security roles defined in the @DeclareRoles and @RolesAllowed annotations.

  The @DeclareRoles annotation is specified on a bean class, where it serves to declare roles that can be tested (for example, by calling isCallerInRole) from within the methods of the annotated class. When declaring the name of a role used as a parameter to the isCallerInRole(String roleName) method, the declared name must be the same as the parameter value.

  The following example code demonstrates the use of the @DeclareRoles annotation:

```
@DeclareRoles("BusinessAdmin")
public class Calculator {
    ...
}
```

  The syntax for declaring more than one role is as shown in the following example:

```
@DeclareRoles({"Administrator", "Manager", "Employee"})
```

- @RolesAllowed("*list-of-roles*"): Specifies the security roles permitted to access methods in an application. This annotation can be specified on a class or on one or more methods. When specified at the class level, the annotation applies to all methods in the class. When specified on a method, the annotation applies to that method only and overrides any values specified at the class level.

  To specify that no roles are authorized to access methods in an application, use the @DenyAll annotation. To specify that a user in any role is authorized to access the application, use the @PermitAll annotation.

When used in conjunction with the @DeclareRoles annotation, the combined set of security roles is used by the application.

The following example code demonstrates the use of the @RolesAllowed annotation:

```
@DeclareRoles({"Administrator", "Manager", "Employee"})
public class Calculator {

    @RolesAllowed("Administrator")
    public void setNewRate(int rate) {
        ...
    }
}
```

- @PermitAll: Specifies that *all* security roles are permitted to execute the specified method or methods. The user is not checked against a database to ensure that he or she is authorized to access this application.

  This annotation can be specified on a class or on one or more methods. Specifying this annotation on the class means that it applies to all methods of the class. Specifying it at the method level means that it applies to only that method.

  The following example code demonstrates the use of the @PermitAll annotation:

```
import javax.annotation.security.*;
@RolesAllowed("RestrictedUsers")
public class Calculator {

    @RolesAllowed("Administrator")
    public void setNewRate(int rate) {
        //...
    }
    @PermitAll
    public long convertCurrency(long amount) {
        //...
    }
}
```

- @DenyAll: Specifies that *no* security roles are permitted to execute the specified method or methods. This means that these methods are excluded from execution in the Java EE container.

The following example code demonstrates the use of the `@DenyAll` annotation:

```
import javax.annotation.security.*;
@RolesAllowed("Users")
public class Calculator {
    @RolesAllowed("Administrator")
    public void setNewRate(int rate) {
        //...
    }
    @DenyAll
    public long convertCurrency(long amount) {
        //...
    }
}
```

The following code snippet demonstrates the use of the `@DeclareRoles` annotation with the `isCallerInRole` method. In this example, the `@DeclareRoles` annotation declares a role that the enterprise bean `PayrollBean` uses to make the security check by using `isCallerInRole("payroll")` to verify that the caller is authorized to change salary data:

```
@DeclareRoles("payroll")
@Stateless public class PayrollBean implements Payroll {
    @Resource SessionContext ctx;

    public void updateEmployeeInfo(EmplInfo info) {

        oldInfo = ... read from database;

        // The salary field can be changed only by callers
        // who have the security role "payroll"
        Principal callerPrincipal = ctx.getCallerPrincipal();
        if (info.salary != oldInfo.salary && !ctx.isCallerInRole("payroll")) {
            throw new SecurityException(...);
        }
        ...
    }
    ...
}
```

The following example code illustrates the use of the `@RolesAllowed` annotation:

```
@RolesAllowed("admin")
public class SomeClass {
    public void aMethod () { ... }
    public void bMethod () { ... }
```

```
    . . .
}

@Stateless public class MyBean extends SomeClass implements A  {

    @RolesAllowed("HR")
    public void aMethod () { ... }

    public void cMethod () { ... }
    . . .
}
```

In this example, assuming that aMethod, bMethod, and cMethod are methods of business interface A, the method permissions values of methods aMethod and bMethod are @RolesAllowed("HR") and @RolesAllowed("admin"), respectively. The method permissions for method cMethod have not been specified.

To clarify, the annotations are not inherited by the subclass itself. Instead, the annotations apply to methods of the superclass that are inherited by the subclass.

20.2.1.2 Specifying an Authentication Mechanism and Secure Connection

When method permissions are specified, basic user name/password authentication will be invoked by GlassFish Server.

To use a different type of authentication or to require a secure connection using SSL, specify this information in an application deployment descriptor.

20.2.2 Securing an Enterprise Bean Programmatically

Programmatic security, code that is embedded in a business method, is used to access a caller's identity programmatically and uses this information to make security decisions within the method itself.

20.2.2.1 Accessing an Enterprise Bean Caller's Security Context

In general, security management should be enforced by the container in a manner that is transparent to the enterprise bean's business methods. The security API described in this section should be used only in the less frequent situations in which the enterprise bean business methods need to access the security context information, such as when you want to restrict access to a particular time of day.

The `javax.ejb.EJBContext` interface provides two methods that allow the bean provider to access security information about the enterprise bean's caller.

- `getCallerPrincipal` allows the enterprise bean methods to obtain the current caller principal's name. The methods might, for example, use the name as a key to information in a database.

  The following code sample illustrates the use of the `getCallerPrincipal` method:

  ```
  @Stateless public class EmployeeServiceBean implements EmployeeService {
      @Resource SessionContext ctx;
      @PersistenceContext EntityManager em;

      public void changePhoneNumber(...) {
          ...
          // obtain the caller principal
          callerPrincipal = ctx.getCallerPrincipal();

          // obtain the caller principal's name
          callerKey = callerPrincipal.getName();

          // use callerKey as primary key to find EmployeeRecord
          EmployeeRecord myEmployeeRecord =
              em.find(EmployeeRecord.class, callerKey);

          // update phone number
          myEmployeeRecord.setPhoneNumber(...);

          ...
      }
  }
  ```

  In this example, the enterprise bean obtains the principal name of the current caller and uses it as the primary key to locate an `EmployeeRecord` entity. This example assumes that application has been deployed such that the current caller principal contains the primary key used for the identification of employees (for example, employee number).

- `isCallerInRole` allows the developer to code the security checks that cannot be easily defined using method permissions. Such a check might impose a role-based limit on a request, or it might depend on information stored in the database.

  The enterprise bean code can use the `isCallerInRole` method to test whether the current caller has been assigned to a given security role. Security roles are defined by the bean provider or the application assembler and are assigned by the deployer to principals or principal groups that exist in the operational environment.

The following code sample illustrates the use of the `isCallerInRole` method:

```
@Stateless public class PayrollBean implements Payroll {
    @Resource SessionContext ctx;

    public void updateEmployeeInfo(EmplInfo info) {

        oldInfo = ... read from database;

        // The salary field can be changed only by callers
        // who have the security role "payroll"
        if (info.salary != oldInfo.salary &&
            !ctx.isCallerInRole("payroll")) {
                throw new SecurityException(...);
        }
        ...
    }
    ...
}
```

You would use programmatic security in this way to dynamically control access to a method, for example, when you want to deny access except during a particular time of day. An example application that uses the `getCallerPrincipal` and `isCallerInRole` methods is described in Section 20.3.2, "The converter-secure Example: Securing an Enterprise Bean with Programmatic Security."

20.2.3 Propagating a Security Identity (Run-As)

You can specify whether a caller's security identity should be used for the execution of specified methods of an enterprise bean or whether a specific run-as identity should be used. Figure 20–1 illustrates this concept.

Figure 20–1   Security Identity Propagation

In this illustration, an application client is making a call to an enterprise bean method in one EJB container. This enterprise bean method, in turn, makes a call to an enterprise bean method in another container. The security identity during the first call is the identity of the caller. The security identity during the second call can be any of the following options.

- By default, the identity of the caller of the intermediate component is propagated to the target enterprise bean. This technique is used when the target container trusts the intermediate container.

- A *specific* identity is propagated to the target enterprise bean. This technique is used when the target container expects access using a specific identity.

To propagate an identity to the target enterprise bean, configure a run-as identity for the bean, as described in Section 20.2.3.1, "Configuring a Component's Propagated Security Identity." Establishing a run-as identity for an enterprise bean does not affect the identities of its callers, which are the identities tested for permission to access the methods of the enterprise bean. The run-as identity establishes the identity that the enterprise bean will use when it makes calls.

The run-as identity applies to the enterprise bean as a whole, including all the methods of the enterprise bean's business interface, local and remote interfaces, component interface, and web service endpoint interfaces, the message listener methods of a message-driven bean, the timeout method of an enterprise bean, and all internal methods of the bean that might be called in turn.

20.2.3.1 Configuring a Component's Propagated Security Identity

You can configure an enterprise bean's run-as, or propagated, security identity by using the @RunAs annotation, which defines the role of the application during execution in a Java EE container. The annotation can be specified on a class, allowing developers to execute an application under a particular role. The role must map to the user/group information in the container's security realm. The @RunAs annotation specifies the name of a security role as its parameter.

The following code demonstrates the use of the @RunAs annotation:

```
@RunAs("Admin")
public class Calculator {
    //....
}
```

You will have to map the run-as role name to a given principal defined in GlassFish Server if the given roles are associated with more than one user principal.

20.2.3.2 Trust between Containers

When an enterprise bean is designed so that either the original caller identity or a designated identity is used to call a target bean, the target bean will receive the propagated identity only. The target bean will not receive any authentication data.

There is no way for the target container to authenticate the propagated security identity. However, because the security identity is used in authorization checks (for example, method permissions or with the isCallerInRole method), it is vitally important that the security identity be authentic. Because no authentication data is available to authenticate the propagated identity, the target must trust that the calling container has propagated an authenticated security identity.

By default, GlassFish Server is configured to trust identities that are propagated from different containers. Therefore, you do not need to take any special steps to set up a trust relationship.

20.2.4 Deploying Secure Enterprise Beans

The deployer is responsible for ensuring that an assembled application is secure after it has been deployed in the target operational environment. If a security view has been provided to the deployer through the use of security annotations and/or a deployment descriptor, the security view is mapped to the mechanisms and policies used by the security domain in the target operational environment, which in this case is GlassFish Server. If no security view is provided, the deployer must set up the appropriate security policy for the enterprise bean application.

Deployment information is specific to a web or application server.

20.3 Examples: Securing Enterprise Beans

The following examples show how to secure enterprise beans using declarative and programmatic security.

20.3.1 The cart-secure Example: Securing an Enterprise Bean with Declarative Security

This section discusses how to configure an enterprise bean for basic user name/password authentication. When a bean that is constrained in this way is requested, the server requests a user name and password from the client and verifies that the user name and password are valid by comparing them against a database of authorized users in GlassFish Server.

If the topic of authentication is new to you, see Section 19.2.2, "Specifying Authentication Mechanisms."

This example demonstrates security by starting with the unsecured enterprise bean application, `cart`, which is found in the *tut-install*/examples/ejb/cart/ directory and is discussed in Section 5.1, "The cart Example."

In general, the following steps are necessary to add user name/password authentication to an existing application that contains an enterprise bean. In the example application included with this tutorial, these steps have been completed for you and are listed here simply to show what needs to be done should you wish to create a similar application.

1. Create an application like the one in Section 5.1, "The cart Example." The example in this tutorial starts with this example and demonstrates adding basic authentication of the client to this application. The example application discussed in this section can be found at *tut-install*/examples/security/ cart-secure/.

2. If you have not already done so, complete the steps in Section 19.4.1, "To Set Up Your System for Running the Security Examples," to configure your system for running the tutorial applications.

3. Modify the source code for the enterprise bean, `CartBean.java`, to specify which roles are authorized to access which protected methods. This step is discussed in Section 20.3.1.1, "Annotating the Bean."

4. Build, package, and deploy the enterprise bean; then build and run the client application by following the steps in Section 20.3.1.2, "To Run the cart-secure Example Using NetBeans IDE," or Section 20.3.1.3, "To Run the cart-secure Example Using Maven."

20.3.1.1 Annotating the Bean

The source code for the original `cart` application was modified as shown in the following code snippet (modifications in **bold**). The resulting file can be found in the file *tut-install*/examples/security/cart-secure/cart-secure-ejb/src/main/ java/javaeetutorial/cart/ejb/CartBean.java.

The code snippet is as follows:

```
package javaeetutorial.cartsecure.ejb;

import java.io.Serializable;
import java.util.ArrayList;
import java.util.List;
import javaeetutorial.cart.util.BookException;
import javaeetutorial.cart.util.IdVerifier;
```

```
import javax.ejb.Remove;
import javax.ejb.Stateful;
import javax.annotation.security.DeclareRoles;
import javax.annotation.security.RolesAllowed;

@Stateful
@DeclareRoles("TutorialUser")
public class CartBean implements Cart, Serializable {
    List<String> contents;
    String customerId;
    String customerName;

    @Override
    public void initialize(String person) throws BookException {
        if (person == null) {
            throw new BookException("Null person not allowed.");
        } else {
            customerName = person;
        }

        customerId = "0";
        contents = new ArrayList<>();
    }

    @Override
    public void initialize(String person, String id) throws BookException {
        if (person == null) {
            throw new BookException("Null person not allowed.");
        } else {
            customerName = person;
        }
        IdVerifier idChecker = new IdVerifier();

        if (idChecker.validate(id)) {
            customerId = id;
        } else {
            throw new BookException("Invalid id: " + id);
        }

        contents = new ArrayList<>();
    }

    @Override
    @RolesAllowed("TutorialUser")
    public void addBook(String title) {
        contents.add(title);
    }
```

```
@Override
@RolesAllowed("TutorialUser")
public void removeBook(String title) throws BookException {
    boolean result = contents.remove(title);

    if (result == false) {
        throw new BookException("\"" + title + "\" not in cart.");
    }
}

@Override
@RolesAllowed("TutorialUser")
public List<String> getContents() {
    return contents;
}

@Override
@Remove()
@RolesAllowed("TutorialUser")
public void remove() {
    contents = null;
}
}
```

The @RolesAllowed annotation is specified on methods for which you want to restrict access. In this example, only users in the role of TutorialUser will be allowed to add and remove books from the cart and to list the contents of the cart. A @RolesAllowed annotation implicitly declares a role that will be referenced in the application; therefore, no @DeclareRoles annotation is required. The presence of the @RolesAllowed annotation also implicitly declares that authentication will be required for a user to access these methods. If no authentication method is specified in the deployment descriptor, the type of authentication will be user name/password authentication.

20.3.1.2 To Run the cart-secure Example Using NetBeans IDE

1. Follow the steps in Section 19.4.1, "To Set Up Your System for Running the Security Examples."

2. From the **File** menu, choose **Open Project**.

3. In the Open Project dialog box, navigate to:

   tut-install/examples/security

4. Select the cart-secure folder.

5. Select the **Open Required Projects** check box.

6. Click **Open Project**.

7. In the **Projects** tab, right-click the `cart-secure` project and select **Build**.

   This step builds and packages the application into `cart-secure.ear`, located in the `cart-secure-ear/target` directory, and deploys this EAR file to your GlassFish Server instance, retrieves the client stubs, and runs the client.

8. In the **Login for user:** dialog box, enter the user name and password of a `file` realm user created in GlassFish Server and assigned to the group `TutorialUser`; then click **OK**.

   If the user name and password you enter are authenticated, the output of the application client appears in the **Output** tab:

   ```
   ...
   Retrieving book title from cart: Infinite Jest
   Retrieving book title from cart: Bel Canto
   Retrieving book title from cart: Kafka on the Shore
   Removing "Gravity's Rainbow" from cart.
   Caught a BookException: "Gravity's Rainbow" not in cart.
   Java Result: 1
   ...
   ```

   If the user name and password are not authenticated, the dialog box reappears until you enter correct values.

20.3.1.3 To Run the cart-secure Example Using Maven

1. Follow the steps in Section 19.4.1, "To Set Up Your System for Running the Security Examples."

2. In a terminal window, go to:

   `tut-install/examples/security/cart-secure/`

3. To build the application, package it into an EAR file in the `cart-secure-ear/target` subdirectory, deploy it, and run it, enter the following command at the terminal window or command prompt:

   ```
   mvn install
   ```

4. In the **Login for user:** dialog box, enter the user name and password of a `file` realm user created in GlassFish Server and assigned to the group `TutorialUser`; then click **OK**.

If the user name and password you enter are authenticated, the output of the application client appears in the **Output** tab:

```
...
Retrieving book title from cart: Infinite Jest
Retrieving book title from cart: Bel Canto
Retrieving book title from cart: Kafka on the Shore
Removing "Gravity's Rainbow" from cart.
Caught a BookException: "Gravity's Rainbow" not in cart.
Java Result: 1
...
```

If the user name and password are not authenticated, the dialog box reappears until you enter correct values.

20.3.2 The converter-secure Example: Securing an Enterprise Bean with Programmatic Security

This example demonstrates how to use the `getCallerPrincipal` and `isCallerInRole` methods with an enterprise bean. This example starts with a very simple EJB application, `converter`, and modifies the methods of the `ConverterBean` so that currency conversion will occur only when the requester is in the role of `TutorialUser`.

This example can be found in the *tut-install*/examples/security/ converter-secure directory. This example is based on the unsecured enterprise bean application, `converter`, which is discussed in Chapter 4, "Getting Started with Enterprise Beans," and is found in the *tut-install*/examples/ejb/converter/ directory. This section builds on the example by adding the necessary elements to secure the application by using the `getCallerPrincipal` and `isCallerInRole` methods, which are discussed in more detail in Section 20.2.2.1, "Accessing an Enterprise Bean Caller's Security Context."

In general, the following steps are necessary when using the `getCallerPrincipal` and `isCallerInRole` methods with an enterprise bean. In the example application included with this tutorial, many of these steps have been completed for you and are listed here simply to show what needs to be done should you wish to create a similar application.

1. Create a simple enterprise bean application.

2. Set up a user in GlassFish Server in the `file` realm, in the group `TutorialUser`, and set up default principal to role mapping. To do this, follow the steps in Section 19.4.1, "To Set Up Your System for Running the Security Examples."

3. Modify the bean to add the `getCallerPrincipal` and `isCallerInRole` methods.

4. If the application contains a web client that is a servlet, specify security for the servlet, as described in Section 19.4.2.1, "Specifying Security for Basic Authentication Using Annotations."

5. Build, package, deploy, and run the application.

20.3.2.1 Modifying ConverterBean

The source code for the original `ConverterBean` class was modified to add the `if..else` clause that tests whether the caller is in the role of `TutorialUser`. If the user is in the correct role, the currency conversion is computed and displayed. If the user is not in the correct role, the computation is not performed, and the application displays the result as 0. The code example can be found in `converter-secure-ejb/src/main/java/javaeetutorial/converter/ejb/ConverterBean.java`.

The code snippet (with modifications shown in **bold**) is as follows:

```java
package javaeetutorial.convertersecure.ejb;

import java.math.BigDecimal;
import java.security.Principal;
import javax.ejb.Stateless;
import javax.annotation.Resource;
import javax.ejb.SessionContext;
import javax.annotation.security.DeclareRoles;
import javax.annotation.security.RolesAllowed;
@Stateless()
@DeclareRoles("TutorialUser")
public class ConverterBean{

    @Resource SessionContext ctx;
    private final BigDecimal yenRate = new BigDecimal("104.34");
    private final BigDecimal euroRate = new BigDecimal("0.007");

    @RolesAllowed("TutorialUser")
     public BigDecimal dollarToYen(BigDecimal dollars) {
        BigDecimal result = new BigDecimal("0.0");
        Principal callerPrincipal = ctx.getCallerPrincipal();
        if (ctx.isCallerInRole("TutorialUser")) {
            result = dollars.multiply(yenRate);
            return result.setScale(2, BigDecimal.ROUND_UP);
        } else {
            return result.setScale(2, BigDecimal.ROUND_UP);
```

```
        }
    }

@RolesAllowed("TutorialUser")
public BigDecimal yenToEuro(BigDecimal yen) {
    BigDecimal result = new BigDecimal("0.0");
    Principal callerPrincipal = ctx.getCallerPrincipal();
    if (ctx.isCallerInRole("TutorialUser")) {
        result = yen.multiply(euroRate);
        return result.setScale(2, BigDecimal.ROUND_UP);
    } else {
        return result.setScale(2, BigDecimal.ROUND_UP);
    }
    }
}
```

20.3.2.2 Modifying ConverterServlet

The following annotations specify security for the `converter` web client, `ConverterServlet`:

```
@WebServlet(urlPatterns = {"/"})
@ServletSecurity(
@HttpConstraint(transportGuarantee = TransportGuarantee.CONFIDENTIAL,
    rolesAllowed = {"TutorialUser"}))
```

20.3.2.3 To Run the converter-secure Example Using NetBeans IDE

1. Follow the steps in Section 19.4.1, "To Set Up Your System for Running the Security Examples."

2. From the **File** menu, choose **Open Project**.

3. In the Open Project dialog box, navigate to:

   tut-install/examples/security

4. Select the `converter-secure` folder.

5. Click **Open Project**.

6. In the **Projects** tab, right-click the `converter-secure` project and select **Build**.

   This command builds and deploys the example application to your GlassFish Server instance.

20.3.2.4 To Run the converter-secure Example Using Maven

1. Follow the steps in Section 19.4.1, "To Set Up Your System for Running the Security Examples."

2. In a terminal window, go to:

   tut-install/examples/security/converter-secure/

3. Enter the following command:

   ```
   mvn install
   ```

   This command builds and packages the application into a WAR file, converter-secure.war, located in the target directory, and deploys the WAR file.

20.3.2.5 To Run the converter-secure Example

1. Open a web browser to the following URL:

   ```
   http://localhost:8080/converter-secure
   ```

   An Authentication Required dialog box appears.

2. Enter a user name and password combination that corresponds to a user who has already been created in the file realm of GlassFish Server and has been assigned to the group of TutorialUser; then click **OK**.

3. Enter 100 in the input field and click **Submit**.

   A second page appears, showing the converted values.

21

Java EE Security: Advanced Topics

This chapter provides advanced information on securing Java EE applications.

The following topics are addressed here:

- Working with Digital Certificates
- Authentication Mechanisms
- Using the JDBC Realm for User Authentication
- Securing HTTP Resources
- Securing Application Clients
- Securing Enterprise Information Systems Applications
- Configuring Security Using Deployment Descriptors
- Further Information about Advanced Security Topics

21.1 Working with Digital Certificates

Digital certificates for GlassFish Server have already been generated and can be found in the directory *domain-dir*/`config/`. These digital certificates are self-signed and are intended for use in a development environment; they are not intended for production purposes. For production purposes, generate your own certificates and have them signed by a Certificate Authority (CA).

To use the Secure Sockets Layer (SSL), an application or web server must have an associated certificate for each external interface, or IP address, that accepts secure connections. The theory behind this design is that a server should provide some kind of reasonable assurance that its owner is who you think it is, particularly before receiving any sensitive information. It may be useful to think of a certificate as a "digital driver's license" for an Internet address. The certificate states with which company the site is associated, along with some basic contact information about the site owner or administrator.

The digital certificate is cryptographically signed by its owner and is difficult for anyone else to forge. For sites involved in e-commerce or in any other business transaction in which authentication of identity is important, a certificate can be purchased from a well-known CA such as VeriSign or Thawte. If your server certificate is self-signed, you must install it in the GlassFish Server keystore file (keystore.jks). If your client certificate is self-signed, you should install it in the GlassFish Server truststore file (cacerts.jks).

Sometimes, authentication is not really a concern. For example, an administrator might simply want to ensure that data being transmitted and received by the server is private and cannot be snooped by anyone eavesdropping on the connection. In such cases, you can save the time and expense involved in obtaining a CA certificate and simply use a self-signed certificate.

SSL uses **public-key cryptography**, which is based on key pairs. **Key pairs** contain one public key and one private key. Data encrypted with one key can be decrypted only with the other key of the pair. This property is fundamental to establishing trust and privacy in transactions. For example, using SSL, the server computes a value and encrypts it by using its private key. The encrypted value is called a **digital signature**. The client decrypts the encrypted value by using the server's public key and compares the value to its own computed value. If the two values match, the client can trust that the signature is authentic, because only the private key could have been used to produce such a signature.

Digital certificates are used with HTTPS to authenticate web clients. The HTTPS service of most web servers will not run unless a digital certificate has been installed. Use the procedure outlined in Section 21.1.1, "Creating a Server Certificate," to set up a digital certificate that can be used by your application or web server to enable SSL.

One tool that can be used to set up a digital certificate is keytool, a key and certificate management utility that ships with the JDK. This tool enables users to administer their own public/private key pairs and associated certificates for use in self-authentication, whereby the user authenticates himself or herself to other users or services, or data integrity and authentication services, using digital signatures. The tool also allows users to cache the public keys, in the form of certificates, of their communicating peers.

For a better understanding of keytool and public-key cryptography, see Section 21.8, "Further Information about Advanced Security Topics," for a link to the keytool documentation.

21.1.1 Creating a Server Certificate

A server certificate has already been created for GlassFish Server and can be found in the *domain-dir*/config/ directory. The server certificate is in keystore.jks. The cacerts.jks file contains all the trusted certificates, including client certificates.

If necessary, you can use keytool to generate certificates. The keytool utility stores the keys and certificates in a file termed a **keystore**, a repository of certificates used for identifying a client or a server. Typically, a keystore is a file that contains one client's or one server's identity. The keystore protects private keys by using a password.

If you don't specify a directory when specifying the keystore file name, the keystores are created in the directory from which the keytool command is run. This can be the directory where the application resides, or it can be a directory common to many applications.

The general steps for creating a server certificate are as follows.

1. Create the keystore.

2. Export the certificate from the keystore.

3. Sign the certificate.

4. Import the certificate into a **truststore**: a repository of certificates used for verifying the certificates. A truststore typically contains more than one certificate.

The next section provides specific information on using the keytool utility to perform these steps.

21.1.1.1 To Use keytool to Create a Server Certificate

Run keytool to generate a new key pair in the default development keystore file, keystore.jks. This example uses the alias server-alias to generate a new public/private key pair and wrap the public key into a self-signed certificate inside keystore.jks. The key pair is generated by using an algorithm of type RSA, with a default password of changeit. For more information and other examples of creating and managing keystore files, read the keytool documentation.

> **Note:** RSA is public-key encryption technology developed by RSA Data Security, Inc.

From the directory in which you want to create the key pair, run `keytool` as shown in the following steps.

1. Generate the server certificate.

   Enter the `keytool` command all on one line:

   ```
   java-home/bin/keytool -genkey -alias server-alias -keyalg RSA
   -keypass changeit -storepass changeit -keystore keystore.jks
   ```

   When you press **Enter**, `keytool` prompts you to enter the server name, organizational unit, organization, locality, state, and country code.

   You must enter the server name in response to `keytool`'s first prompt, in which it asks for first and last names. For testing purposes, this can be `localhost`.

2. Export the generated server certificate in `keystore.jks` into the file `server.cer`.

   Enter the `keytool` command all on one line:

   ```
   java-home/bin/keytool -export -alias server-alias -storepass changeit
   -file server.cer -keystore keystore.jks
   ```

3. If you want to have the certificate signed by a CA, read the example in the `keytool` documentation.

4. To add the server certificate to the truststore file, `cacerts.jks`, run `keytool` from the directory where you created the keystore and server certificate.

   Use the following parameters:

   ```
   java-home/bin/keytool -import -v -trustcacerts -alias server-alias
   -file server.cer -keystore cacerts.jks -keypass changeit
   -storepass changeit
   ```

   Information on the certificate, such as that shown next, will appear:

   ```
   Owner: CN=localhost, OU=My Company, O=Software, L=Santa Clara, ST=CA, C=US
   Issuer: CN=localhost, OU=My Company, O=Software, L=Santa Clara, ST=CA,
     C=US
   Serial number: 3e932169
   Valid from: Mon Nov 26 18:15:47 EST 2012 until: Sun Feb 24 18:15:47 EST
     2013
   Certificate fingerprints:
           MD5: 52:9F:49:68:ED:78:6F:39:87:F3:98:B3:6A:6B:0F:90
           SHA1: EE:2E:2A:A6:9E:03:9A:3A:1C:17:4A:28:5E:97:20:78:3F:
           SHA256: 80:05:EC:7E:50:50:5D:AA:A3:53:F1:11:9B:19:EB:0D:20:67:
           C1:12:AF:42:EC:CD:66:8C:BD:99:AD:D9:76:95
   ```

```
            Signature algorithm name: SHA256withRSA
            Version: 3
            ...
Trust this certificate? [no]:
```

5. Enter yes, then press the **Enter** or **Return** key.

    The following information appears:

    ```
    Certificate was added to keystore
    [Storing cacerts.jks]
    ```

21.1.2 Adding Users to the Certificate Realm

In the certificate realm, user identity is set up in the GlassFish Server security context and populated with user data obtained from cryptographically verified client certificates. For step-by-step instructions for creating this type of certificate, see Section 21.1, "Working with Digital Certificates."

21.1.3 Using a Different Server Certificate with GlassFish Server

Follow the steps in Section 21.1.1, "Creating a Server Certificate," to create your own server certificate, have it signed by a CA, and import the certificate into keystore.jks.

Make sure that when you create the certificate, you follow these rules.

■   When you create the server certificate, keytool prompts you to enter your first and last name. In response to this prompt, you must enter the name of your server. For testing purposes, this can be localhost.

■   If you want to replace the existing keystore.jks, you must either change your keystore's password to the default password (changeit) or change the default password to your keystore's password.

21.1.3.1 To Specify a Different Server Certificate

To specify that GlassFish Server should use the new keystore for authentication and authorization decisions, you must set the JVM options for GlassFish Server so that they recognize the new keystore. To use a different keystore from the one provided for development purposes, follow these steps.

1. Start GlassFish Server if you haven't already done so. Information on starting GlassFish Server can be found in Section 2.2, "Starting and Stopping GlassFish Server."

2. Open the GlassFish Server Administration Console in a web browser at `http://localhost:4848`.

3. Expand **Configurations**, then expand **server-config**, then click **JVM Settings**.

4. Click the **JVM Options** tab.

5. Change the following JVM options so that they point to the location and name of the new keystore. The current settings are shown below:

```
-Djavax.net.ssl.keyStore=${com.sun.aas.instanceRoot}/config/keystore.jks
-Djavax.net.ssl.trustStore=${com.sun.aas.instanceRoot}/config/cacerts.jks
```

6. If you've changed the keystore password from its default value, you need to add the password option as well:

```
-Djavax.net.ssl.keyStorePassword=your-new-password
```

7. Click **Save**, then restart GlassFish Server.

21.2 Authentication Mechanisms

This section discusses the client authentication and mutual authentication mechanisms.

21.2.1 Client Authentication

With **client authentication**, the web server authenticates the client by using the client's public key certificate. Client authentication is a more secure method of authentication than either basic or form-based authentication. It uses HTTP over SSL (HTTPS), in which the server authenticates the client using the client's public key certificate. SSL technology provides data encryption, server authentication, message integrity, and optional client authentication for a TCP/IP connection. You can think of a public key certificate as the digital equivalent of a passport. The certificate is issued by a trusted organization, a certificate authority (CA), and provides identification for the bearer.

Before using client authentication, make sure that the client has a valid public key certificate. For more information on creating and using public key certificates, read Section 21.1, "Working with Digital Certificates."

The following example shows how to declare client authentication in your deployment descriptor:

```
<login-config>
    <auth-method>CLIENT-CERT</auth-method>
</login-config>
```

21.2.2 Mutual Authentication

With **mutual authentication**, the server and the client authenticate each other. Mutual authentication is of two types:

- Certificate-based (see Figure 21–1)
- User name/password-based (see Figure 21–2)

When using certificate-based mutual authentication, the following actions occur.

1. A client requests access to a protected resource.
2. The web server presents its certificate to the client.
3. The client verifies the server's certificate.
4. If successful, the client sends its certificate to the server.
5. The server verifies the client's credentials.
6. If successful, the server grants access to the protected resource requested by the client.

Figure 21–1 shows what occurs during certificate-based mutual authentication.

Figure 21–1   Certificate-Based Mutual Authentication

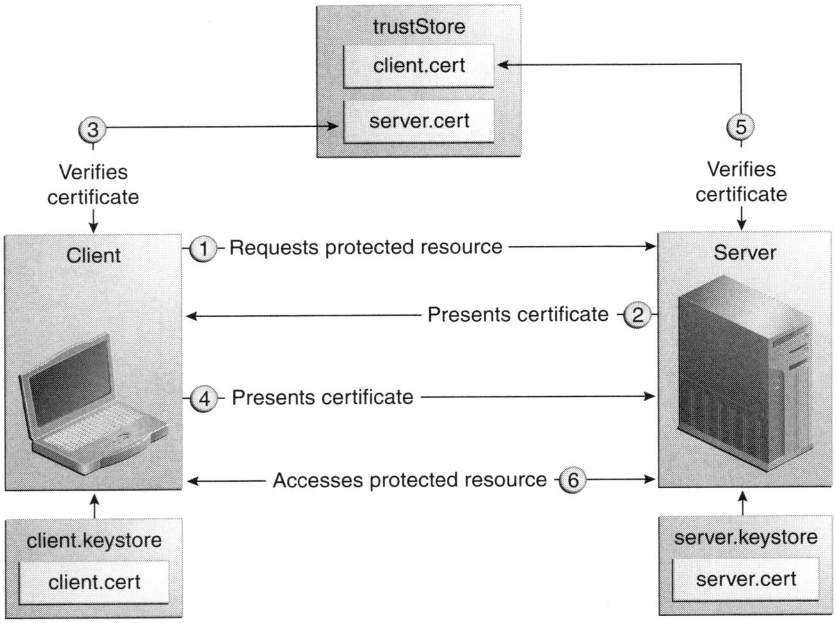

In user name/password-based mutual authentication, the following actions occur.

1. A client requests access to a protected resource.

2. The web server presents its certificate to the client.

3. The client verifies the server's certificate.

4. If successful, the client sends its user name and password to the server.

5. The server verifies the client's credentials

6. If the verification is successful, the server grants access to the protected resource requested by the client.

Figure 21–2 shows what occurs during user name/password-based mutual authentication.

Figure 21–2   User Name/Password-Based Mutual Authentication

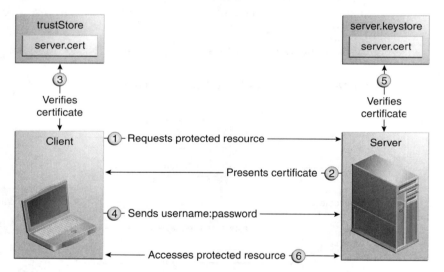

21.2.2.1 Enabling Mutual Authentication over SSL

This section discusses setting up client-side authentication. Enabling both server-side and client-side authentication is called mutual, or two-way, authentication. In client authentication, clients are required to submit certificates issued by a certificate authority that you choose to accept.

There are at least two ways to enable mutual authentication over SSL.

- The preferred method is to set the method of authentication in the `web.xml` application deployment descriptor to `CLIENT-CERT`. This enforces mutual authentication by modifying the deployment descriptor of the given application. In this way, client authentication is enabled only for a specific resource controlled by the security constraint, and the check is performed only when the application requires client authentication.

- A less commonly used method is to set the `clientAuth` property in the `certificate` realm to `true` if you want the SSL stack to require a valid certificate chain from the client before accepting a connection. A `false` value (which is the default) will not require a certificate chain unless the client requests a resource protected by a security constraint that uses `CLIENT-CERT` authentication. When you enable client authentication by setting the `clientAuth` property to `true`, client authentication will be required for all the requests going through the specified SSL port. If you turn `clientAuth` on, it is on all of the time, which can severely degrade performance.

When client authentication is enabled in both of these ways, client authentication will be performed twice.

21.2.2.2 Creating a Client Certificate for Mutual Authentication

If you have a certificate signed by a trusted Certificate Authority (CA) such as Verisign, and the GlassFish Server `cacerts.jks` file already contains a certificate verified by that CA, you do not need to complete this step. You need to install your certificate in the GlassFish Server certificate file only when your certificate is self-signed.

From the directory where you want to create the client certificate, run `keytool` as outlined here. When you press Enter, `keytool` prompts you to enter the server name, organizational unit, organization, locality, state, and country code.

You must enter the server name in response to `keytool`'s first prompt, in which it asks for first and last names. For testing purposes, this can be `localhost`. If this example is to verify mutual authentication and you receive a runtime error stating that the HTTPS host name is wrong, re-create the client certificate, being sure to use the same host name you will use when running the example. For example, if your machine name is `duke`, then enter `duke` as the certificate CN or when prompted for first and last names. When accessing the application, enter a URL that points to the same location (for example, `https://duke:8181/mutualauth/hello`). This is necessary because during SSL handshake, the server verifies the client certificate by comparing the certificate name to the host name from which it originates.

To create a keystore named `client_keystore.jks` that contains a client certificate named `client.cer`, follow these steps.

1. Create a backup copy of the server truststore file. To do this,

   a. Change to the directory containing the server's keystore and truststore files, *domain-dir*\config.

   b. Copy `cacerts.jks` to `cacerts.backup.jks`.

   c. Copy `keystore.jks` to `keystore.backup.jks`.

   Do not put client certificates in the `cacerts.jks` file. Any certificate you add to the `cacerts` file effectively can be a trusted root for any and all certificate chains. After you have completed development, delete the development version of the `cacerts` file and replace it with the original copy.

2. Generate the client certificate. Enter the following command from the directory where you want to generate the client certificate:

```
java-home\bin\keytool -genkey -alias client-alias -keyalg RSA
-keypass changeit -storepass changeit -keystore client_keystore.jks
```

3. Export the generated client certificate into the file `client.cer`:

```
java-home\bin\keytool -export -alias client-alias -storepass changeit
-file client.cer -keystore client_keystore.jks
```

4. Add the certificate to the truststore file *domain-dir*/config/cacerts.jks. Run `keytool` from the directory where you created the keystore and client certificate. Use the following parameters:

```
java-home\bin\keytool -import -v -trustcacerts -alias client-alias
-file client.cer -keystore domain-dir/config/cacerts.jks
-keypass changeit -storepass changeit
```

The `keytool` utility returns a message like this one:

```
Owner: CN=localhost, OU=My Company, O=Software, L=Santa Clara, ST=CA, C=US
Issuer: CN=localhost, OU=My Company, O=Software, L=Santa Clara, ST=CA,
 C=US
Serial number: 3e39e66a
Valid from: Tue Nov 27 12:22:47 EST 2012 until: Mon Feb 25 12:22:47 EST
 2013
Certificate fingerprints:
    MD5: 5A:B0:4C:88:4E:F8:EF:E9:E5:8B:53:BD:D0:AA:8E:5A
    SHA1:90:00:36:5B:E0:A7:A2:BD:67:DB:EA:37:B9:61:3E:26:B3:89:46:32
    Signature algorithm name: SHA1withRSA
```

```
                    Version: 3
                    Trust this certificate? [no]: yes
                    Certificate was added to keystore
                    [Storing cacerts.jks]
```

5. Restart GlassFish Server.

21.3 Using the JDBC Realm for User Authentication

An authentication realm, sometimes called a *security policy domain* or *security domain*, is a scope over which an application server defines and enforces a common security policy. A realm contains a collection of users, who may or may not be assigned to a group. GlassFish Server comes preconfigured with the file, certificate, and administration realms. An administrator can also set up LDAP, JDBC, digest, or custom realms.

An application can specify in its deployment descriptor which realm to use. If the application does not specify a realm, GlassFish Server uses its default realm, the file realm. If an application specifies that a JDBC realm is to be used for user authentication, GlassFish Server will retrieve user credentials from a database. The application server uses the database information and the enabled JDBC realm option in the configuration file.

A database provides an easy way to add, edit, or delete users at runtime and enables users to create their own accounts without any administrative assistance. Using a database has an additional benefit: providing a place to securely store any extra user information. A realm can be thought of as a database of user names and passwords that identify valid users of a web application or set of web applications with an enumeration of the list of roles associated with each valid user. Access to specific web application resources is granted to all users in a particular role, instead of enumerating a list of associated users. A user name can have any number of roles associated with it.

Two of the tutorial case studies, Chapter 29, "Duke's Tutoring Case Study Example," and Chapter 30, "Duke's Forest Case Study Example," use a JDBC realm for user authentication.

21.3.1 To Configure a JDBC Authentication Realm

GlassFish Server enables administrators to specify a user's credentials (user name and password) in the JDBC realm instead of in the connection pool. This prevents other applications from browsing the database tables for user credentials. By default, storing passwords as clear text is not supported in the JDBC realm. Under normal circumstances, passwords should not be stored as clear text.

1. Create the database tables in which user credentials for the realm will be stored.

2. Add user credentials to the database tables you created.

3. Create a JDBC connection pool for the database.

   You can use the Administration Console or the command line to create a connection pool.

4. Create a JDBC resource for the database.

   You can use the Administration Console or the command line to create a JDBC resource.

5. Create a realm.

   This step needs to associate the resource with the realm, define the tables and columns for users and groups used for authentication, and define the digest algorithm that will be used for storing passwords in the database.

   You can use the Administration Console or the command line to create a realm.

6. Modify the deployment descriptor for your application to specify the JDBC realm.

   - For an enterprise application in an EAR file, modify the `glassfish-application.xml` file.

   - For a web application in a WAR file, modify the `web.xml` file.

   - For an enterprise bean in an EJB JAR file, modify the `glassfish-ejb-jar.xml` file.

   For example, for a hypothetical application, the `web.xml` file could specify the `jdbcRealm` realm, as follows:

```
<login-config>
    <auth-method>FORM</auth-method>
    <realm-name>jdbcRealm</realm-name>
    <form-login-config>
        <form-login-page>/login.xhtml</form-login-page>
        <form-error-page>/login.xhtml</form-error-page>
    </form-login-config>
</login-config>
<security-constraint>
    <web-resource-collection>
        <web-resource-name>Secure Pages</web-resource-name>
        <description/>
        <url-pattern>/admin/*</url-pattern>
```

```
    </web-resource-collection>
    <auth-constraint>
        <role-name>ADMINS</role-name>
    </auth-constraint>
</security-constraint>
```

Form-based login is specified for all web pages under /admin. Access to those pages will be allowed only to users in the ADMINS role.

7. Assign security roles to users or groups of users in the realm.

To assign a security role to a group or to a user, add a security-role-mapping element to the application server-specific deployment descriptor, in this case glassfish-web.xml:

```
<security-role-mapping>
    <role-name>USERS</role-name>
    <group-name>USERS</group-name>
</security-role-mapping>
<security-role-mapping>
    <role-name>ADMINS</role-name>
    <group-name>ADMINS</group-name>
</security-role-mapping>
```

Since GlassFish Server users are assigned to groups during the user creation process, this is more efficient than mapping security roles to individual users.

21.4 Securing HTTP Resources

When a request URI is matched by multiple constrained URL patterns, the constraints that apply to the request are those that are associated with the best matching URL pattern. The servlet matching rules defined in Chapter 12, "Mapping Requests To Servlets," in the Java Servlet 3.1 Specification, are used to determine the best matching URL pattern to the request URI. No protection requirements apply to a request URI that is not matched by a constrained URL pattern. The HTTP method of the request plays no role in selecting the best matching URL pattern for a request.

When HTTP methods are listed within a constraint definition, the protections defined by the constraint are applied to the listed methods only.

When HTTP methods are not listed within a constraint definition, the protections defined by the constraint apply to the complete set of HTTP methods, including HTTP extension methods.

When constraints with different protection requirements apply to the same combination of URL patterns and HTTP methods, the rules for combining the protection requirements are as defined in Section 13.8.1, "Combining Constraints," in the Java Servlet 3.1 Specification.

Follow these guidelines to properly secure a web application.

- Do not list HTTP methods within constraint definitions. This is the simplest way to ensure that you are not leaving HTTP methods unprotected. For example:

```
<!-- SECURITY CONSTRAINT #1 -->
<security-constraint>
    <display-name>Do not enumerate Http Methods</display-name>
    <web-resource-collection>
        <url-pattern>/company/*</url-pattern>
    </web-resource-collection>
    <auth-constraint>
        <role-name>sales</role-name>
    </auth-constraint>
</security-constraint>
```

If you list methods in a constraint, all non-listed methods of the effectively infinite set of possible HTTP methods, including extension methods, will be *unprotected*. Use such a constraint *only* if you are certain that this is the protection scheme you intend to define. The following example shows a constraint that lists the GET method and thus defines no protection on any of the other possible HTTP methods:

```
<!-- SECURITY CONSTRAINT #2 -->
<security-constraint>
    <display-name>
        Protect GET only, leave all other methods unprotected
    </display-name>
    <web-resource-collection>
        <url-pattern>/company/*</url-pattern>
        <http-method>GET</http-method>
    </web-resource-collection>
    <auth-constraint>
        <role-name>sales</role-name>
    </auth-constraint>
</security-constraint>
```

- If you need to apply specific types of protection to specific HTTP methods, make sure that you define constraints to cover every method that you want to permit, with or without constraint, at the corresponding URL patterns. If there are any methods that you do not want to permit, you must also create a constraint that denies access to those methods at the same patterns; for an example, see security constraint #5 in the next bullet.

For example, to permit GET and POST, where POST requires authentication and GET is permitted without constraint, you could define the following constraints:

```
<!-- SECURITY CONSTRAINT #3 -->
<security-constraint>
    <display-name>Allow unprotected GET</display-name>
    <web-resource-collection>
        <url-pattern>/company/*</url-pattern>
        <http-method>GET</http-method>
    </web-resource-collection>
</security-constraint>


<!-- SECURITY CONSTRAINT #4 -->
<security-constraint>
    <display-name>Require authentication for POST</display-name>
    <web-resource-collection>
        <url-pattern>/company/*</url-pattern>
        <http-method>POST</http-method>
    </web-resource-collection>
    <auth-constraint>
        <role-name>sales</role-name>
    </auth-constraint>
</security-constraint>
```

- The simplest way to ensure that you deny all HTTP methods except those that you want to be permitted is to use http-method-omission elements to omit those HTTP methods from the security constraint, and also to define an auth-constraint that names no roles. The security constraint will apply to all methods except those that were named in the omissions, and the constraint will apply only to the resources matched by the patterns in the constraint.

For example, the following constraint excludes access to all methods except GET and POST at the resources matched by the pattern /company/*:

```
<!-- SECURITY CONSTRAINT #5 -->
<security-constraint>
    <display-name>Deny all HTTP methods except GET and POST</display-name>
    <web-resource-collection>
        <url-pattern>/company/*</url-pattern>
        <http-method-omission>GET</http-method-omission>
        <http-method-omission>POST</http-method-omission>
    </web-resource-collection>
    <auth-constraint/>
</security-constraint>
```

If you want to extend these exclusions to the unconstrained parts of your application, also include the URL pattern / (forward slash):

```
<!-- SECURITY CONSTRAINT #6 -->
<security-constraint>
    <display-name>Deny all HTTP methods except GET and POST</display-name>
    <web-resource-collection>
        <url-pattern>/company/*</url-pattern>
        <url-pattern>/</url-pattern>
        <http-method-omission>GET</http-method-omission>
        <http-method-omission>POST</http-method-omission>
    </web-resource-collection>
    <auth-constraint/>
</security-constraint>
```

- If, for your web application, you do not want any resource to be accessible unless you explicitly define a constraint that permits access to it, you can define an `auth-constraint` that names no roles and associate it with the URL pattern /. The URL pattern / is the weakest matching pattern. Do not list any HTTP methods in this constraint:

```
<!-- SECURITY CONSTRAINT #7 -->
<security-constraint>
    <display-name>
        Switch from Constraint to Permission model
        (where everything is denied by default)
    </display-name>
    <web-resource-collection>
        <url-pattern>/</url-pattern>
    </web-resource-collection>
    <auth-constraint/>
</security-constraint>
```

21.5 Securing Application Clients

The Java EE authentication requirements for application clients are the same as for other Java EE components, and the same authentication techniques can be used as for other Java EE application components. No authentication is necessary when accessing unprotected web resources.

When accessing protected web resources, the usual varieties of authentication can be used: HTTP basic authentication, HTTP login-form authentication, or SSL client authentication. Section 19.2.3, "Specifying an Authentication Mechanism in the Deployment Descriptor," describes how to specify HTTP basic authentication and HTTP login-form authentication. Section 21.2.1, "Client Authentication," describes how to specify SSL client authentication.

Authentication is required when accessing protected enterprise beans. The authentication mechanisms for enterprise beans are discussed in Section 20.2, "Securing Enterprise Beans."

An application client makes use of an authentication service provided by the application client container for authenticating its users. The container's service can be integrated with the native platform's authentication system so that a single sign-on capability is used. The container can authenticate the user either when the application is started or when a protected resource is accessed.

An application client can provide a class, called a **login module**, to gather authentication data. If so, the `javax.security.auth.callback.CallbackHandler` interface must be implemented, and the class name must be specified in its deployment descriptor. The application's callback handler must fully support `Callback` objects specified in the `javax.security.auth.callback` package.

21.5.1 Using Login Modules

An application client can use the Java Authentication and Authorization Service (JAAS) to create login modules for authentication. A JAAS-based application implements the `javax.security.auth.callback.CallbackHandler` interface so that it can interact with users to enter specific authentication data, such as user names or passwords, or to display error and warning messages.

Applications implement the `CallbackHandler` interface and pass it to the login context, which forwards it directly to the underlying login modules. A login module uses the callback handler both to gather input, such as a password or smart card PIN, from users and to supply information, such as status information, to users. Because the application specifies the callback handler, an underlying login module can remain independent of the various ways applications interact with users.

For example, the implementation of a callback handler for a GUI application might display a window to solicit user input, or the implementation of a callback handler for a command-line tool might simply prompt the user for input directly from the command line.

The login module passes an array of appropriate callbacks to the callback handler's `handle` method, such as a `NameCallback` for the user name and a `PasswordCallback` for the password; the callback handler performs the requested user interaction and sets appropriate values in the callbacks. For example, to process a `NameCallback`, the `CallbackHandler` might prompt for a name, retrieve the value from the user, and call the `setName` method of the `NameCallback` to store the name.

For more information on using JAAS for authentication in login modules, refer to the documentation listed in Section 21.8, "Further Information about Advanced Security Topics."

21.5.2 Using Programmatic Login

Programmatic login enables the client code to supply user credentials. If you are using an EJB client, you can use the `com.sun.appserv.security.ProgrammaticLogin` class with its convenient `login` and `logout` methods. Programmatic login is specific to a server.

21.6 Securing Enterprise Information Systems Applications

In Enterprise Information Systems (EIS) applications, components request a connection to an EIS resource. As part of this connection, the EIS can require a sign-on for the requester to access the resource. The application component provider has two choices for the design of the EIS sign-on.

- **Container-managed sign-on**: The application component lets the container take the responsibility of configuring and managing the EIS sign-on. The container determines the user name and password for establishing a connection to an EIS instance. For more information, see Section 21.6.1, "Container-Managed Sign-On."

- **Component-managed sign-on**: The application component code manages EIS sign-on by including code that performs the sign-on process to an EIS. For more information, see Section 21.6.2, "Component-Managed Sign-On."

You can also configure security for resource adapters. See Section 21.6.3, "Configuring Resource Adapter Security."

21.6.1 Container-Managed Sign-On

In container-managed sign-on, an application component does not have to pass any sign-on security information to the `getConnection()` method. The security information is supplied by the container, as shown in the following example (the method call is highlighted in **bold**):

```
// Business method in an application component
Context initctx = new InitialContext();
// Perform JNDI lookup to obtain a connection factory
javax.resource.cci.ConnectionFactory cxf =
    (javax.resource.cci.ConnectionFactory)initctx.lookup(
    "java:comp/env/eis/MainframeCxFactory");
```

```
// Invoke factory to obtain a connection. The security
// information is not passed in the getConnection method
javax.resource.cci.Connection cx = cxf.getConnection();
...
```

21.6.2 Component-Managed Sign-On

In component-managed sign-on, an application component is responsible for passing the needed sign-on security information for the resource to the `getConnection` method. For example, security information might be a user name and password, as shown here (the method call is highlighted in **bold**):

```
// Method in an application component
Context initctx = new InitialContext();

// Perform JNDI lookup to obtain a connection factory
javax.resource.cci.ConnectionFactory cxf =
    (javax.resource.cci.ConnectionFactory)initctx.lookup(
    "java:comp/env/eis/MainframeCxFactory");

// Get a new ConnectionSpec
com.myeis.ConnectionSpecImpl properties = //..

// Invoke factory to obtain a connection
properties.setUserName("...");
properties.setPassword("...");
javax.resource.cci.Connection cx =
    cxf.getConnection(properties);
...
```

21.6.3 Configuring Resource Adapter Security

A resource adapter is a system-level software component that typically implements network connectivity to an external resource manager. A resource adapter can extend the functionality of the Java EE platform either by implementing one of the Java EE standard service APIs, such as a JDBC driver, or by defining and implementing a resource adapter for a connector to an external application system. Resource adapters can also provide services that are entirely local, perhaps interacting with native resources. Resource adapters interface with the Java EE platform through the Java EE service provider interfaces (Java EE SPI). A resource adapter that uses the Java EE SPIs to attach to the Java EE platform will be able to work with all Java EE products.

To configure the security settings for a resource adapter, you need to edit the resource adapter descriptor file, `ra.xml`. Here is an example of the part of an `ra.xml` file that configures security properties for a resource adapter:

```
<authentication-mechanism>
    <authentication-mechanism-type>
        BasicPassword
    </authentication-mechanism-type>
    <credential-interface>
        javax.resource.spi.security.PasswordCredential
    </credential-interface>
</authentication-mechanism>
<reauthentication-support>false</reauthentication-support>
```

You can find out more about the options for configuring resource adapter security by reviewing *as-install*/`lib/schemas/connector_1_7.xsd`. You can configure the following elements in the resource adapter deployment descriptor file.

- **Authentication mechanisms**: Use the `authentication-mechanism` element to specify an authentication mechanism supported by the resource adapter. This support is for the resource adapter, not for the underlying EIS instance.

  There are two supported mechanism types:

  - `BasicPassword`, which supports the following interface:

    `javax.resource.spi.security.PasswordCredential`

  - `Kerbv5`, which supports the following interface:

    `javax.resource.spi.security.GenericCredential`

    GlassFish Server does not currently support this mechanism type.

- **Reauthentication support**: Use the `reauthentication-support` element to specify whether the resource adapter implementation supports reauthentication of existing `Managed-Connection` instances. Options are `true` or `false`.

- **Security permissions**: Use the `security-permission` element to specify a security permission that is required by the resource adapter code. Support for security permissions is optional and is not supported in the current release of GlassFish Server. You can, however, manually update the `server.policy` file to add the relevant permissions for the resource adapter.

  The security permissions listed in the deployment descriptor are different from those required by the default permission set as specified in the connector specification.

For more information on the implementation of the security permission specification, see the security policy file documentation listed in Section 21.8, "Further Information about Advanced Security Topics."

In addition to specifying resource adapter security in the `ra.xml` file, you can create a security map for a connector connection pool to map an application principal or a user group to a back-end EIS principal. The security map is usually used if one or more EIS back-end principals are used to execute operations (on the EIS) initiated by various principals or user groups in the application.

21.6.4 Mapping an Application Principal to EIS Principals

When using GlassFish Server, you can use security maps to map the caller identity of the application (principal or user group) to a suitable EIS principal in container-managed transaction-based scenarios. When an application principal initiates a request to an EIS, GlassFish Server first checks for an exact principal by using the security map defined for the connector connection pool to determine the mapped back-end EIS principal. If there is no exact match, GlassFish Server uses the wildcard character specification, if any, to determine the mapped back-end EIS principal. Security maps are used when an application user needs to execute an EIS operation that requires execution as a specific identity in the EIS.

To work with security maps, use the Administration Console. From the Administration Console, follow these steps to get to the security maps page.

1. In the navigation tree, expand the **Resources** node.

2. Expand the **Connectors** node.

3. Select the **Connector Connection Pools** node.

4. On the Connector Connection Pools page, click the name of the connection pool for which you want to create a security map.

5. Click the **Security Maps** tab.

6. Click **New** to create a new security map for the connection pool.

7. Enter a name by which you will refer to the security map, as well as the other required information.

   Click **Help** for more information on the individual options.

21.7 Configuring Security Using Deployment Descriptors

The recommended way to configure security in the Java EE 7 platform is with annotations. If you wish to override the security settings at deployment time, you can use security elements in the web.xml deployment descriptor to do so. This section describes how to use the deployment descriptor to specify basic authentication and to override default principal-to-role mapping.

21.7.1 Specifying Security for Basic Authentication in the Deployment Descriptor

The elements of the deployment descriptor that add basic authentication to an example tell the server or browser to perform the following tasks.

- Send a standard login dialog box to collect user name and password data.

- Verify that the user is authorized to access the application.

- If authorized, display the servlet to the user.

The following sample code shows the security elements for a deployment descriptor that could be used in the example of basic authentication found in the *tut-install*/examples/security/hello2_basicauth/ directory:

```
<security-constraint>
    <display-name>SecurityConstraint</display-name>
    <web-resource-collection>
        <web-resource-name>WRCollection</web-resource-name>
        <url-pattern>/greeting</url-pattern>
    </web-resource-collection>
    <auth-constraint>
        <role-name>TutorialUser</role-name>
    </auth-constraint>
    <user-data-constraint>
        <transport-guarantee>CONFIDENTIAL</transport-guarantee>
    </user-data-constraint>
</security-constraint>
<login-config>
    <auth-method>BASIC</auth-method>
    <realm-name>file</realm-name>
</login-config>
<security-role>
    <role-name>TutorialUser</role-name>
</security-role>
```

This deployment descriptor specifies that the request URI /greeting can be accessed only by users who have entered their user names and passwords and have been authorized to access this URL because they have been verified to be in the role TutorialUser. The user name and password data will be sent over a protected transport in order to keep it from being read in transit.

21.7.2 Specifying Non-Default Principal-to-Role Mapping in the Deployment Descriptor

To map a role name permitted by the application or module to principals (users) and groups defined on the server, use the `security-role-mapping` element in the runtime deployment descriptor file (`glassfish-application.xml`, `glassfish-web.xml`, or `glassfish-ejb-jar.xml`). The entry needs to declare a mapping between a security role used in the application and one or more groups or principals defined for the applicable realm of GlassFish Server. An example for the `glassfish-web.xml` file is shown below:

```
<glassfish-web-app>
    <security-role-mapping>
        <role-name>DIRECTOR</role-name>
        <principal-name>schwartz</principal-name>
    </security-role-mapping>
    <security-role-mapping>
        <role-name>DEPT-ADMIN</role-name>
        <group-name>dept-admins</group-name>
    </security-role-mapping>
</glassfish-web-app>
```

The role name can be mapped to either a specific principal (user), a group, or both. The principal or group names referenced must be valid principals or groups in the current default realm of GlassFish Server. The `role-name` in this example must exactly match the `role-name` in the `security-role` element of the corresponding `web.xml` file or the role name defined in the `@DeclareRoles` and/or `@RolesAllowed` annotations.

21.8 Further Information about Advanced Security Topics

For more information about the security topics covered in this chapter, see

- Documentation on the `keytool` command:

  `http://docs.oracle.com/javase/7/docs/technotes/tools/solaris/keytool.html`

- *Java Authentication and Authorization Service (JAAS) Reference Guide*:

  `http://docs.oracle.com/javase/7/docs/technotes/guides/security/jaas/JAASRefGuide.html`

- *Java Authentication and Authorization Service (JAAS): LoginModule Developer's Guide*:

  http://docs.oracle.com/javase/7/docs/technotes/guides/
  security/jaas/JAASLMDevGuide.html

- Documentation on security policy file syntax:

  http://docs.oracle.com/javase/7/docs/technotes/guides/
  security/PolicyFiles.html#FileSyntax

Part VI

Java EE Supporting Technologies

Part VI explores several technologies that support the Java EE platform. This part contains the following chapters:

- Chapter 22, "Transactions"
- Chapter 23, "Resource Adapters and Contracts"
- Chapter 24, "The Resource Adapter Examples"
- Chapter 25, "Using Java EE Interceptors"
- Chapter 26, "Batch Processing"
- Chapter 27, "Concurrency Utilities for Java EE"

22

Transactions

A typical enterprise application accesses and stores information in one or more databases. Because this information is critical for business operations, it must be accurate, current, and reliable. Data integrity would be lost if multiple programs were allowed to update the same information simultaneously or if a system that failed while processing a business transaction were to leave the affected data only partially updated. By preventing both of these scenarios, software transactions ensure data integrity. Transactions control the concurrent access of data by multiple programs. In the event of a system failure, transactions make sure that after recovery, the data will be in a consistent state.

The following topics are addressed here:

- Transactions in Java EE Applications

- What Is a Transaction?

- Container-Managed Transactions

- Bean-Managed Transactions

- Transaction Timeouts

- Updating Multiple Databases

- Transactions in Web Components

- Further Information about Transactions

22.1 Transactions in Java EE Applications

In a Java EE application, a transaction is a series of actions that must all complete successfully, or else all the changes in each action are backed out. Transactions end in either a commit or a rollback.

The Java Transaction API (JTA) allows applications to access transactions in a manner that is independent of specific implementations. JTA specifies standard Java interfaces between a transaction manager and the parties involved in a distributed transaction system: the transactional application, the Java EE server, and the manager that controls access to the shared resources affected by the transactions.

The JTA defines the `UserTransaction` interface that applications use to start, commit, or roll back transactions. Application components get a `UserTransaction` object through a JNDI lookup by using the name `java:comp/UserTransaction` or by requesting injection of a `UserTransaction` object. An application server uses a number of JTA-defined interfaces to communicate with a transaction manager; a transaction manager uses JTA-defined interfaces to interact with a resource manager.

The JTA 1.2 specification is available at `http://jcp.org/en/jsr/detail?id=907`.

22.2 What Is a Transaction?

To emulate a business transaction, a program may need to perform several steps. A financial program, for example, might transfer funds from a checking account to a savings account by using the steps listed in the following pseudocode:

```
begin transaction
    debit checking account
    credit savings account
    update history log
commit transaction
```

Either all or none of the three steps must complete. Otherwise, data integrity is lost. Because the steps within a transaction are a unified whole, a **transaction** is often defined as an indivisible unit of work.

A transaction can end in two ways: with a commit or with a rollback. When a transaction commits, the data modifications made by its statements are saved. If a statement within a transaction fails, the transaction rolls back, undoing the effects of all statements in the transaction. In the pseudocode, for example, if a disk drive were to crash during the `credit` step, the transaction would roll back and undo the data modifications made by the `debit` statement. Although the transaction fails, data integrity would be intact because the accounts still balance.

In the preceding pseudocode, the `begin` and `commit` statements mark the boundaries of the transaction. When designing an enterprise bean, you determine how the boundaries are set by specifying either container-managed or bean-managed transactions.

22.3 Container-Managed Transactions

In an enterprise bean with **container-managed transaction demarcation**, the EJB container sets the boundaries of the transactions. You can use container-managed transactions with any type of enterprise bean: session or message-driven. Container-managed transactions simplify development because the enterprise bean code does not explicitly mark the transaction's boundaries. The code does not include statements that begin and end the transaction. By default, if no transaction demarcation is specified, enterprise beans use container-managed transaction demarcation.

Typically, the container begins a transaction immediately before an enterprise bean method starts and commits the transaction just before the method exits. Each method can be associated with a single transaction. Nested or multiple transactions are not allowed within a method.

Container-managed transactions do not require all methods to be associated with transactions. When developing a bean, you can set the transaction attributes to specify which of the bean's methods are associated with transactions.

Enterprise beans that use container-managed transaction demarcation must not use any transaction-management methods that interfere with the container's transaction demarcation boundaries. Examples of such methods are the `commit`, `setAutoCommit`, and `rollback` methods of `java.sql.Connection` or the `commit` and `rollback` methods of `javax.jms.Session`. If you require control over the transaction demarcation, you must use application-managed transaction demarcation.

Enterprise beans that use container-managed transaction demarcation also must not use the `javax.transaction.UserTransaction` interface.

22.3.1 Transaction Attributes

A **transaction attribute** controls the scope of a transaction. Figure 22–1 illustrates why controlling the scope is important. In the diagram, `method-A` begins a transaction and then invokes `method-B` of `Bean-2`. When `method-B` executes, does it run within the scope of the transaction started by method-A, or does it execute with a new transaction? The answer depends on the transaction attribute of method-B.

Figure 22–1   Transaction Scope

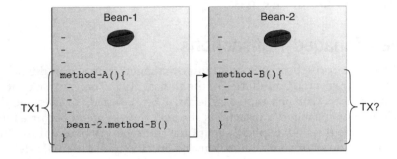

A transaction attribute can have one of the following values:

- Required
- RequiresNew
- Mandatory
- NotSupported
- Supports
- Never

22.3.1.1 Required Attribute

If the client is running within a transaction and invokes the enterprise bean's method, the method executes within the client's transaction. If the client is not associated with a transaction, the container starts a new transaction before running the method.

The Required attribute is the implicit transaction attribute for all enterprise bean methods running with container-managed transaction demarcation. You typically do not set the Required attribute unless you need to override another transaction attribute. Because transaction attributes are declarative, you can easily change them later.

22.3.1.2 RequiresNew Attribute

If the client is running within a transaction and invokes the enterprise bean's method, the container takes the following steps:

1. Suspends the client's transaction

2. Starts a new transaction

3. Delegates the call to the method

4. Resumes the client's transaction after the method completes

If the client is not associated with a transaction, the container starts a new transaction before running the method.

You should use the `RequiresNew` attribute when you want to ensure that the method always runs within a new transaction.

22.3.1.3 Mandatory Attribute

If the client is running within a transaction and invokes the enterprise bean's method, the method executes within the client's transaction. If the client is not associated with a transaction, the container throws a `TransactionRequiredException`.

Use the `Mandatory` attribute if the enterprise bean's method must use the transaction of the client.

22.3.1.4 NotSupported Attribute

If the client is running within a transaction and invokes the enterprise bean's method, the container suspends the client's transaction before invoking the method. After the method has completed, the container resumes the client's transaction.

If the client is not associated with a transaction, the container does not start a new transaction before running the method.

Use the `NotSupported` attribute for methods that don't need transactions. Because transactions involve overhead, this attribute may improve performance.

22.3.1.5 Supports Attribute

If the client is running within a transaction and invokes the enterprise bean's method, the method executes within the client's transaction. If the client is not associated with a transaction, the container does not start a new transaction before running the method.

Because the transactional behavior of the method may vary, you should use the `Supports` attribute with caution.

22.3.1.6 Never Attribute

If the client is running within a transaction and invokes the enterprise bean's method, the container throws a `RemoteException`. If the client is not associated with a transaction, the container does not start a new transaction before running the method.

22.3.1.7 Summary of Transaction Attributes

Table 22–1 summarizes the effects of the transaction attributes. Both the T1 and the T2 transactions are controlled by the container. A T1 transaction is associated with the client that calls a method in the enterprise bean. In most cases, the client is another enterprise bean. A T2 transaction is started by the container just before the method executes.

In the last column of Table 22–1, the word "None" means that the business method does not execute within a transaction controlled by the container. However, the database calls in such a business method might be controlled by the transaction manager of the database management system.

Table 22–1   Transaction Attributes and Scope

Transaction Attribute	Client's Transaction	Business Method's Transaction
Required	None	T2
Required	T1	T1
RequiresNew	None	T2
RequiresNew	T1	T2
Mandatory	None	Error
Mandatory	T1	T1
NotSupported	None	None
NotSupported	T1	None
Supports	None	None
Supports	T1	T1
Never	None	None
Never	T1	Error

22.3.1.8 Setting Transaction Attributes

Transaction attributes are specified by decorating the enterprise bean class or method with a `javax.ejb.TransactionAttribute` annotation and setting it to one of the `javax.ejb.TransactionAttributeType` constants.

If you decorate the enterprise bean class with `@TransactionAttribute`, the specified `TransactionAttributeType` is applied to all the business methods in the class. Decorating a business method with `@TransactionAttribute` applies the `TransactionAttributeType` only to that method. If a `@TransactionAttribute` annotation decorates both the class and the method, the method `TransactionAttributeType` overrides the class `TransactionAttributeType`.

The `TransactionAttributeType` constants shown in Table 22–2 encapsulate the transaction attributes described earlier in this section.

Table 22–2   TransactionAttributeType Constants

Transaction Attribute	TransactionAttributeType Constant
Required	TransactionAttributeType.REQUIRED
RequiresNew	TransactionAttributeType.REQUIRES_NEW
Mandatory	TransactionAttributeType.MANDATORY
NotSupported	TransactionAttributeType.NOT_SUPPORTED
Supports	TransactionAttributeType.SUPPORTS
Never	TransactionAttributeType.NEVER

The following code snippet demonstrates how to use the `@TransactionAttribute` annotation:

```
@TransactionAttribute(NOT_SUPPORTED)
@Stateful
public class TransactionBean implements Transaction {
...
    @TransactionAttribute(REQUIRES_NEW)
    public void firstMethod() { ... }

    @TransactionAttribute(REQUIRED)
    public void secondMethod() { ... }

    public void thirdMethod() { ... }

    public void fourthMethod() { ... }
}
```

In this example, the `TransactionBean` class's transaction attribute has been set to `NotSupported`, `firstMethod` has been set to `RequiresNew`, and `secondMethod` has been set to `Required`. Because a `@TransactionAttribute` set on a method overrides the class `@TransactionAttribute`, calls to `firstMethod` will create a new transaction, and calls to `secondMethod` will either run in the current transaction or start a new transaction. Calls to `thirdMethod` or `fourthMethod` do not take place within a transaction.

22.3.2 Rolling Back a Container-Managed Transaction

There are two ways to roll back a container-managed transaction. First, if a system exception is thrown, the container will automatically roll back the transaction. Second, by invoking the `setRollbackOnly` method of the `EJBContext` interface, the bean method instructs the container to roll back the transaction. If the bean throws an application exception, the rollback is not automatic but can be initiated by a call to `setRollbackOnly`.

22.3.3 Synchronizing a Session Bean's Instance Variables

The `SessionSynchronization` interface, which is optional, allows stateful session bean instances to receive transaction synchronization notifications. For example, you could synchronize the instance variables of an enterprise bean with their corresponding values in the database. The container invokes the `SessionSynchronization` methods (`afterBegin`, `beforeCompletion`, and `afterCompletion`) at each of the main stages of a transaction.

The `afterBegin` method informs the instance that a new transaction has begun. The container invokes `afterBegin` immediately before it invokes the business method.

The container invokes the `beforeCompletion` method after the business method has finished but just before the transaction commits. The `beforeCompletion` method is the last opportunity for the session bean to roll back the transaction (by calling `setRollbackOnly`).

The `afterCompletion` method indicates that the transaction has completed. This method has a single `boolean` parameter whose value is `true` if the transaction was committed and `false` if it was rolled back.

22.3.4 Methods Not Allowed in Container-Managed Transactions

You should not invoke any method that might interfere with the transaction boundaries set by the container. The following methods are prohibited:

- The `commit`, `setAutoCommit`, and `rollback` methods of `java.sql.Connection`
- The `getUserTransaction` method of `javax.ejb.EJBContext`
- Any method of `javax.transaction.UserTransaction`

You can, however, use these methods to set boundaries in application-managed transactions.

22.4 Bean-Managed Transactions

In **bean-managed transaction demarcation**, the code in the session or message-driven bean explicitly marks the boundaries of the transaction. Although beans with container-managed transactions require less coding, they have one limitation: When a method is executing, it can be associated with either a single transaction or no transaction at all. If this limitation will make coding your bean difficult, you should consider using bean-managed transactions.

The following pseudocode illustrates the kind of fine-grained control you can obtain with application-managed transactions. By checking various conditions, the pseudocode decides whether to start or stop certain transactions within the business method:

```
begin transaction
...
    update table-a
...
    if (condition-x)
    commit transaction
     else if (condition-y)
    update table-b
    commit transaction
     else
    rollback transaction
    begin transaction
    update table-c
    commit transaction
```

When coding an application-managed transaction for session or message-driven beans, you must decide whether to use Java Database Connectivity or JTA transactions. The sections that follow discuss both types of transactions.

22.4.1 JTA Transactions

JTA, or the Java Transaction API, allows you to demarcate transactions in a manner that is independent of the transaction manager implementation. GlassFish Server implements the transaction manager with the Java Transaction Service (JTS). However, your code doesn't call the JTS methods directly but instead invokes the JTA methods, which then call the lower-level JTS routines.

A **JTA transaction** is controlled by the Java EE transaction manager. You may want to use a JTA transaction because it can span updates to multiple databases from different vendors. A particular DBMS's transaction manager may not work with heterogeneous databases. However, the Java EE transaction manager does have one limitation: It does not support nested transactions. In other words, it cannot start a transaction for an instance until the preceding transaction has ended.

To demarcate a JTA transaction, you invoke the `begin`, `commit`, and `rollback` methods of the `javax.transaction.UserTransaction` interface.

22.4.2 Returning without Committing

In a stateless session bean with bean-managed transactions, a business method must commit or roll back a transaction before returning. However, a stateful session bean does not have this restriction.

In a stateful session bean with a JTA transaction, the association between the bean instance and the transaction is retained across multiple client calls. Even if each business method called by the client opens and closes the database connection, the association is retained until the instance completes the transaction.

In a stateful session bean with a JDBC transaction, the JDBC connection retains the association between the bean instance and the transaction across multiple calls. If the connection is closed, the association is not retained.

22.4.3 Methods Not Allowed in Bean-Managed Transactions

Do not invoke the `getRollbackOnly` and `setRollbackOnly` methods of the `EJBContext` interface in bean-managed transactions. These methods should be used only in container-managed transactions. For bean-managed transactions, invoke the `getStatus` and `rollback` methods of the `UserTransaction` interface.

22.5 Transaction Timeouts

For container-managed transactions, you can use the Administration Console to configure the transaction timeout interval. See Section 2.3, "Starting the Administration Console."

For enterprise beans with bean-managed JTA transactions, you invoke the `setTransactionTimeout` method of the `UserTransaction` interface.

22.5.1 To Set a Transaction Timeout

1. In the Administration Console, expand the **Configurations** node, then expand the **server-config** node and select **Transaction Service**.

2. On the Transaction Service page, set the value of the **Transaction Timeout** field to the value of your choice (for example, 5).

   With this setting, if the transaction has not completed within 5 seconds, the EJB container rolls it back.

   The default value is 0, meaning that the transaction will not time out.

3. Click **Save**.

22.6 Updating Multiple Databases

The Java EE transaction manager controls all enterprise bean transactions except for bean-managed JDBC transactions. The Java EE transaction manager allows an enterprise bean to update multiple databases within a transaction. Figure 22–2 and Figure 22–3 show two scenarios for updating multiple databases in a single transaction.

In Figure 22–2, the client invokes a business method in `Bean-A`. The business method begins a transaction, updates Database X, updates Database Y, and invokes a business method in `Bean-B`. The second business method updates Database Z and returns control to the business method in `Bean-A`, which commits the transaction. All three database updates occur in the same transaction.

In Figure 22–3, the client calls a business method in `Bean-A`, which begins a transaction and updates Database X. Then `Bean-A` invokes a method in `Bean-B`, which resides in a remote Java EE server. The method in `Bean-B` updates Database Y. The transaction managers of the Java EE servers ensure that both databases are updated in the same transaction.

Figure 22–2   Updating Multiple Databases

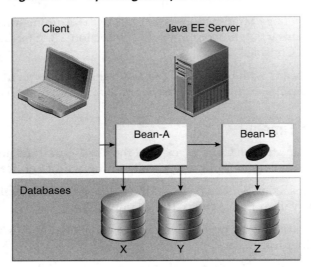

Figure 22–3   Updating Multiple Databases Across Java EE Servers

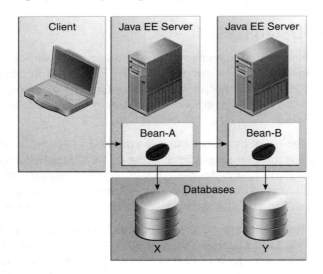

22.7 Transactions in Web Components

You can demarcate a transaction in a web component by using either the java.sql.Connection or the javax.transaction.UserTransaction interface.

These are the same interfaces that a session bean with bean-managed transactions can use. Transactions demarcated with the `UserTransaction` interface are discussed in Section 22.4.1, "JTA Transactions."

22.8 Further Information about Transactions

For more information about transactions, see the Java Transaction API 1.2 specification at `https://www.jcp.org/en/jsr/detail?id=907`.

23

Resource Adapters and Contracts

This chapter examines resource adapters and explains how communications between Java EE servers and EIS systems are mediated by them.

The following topics are addressed here:

- What Is a Resource Adapter?
- Metadata Annotations
- Common Client Interface
- Using Resource Adapters with Contexts and Dependency Injection for Java EE (CDI)
- Further Information about Resource Adapters

23.1 What Is a Resource Adapter?

A resource adapter is a Java EE component that implements the Java EE Connector Architecture for a specific EIS. Examples of EISs include enterprise resource planning, mainframe transaction processing, and database systems. In a Java EE server, the Java Message Server and JavaMail also act as EISs that you access using resource adapters. As illustrated in Figure 23–1, the resource adapter facilitates communication between a Java EE application and an EIS.

Stored in a Resource Adapter Archive (RAR) file, a resource adapter can be deployed on any Java EE server, much like a Java EE application. A RAR file may be contained in an Enterprise Archive (EAR) file, or it may exist as a separate file.

Figure 23–1   Resource Adapters

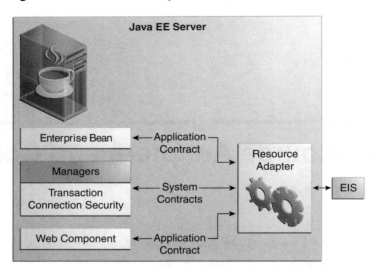

A resource adapter is analogous to a JDBC driver. Both provide a standard API through which an application can access a resource that is outside the Java EE server. For a resource adapter, the target system is an EIS; for a JDBC driver, it is a DBMS. Resource adapters and JDBC drivers are rarely created by application developers. In most cases, both types of software are built by vendors that sell tools, servers, or integration software.

The resource adapter mediates communication between the Java EE server and the EIS by means of contracts. The application contract defines the API through which a Java EE component, such as an enterprise bean, accesses the EIS. This API is the only view that the component has of the EIS. The system contracts link the resource adapter to important services that are managed by the Java EE server. The resource adapter itself and its system contracts are transparent to the Java EE component.

23.1.1 Management Contracts

The Java EE Connector Architecture defines system contracts that enable resource adapter lifecycle and thread management.

23.1.1.1 Lifecycle Management

The Connector Architecture specifies a lifecycle management contract that allows an application server to manage the lifecycle of a resource adapter. This contract provides a mechanism for the application server to bootstrap a resource adapter instance during the deployment or application server startup. This contract also provides a means for the application server to notify the resource adapter instance when it is undeployed or when an orderly shutdown of the application server takes place.

23.1.1.2 Work Management Contract

The Connector Architecture work management contract ensures that resource adapters use threads in the proper, recommended manner. This contract also enables an application server to manage threads for resource adapters.

Resource adapters that improperly use threads can jeopardize the entire application server environment. For example, a resource adapter might create too many threads or might not properly release threads it has created. Poor thread handling inhibits application server shutdown and impacts the application server's performance because creating and destroying threads are expensive operations.

The work management contract establishes a means for the application server to pool and reuse threads, similar to pooling and reusing connections. By adhering to this contract, the resource adapter does not have to manage threads itself. Instead, the resource adapter has the application server create and provide needed threads. When it is finished with a given thread, the resource adapter returns the thread to the application server. The application server manages the thread, either returning it to a pool for later reuse or destroying it. Handling threads in this manner results in increased application server performance and more efficient use of resources.

In addition to moving thread management to the application server, the Connector Architecture provides a flexible model for a resource adapter that uses threads.

- The requesting thread can choose to block (stop its own execution) until the work thread completes.

- The requesting thread can block while it waits to get the work thread. When the application server provides a work thread, the requesting thread and the work thread execute in parallel.

- The resource adapter can opt to submit the work for the thread to a queue. The thread executes the work from the queue at some later point. The resource adapter continues its own execution from the point it submitted the work to the queue, no matter when the thread executes it.

With the latter two approaches, the submitting thread and the work thread may execute simultaneously or independently. For these approaches, the contract specifies a listener mechanism to notify the resource adapter that the thread has completed its operation. The resource adapter can also specify the execution context for the thread, and the work management contract controls the context in which the thread executes.

23.1.2 Generic Work Context Contract

The work management contract between the application server and a resource adapter enables a resource adapter to do a task, such as communicating with the EIS or delivering messages, by delivering Work instances for execution.

A generic work context contract enables a resource adapter to control the contexts in which the Work instances that it submits are executed by the application server's WorkManager. A generic work context mechanism also enables an application server to support message inflow and delivery schemes. It also provides a richer contextual Work execution environment to the resource adapter while still maintaining control over concurrent behavior in a managed environment.

The generic work context contract standardizes the transaction context and the security context.

23.1.3 Outbound and Inbound Contracts

The Connector Architecture defines the following outbound contracts, system-level contracts between an application server and an EIS that enable outbound connectivity to an EIS.

- The connection management contract supports connection pooling, a technique that enhances application performance and scalability. Connection pooling is transparent to the application, which simply obtains a connection to the EIS.

- The transaction management contract extends the connection management contract and provides support for management of both local and XA transactions.

  A local transaction is limited in scope to a single EIS system, and the EIS resource manager itself manages such a transaction. An XA transaction or global transaction can span multiple resource managers. This form of transaction requires transaction coordination by an external transaction manager, typically bundled with an application server. A transaction manager uses a two-phase commit protocol to manage a transaction that spans multiple resource managers or EISs, and uses one-phase commit optimization if only one resource manager is participating in an XA transaction.

- The security management contract provides mechanisms for authentication, authorization, and secure communication between a Java EE server and an EIS to protect the information in the EIS.

  A work security map matches EIS identities to the application server domain's identities.

Inbound contracts are system contracts between a Java EE server and an EIS that enable inbound connectivity from the EIS: pluggability contracts for message providers and contracts for importing transactions.

23.2 Metadata Annotations

Java EE Connector Architecture provides a set of annotations to minimize the need for deployment descriptors.

- The @Connector annotation can be used by the resource adapter developer to specify that the JavaBeans component is a resource adapter JavaBeans component. This annotation is used for providing metadata about the capabilities of the resource adapter. Optionally, you can provide a JavaBeans component implementing the ResourceAdapter interface, as in the following example:

```
@Connector(
    displayName = "TrafficResourceAdapter",
    vendorName = "Java EE Tutorial",
    version = "7.0"
)
public class TrafficResourceAdapter implements ResourceAdapter,
                                               Serializable {

    ...

}
```

- The @ConnectionDefinition annotation defines a set of connection interfaces and classes pertaining to a particular connection type, as in the following example:

```
@ConnectionDefinition(
    connectionFactory = ConnectionFactory.class,
    connectionFactoryImpl = TradeConnectionFactory.class,
    connection = Connection.class,
    connectionImpl = TradeConnection.class
)
public class TradeManagedConnectionFactory ... {

    ...

}
```

- The @AdministeredObject annotation designates a JavaBeans component as an administered object.

- The @Activation annotation contains configuration information pertaining to inbound connectivity from an EIS instance, as in the following example:

```
@Activation(
        messageListeners = { TrafficListener.class }
)
public class TrafficActivationSpec implements ActivationSpec,
                                              Serializable {

    ...
    @ConfigProperty()
    /* port to listen to requests from the EIS */
    private String port;

    ...
}
```

- The @ConfigProperty annotation can be used on JavaBeans components to provide additional configuration information that may be used by the deployer and resource adapter provider. The preceding example code shows several @ConfigProperty annotations.

- The @ConnectionFactoryDefinition annotation is a resource definition annotation that is used to define a connector connection factory and register it in JNDI under the name specified in the mandatory name annotation element. The mandatory interfaceName annotation element specifies the fully qualified name of the connection factory interface class. The transactionSupport annotation element specifies the level of transaction support the connection factory needs to support. The minPoolSize and maxPoolSize annotation elements specify the minimum or maximum number of connections that should be allocated for a connection pool that backs this connection factory resource. Additional properties associated with the connection factory being defined can be specified through the properties element.

  Since repeated annotations are not allowed, the @ConnectionFactoryDefinitions annotation acts as a container for multiple connector connection factory definitions. The value annotation element contains the multiple connector connection factory definitions.

- The @AdministeredObjectDefinition annotation is a resource definition annotation that is used to define an administered object and register it in JNDI under the name specified in the mandatory name annotation element. The mandatory fully qualified name of the administered object's class must be indicated by the className element. Additional properties that must be configured in the administered object can be specified through the `properties` element.

Since repeated annotations are not allowed, the `@AdministeredObjectDefinitions` annotation acts as a container for multiple administered object definitions. The `value` annotation element contains the multiple administered object definitions.

The specification allows a resource adapter to be developed in mixed-mode form, that is the ability for a resource adapter developer to use both metadata annotations and deployment descriptors in applications. An application assembler or deployer may use the deployment descriptor to override the metadata annotations specified by the resource adapter developer.

The deployment descriptor for a resource adapter, if present, is named `ra.xml`. The `metadata-complete` attribute defines whether the deployment descriptor for the resource adapter module is complete or whether the class files available to the module and packaged with the resource adapter need to be examined for annotations that specify deployment information.

For the complete list of annotations and JavaBeans components provided in the Java EE 7 platform, see the Java EE Connector Architecture 1.7 specification.

23.3 Common Client Interface

This section explains how components use the Connector Architecture Common Client Interface (CCI) API and a resource adapter to access data from an EIS. The CCI API defines a set of interfaces and classes whose methods allow a client to perform typical data access operations. The CCI interfaces and classes are as follows.

- `ConnectionFactory`: Provides an application component with a `Connection` instance to an EIS.

- `Connection`: Represents the connection to the underlying EIS.

- `ConnectionSpec`: Provides a means for an application component to pass connection-request-specific properties to the `ConnectionFactory` when making a connection request.

- `Interaction`: Provides a means for an application component to execute EIS functions, such as database stored procedures.

- `InteractionSpec`: Holds properties pertaining to an application component's interaction with an EIS.

- `Record`: The superinterface for the various kinds of record instances. Record instances can be `MappedRecord`, `IndexedRecord`, or `ResultSet` instances, all of which inherit from the `Record` interface.

- `RecordFactory`: Provides an application component with a `Record` instance.

- `IndexedRecord`: Represents an ordered collection of `Record` instances based on the `java.util.List` interface.

A client or application component that uses the CCI to interact with an underlying EIS does so in a prescribed manner. The component must establish a connection to the EIS's resource manager, and it does so using the `ConnectionFactory`. The `Connection` object represents the connection to the EIS and is used for subsequent interactions with the EIS.

The component performs its interactions with the EIS, such as accessing data from a specific table, using an `Interaction` object. The application component defines the Interaction object by using an `InteractionSpec` object. When it reads data from the EIS, such as from database tables, or writes to those tables, the application component does so by using a particular type of `Record` instance: a `MappedRecord`, an `IndexedRecord`, or a `ResultSet` instance.

Note, too, that a client application that relies on a CCI resource adapter is very much like any other Java EE client that uses enterprise bean methods.

23.4 Using Resource Adapters with Contexts and Dependency Injection for Java EE (CDI)

For details about CDI, see Chapter 23, "Introduction to Contexts and Dependency Injection for Java EE," and Chapter 25, "Contexts and Dependency Injection for Java EE: Advanced Topics," both in *The Java EE 7 Tutorial, Volume 1*.

Do not specify the following classes in the resource adapter as CDI managed beans (that is, do not inject them), because the behavior of these classes as CDI managed beans has not been portably defined.

- **Resource adapter beans**: These beans are classes that are annotated with the `javax.resource.spi.Connector` annotation or are declared as corresponding elements in the resource adapter deployment descriptor, `ra.xml`.

- **Managed connection factory beans**: These beans are classes that are annotated with the `javax.resource.spi.ConnectorDefinition` annotation or the `javax.resource.spi.ConnectorDefinitions` annotation or are declared as corresponding elements in `ra.xml`.

- **Activation specification beans**: These beans are classes that are annotated with the `javax.resource.spi.Activation` annotation or are declared as corresponding elements in `ra.xml`.

- **Administered object beans**: These beans are classes that are annotated with the `javax.resource.spi.AdministeredObject` annotation or are declared as corresponding elements in `ra.xml`.

Other types of classes in the resource adapter can be CDI managed beans and will behave in a portable manner.

23.5 Further Information about Resource Adapters

For more information about resource adapters and annotations, see

- Java EE 7 Platform Specification (JSR 342):

  `http://jcp.org/en/jsr/detail?id=342`

- Java EE Connector Architecture 1.7 specification:

  `http://jcp.org/en/jsr/detail?id=322`

- EJB 3.2 specification:

  `http://jcp.org/en/jsr/detail?id=345`

- Common Annotations for the Java Platform:

  `http://www.jcp.org/en/jsr/detail?id=250`

24

The Resource Adapter Examples

This chapter describes two examples that demonstrate how to use resource adapters in Java EE applications and how to implement simple resource adapters. The `trading` example shows how to use a simple custom client interface to connect to an EIS from a web application. The resource adapter in this example implements the outbound contract and the custom client interface. The `traffic` example shows how to use a message-driven bean (MDB) to process traffic information updates from an EIS. The resource adapter in this example implements the inbound and work management contracts.

The following topics are addressed here:

- The trading Example
- The traffic Example

24.1 The trading Example

The `trading` example demonstrates how to implement and use a simple outbound resource adapter that submits requests to a legacy EIS using a TCP socket. The example demonstrates the scenario in Figure 24–1 and consists of the following modules:

- `trading-eis`: A Java SE program that simulates a legacy EIS
- `trading-rar`: The outbound resource adapter implementation
- `trading-war`: A web application that uses the resource adapter
- `trading-ear`: An enterprise archive that contains the resource adapter and the web application

Figure 24–1   The trading Example

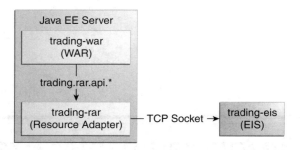

The `trading-eis` module is an auxiliary project that resembles a legacy stock trading execution platform. It contains a Java SE program that listens for trading requests in plain text on a TCP socket. The program replies to trading requests with a status value, a confirmation number, and the dollar amounts for the requested shares and fees. For example, a request-response pair would look like this:

```
>> BUY 1000 ZZZZ MARKET
<< EXECUTED #1234567 TOTAL 50400.00 FEE 252.00
```

The `trading-rar` module implements the outbound contract of the Java EE Connector Architecture to submit requests and obtain responses from the legacy stock trading execution platform. The `trading-rar` module provides and implements a custom client interface for Java EE applications to use. This interface is simpler than the Common Client Interface (CCI).

The `trading-war` module is a web application with a JavaServer Faces interface and a managed bean. This application enables clients to submit trades to the EIS using the resource adapter provided by the `trading-rar` module. The `trading-war` module uses the custom client interface provided by the resource adapter to obtain connections to the EIS.

24.1.1 Using the Outbound Resource Adapter

In most cases, Java EE application developers use outbound resource adapters developed by a third party. Outbound resource adapters either implement the Common Client Interface (CCI) or provide a custom interface for applications to interact with the EIS. Outbound resource adapters provide Java EE applications with the following elements:

- Connection factories
- Connection handles
- Other interfaces and objects specific to the EIS domain

Java EE applications obtain an instance of the connection factory via resource injection and then use the factory object to obtain connection handles to the EIS. The connection handles enable the application to make requests and obtain information from the EIS.

The `trading-rar` module provides a custom client interface that consists of the classes listed in Table 24–1.

Table 24–1   Classes and Interfaces in the javaeetutorial.trading.rar.api Package

API Component	Description
TradeOrder	Represents a trade order for the EIS
TradeResponse	Represents a response from the EIS to a trade request
TradeConnection	Represents a connection handle to the EIS
	Provides a method for applications to submit trades to the EIS
TradeConnectionFactory	Enables applications to obtain connection handles to the EIS
TradeProcessingException	Indicates that a problem occurred processing a trade request

The `ResourceAccessBean` managed bean in the `trading-war` module configures a connection factory for the `trading-rar` resource adapter by using the `@ConnectionFactoryDefinition` annotation as follows:

```
@Named
@SessionScoped
@ConnectionFactoryDefinition(
    name = "java:comp/env/eis/TradeConnectionFactory",
    interfaceName = "javaeetutorial.trading.rar.api.TradeConnectionFactory",
    resourceAdapter = "#trading-rar",
    minPoolSize = 5,
    transactionSupport =
            TransactionSupport.TransactionSupportLevel.NoTransaction
)
public class ResourceAccessBean implements Serializable { ... }
```

The name parameter specifies the JNDI name for the connection factory. This example registers the connection factory in the java:comp scope. You can use the ConnectionFactoryDefinition annotation to specify a different scope, such as java:global, java:app, or java:module. The AdministeredObjectDefinition annotation also enables you to register administered connector objects in the JNDI namespace.

The interfaceName parameter specifies the interface implemented by the connection factory included in the resource adapter. In this example, this is a custom interface.

The resourceAdapter parameter specifies the name of the resource adapter that contains the connection factory implementation. The # prefix in #trading-rar indicates that trading-rar is an embedded resource adapter that is bundled in the same EAR as this web application.

> **Note:** You can also configure a connection factory for a previously deployed outbound resource adapter using the administration commands from your application server. However, this is a vendor-specific procedure.

The managed bean obtains a connection factory object using resource injection as follows:

```
...
public class ResourceAccessBean implements Serializable {
    @Resource(lookup = "java:comp/env/eis/TradeConnectionFactory")
    private TradeConnectionFactory connectionFactory;
    ...
}
```

The managed bean uses the connection factory to obtain connection handles as follows:

```
TradeConnection connection = connectionFactory.getConnection();
```

The resource adapter returns a connection handle associated with a physical connection to the EIS. Once a connection handle is available, the managed bean submits a trade and obtains the response as follows:

```
TradeOrder order = new TradeOrder();
order.setNShares(1000);
order.setTicker(TradeOrder.Ticker.YYYY);
```

```
order.setOrderType(TradeOrder.OrderType.BUY);
order.setOrderClass(TradeOrder.OrderClass.MARKET);
...
try {
    TradeResponse response = connection.submitOrder(order);
    ...
} catch (TradeProcessingException ex) { ... }
```

24.1.2 Implementing the Outbound Resource Adapter

The trading-rar module implements the outbound contract and a custom client interface for the simple legacy stock trading platform EIS used in this example. The architecture of the outbound resource adapter is shown in Figure 24–2.

Figure 24–2   Architecture of the trading Example

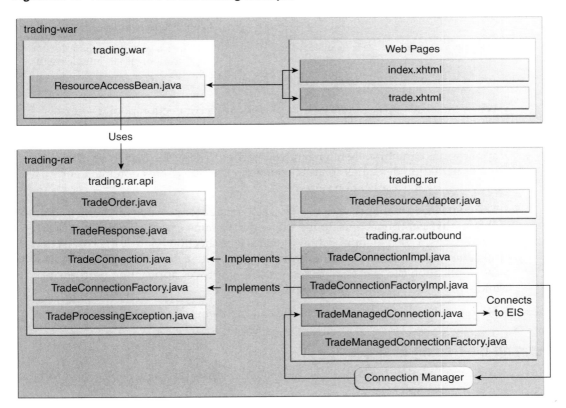

The `trading-rar` module implements the interfaces listed in Table 24–2.

Table 24–2   Interfaces Implemented in the trading-rar Module

Package	Interface	Description
javax.resource.spi	ResourceAdapter	Defines the lifecycle methods of the resource adapter
javax.resource.spi	ManagedConnectionFactory	Defines a connection factory that the connection manager from the application server uses to obtain physical connections to the EIS
javax.resource.spi	ManagedConnection	Defines a physical connection to the EIS that can be managed by the connection manager
trading.rar.api	TradeConnectionFactory	Defines a connection factory that applications use to obtain connection handles
trading.rar.api	TradeConnection	Defines a connection handle that applications use to interact with the EIS

When the `trading-ear` archive is deployed and a connection pool resource is configured as described in Section 24.1.1, "Using the Outbound Resource Adapter," the application server creates `TradeConnectionFactory` objects that applications can obtain using resource injection. The `TradeConnectionFactory` implementation delegates creating connections to the connection manager provided by the application server.

The connection manager uses the `ManagedConnectionFactory` implementation to obtain physical connections to the EIS and maintains a pool of active physical connections. When an application requests a connection handle, the connection manager associates a connection from the pool with a new connection handle that the application can use. Connection pooling improves application performance and simplifies resource adapter development.

For more details, see the code and the comments in the `trading-rar` module.

24.1.3 Running the trading Example

You can use either NetBeans IDE or Maven to build, package, deploy, and run the `trading` example.

24.1.3.1 To Run the trading Example Using NetBeans IDE

1. Make sure that GlassFish Server has been started (see Section 2.2, "Starting and Stopping GlassFish Server").

2. From the **File** menu, choose **Open Project**.

3. In the Open Project dialog box, navigate to:

   tut-install/examples/connectors

4. Select the trading folder.

5. Click **Open Project**.

6. In the **Projects** tab, expand the trading node.

7. Right-click the trading-eis module and select **Open Project**.

8. Right-click the trading-eis project and select **Run**.

   The messages from the EIS appear in the **Output** tab:

   ```
   Trade execution server listening on port 4004.
   ```

9. Right-click the trading-ear project and select **Build**.

   This command packages the resource adapter and the web application in an EAR file and deploys it to GlassFish Server.

10. Open the following URL in a web browser:

    ```
    http://localhost:8080/trading/
    ```

    The web interface enables you to connect to the EIS and submit trades. The server log shows the requests from the web application and the call sequence that provides connection handles from the resource adapter.

11. Before undeploying the trading-ear application, close the trading-eis application from the status bar.

24.1.3.2 To Run the trading Example Using Maven

1. Make sure that GlassFish Server has been started (see Section 2.2, "Starting and Stopping GlassFish Server").

2. In a terminal window, go to:

   tut-install/examples/connectors/trading/

3. Enter the following command:

   ```
   mvn install
   ```

This command builds and packages the resource adapter and the web application into an EAR archive and deploys it to GlassFish Server.

4. In the same terminal window, go to the `trading-eis` directory:

```
cd trading-eis
```

5. Enter the following command to run the trade execution platform:

```
mvn exec:java
```

The messages from the EIS appear in the terminal window:

```
Trade execution server listening on port 4004.
```

6. Open the following URL in a web browser:

```
http://localhost:8080/trading/
```

The web interface enables you to connect to the EIS and submit trades. The server log shows the requests from the web application and the call sequence that provides connection handles from the resource adapter.

7. Before undeploying the `trading-ear` application, press **Ctrl+C** on the terminal window to close the `trading-eis` application.

24.2 The traffic Example

The `traffic` example demonstrates how to implement and use a simple inbound resource adapter that receives data from a legacy EIS using a TCP socket.

The example is in the *tut-install*/examples/connectors/traffic directory. See Chapter 2, "Using the Tutorial Examples," for basic information on building and running sample applications.

The example demonstrates the scenario in Figure 24–3 and consists of the following modules:

- `traffic-eis`: A Java SE program that simulates an EIS
- `traffic-rar`: The inbound resource adapter implementation
- `traffic-ejb`: A message-driven bean that is the endpoint for incoming messages
- `traffic-war`: A web application that displays information from the message-driven bean
- `traffic-ear`: An enterprise archive that contains the resource adapter, the message-driven bean, and the web application

Figure 24–3   The traffic Example

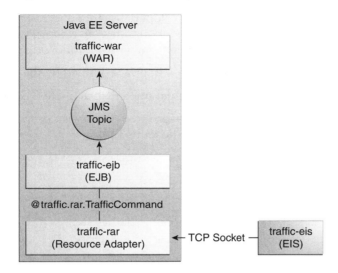

The `traffic-eis` module is an auxiliary project that resembles a legacy traffic information system. It contains a Java SE program that sends traffic status updates for several cities to any subscribed client. The program sends the updates in JSON format over a TCP socket. For example, a traffic update looks like this:

```
{"report":[
    {"city":"City1", "access":"AccessA", "status":"GOOD"},
    {"city":"City1", "access":"AccessB", "status":"CONGESTED"},
    ...
    {"city":"City5", "access":"AccessE", "status":"SLOW"}
]}
```

The `traffic-rar` module implements the inbound contract of the Java EE Connector Architecture. This module subscribes to the traffic information system using the TCP port indicated by the configuration provided by the MDB and invokes the methods of the MDB to process traffic information updates.

The `traffic-ejb` module contains a message-driven bean that activates the resource adapter with a configuration parameter (the TCP port to subscribe to the traffic information system). The MDB contains a method to process the traffic information updates. This method filters the updates for a particular city and publishes the results to a Java Message Service (JMS) topic.

The `traffic-war` module contains a message-driven bean that receives filtered traffic information updates from the JMS topic asynchronously and sends them to the clients using a WebSocket endpoint.

24.2.1 Using the Inbound Resource Adapter

In most cases, Java EE application developers use inbound resource adapters developed by a third party. To use an inbound resource adapter, a Java EE application includes a message-driven bean with the following characteristics.

- The MDB implements the business interface defined by the resource adapter.

- The MDB specifies configuration parameters to activate the resource adapter.

The business interface defined by the resource adapter is not specified in the Java EE Connector Architecture; it is specific to the EIS.

The MDB in this example is defined as follows:

```
@MessageDriven(
    activationConfig = {
      @ActivationConfigProperty(propertyName = "port",
                                propertyValue = "4008")
    }
)
public class TrafficMdb implements TrafficListener { ... }
```

The TrafficListener interface is defined in the API package of the resource adapter. The resource adapter requires the MDB to provide the port property.

When the MDB is deployed, it activates the traffic-rar resource adapter, which invokes the methods of the MDB to process traffic information updates. Then the MDB filters the updates for a particular city and publishes the results to a JMS topic.

In this particular example, the TrafficListener interface is empty. In addition to this interface, the resource adapter provides the TrafficCommand annotation and uses reflection to discover which methods in the MDB are decorated with this annotation:

```
@MessageDriven(...)
public class TrafficMdb implements TrafficListener {
    @TrafficCommand(name="report", info="Process report")
    public void processReport(String jsonReport) { ... }
    ...
}
```

This approach enables you to adapt the MDB to support new features in the EIS without having to modify the TrafficListener interface or the resource adapter module.

24.2.2 Implementing the Inbound Resource Adapter

The traffic-rar module implements the inbound resource adapter contract from the Java EE Connector Architecture for the simple traffic information system (EIS) used in this example. The architecture of the inbound resource adapter is shown in Figure 24–4.

Figure 24–4 Architecture of the traffic Example

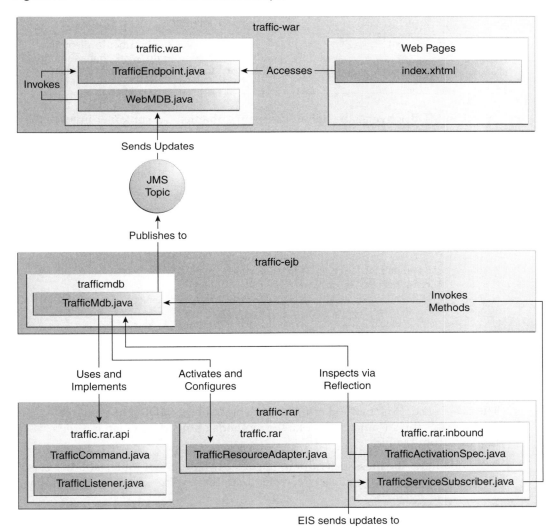

The `traffic-rar` module implements the interfaces listed in Table 24–3.

Table 24–3   Interfaces Implemented in the traffic-rar Module

Package	Interface	Description
javax.resource.spi	ResourceAdapter	Defines the lifecycle methods of the resource adapter.
javax.resource.spi	ActivationSpec	Defines the configuration parameters that the MDB provides to activate the inbound resource adapter.
javax.resource.spi	Work	The traffic service subscriber implements this interface from the work management contract to wait for traffic updates on a separate thread.

When an MDB activates the inbound resource adapter, the container invokes the `endpointActivation` method in the `TrafficResourceAdapter` class:

```
@Connector(...)
public class TrafficResourceAdapter implements ResourceAdapter, Serializable {
    ...
    @Override
    public void endpointActivation(MessageEndpointFactory endpointFactory,
                                   ActivationSpec spec)
                                   throws ResourceException {
        ...
        Class endpointClass = endpointFactory.getEndpointClass();
        /* this method is called from a new thread in the example:
        MessageEndpoint endpoint = endpointFactory.createEndpoint(null); */
    }
}
```

The `getEndpointClass` method returns the `Class` type of the MDB performing the activation, which enables the resource adapter to use reflection to find methods annotated with `@TrafficCommand` in the MDB.

The `createEndpoint` method returns an instance of the MDB. The resource adapter uses this instance to invoke the methods of the MDB when it receives requests from the EIS.

After obtaining the message endpoint instance (MDB), the resource adapter uses the work management contract to create the traffic service subscriber thread that receives traffic updates from the EIS. The resource adapter obtains the `WorkManager` instance from the bootstrap context as follows:

```
WorkManager workManager;
...
@Override
public void start(BootstrapContext ctx) ... {
    workManager = ctx.getWorkManager();
}
```

The resource adapter schedules the traffic service subscriber thread using the work manager:

```
tSubscriber = new TrafficServiceSubscriber(tSpec, endpoint);
workManager.scheduleWork(tSubscriber);
```

The `TrafficServiceSubscriber` class implements the `javax.resource.spi.Work` interface from the work management contract.

The traffic service subscriber thread uses reflection to invoke the methods in the MDB:

```
private String callMdb(MessageEndpoint mdb, Method command,
                       String... params) ... {
    String resp;
    /* this code contains proper exception handling in the sources */
    mdb.beforeDelivery(command);
    Object ret = command.invoke(mdb, (Object[]) params);
    resp = (String) ret;
    mdb.afterDelivery();
    return resp;
}
```

For more details, see the code and the comments in the `traffic-rar` module.

24.2.3 Running the traffic Example

You can use either NetBeans IDE or Maven to build, package, deploy, and run the `traffic` example.

24.2.3.1 To Run the traffic Example Using NetBeans IDE

1. Make sure that GlassFish Server has been started (see Section 2.2, "Starting and Stopping GlassFish Server").

2. From the **File** menu, choose **Open Project**.

3. In the Open Project dialog box, navigate to:

   `tut-install`/examples/connectors

4. Select the `traffic` folder.

5. Click **Open Project**.

6. In the **Projects** tab, expand the `traffic` node.

7. Right-click the `traffic-eis` module and select **Open Project**.

8. Right-click the `traffic-eis` project and select **Run**.

   The messages from the EIS appear on the Output tab:

   `Traffic EIS accepting connections on port 4008`

9. In the **Projects** tab, right-click the `traffic` project and select **Clean and Build**.

   This command builds and packages the resource adapter, the MDB, and the web application into an EAR archive and deploys it. The server log shows the call sequence that activates the resource adapter and the filtered traffic updates for City1.

10. Open the following URL in a web browser:

    `http://localhost:8080/traffic/`

    The web interface shows filtered traffic updates for City1 every few seconds.

11. After undeploying the `traffic-ear` application, close the `traffic-eis` application from the status bar.

24.2.3.2 To Run the traffic Example Using Maven

1. Make sure that GlassFish Server has been started (see Section 2.2, "Starting and Stopping GlassFish Server").

2. In a terminal window, go to:

   `tut-install`/examples/connectors/traffic/traffic-eis

3. Enter the following command in the terminal window:

   `mvn install`

   This command builds and packages the traffic EIS.

4. Enter the following command in the terminal window:

   `mvn exec:java`

The messages from the EIS appear in the terminal window:

```
Traffic EIS accepting connections on port 4008
```

Leave this terminal window open.

5. Open a new terminal window and go to:

   tut-install/examples/connectors/traffic/

6. Enter the following command:

   ```
   mvn install
   ```

   This command builds and packages the resource adapter, the MDB, and the web application into an EAR archive and deploys it. The server log shows the call sequence that activates the resource adapter and the filtered traffic updates for City1.

7. Open the following URL in a web browser:

   http://localhost:8080/traffic/

   The web interface shows the filtered traffic updates for City1 every few seconds.

8. After undeploying the traffic-ear application, press **Ctrl+C** in the first terminal window to close the traffic-eis application.

25

Using Java EE Interceptors

This chapter discusses how to create interceptor classes and methods that interpose on method invocations or lifecycle events on a target class.

The following topics are addressed here:

- Overview of Interceptors
- Using Interceptors
- The interceptor Example Application

25.1 Overview of Interceptors

Interceptors are used in conjunction with Java EE managed classes to allow developers to invoke interceptor methods on an associated **target class**, in conjunction with method invocations or lifecycle events. Common uses of interceptors are logging, auditing, and profiling.

Although interceptors are part of Enterprise JavaBeans 3.2 and Contexts and Dependency Injection for Java EE 1.1, the Interceptors 1.2 specification is downloadable as part of a maintenance release of JSR 318, Enterprise JavaBeans 3.1, available from `http://jcp.org/en/jsr/detail?id=318`. You can use interceptors with session beans, message-driven beans, and CDI managed beans. In all of these cases, the interceptor target class is the bean class.

An interceptor can be defined within a target class as an **interceptor method**, or in an associated class called an **interceptor class**. Interceptor classes contain methods that are invoked in conjunction with the methods or lifecycle events of the target class.

Interceptor classes and methods are defined using metadata annotations, or in the deployment descriptor of the application that contains the interceptors and target classes.

> **Note:** Applications that use the deployment descriptor to define interceptors are not portable across Java EE servers.

Interceptor methods within the target class or in an interceptor class are annotated with one of the metadata annotations defined in Table 25–1.

Table 25–1   Interceptor Metadata Annotations

Interceptor Metadata Annotation	Description
`javax.interceptor.AroundConstruct`	Designates the method as an interceptor method that receives a callback after the target class is constructed
`javax.interceptor.AroundInvoke`	Designates the method as an interceptor method
`javax.interceptor.AroundTimeout`	Designates the method as a timeout interceptor for interposing on timeout methods for enterprise bean timers
`javax.annotation.PostConstruct`	Designates the method as an interceptor method for post-construct lifecycle events
`javax.annotation.PreDestroy`	Designates the method as an interceptor method for pre-destroy lifecycle events

25.1.1 Interceptor Classes

Interceptor classes may be designated with the optional `javax.interceptor.Interceptor` annotation, but interceptor classes are not required to be so annotated. An interceptor class *must* have a public, no-argument constructor.

The target class can have any number of interceptor classes associated with it. The order in which the interceptor classes are invoked is determined by the order in which the interceptor classes are defined in the `javax.interceptor.Interceptors` annotation. However, this order can be overridden in the deployment descriptor.

Interceptor classes may be targets of dependency injection. Dependency injection occurs when the interceptor class instance is created, using the naming context of the associated target class, and before any @PostConstruct callbacks are invoked.

25.1.2 Interceptor Lifecycle

Interceptor classes have the same lifecycle as their associated target class. When a target class instance is created, an interceptor class instance is also created for each declared interceptor class in the target class. That is, if the target class declares multiple interceptor classes, an instance of each class is created when the target class instance is created. The target class instance and all interceptor class instances are fully instantiated before any @PostConstruct callbacks are invoked, and any @PreDestroy callbacks are invoked before the target class and interceptor class instances are destroyed.

25.1.3 Interceptors and CDI

Contexts and Dependency Injection for Java EE (CDI) builds on the basic functionality of Java EE interceptors. For information on CDI interceptors, including a discussion of interceptor binding types, see Section 25.6, "Using Interceptors in CDI Applications,"in *The Java EE 7 Tutorial, Volume 1*.

25.2 Using Interceptors

To define an interceptor, use one of the interceptor metadata annotations listed in Table 25–1 within the target class, or in a separate interceptor class. The following code declares an @AroundTimeout interceptor method within a target class:

```
@Stateless
public class TimerBean {
    ...
    @Schedule(minute="*/1", hour="*")
    public void automaticTimerMethod() { ... }

    @AroundTimeout
    public void timeoutInterceptorMethod(InvocationContext ctx) { ... }
    ...
}
```

If you are using interceptor classes, use the javax.interceptor.Interceptors annotation to declare one or more interceptors at the class or method level of the target class. The following code declares interceptors at the class level:

```
@Stateless
@Interceptors({PrimaryInterceptor.class, SecondaryInterceptor.class})
public class OrderBean { ... }
```

The following code declares a method-level interceptor class:

```
@Stateless
public class OrderBean {
    ...
    @Interceptors(OrderInterceptor.class)
    public void placeOrder(Order order) { ... }
    ...
}
```

25.2.1 Intercepting Method Invocations

Use the @AroundInvoke annotation to designate interceptor methods for managed object methods. Only one around-invoke interceptor method per class is allowed. Around-invoke interceptor methods have the following form:

```
@AroundInvoke
visibility Object method-name(InvocationContext) throws Exception { ... }
```

For example:

```
@AroundInvoke
public void interceptOrder(InvocationContext ctx) { ... }
```

Around-invoke interceptor methods can have public, private, protected, or package-level access, and must not be declared static or final.

An around-invoke interceptor can call any component or resource that is callable by the target method on which it interposes, can have the same security and transaction context as the target method, and can run in the same Java virtual machine call stack as the target method.

Around-invoke interceptors can throw runtime exceptions and any exception allowed by the throws clause of the target method. They may catch and suppress exceptions, and then recover by calling the InvocationContext.proceed method.

25.2.1.1 Using Multiple Method Interceptors

Use the @Interceptors annotation to declare multiple interceptors for a target method or class:

```
@Interceptors({PrimaryInterceptor.class, SecondaryInterceptor.class,
        LastInterceptor.class})
public void updateInfo(String info) { ... }
```

The order of the interceptors in the @Interceptors annotation is the order in which the interceptors are invoked.

You can also define multiple interceptors in the deployment descriptor. The order of the interceptors in the deployment descriptor is the order in which the interceptors will be invoked:

```
...
<interceptor-binding>
    <target-name>myapp.OrderBean</target-name>
    <interceptor-class>myapp.PrimaryInterceptor.class</interceptor-class>
    <interceptor-class>myapp.SecondaryInterceptor.class</interceptor-class>
    <interceptor-class>myapp.LastInterceptor.class</interceptor-class>
    <method-name>updateInfo</method-name>
</interceptor-binding>
...
```

To explicitly pass control to the next interceptor in the chain, call the `InvocationContext.proceed` method.

Data can be shared across interceptors.

- The same `InvocationContext` instance is passed as an input parameter to each interceptor method in the interceptor chain for a particular target method. The `InvocationContext` instance's `contextData` property is used to pass data across interceptor methods. The `contextData` property is a `java.util.Map<String, Object>` object. Data stored in `contextData` is accessible to interceptor methods further down the interceptor chain.

- The data stored in `contextData` is not sharable across separate target class method invocations. That is, a different `InvocationContext` object is created for each invocation of the method in the target class.

25.2.1.2 Accessing Target Method Parameters from an Interceptor Class

You can use the `InvocationContext` instance passed to each around-invoke method to access and modify the parameters of the target method. The `parameters` property of `InvocationContext` is an array of `Object` instances that corresponds to the parameter order of the target method. For example, for the following target method, the `parameters` property, in the `InvocationContext` instance passed to the around-invoke interceptor method in `PrimaryInterceptor`, is an `Object` array containing two `String` objects (`firstName` and `lastName`) and a `Date` object (`date`):

```
@Interceptors(PrimaryInterceptor.class)
public void updateInfo(String firstName, String lastName, Date date) { ... }
```

You can access and modify the parameters by using the `InvocationContext.getParameters` and `InvocationContext.setParameters` methods, respectively.

25.2.2 Intercepting Lifecycle Callback Events

Interceptors for lifecycle callback events (around-construct, post-construct, and pre-destroy) may be defined in the target class or in interceptor classes. The `javax.interceptor.AroundConstruct` annotation designates the method as an interceptor method that interposes on the invocation of the target class's constructor. The `javax.annotation.PostConstruct` annotation is used to designate a method as a post-construct lifecycle event interceptor. The `javax.annotation.PreDestroy` annotation is used to designate a method as a pre-destroy lifecycle event interceptor.

Lifecycle event interceptors defined within the target class have the following form:

```
void method-name() { ... }
```

For example:

```
@PostConstruct
void initialize() { ... }
```

Lifecycle event interceptors defined in an interceptor class have the following form:

```
void method-name(InvocationContext) { ... }
```

For example:

```
@PreDestroy
void cleanup(InvocationContext ctx) { ... }
```

Lifecycle interceptor methods can have public, private, protected, or package-level access, and must not be declared static or final. Lifecycle interceptors may throw runtime exceptions but cannot throw checked exceptions.

Lifecycle interceptor methods are called in an unspecified security and transaction context. That is, portable Java EE applications should not assume the lifecycle event interceptor method has access to a security or transaction context. Only one interceptor method for each lifecycle event (post-create and pre-destroy) is allowed per class.

25.2.2.1 Using AroundConstruct Interceptor Methods

`@AroundConstruct` methods are interposed on the invocation of the target class's constructor. Methods decorated with `@AroundConstruct` may only be defined within interceptor classes or superclasses of interceptor classes. You may not use `@AroundConstruct` methods within the target class.

The @AroundConstruct method is called after dependency injection has been completed for all interceptors associated with the target class. The target class is created and the target class's constructor injection is performed after all associated @AroundConstruct methods have called the Invocation.proceed method. At that point, dependency injection for the target class is completed, and then any @PostConstruct callback methods are invoked.

@AroundConstruct methods can access the constructed target instance after calling Invocation.proceed by calling the InvocationContext.getTarget method.

> **Caution:** Calling methods on the target instance from an @AroundConstruct method is dangerous because dependency injection may not have completed on the target instance.

@AroundConstruct methods must call Invocation.proceed in order to create the target instance. If an @AroundConstruct method does not call Invocation.proceed, the target instance will not be created.

25.2.2.2 Using Multiple Lifecycle Callback Interceptors

You can define multiple lifecycle interceptors for a target class by specifying the interceptor classes in the @Interceptors annotation:

```
@Interceptors({PrimaryInterceptor.class, SecondaryInterceptor.class,
        LastInterceptor.class})
@Stateless
public class OrderBean { ... }
```

Data stored in the contextData property of InvocationContext is not sharable across different lifecycle events.

25.2.3 Intercepting Timeout Events

You can define interceptors for EJB timer service timeout methods by using the @AroundTimeout annotation on methods in the target class or in an interceptor class. Only one @AroundTimeout method per class is allowed.

Timeout interceptors have the following form:

```
Object method-name(InvocationContext) throws Exception { ... }
```

For example:

```
@AroundTimeout
protected void timeoutInterceptorMethod(InvocationContext ctx) { ... }
```

Timeout interceptor methods can have public, private, protected, or package-level access, and must not be declared static or final.

Timeout interceptors can call any component or resource callable by the target timeout method, and are invoked in the same transaction and security context as the target method.

Timeout interceptors may access the timer object associated with the target timeout method through the InvocationContext instance's getTimer method.

25.2.3.1 Using Multiple Timeout Interceptors

You can define multiple timeout interceptors for a given target class by specifying the interceptor classes containing @AroundTimeout interceptor methods in an @Interceptors annotation at the class level.

If a target class specifies timeout interceptors in an interceptor class, and also has an @AroundTimeout interceptor method within the target class itself, the timeout interceptors in the interceptor classes are called first, followed by the timeout interceptors defined in the target class. In the following example, assume that both the PrimaryInterceptor and SecondaryInterceptor classes have timeout interceptor methods:

```
@Interceptors({PrimaryInterceptor.class, SecondaryInterceptor.class})
@Stateful
public class OrderBean {
    ...
    @AroundTimeout
    private void last(InvocationContext ctx) { ... }
    ...
}
```

The timeout interceptor in PrimaryInterceptor will be called first, followed by the timeout interceptor in SecondaryInterceptor, and finally the last method defined in the target class.

25.2.4 Binding Interceptors to Components

Interceptor binding types are annotations that may be applied to components to associate them with a particular interceptor. Interceptor binding types are typically custom runtime annotation types that specify the interceptor target. Use the javax.interceptor.InterceptorBinding annotation on the custom annotation definition and specify the target by using @Target, setting one or more of TYPE (class-level interceptors), METHOD (method-level interceptors), CONSTRUCTOR (around-construct interceptors), or any other valid target:

```
@InterceptorBinding
@Target({TYPE, METHOD})
@Retention(RUNTIME)
@Inherited
pubic @interface Logged { ... }
```

Interceptor binding types may also be applied to other interceptor binding types:

```
@Logged
@InterceptorBinding
@Target({TYPE, METHOD})
@Retention(RUNTIME)
@Inherited
public @interface Secured { ... }
```

25.2.4.1 Declaring the Interceptor Bindings on an Interceptor Class

Annotate the interceptor class with the interceptor binding type and @Interceptor to associate the interceptor binding with the interceptor class:

```
@Logged
@Interceptor
public class LoggingInterceptor {
    @AroundInvoke
    public Object logInvocation(InvocationContext ctx) throws Exception { ... }
    ...
}
```

An interceptor class may declare multiple interceptor binding types, and more than one interceptor class may declare an interceptor binding type.

If the interceptor class intercepts lifecycle callbacks, it can only declare interceptor binding types with Target(TYPE), or in the case of @AroundConstruct lifecycle callbacks, Target(CONSTRUCTOR).

25.2.4.2 Binding a Component to an Interceptor

Add the interceptor binding type annotation to the target component's class, method, or constructor. Interceptor binding types are applied using the same rules as @Interceptor annotations:

```
@Logged
public class Message {
    ...
```

```
@Secured
public void getConfidentialMessage() { ... }
    ...
}
```

If the component has a class-level interceptor binding, it must not be `final` or have any non-`static`, non-`private` `final` methods. If a non-`static`, non-`private` method has an interceptor binding applied to it, it must not be `final`, and the component class cannot be `final`.

25.2.5 Ordering Interceptors

The order in which multiple interceptors are invoked is determined by the following rules.

- Default interceptors are defined in a deployment descriptor, and are invoked first. They may specify the invocation order or override the order specified using annotations. Default interceptors are invoked in the order in which they are defined in the deployment descriptor.

- The order in which the interceptor classes are listed in the `@Interceptors` annotation defines the order in which the interceptors are invoked. Any `@Priority` settings for interceptors listed within an `@Interceptors` annotation are ignored.

- If the interceptor class has superclasses, the interceptors defined on the superclasses are invoked first, starting with the most general superclass.

- Interceptor classes may set the priority of the interceptor methods by setting a value within a `javax.annotation.Priority` annotation.

- After the interceptors defined within interceptor classes have been invoked, the target class's constructor, around-invoke, or around-timeout interceptors are invoked in the same order as the interceptors within the `@Interceptors` annotation.

- If the target class has superclasses, any interceptors defined on the superclasses are invoked first, starting with the most general superclass.

The `@Priority` annotation requires an `int` value as an element. The lower the number, the higher the priority of the associated interceptor.

Note: The invocation order of interceptors with the same priority value is implementation-specific.

The `javax.interceptor.Interceptor.Priority` class defines the priority constants listed in Table 25–2.

Table 25–2   Interceptor Priority Constants

Priority Constant	Value	Description
PLATFORM_BEFORE	0	Interceptors defined by the Java EE Platform and intended to be invoked early in the invocation chain should use the range between PLATFORM_BEFORE and LIBRARY_BEFORE. These interceptors have the highest priority.
LIBRARY_BEFORE	1000	Interceptors defined by extension libraries that should be invoked early in the interceptor chain should use the range between LIBRARY_BEFORE and APPLICATION.
APPLICATION	2000	Interceptors defined by applications should use the range between APPLICATION and LIBRARY_AFTER.
LIBRARY_AFTER	3000	Low priority interceptors defined by extension libraries should use the range between LIBRARY_AFTER and PLATFORM_AFTER.
PLATFORM_AFTER	4000	Low priority interceptors defined by the Java EE Platform should have values higher than PLATFORM_AFTER.

Note: Negative priority values are reserved by the Interceptors specification for future use, and should not be used.

The following code snippet shows how to use the priority constants in an application-defined interceptor:

```
@Interceptor
@Priority(Interceptor.Priority.APPLICATION+200
public class MyInterceptor { ... }
```

25.3 The interceptor Example Application

The `interceptor` example demonstrates how to use an interceptor class, containing an `@AroundInvoke` interceptor method, with a stateless session bean.

The `HelloBean` stateless session bean is a simple enterprise bean with two business methods, `getName` and `setName`, to retrieve and modify a string. The setName business method has an @Interceptors annotation that specifies an interceptor class, HelloInterceptor, for that method:

```
@Interceptors(HelloInterceptor.class)
public void setName(String name) {
    this.name = name;
}
```

The HelloInterceptor class defines an @AroundInvoke interceptor method, modifyGreeting, that converts the string passed to HelloBean.setName to lowercase:

```
@AroundInvoke
public Object modifyGreeting(InvocationContext ctx) throws Exception {
    Object[] parameters = ctx.getParameters();
    String param = (String) parameters[0];
    param = param.toLowerCase();
    parameters[0] = param;
    ctx.setParameters(parameters);
    try {
        return ctx.proceed();
    } catch (Exception e) {
        logger.warning("Error calling ctx.proceed in modifyGreeting()");
        return null;
    }
}
```

The parameters to HelloBean.setName are retrieved and stored in an Object array by calling the InvocationContext.getParameters method. Because setName only has one parameter, it is the first and only element in the array. The string is set to lowercase and stored in the parameters array, then passed to InvocationContext.setParameters. To return control to the session bean, InvocationContext.proceed is called.

The user interface of interceptor is a JavaServer Faces web application that consists of two Facelets views: index.xhtml, which contains a form for entering the name, and response.xhtml, which displays the final name.

25.3.1 Running the interceptor Example

You can use either NetBeans IDE or Maven to build, package, deploy, and run the interceptor example.

25.3.1.1 To Run the interceptor Example Using NetBeans IDE

1. Make sure that GlassFish Server has been started (see Section 2.2, "Starting and Stopping GlassFish Server").

2. From the **File** menu, choose **Open Project**.

3. In the Open Project dialog box, navigate to:

   tut-install/examples/ejb

4. Select the interceptor folder and click **Open Project**.

5. In the **Projects** tab, right-click the interceptor project and select **Run**.

   This will compile, deploy, and run the interceptor example, opening a web browser to the following URL:

   http://localhost:8080/interceptor/

6. Enter a name into the form and click **Submit**.

   The name will be converted to lowercase by the method interceptor defined in the HelloInterceptor class.

25.3.1.2 To Run the interceptor Example Using Maven

1. Make sure that GlassFish Server has been started (see Section 2.2, "Starting and Stopping GlassFish Server").

2. In a terminal window, go to:

   tut-install/examples/ejb/interceptor/

3. To compile the source files and package the application, use the following command:

   ```
   mvn install
   ```

   This command builds and packages the application into a WAR file, interceptor.war, located in the target directory. The WAR file is then deployed to GlassFish Server.

4. Open the following URL in a web browser:

   http://localhost:8080/interceptor/

5. Enter a name into the form and click **Submit**.

   The name will be converted to lowercase by the method interceptor defined in the HelloInterceptor class.

26

Batch Processing

This chapter describes Batch Applications for the Java Platform (JSR 352), which provides support for defining, implementing, and running batch jobs. Batch jobs are tasks that can be executed without user interaction. The batch framework is composed of a job specification language based on XML, a Java API, and a batch runtime.

Some enterprise applications contain tasks that can be executed without user interaction. These tasks are executed periodically or when resource usage is low, and they often process large amounts of information such as log files, database records, or images. Examples include billing, report generation, data format conversion, and image processing. These tasks are called **batch jobs**.

Batch processing refers to running batch jobs on a computer system. Java EE includes a batch processing framework that provides the batch execution infrastructure common to all batch applications, enabling developers to concentrate on the business logic of their batch applications. The batch framework consists of a job specification language based on XML, a set of batch annotations and interfaces for application classes that implement the business logic, a batch container that manages the execution of batch jobs, and supporting classes and interfaces to interact with the batch container.

The following topics are addressed here:

- Introduction to Batch Processing
- Batch Processing in Java EE
- Simple Use Case
- Using the Job Specification Language
- Creating Batch Artifacts

- Submitting Jobs to the Batch Runtime

- Packaging Batch Applications

- The webserverlog Example Application

- The phonebilling Example Application

- Further Information about Batch Processing

26.1 Introduction to Batch Processing

A batch job can be completed without user intervention. For example, consider a telephone billing application that reads phone call records from the enterprise information systems and generates a monthly bill for each account. Since this application does not require any user interaction, it can run as a batch job.

The phone billing application consists of two phases: The first phase associates each call from the registry with a monthly bill, and the second phase calculates the tax and total amount due for each bill. Each of these phases is a **step** of the batch job.

Batch applications specify a set of steps and their execution order. Different batch frameworks may specify additional elements, like decision elements or groups of steps that run in parallel. The following sections describe steps in more detail and provide information about other common characteristics of batch frameworks.

26.1.1 Steps in Batch Jobs

A step is an independent and sequential phase of a batch job. Batch jobs contain chunk-oriented steps and task-oriented steps.

- **Chunk-oriented steps** (chunk steps) process data by reading items from a data source, applying some business logic to each item, and storing the results. Chunk steps read and process one item at a time and group the results into a chunk. The results are stored when the chunk reaches a configurable size. Chunk-oriented processing makes storing results more efficient and facilitates transaction demarcation.

  Chunk steps have three parts.

  - The input retrieval part reads one item at a time from a data source, such as entries on a database, files in a directory, or entries in a log file.

  - The business processing part manipulates one item at a time using the business logic defined by the application. Examples include filtering, formatting, and accessing data from the item for computing a result.

– The output writing part stores a chunk of processed items at a time.

Chunk steps are often long-running because they process large amounts of data. Batch frameworks enable chunk steps to bookmark their progress using **checkpoints**. A chunk step that is interrupted can be restarted from the last checkpoint. The input retrieval and output writing parts of a chunk step save their current position after the processing of each chunk, and can recover it when the step is restarted.

Figure 26–1 shows the three parts of two chunk steps in a batch job.

Figure 26–1   Chunk Steps in a Batch Job

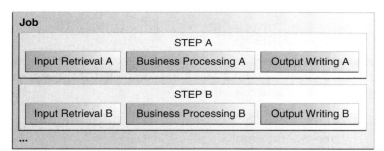

■ **Task-oriented steps** (task steps) execute tasks other than processing items from a data source. Examples include creating or removing directories, moving files, creating or dropping database tables, configuring resources, and so on. Task steps are not usually long-running compared to chunk steps.

For example, the phone billing application consists of two chunk steps.

■ In the first step, the input retrieval part reads call records from the registry; the business processing part associates each call with a bill and creates a bill if one does not exist for an account; and the output writing part stores each bill in a database.

■ In the second step, the input retrieval part reads bills from the database; the business processing part calculates the tax and total amount due for each bill; and the output writing part updates the database records and generates printable versions of each bill.

This application could also contain a task step that cleaned up the files from the bills generated for the previous month.

26.1.2 Parallel Processing

Batch jobs often process large amounts of data or perform computationally expensive operations. Batch applications can benefit from parallel processing in two scenarios.

- Steps that do not depend on each other can run on different threads.

- Chunk-oriented steps where the processing of each item does not depend on the results of processing previous items can run on more than one thread.

Batch frameworks provide mechanisms for developers to define groups of independent steps and to split chunk-oriented steps in parts that can run in parallel.

26.1.3 Status and Decision Elements

Batch frameworks keep track of a **status** for every step in a job. The status indicates if a step is running or if it has completed. If the step has completed, the status indicates one of the following.

- The execution of the step was successful.

- The step was interrupted.

- An error occurred in the execution of the step.

In addition to steps, batch jobs can also contain **decision elements**. Decision elements use the exit status of the previous step to determine the next step or to terminate the batch job. Decision elements set the status of the batch job when terminating it. Like a step, a batch job can terminate successfully, be interrupted, or fail.

Figure 26–2 shows an example of a job that contains chunk steps, task steps and a decision element.

Figure 26–2   Steps and Decision Elements in a Job

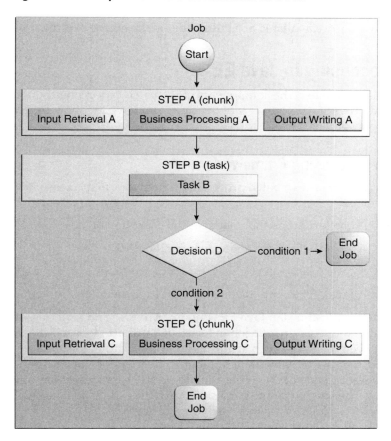

26.1.4 Batch Framework Functionality

Batch applications have the following common requirements.

- Define jobs, steps, decision elements, and the relationships between them.
- Execute some groups of steps or parts of a step in parallel.
- Maintain state information for jobs and steps.
- Launch jobs and resume interrupted jobs.
- Handle errors.

Batch frameworks provide the batch execution infrastructure that addresses the common requirements of all batch applications, enabling developers to concentrate on the business logic of their applications. Batch frameworks consist of a format to specify jobs and steps, an application programming interface (API), and a service available at runtime that manages the execution of batch jobs.

26.2 Batch Processing in Java EE

This section lists the components of the batch processing framework in Java EE and provides an overview of the steps you have to follow to create a batch application.

26.2.1 The Batch Processing Framework

Java EE includes a batch processing framework that consists of the following elements:

- A batch runtime that manages the execution of jobs
- A job specification language based on XML
- A Java API to interact with the batch runtime
- A Java API to implement steps, decision elements, and other batch artifacts

Batch applications in Java EE contain XML files and Java classes. The XML files define the structure of a job in terms of batch artifacts and the relationships between them. (A batch artifact is a part of a chunk-oriented step, a task-oriented step, a decision element, or another component of a batch application). The Java classes implement the application logic of the batch artifacts defined in the XML files. The batch runtime parses the XML files and loads the batch artifacts as Java classes to run the jobs in a batch application.

26.2.2 Creating Batch Applications

The process for creating a batch application in Java EE is the following.

1. Design the batch application.

    a. Identify the input sources, the format of the input data, the desired final result, and the required processing phases.

    b. Organize the application as a job with chunk-oriented steps, task-oriented steps, and decision elements. Determine the dependencies between them.

    c. Determine the order of execution in terms of transitions between steps.

    d. Identify steps that can run in parallel and steps that can run in more than one thread.

2. Create the batch artifacts as Java classes by implementing the interfaces specified by the framework for steps, decision elements, and so on. These Java classes contain the code to read data from input sources, format items, process items, and store results. Batch artifacts can access context objects from the batch runtime using dependency injection.

3. Define jobs, steps, and their execution flow in XML files using the Job Specification Language. The elements in the XML files reference batch artifacts implemented as Java classes. The batch artifacts can access properties declared in the XML files, such as names of files and databases.

4. Use the Java API provided by the batch runtime to launch the batch application.

The following sections describe in detail how to use the components of the batch processing framework in Java EE to create batch applications.

26.2.3 Elements of a Batch Job

A batch job can contain one or more of the following elements:

- Steps
- Flows
- Splits
- Decision elements

Steps are described in Section 26.1, "Introduction to Batch Processing," and can be chunk-oriented or task-oriented. Chunk-oriented steps can be **partitioned steps**. In a partitioned chunk step, the processing of one item does not depend on other items, so these steps can run in more than one thread.

A **flow** is a sequence of steps that execute as a unit. A sequence of related steps can be grouped together into a flow. The steps in a flow cannot transition to steps outside the flow. The flow transitions to the next element when its last step completes.

A **split** is a set of flows that execute in parallel; each flow runs on a separate thread. The split transitions to the next element when all its flows complete.

Decision elements use the exit status of the previous step to determine the next step or to terminate the batch job.

26.2.4 Properties and Parameters

Jobs and steps can have a number of **properties** associated with them. You define properties in the job definition file, and batch artifacts access these properties using context objects from the batch runtime. Using properties in this manner enables you to decouple static parameters of the job from the business logic and to reuse batch artifacts in different job definition files.

Specifying properties is described in Section 26.4, "Using the Job Specification Language," and accessing properties in batch artifacts is described in Section 26.5, "Creating Batch Artifacts."

Java EE applications can also pass **parameters** to a job when they submit it to the batch runtime. This enables you to specify dynamic parameters that are only known at runtime. Parameters are also necessary for partitioned steps, since each partition needs to know, for example, what range of items to process.

Specifying parameters when submitting jobs is described in Section 26.6, "Submitting Jobs to the Batch Runtime." Specifying parameters for partitioned steps and accessing them in batch artifacts is demonstrated in Section 26.9, "The phonebilling Example Application."

26.2.5 Job Instances and Job Executions

A job definition can have multiple **instances**, each with different parameters. A job **execution** is an attempt to run a job instance. The batch runtime maintains information about job instances and job executions, as described in Section 26.6.2, "Checking the Status of a Job."

26.2.6 Batch and Exit Status

The state of jobs, steps, splits, and flows is represented in the batch runtime as a **batch status** value. Batch status values are listed in Table 26–1. They are represented as strings.

Table 26–1   Batch Status Values

Value	Description
STARTING	The job has been submitted to the batch runtime.
STARTED	The job is running.
STOPPING	The job has been requested to stop.
STOPPED	The job has stopped.
FAILED	The job finished executing because of an error.

Table 26–1   (Cont.) Batch Status Values

Value	Description
COMPLETED	The job finished executing successfully.
ABANDONED	The job was marked abandoned.

Java EE applications can submit jobs and access the batch status of a job using the JobOperator interface, as described in Section 26.6, "Submitting Jobs to the Batch Runtime." Job definition files can refer to batch status values using the Job Specification Language (JSL), as described in Section 26.4, "Using the Job Specification Language." Batch artifacts can access batch status values using context objects, as described in Section 26.5.3, "Using the Context Objects from the Batch Runtime."

For flows, the batch status is that of its last step. For splits, the batch status is the following:

- COMPLETED: If all its flows have a batch status of COMPLETED
- FAILED: If any flow has a batch status of FAILED
- STOPPED: If any flow has a batch status of STOPPED, and no flows have a batch status of FAILED

The batch status for jobs, steps, splits, and flows is set by the batch runtime. Jobs, steps, splits, and flows also have an **exit status**, which is a user-defined value based on the batch status. You can set the exit status inside batch artifacts or in the job definition file. You can access the exit status in the same manner as the batch status, described above. The default value for the exit status is the same as the batch status.

26.3 Simple Use Case

This section demonstrates how to define a simple job using the Job Specification Language (JSL) and how to implement the corresponding batch artifacts. Refer to the rest of the sections in this chapter for detailed descriptions of the elements in the batch framework.

The following job definition specifies a chunk step and a task step as follows:

```
<job id="simplejob" xmlns="http://xmlns.jcp.org/xml/ns/javaee"
                    version="1.0">
  <properties>
    <property name="input_file" value="input.txt"/>
    <property name="output_file" value="output.txt"/>
  </properties>
```

```
      <step id="mychunk" next="mytask">
        <chunk>
          <reader ref="MyReader"></reader>
          <processor ref="MyProcessor"></processor>
          <writer ref="MyWriter"></writer>
        </chunk>
      </step>
      <step id="mytask">
        <batchlet ref="MyBatchlet"></batchlet>
        <end on="COMPLETED"/>
      </step>
    </job>
```

26.3.1 Chunk Step

In most cases, you have to implement a checkpoint class for chunk-oriented steps. The following class just keeps track of the line number in a text file:

```
public class MyCheckpoint implements Serializable {
    private long lineNum = 0;
    public void increase() { lineNum++; }
    public long getLineNum() { return lineNum; }
}
```

The following item reader implementation continues reading the input file from the provided checkpoint if the job was restarted. The items consist of each line in the text file (in more complex scenarios, the items are custom Java types and the input source can be a database):

```
@Dependent
@Named("MyReader")
public class MyReader implements javax.batch.api.chunk.ItemReader {
    private MyCheckpoint checkpoint;
    private BufferedReader breader;
    @Inject
    JobContext jobCtx;

    public MyReader() {}

    @Override
    public void open(Serializable ckpt) throws Exception {
        if (ckpt == null)
            checkpoint = new MyCheckpoint();
        else
            checkpoint = (MyCheckpoint) ckpt;
        String fileName = jobCtx.getProperties()
                                .getProperty("input_file");
```

```
        breader = new BufferedReader(new FileReader(fileName));
        for (long i = 0; i < checkpoint.getLineNum(); i++)
            breader.readLine();
    }

    @Override
    public void close() throws Exception {
        breader.close();
    }

    @Override
    public Object readItem() throws Exception {
        String line = breader.readLine();
        return line;
    }
}
```

In the following case, the item processor only converts the line to uppercase. More complex examples can process items in different ways or transform them into custom output Java types:

```
@Dependent
@Named("MyProcessor")
public class MyProcessor implements javax.batch.api.chunk.ItemProcessor {

    public MyProcessor() {}

    @Override
    public Object processItem(Object obj) throws Exception {
        String line = (String) obj;
        return line.toUpperCase();
    }
}
```

> **Note:** The batch processing API does not support generics. In most cases, you need to cast items to their specific type before processing them.

The item writer writes the processed items to the output file. It overwrites the output file if no checkpoint is provided; otherwise, it resumes writing at the end of the file. Items are written in chunks:

```
@Dependent
@Named("MyWriter")
public class MyWriter implements javax.batch.api.chunk.ItemWriter {
```

```
                    private BufferedWriter bwriter;
                    @Inject
                    private JobContext jobCtx;

                    @Override
                    public void open(Serializable ckpt) throws Exception {
                        String fileName = jobCtx.getProperties()
                                             .getProperty("output_file");
                        bwriter = new BufferedWriter(new FileWriter(fileName,
                                                         (ckpt != null)));
                    }

                    @Override
                    public void writeItems(List<Object> items) throws Exception {
                        for (int i = 0; i < items.size(); i++) {
                            String line = (String) items.get(i);
                            bwriter.write(line);
                            bwriter.newLine();
                        }
                    }

                    @Override
                    public Serializable checkpointInfo() throws Exception {
                        return new MyCheckpoint();
                    }
                }
```

26.3.2 Task Step

The task step displays the length of the output file. In more complex scenarios, task steps perform any task that does not fit the chunk processing programming model:

```
@Dependent
@Named("MyBatchlet")
public class MyBatchlet implements javax.batch.api.chunk.Batchlet {
    @Inject
    private JobContext jobCtx;

    @Override
    public String process() throws Exception {
        String fileName = jobCtx.getProperties()
                             .getProperty("output_file");
        System.out.println(""+(new File(fileName)).length());
        return "COMPLETED";
    }
}
```

26.4 Using the Job Specification Language

The Job Specification Language (JSL) enables you to define the steps in a job and their execution order using an XML file. The following example shows how to define a simple job that contains one chunk step and one task step:

```xml
<job id="loganalysis" xmlns="http://xmlns.jcp.org/xml/ns/javaee"
                      version="1.0">
  <properties>
    <property name="input_file" value="input1.txt"/>
    <property name="output_file" value="output2.txt"/>
  </properties>

  <step id="logprocessor" next="cleanup">
    <chunk checkpoint-policy="item" item-count="10">
      <reader ref="com.example.pkg.LogItemReader"></reader>
      <processor ref="com.example.pkg.LogItemProcessor"></processor>
      <writer ref="com.example.pkg.LogItemWriter"></writer>
    </chunk>
  </step>

  <step id="cleanup">
    <batchlet ref="com.example.pkg.CleanUp"></batchlet>
    <end on="COMPLETED"/>
  </step>
</job>
```

This example defines the `loganalysis` batch job, which consists of the `logprocessor` chunk step and the `cleanup` task step. The `logprocessor` step transitions to the `cleanup` step, which terminates the job when completed.

The `job` element defines two properties, `input_file` and `output_file`. Specifying properties in this manner enables you to run a batch job with different configuration parameters without having to recompile its Java batch artifacts. The batch artifacts can access these properties using the context objects from the batch runtime.

The `logprocessor` step is a chunk step that specifies batch artifacts for the reader (`LogItemReader`), the processor (`LogItemProcessor`), and the writer (`LogItemWriter`). This step creates a checkpoint for every ten items processed.

The `cleanup` step is a task step that specifies the `CleanUp` class as its batch artifact. The job terminates when this step completes.

The following sections describe the elements of the Job Specification Language (JSL) in more detail and show the most common attributes and child elements.

26.4.1 The job Element

The job element is always the top-level element in a job definition file. Its main attributes are id and restartable. The job element can contain one properties element and zero or more of each of the following elements: listener, step, flow, and split. For example:

```
<job id="jobname" restartable="true">
  <listeners>
    <listener ref="com.example.pkg.ListenerBatchArtifact"/>
  </listeners>
  <properties>
    <property name="propertyName1" value="propertyValue1"/>
    <property name="propertyName2" value="propertyValue2"/>
  </properties>
  <step ...> ... </step>
  <step ...> ... </step>
  <decision ...> ... </decision>
  <flow ...> ... </flow>
  <split ...> ... </split>
</job>
```

The listener element specifies a batch artifact whose methods are invoked before and after the execution of the job. The batch artifact is an implementation of the javax.batch.api.listener.JobListener interface. See Section 26.8.1.4, "The Listener Batch Artifacts," for an example of a job listener implementation.

The first step, flow, or split element inside the job element executes first.

26.4.2 The step Element

The step element can be a child of the job and flow elements. Its main attributes are id and next. The step element can contain the following elements.

- One chunk element for chunk-oriented steps or one batchlet element for task-oriented steps.

- One properties element (optional).

  This element specifies a set of properties that batch artifacts can access using batch context objects.

- One listener element (optional); one listeners element if more than one listener is specified.

  This element specifies listener artifacts that intercept various phases of step execution.

For chunk steps, the batch artifacts for these listeners can be implementations of the following interfaces: `StepListener`, `ItemReadListener`, `ItemProcessListener`, `ItemWriteListener`, `ChunkListener`, `RetryReadListener`, `RetryProcessListener`, `RetryWriteListener`, `SkipReadListener`, `SkipProcessListener`, and `SkipWriteListener`.

For task steps, the batch artifact for these listeners must be an implementation of the `StepListener` interface.

See Section 26.8.1.4, "The Listener Batch Artifacts," for an example of an item processor listener implementation.

- One `partition` element (optional).

  This element is used in partitioned steps which execute in more than one thread.

- One `end` element if this is the last step in a job.

  This element sets the batch status to `COMPLETED`.

- One `stop` element (optional) to stop a job at this step.

  This element sets the batch status to `STOPPED`.

- One `fail` element (optional) to terminate a job at this step.

  This element sets the batch status to `FAILED`.

- One or more `next` elements if the `next` attribute is not specified.

  This element is associated with an exit status and refers to another step, a flow, a split, or a decision element.

The following is an example of a chunk step:

```
<step id="stepA" next="stepB">
  <properties> ... </properties>
  <listeners>
    <listener ref="MyItemReadListenerImpl"/>
    ...
  </listeners>
  <chunk ...> ... </chunk>
  <partition> ... </partition>
  <end on="COMPLETED" exit-status="MY_COMPLETED_EXIT_STATUS"/>
  <stop on="MY_TEMP_ISSUE_EXIST_STATUS" restart="step0"/>
  <fail on="MY_ERROR_EXIT_STATUS" exit-status="MY_ERROR_EXIT_STATUS"/>
</step>
```

The following is an example of a task step:

```
<step id="stepB" next="stepC">
  <batchlet ...> ... </batchlet>
  <properties> ... </properties>
  <listener ref="MyStepListenerImpl"/>
</step>
```

26.4.2.1 The chunk Element

The chunk element is a child of the step element for chunk-oriented steps. The attributes of this element are listed in Table 26–2.

Table 26–2   Attributes of the chunk Element

Attribute Name	Description	Default Value
checkpoint-policy	Specifies how to commit the results of processing each chunk: ■ "item": the chunk is committed after processing item-count items ■ "custom": the chunk is committed according to a checkpoint algorithm specified with the checkpoint-algorithm element The checkpoint is updated when the results of a chunk are committed. *Every chunk is processed in a global Java EE transaction.* If the processing of one item in the chunk fails, the transaction is rolled back and no processed items from this chunk are stored.	"item"
item-count	Specifies the number of items to process before committing the chunk and taking a checkpoint.	10
time-limit	Specifies the number of seconds before committing the chunk and taking a checkpoint when checkpoint-policy="item". If item-count items have not been processed by time-limit seconds, the chunk is committed and a checkpoint is taken.	0 (no limit)
buffer-items	Specifies if processed items are buffered until it is time to take a checkpoint. If true, a single call to the item writer is made with a list of the buffered items before committing the chunk and taking a checkpoint.	true
skip-limit	Specifies the number of skippable exceptions to skip in this step during chunk processing. Skippable exception classes are specified with the skippable-exception-classes element.	No limit
retry-limit	Specifies the number of attempts to execute this step if retryable exceptions occur. Retryable exception classes are specified with the retryable-exception-classes element.	No limit

The `chunk` element can contain the following elements.

- One `reader` element.

  This element specifies a batch artifact that implements the `ItemReader` interface.

- One `processor` element.

  This element specifies a batch artifact that implements the `ItemProcessor` interface.

- One `writer` element.

  This element specifies a batch artifact that implements the `ItemWriter` interface.

- One `checkpoint-algorithm` element (optional).

  This element specifies a batch artifact that implements the `CheckpointAlgorithm` interface and provides a custom checkpoint policy.

- One `skippable-exception-classes` element (optional).

  This element specifies a set of exceptions thrown from the reader, writer, and processor batch artifacts that chunk processing should skip. The `skip-limit` attribute from the `chunk` element specifies the maximum number of skipped exceptions.

- One `retryable-exception-classes` element (optional).

  This element specifies a set of exceptions thrown from the reader, writer, and processor batch artifacts that chunk processing will retry. The `retry-limit` attribute from the `chunk` element specifies the maximum number of attempts.

- One `no-rollback-exception-classes` element (optional).

  This element specifies a set of exceptions thrown from the reader, writer, and processor batch artifacts that should cause the batch runtime not to roll back the current chunk, but to retry the current operation without a rollback.

  For exception types not specified in this element, the current chunk is rolled back by default when an exception occurs.

The following is an example of a chunk-oriented step:

```
<step id="stepC" next="stepD">
  <chunk checkpoint-policy="item" item-count="5" time-limit="180"
       buffer-items="true" skip-limit="10" retry-limit="3">
    <reader ref="pkg.MyItemReaderImpl"></reader>
    <processor ref="pkg.MyItemProcessorImpl"></processor>
    <writer ref="pkg.MyItemWriterImpl"></writer>
```

```
      <skippable-exception-classes>
        <include class="pkg.MyItemException"/>
        <exclude class="pkg.MyItemSeriousSubException"/>
      </skippable-exception-classes>
      <retryable-exception-classes>
        <include class="pkg.MyResourceTempUnavailable"/>
      </retryable-exception-classes>
    </chunk>
</step>
```

This example defines a chunk step and specifies its reader, processor, and writer artifacts. The step updates a checkpoint and commits each chunk after processing five items. It skips all `MyItemException` exceptions and all its subtypes, except for `MyItemSeriousSubException`, up to a maximum of ten skipped exceptions. The step retries a chunk when a `MyResourceTempUnavailable` exception occurs, up to a maximum of three attempts.

26.4.2.2 The batchlet Element

The `batchlet` element is a child of the `step` element for task-oriented steps. This element only has the `ref` attribute, which specifies a batch artifact that implements the `Batchlet` interface. The `batch` element can contain a `properties` element.

The following is an example of a task-oriented step:

```
<step id="stepD" next="stepE">
  <batchlet ref="pkg.MyBatchletImpl">
    <properties>
      <property name="pname" value="pvalue"/>
    </properties>
  </batchlet>
</step>
```

This example defines a batch step and specifies its batch artifact.

26.4.2.3 The partition Element

The `partition` element is a child of the `step` element. It indicates that a step is partitioned. Most partitioned steps are chunk steps where the processing of each item does not depend on the results of processing previous items. You specify the number of partitions in a step and provide each partition with specific information on which items to process, such as the following.

- A range of items. For example, partition 1 processes items 1 through 500, and partition 2 processes items 501 through 1000.

- An input source. For example, partition 1 processes the items in `input1.txt` and partition 2 processes the items in `input2.txt`.

When the number of partitions, the number of items, and the input sources for a partitioned step are known at development or deployment time, you can use partition properties in the job definition file to specify partition-specific information and access these properties from the step batch artifacts. The runtime creates as many instances of the step batch artifacts (reader, processor, and writer) as partitions, and each artifact instance receives the properties specific to its partition.

In most cases, the number of partitions, the number of items, or the input sources for a partitioned step can only be determined at runtime. Instead of specifying partition-specific properties statically in the job definition file, you provide a batch artifact that can access your data sources at runtime and determine how many partitions are needed and what range of items each partition should process. This batch artifact is an implementation of the `PartitionMapper` interface. The batch runtime invokes this artifact and then uses the information it provides to instantiate the step batch artifacts (reader, writer, and processor) for each partition and to pass them partition-specific data as parameters.

The rest of this section describes the `partition` element in detail and shows two examples of job definition files: one that uses partition properties to specify a range of items for each partition, and one that relies on a `PartitionMapper` implementation to determine partition-specific information.

See Section 26.9.1.4, "The Phone Billing Chunk Step," for a complete example of a partitioned chunk step.

The `partition` element can contain the following elements.

- One `plan` element, if the `mapper` element is not specified.

  This element defines the number of partitions, the number of threads, and the properties for each partition in the job definition file. The `plan` element is useful when this information is known at development or deployment time.

- One `mapper` element, if the `plan` element is not specified.

  This element specifies a batch artifact that provides the number of partitions, the number of threads, and the properties for each partition. The batch artifact is an implementation of the `PartitionMapper` interface. You use this option when the information required for each partition is only known at runtime.

- One `reducer` element (optional).

  This element specifies a batch artifact that receives control when a partitioned step begins, ends, or rolls back. The batch artifact enables you to merge results from different partitions and perform other related operations. The batch artifact is an implementation of the PartitionReducer interface.

- One collector element (optional).

  This element specifies a batch artifact that sends intermediary results from each partition to a partition analyzer. The batch artifact sends the intermediary results after each checkpoint for chunk steps and at the end of the step for task steps. The batch artifact is an implementation of the PartitionCollector interface.

- One analyzer element (optional).

  This element specifies a batch artifact that analyzes the intermediary results from the partition collector instances. The batch artifact is an implementation of the PartitionAnalyzer interface.

The following is an example of a partitioned step using the plan element:

```
<step id="stepE" next="stepF">
  <chunk>
    <reader ...></reader>
    <processor ...></processor>
    <writer ...></writer>
  </chunk>
  <partition>
    <plan partitions="2" threads="2">
      <properties partition="0">
        <property name="firstItem" value="0"/>
        <property name="lastItem" value="500"/>
      </properties>
      <properties partition="1">
        <property name="firstItem" value="501"/>
        <property name="lastItem" value="999"/>
      </properties>
    </plan>
  </partition>
  <reducer ref="MyPartitionReducerImpl"/>
  <collector ref="MyPartitionCollectorImpl"/>
  <analyzer ref="MyPartitionAnalyzerImpl"/>
</step>
```

In this example, the plan element specifies the properties for each partition in the job definition file.

The following example uses a `mapper` element instead of a `plan` element. The `PartitionMapper` implementation dynamically provides the same information as the `plan` element provides in the job definition file:

```
<step id="stepE" next="stepF">
  <chunk>
    <reader ...></reader>
    <processor ...></processor>
    <writer ...></writer>
  </chunk>
  <partition>
    <mapper ref="MyPartitionMapperImpl"/>
    <reducer ref="MyPartitionReducerImpl"/>
    <collector ref="MyPartitionCollectorImpl"/>
    <analyzer ref="MyPartitionAnalyzerImpl"/>
  </partition>
</step>
```

Refer to Section 26.9, "The phonebilling Example Application," for an example implementation of the `PartitionMapper` interface.

26.4.3 The flow Element

The `flow` element can be a child of the `job`, `flow`, and `split` elements. Its attributes are `id` and `next`. Flows can transition to flows, steps, splits, and decision elements. The `flow` element can contain the following elements:

- One or more `step` elements
- One or more `flow` elements (optional)
- One or more `split` elements (optional)
- One or more `decision` elements (optional)

The last `step` in a flow is the one with no `next` attribute or `next` element. Steps and other elements in a flow cannot transition to elements outside the flow.

The following is an example of the `flow` element:

```
<flow id="flowA" next="stepE">
  <step id="flowAstepA" next="flowAstepB">...</step>
  <step id="flowAstepB" next="flowAflowC">...</step>
  <flow id="flowAflowC" next="flowAsplitD">...</flow>
  <split id="flowAsplitD" next="flowAstepE">...</split>
  <step id="flowAstepE">...</step>
</flow>
```

This example flow contains three steps, one flow, and one split. The last step does not have the `next` attribute. The flow transitions to `stepE` when its last step completes.

26.4.4 The split Element

The `split` element can be a child of the `job` and `flow` elements. Its attributes are `id` and `next`. Splits can transition to splits, steps, flows, and decision elements. The `split` element can only contain one or more `flow` elements that can only transition to other `flow` elements in the split.

The following is an example of a split with three flows that execute concurrently:

```
<split id="splitA" next="stepB">
  <flow id="splitAflowA">...</flow>
  <flow id="splitAflowB">...</flow>
  <flow id="splitAflowC">...</flow>
</split>
```

26.4.5 The decision Element

The `decision` element can be a child of the `job` and `flow` elements. Its attributes are `id` and `next`. Steps, flows, and splits can transition to a `decision` element. This element specifies a batch artifact that decides the next step, flow, or split to execute based on information from the execution of the previous step, flow, or split. The batch artifact implements the `Decider` interface. The `decision` element can contain the following elements.

- One or more `end` elements (optional).

  This element sets the batch status to `COMPLETED`.

- One or more `stop` elements (optional).

  This element sets the batch status to `STOPPED`.

- One or more `fail` elements (optional).

  This element sets the batch status to `FAILED`.

- One or more `next` elements (optional).

- One `properties` element (optional).

The following is an example of the `decider` element:

```
<decision id="decisionA" ref="MyDeciderImpl">
  <fail on="FAILED" exit-status="FAILED_AT_DECIDER"/>
  <end on="COMPLETED" exit-status="COMPLETED_AT_DECIDER"/>
```

```
    <stop on="MY_TEMP_ISSUE_EXIST_STATUS" restart="step2"/>
</decision>
```

26.5 Creating Batch Artifacts

After you define a job in terms of its batch artifacts using the Job Specification Language (JSL), you create these artifacts as Java classes that implement the interfaces in the `javax.batch.api` package and its subpackages.

This section lists the main batch artifact interfaces, demonstrates how to access context objects from the batch runtime, and provides some examples.

26.5.1 Batch Artifact Interfaces

The following tables list the interfaces that you implement to create batch artifacts. The interface implementations are referenced from the elements described in Section 26.4, "Using the Job Specification Language."

Table 26–3 lists the interfaces to implement batch artifacts for chunk steps, task steps, and decision elements.

Table 26–4 lists the interfaces to implement batch artifacts for partitioned steps.

Table 26–5 lists the interfaces to implement batch artifacts for job and step listeners.

Table 26–3 **Main Batch Artifact Interfaces**

Package	Interface	Description
javax.batch.api	Batchlet	Implements the business logic of a task-oriented step. It is referenced from the `batchlet` element.
javax.batch.api	Decider	Decides the next step, flow, or split to execute based on information from the execution of the previous step, flow, or split. It is referenced from the `decision` element.
javax.batch.api.chunk	CheckPointAlgorithm	Implements a custom checkpoint policy for chunk steps. It is referenced from the `checkpoint-algorithm` element inside the `chunk` element.
javax.batch.api.chunk	ItemReader	Reads items from an input source in a chunk step. It is referenced from the `reader` element inside the `chunk` element.

Table 26–3 *(Cont.) Main Batch Artifact Interfaces*

Package	Interface	Description
`javax.batch.api.chunk`	`ItemProcessor`	Processes input items to obtain output items in chunk steps. It is referenced from the `processor` element inside the `chunk` element.
`javax.batch.api.chunk`	`ItemWriter`	Writes output items in chunk steps. It is referenced from the `writer` element inside the `chunk` element.

Table 26–4 *Partition Batch Artifact Interfaces*

Package	Interface	Description
`javax.batch.api.partition`	`PartitionPlan`	Provides details on how to execute a partitioned step, such as the number of partitions, the number of threads, and the parameters for each partition. This artifact is not referenced directly from the job definition file.
`javax.batch.api.partition`	`PartitionMapper`	Provides a `PartitionPlan` object. It is referenced from the `mapper` element inside the `partition` element.
`javax.batch.api.partition`	`PartitionReducer`	Receives control when a partitioned step begins, ends, or rolls back. It is referenced from the `reducer` element inside the `partition` element.
`javax.batch.api.partition`	`PartitionCollector`	Sends intermediary results from each partition to a partition analyzer. It is referenced from the `collector` element inside the `partition` element.
`javax.batch.api.partition`	`PartitionAnalyzer`	Processes data and final results from each partition. It is referenced from the `analyzer` element inside the `partition` element.

Table 26–5   **Listener Batch Artifact Interfaces**

Package	Interface	Description
`javax.batch.api.listener`	`JobListener`	Intercepts job execution before and after running a job. It is referenced from the `listener` element inside the `job` element.
`javax.batch.api.listener`	`StepListener`	Intercepts step execution before and after running a step. It is referenced from the `listener` element inside the `step` element
`javax.batch.api.chunk.listener`	`ChunkListener`	Intercepts chunk processing in chunk steps before and after processing each chunk, and on errors. It is referenced from the `listener` element inside the `step` element.
`javax.batch.api.chunk.listener`	`ItemReadListener`	Intercepts item reading in chunk steps before and after reading each item, and on errors. It is referenced from the `listener` element inside the `step` element.
`javax.batch.api.chunk.listener`	`ItemProcessListener`	Intercepts item processing in chunk steps before and after processing each item, and on errors. It is referenced from the `listener` element inside the `step` element.
`javax.batch.api.chunk.listener`	`ItemWriteListener`	Intercepts item writing in chunk steps before and after writing each item, and on errors. It is referenced from the `listener` element inside the `step` element.
`javax.batch.api.chunk.listener`	`RetryReadListener`	Intercepts retry item reading in chunk steps when an exception occurs. It is referenced from the `listener` element inside the `step` element.

Table 26–5 (Cont.) Listener Batch Artifact Interfaces

Package	Interface	Description
javax.batch.api.chunk.listener	RetryProcessListener	Intercepts retry item processing in chunk steps when an exception occurs. It is referenced from the listener element inside the step element.
javax.batch.api.chunk.listener	RetryWriteListener	Intercepts retry item writing in chunk steps when an exception occurs. It is referenced from the listener element inside the step element.
javax.batch.api.chunk.listener	SkipReadListener	Intercepts skippable exception handling for item readers in chunk steps. It is referenced from the listener element inside the step element.
javax.batch.api.chunk.listener	SkipProcessListener	Intercepts skippable exception handling for item processors in chunk steps. It is referenced from the listener element inside the step element.
javax.batch.api.chunk.listener	SkipWriteListener	Intercepts skippable exception handling for item writers in chunk steps. It is referenced from the listener element inside the step element.

26.5.2 Dependency Injection in Batch Artifacts

To ensure that Contexts and Dependency Injection (CDI) works in your batch artifacts, follow these steps.

1. Define your batch artifact implementations as CDI named beans using the Named annotation.

    For example, define an item reader implementation in a chunk step as follows:

    ```
    @Named("MyItemReaderImpl")
    public class MyItemReaderImpl implements ItemReader {
    ```

```
        /* ... Override the ItemReader interface methods ... */
}
```

2. Provide a public, empty, no-argument constructor for your batch artifacts.

   For example, provide the following constructor for the artifact above:

   ```
   public MyItemReaderImpl() {}
   ```

3. Specify the CDI name for the batch artifacts in the job definition file, instead of using the fully qualified name of the class.

   For example, define the step for the artifact above as follows:

   ```
   <step id="stepA" next="stepB">
     <chunk>
       <reader ref="MyItemReaderImpl"></reader>
       ...
     </chunk>
   </step>
   ```

   This example uses the CDI name (`MyItemReaderImpl`) instead of the fully qualified name of the class (`com.example.pkg.MyItemReaderImpl`) to specify a batch artifact.

4. Ensure that your module is a CDI bean archive by annotating your batch artifacts with the `javax.enterprise.context.Dependent` annotation or by including an empty `beans.xml` deployment description with your application. For example, the following batch artifact is annotated with @Dependent:

   ```
   @Dependent
   @Named("MyItemReaderImpl")
   public class MyItemReaderImpl implements ItemReader { ... }
   ```

   For more information on bean archives, see Section 25.1, "Packaging CDI Applications," in *The Java EE 7 Tutorial, Volume 1*.

   > **Note:** Contexts and Dependency Injection (CDI) is required in order to access context objects from the batch runtime in batch artifacts.

You may encounter the following errors if you do not follow this procedure.

- The batch runtime cannot locate some batch artifacts.

- The batch artifacts throw null pointer exceptions when accessing injected objects.

26.5.3 Using the Context Objects from the Batch Runtime

The batch runtime provides context objects that implement the JobContext and StepContext interfaces in the javax.batch.runtime.context package. These objects are associated with the current job and step, respectively, and enable you to do the following:

- Get information from the current job or step, such as its name, instance ID, execution ID, batch status, and exit status
- Set the user-defined exit status
- Store user data
- Get property values from the job or step definition

You can inject context objects from the batch runtime inside batch artifact implementations like item readers, item processors, item writers, batchlets, listeners, and so on. The following example demonstrates how to access property values from the job definition file in an item reader implementation:

```
@Dependent
@Named("MyItemReaderImpl")
public class MyItemReaderImpl implements ItemReader {
    @Inject
    JobContext jobCtx;

    public MyItemReaderImpl() {}

    @Override
    public void open(Serializable checkpoint) throws Exception {
        String fileName = jobCtx.getProperties()
                                .getProperty("log_file_name");
        ...
    }
    ...
}
```

See Section 26.5.2, "Dependency Injection in Batch Artifacts," for instructions on how to define your batch artifacts to use dependency injection.

Note: Do *not* access batch context objects inside artifact constructors.

Because the job does not run until you submit it to the batch runtime, the batch context objects are not available when CDI instantiates your artifacts upon loading your application. The instantiation of these beans fails and the batch runtime cannot find your batch artifacts when your application submits the job.

26.6 Submitting Jobs to the Batch Runtime

The JobOperator interface in the javax.batch.operations package enables you to submit jobs to the batch runtime and obtain information about existing jobs. This interface provides the following functionality.

- Obtain the names of all known jobs.

- Start, stop, restart, and abandon jobs.

- Obtain job instances and job executions.

The BatchRuntime class in the javax.batch.runtime package provides the getJobOperator factory method to obtain JobOperator objects.

26.6.1 Starting a Job

The following example code demonstrates how to obtain a JobOperator object and submit a batch job:

```
JobOperator jobOperator = BatchRuntime.getJobOperator();
Properties props = new Properties();
props.setProperty("parameter1", "value1");
...
long execID = jobOperator.start("simplejob", props);
```

The first argument of the JobOperator.start method is the name of the job as specified in its job definition file. The second parameter is a Properties object that represents the parameters for this job execution. You can use job parameters to pass to a job information that is only known at runtime.

26.6.2 Checking the Status of a Job

The JobExecution interface in the javax.batch.runtime package provides methods to obtain information about submitted jobs. This interface provides the following functionality.

- Obtain the batch and exit status of a job execution.

- Obtain the time the execution was started, updated, or ended.

- Obtain the job name.

- Obtain the execution ID.

The following example code demonstrates how to obtain the batch status of a job using its execution ID:

```
JobExecution jobExec = jobOperator.getJobExecution(execID);
String status = jobExec.getBatchStatus().toString();
```

26.6.3 Invoking the Batch Runtime in Your Application

The component from which you invoke the batch runtime depends on the architecture of your particular application. For example, you can invoke the batch runtime from an enterprise bean, a servlet, a managed bean, and so on.

See Section 26.8, "The webserverlog Example Application," and Section 26.9, "The phonebilling Example Application," for details on how to invoke the batch runtime from a managed bean driven by a JavaServer Faces user interface.

26.7 Packaging Batch Applications

Job definition files and batch artifacts do not require separate packaging and can be included in any Java EE application.

Package the batch artifact classes with the rest of the classes of your application, and include the job definition files in one of the following directories:

- META-INF/batch-jobs/ for jar packages

- WEB-INF/classes/META-INF/batch-jobs/ for war packages

The name of each job definition file must match its job ID. For example, if you define a job as follows, and you are packaging your application as a WAR file, include the job definition file in `WEB-INF/classes/META-INF/batch-jobs/` `simplejob.xml`:

```
<job id="simplejob" xmlns="http://xmlns.jcp.org/xml/ns/javaee"
                     version="1.0">
  ...
</job>
```

26.8 The webserverlog Example Application

The `webserverlog` example application, located in the *tut-install*/`examples/` `batch/webserverlog/` directory, demonstrates how to use the batch framework in Java EE to analyze the log file from a web server. This example application reads a log file and finds what percentage of page views from tablet devices are product sales.

26.8.1 Architecture of the webserverlog Example Application

The `webserverlog` example application consists of the following elements.

- A job definition file (`webserverlog.xml`) that uses the Job Specification Language (JSL) to define a batch job with a chunk step and a task step. The chunk step acts as a filter, and the task step calculates statistics on the remaining entries.

- A log file (`log1.txt`) that serves as input data to the batch job.

- Two Java classes (`LogLine` and `LogFilteredLine`) that represent input items and output items for the chunk step.

- Three batch artifacts (`LogLineReader`, `LogLineProcessor`, and `LogFilteredLineWriter`) that implement the chunk step of the application. This step reads items from the web server log file, filters them by the web browser used by the client, and writes the results to a text file.

- Two batch artifacts (`InfoJobListener` and `InfoItemProcessListener`) that implement two simple listeners.

- A batch artifact (`MobileBatchlet.java`) that calculates statistics on the filtered items.

- Two Facelets pages (index.xhtml and jobstarted.xhtml) that provide the front end of the batch application. The first page shows the log file that will be processed by the batch job, and the second page enables the user to check on the status of the job and shows the results.

- A managed bean (JsfBean) that is accessed from the Facelets pages. The bean submits the job to the batch runtime, checks on the status of the job, and reads the results from a text file.

26.8.1.1 The Job Definition File

The webserverlog.xml job definition file is located in the WEB-INF/classes/ META-INF/batch-jobs/ directory. The file specifies seven job-level properties and two steps:

```
<?xml version="1.0" encoding="UTF-8"?>
<job id="webserverlog" xmlns="http://xmlns.jcp.org/xml/ns/javaee"
     version="1.0">
    <properties>
        <property name="log_file_name" value="log1.txt"/>
        <property name="filtered_file_name" value="filtered1.txt"/>
        <property name="num_browsers" value="2"/>
        <property name="browser_1" value="Tablet Browser D"/>
        <property name="browser_2" value="Tablet Browser E"/>
        <property name="buy_page" value="/auth/buy.html"/>
        <property name="out_file_name" value="result1.txt"/>
    </properties>
    <listeners>
        <listener ref="InfoJobListener"/>
    </listeners>
    <step id="mobilefilter" next="mobileanalyzer"> ... </step>
    <step id="mobileanalyzer"> ... </step>
</job>
```

The first step is defined as follows:

```
<step id="mobilefilter" next="mobileanalyzer">
    <listeners>
        <listener ref="InfoItemProcessListeners"/>
    </listeners>
    <chunk checkpoint-policy="item" item-count="10">
        <reader ref="LogLineReader"></reader>
        <processor ref="LogLineProcessor"></processor>
        <writer ref="LogFilteredLineWriter"></writer>
    </chunk>
</step>
```

This step is a normal chunk step that specifies the batch artifacts that implement each phase of the step. The batch artifact names are not fully qualified class names, so the batch artifacts are CDI beans annotated with @Named.

The second step is defined as follows:

```
<step id="mobileanalyzer">
    <batchlet ref="MobileBatchlet"></batchlet>
    <end on="COMPLETED"/>
</step>
```

This step is a task step that specifies the batch artifact that implements it. This is the last step of the job.

26.8.1.2 The LogLine and LogFilteredLine Items

The LogLine class represents entries in the web server log file and it is defined as follows:

```
public class LogLine {
    private final String datetime;
    private final String ipaddr;
    private final String browser;
    private final String url;

    /* ... Constructor, getters, and setters ... */
}
```

The LogFilteredLine class is similar to this class but only has two fields: the IP address of the client and the URL.

26.8.1.3 The Chunk Step Batch Artifacts

The first step is composed of the LogLineReader, LogLineProcessor, and LogFilteredLineWriter batch artifacts.

The LogLineReader artifact reads records from the web server log file:

```
@Dependent
@Named("LogLineReader")
public class LogLineReader implements ItemReader {
    private ItemNumberCheckpoint checkpoint;
    private String fileName;
    private BufferedReader breader;
    @Inject
    private JobContext jobCtx;

    public LogLineReader() { }
```

```
/* ... Override the open, close, readItem, and
 *     checkpointInfo methods ... */
}
```

The open method reads the log_file_name property and opens the log file with a buffered reader. In this example, the log file has been included with the application under webserverlog/WEB-INF/classes/log1.txt:

```
fileName = jobCtx.getProperties().getProperty("log_file_name");
ClassLoader classLoader = Thread.currentThread().getContextClassLoader();
InputStream iStream = classLoader.getResourceAsStream(fileName);
breader = new BufferedReader(new InputStreamReader(iStream));
```

If a checkpoint object is provided, the open method advances the reader up to the last checkpoint. Otherwise, this method creates a new checkpoint object. The checkpoint object keeps track of the line number from the last committed chunk.

The readItem method returns a new LogLine object or null at the end of the log file:

```
@Override
public Object readItem() throws Exception {
    String entry = breader.readLine();
    if (entry != null) {
        checkpoint.nextLine();
        return new LogLine(entry);
    } else {
        return null;
    }
}
```

The LogLineProcessor artifact obtains a list of browsers from the job properties and filters the log entries according to the list:

```
@Override
public Object processItem(Object item) {
    /* Obtain a list of browsers we are interested in */
    if (nbrowsers == 0) {
        Properties props = jobCtx.getProperties();
        nbrowsers = Integer.parseInt(props.getProperty("num_browsers"));
        browsers = new String[nbrowsers];
        for (int i = 1; i < nbrowsers + 1; i++)
            browsers[i - 1] = props.getProperty("browser_" + i);
    }

    LogLine logline = (LogLine) item;
    /* Filter for only the mobile/tablet browsers as specified */
    for (int i = 0; i < nbrowsers; i++) {
```

```
            if (logline.getBrowser().equals(browsers[i])) {
                return new LogFilteredLine(logline);
            }
        }
    }
    return null;
}
```

The `LogFilteredLineWriter` artifact reads the name of the output file from the job properties. The `open` method opens the file for writing. If a checkpoint object is provided, the artifact continues writing at the end of the file; otherwise, it overwrites the file if it exists. The `writeItems` method writes filtered items to the output file:

```
@Override
public void writeItems(List<Object> items) throws Exception {
    /* Write the filtered lines to the output file */
    for (int i = 0; i < items.size(); i++) {
        LogFilteredLine filtLine = (LogFilteredLine) items.get(i);
        bwriter.write(filtLine.toString());
        bwriter.newLine();
    }
}
```

26.8.1.4 The Listener Batch Artifacts

The `InfoJobListener` batch artifact implements a simple listener that writes log messages when the job starts and when it ends:

```
@Dependent
@Named("InfoJobListener")
public class InfoJobListener implements JobListener {
    ...
    @Override
    public void beforeJob() throws Exception {
        logger.log(Level.INFO, "The job is starting");
    }

    @Override
    public void afterJob() throws Exception { ... }
}
```

The `InfoItemProcessListener` batch artifact implements the `ItemProcessListener` interface for chunk steps:

```
@Dependent
@Named("InfoItemProcessListener")
public class InfoItemProcessListener implements ItemProcessListener {
```

```
    ...
    @Override
    public void beforeProcess(Object o) throws Exception {
        LogLine logline = (LogLine) o;
        logger.log(Level.INFO, "Processing entry {0}", logline);
    }
    ...
}
```

26.8.1.5 The Task Step Batch Artifact

The task step is implemented by the `MobileBatchlet` artifact, which computes what percentage of the filtered log entries are purchases:

```
@Override
public String process() throws Exception {
    /* Get properties from the job definition file */
    ...
    /* Count from the output of the previous chunk step */
    breader = new BufferedReader(new FileReader(fileName));
    String line = breader.readLine();
    while (line != null) {
        String[] lineSplit = line.split(", ");
        if (buyPage.compareTo(lineSplit[1]) == 0)
            pageVisits++;
        totalVisits++;
        line = breader.readLine();
    }
    breader.close();
    /* Write the result */
    ...
}
```

26.8.1.6 The JavaServer Faces Pages

The `index.xhtml` page contains a text area that shows the web server log. The page provides a button for the user to submit the batch job and navigate to the next page:

```
<body>
    ...
    <textarea cols="90" rows="25"
            readonly="true">#{jsfBean.getInputLog()}</textarea>
    <p> </p>
    <h:form>
        <h:commandButton value="Start Batch Job"
                    action="#{jsfBean.startBatchJob()}" />
```

```
    </h:form>
</body>
```

This page calls the methods of the managed bean to show the log file and submit the batch job.

The `jobstarted.xhtml` page provides a button to check the current status of the batch job and displays the results when the job finishes:

```
<p>Current Status of the Job: <b>#{jsfBean.jobStatus}</b></p>
<p>#{jsfBean.showResults()}</p>
<h:form>
    <h:commandButton value="Check Status"
                     action="jobstarted"
                     rendered="#{jsfBean.completed==false}" />
</h:form>
```

26.8.1.7 The Managed Bean

The `JsfBean` managed bean submits the job to the batch runtime, checks on the status of the job, and reads the results from a text file.

The `startBatchJob` method submits the job to the batch runtime:

```
/* Submit the batch job to the batch runtime.
 * JSF Navigation method (return the name of the next page) */
public String startBatchJob() {
    jobOperator = BatchRuntime.getJobOperator();
    execID = jobOperator.start("webserverlog", null);
    return "jobstarted";
}
```

The `getJobStatus` method checks the status of the job:

```
/* Get the status of the job from the batch runtime */
public String getJobStatus() {
    return jobOperator.getJobExecution(execID).getBatchStatus().toString();
}
```

The `showResults` method reads the results from a text file.

26.8.2 Running the webserverlog Example Application

You can use either NetBeans IDE or Maven to build, package, deploy, and run the `webserverlog` example application.

26.8.2.1 To Run the webserverlog Example Application Using NetBeans IDE

1. Make sure that GlassFish Server has been started (see Section 2.2, "Starting and Stopping GlassFish Server").

2. From the **File** menu, choose **Open Project**.

3. In the Open Project dialog box, navigate to:

   `tut-install/examples/batch`

4. Select the `webserverlog` folder.

5. Click **Open Project**.

6. In the **Projects** tab, right-click the `webserverlog` project and select **Run**.

   This command builds and packages the application into a WAR file, `webserverlog.war`, located in the `target/` directory; deploys it to the server; and launches a web browser window at the following URL:

   `http://localhost:8080/webserverlog/`

26.8.2.2 To Run the webserverlog Example Application Using Maven

1. Make sure that GlassFish Server has been started (see Section 2.2, "Starting and Stopping GlassFish Server").

2. In a terminal window, go to:

   `tut-install/examples/batch/webserverlog/`

3. Enter the following command to deploy the application:

   `mvn install`

4. Open a web browser window at the following URL:

   `http://localhost:8080/webserverlog/`

26.9 The phonebilling Example Application

The `phonebilling` example application, located in the *tut-install*/examples/ `batch/phonebilling/` directory, demonstrates how to use the batch framework in Java EE to implement a phone billing system. This example application processes a log file of phone calls and creates a bill for each customer.

26.9.1 Architecture of the phonebilling Example Application

The `phonebilling` example application consists of the following elements.

- A job definition file (`phonebilling.xml`) that uses the Job Specification Language (JSL) to define a batch job with two chunk steps. The first step reads call records from a log file and associates them with a bill. The second step computes the amount due and writes each bill to a text file.

- A Java class (`CallRecordLogCreator`) that creates the log file for the batch job. This is an auxiliary component that does not demonstrate any key functionality in this example.

- Two Java Persistence API (JPA) entities (`CallRecord` and `PhoneBill`) that represent call records and customer bills. The application uses a JPA entity manager to store instances of these entities in a database.

- Three batch artifacts (`CallRecordReader`, `CallRecordProcessor`, and `CallRecordWriter`) that implement the first step of the application. This step reads call records from the log file, associates them with a bill, and stores them in a database.

- Four batch artifacts (`BillReader`, `BillProcessor`, `BillWriter`, and `BillPartitionMapper`) that implement the second step of the application. This step is a partitioned step that gets each bill from the database, calculates the amount due, and writes it to a text file.

- Two Facelets pages (`index.xhtml` and `jobstarted.xhtml`) that provide the front end of the batch application. The first page shows the log file that will be processed by the batch job, and the second page enables the user to check on the status of the job and shows the resulting bill for each customer.

- A managed bean (`JsfBean`) that is accessed from the Facelets pages. The bean submits the job to the batch runtime, checks on the status of the job, and reads the text files for each bill.

26.9.1.1 The Job Definition File

The `phonebilling.xml` job definition file is located in the `WEB-INF/classes/META-INF/batch-jobs/` directory. The file specifies three job-level properties and two steps:

```
<job id="phonebilling" xmlns="http://xmlns.jcp.org/xml/ns/javaee"
    version="1.0">
    <properties>
        <property name="log_file_name" value="log1.txt"/>
        <property name="airtime_price" value="0.08"/>
        <property name="tax_rate" value="0.07"/>
```

```
        </properties>
        <step id="callrecords" next="bills"> ... </step>
        <step id="bills"> ... </step>
</job>
```

The first step is defined as follows:

```
<step id="callrecords" next="bills">
    <chunk checkpoint-policy="item" item-count="10">
        <reader ref="CallRecordReader"></reader>
        <processor ref="CallRecordProcessor"></processor>
        <writer ref="CallRecordWriter"></writer>
    </chunk>
</step>
```

This step is a normal chunk step that specifies the batch artifacts that implement each phase of the step. The batch artifact names are not fully qualified class names, so the batch artifacts are CDI beans annotated with @Named.

The second step is defined as follows:

```
<step id="bills">
    <chunk checkpoint-policy="item" item-count="2">
        <reader ref="BillReader"></reader>
        <processor ref="BillProcessor"></processor>
        <writer ref="BillWriter"></writer>
    </chunk>
    <partition>
        <mapper ref="BillPartitionMapper"/>
    </partition>
    <end on="COMPLETED"/>
</step>
```

This step is a partitioned chunk step. The partition plan is specified through the BillPartitionMapper artifact instead of using the plan element.

26.9.1.2 The CallRecord and PhoneBill Entities

The CallRecord entity is defined as follows:

```
@Entity
public class CallRecord implements Serializable {
    @Id @GeneratedValue
    private Long id;
    @Temporal(TemporalType.DATE)
    private Date datetime;
    private String fromNumber;
    private String toNumber;
```

```
        private int minutes;
        private int seconds;
        private BigDecimal price;

        public CallRecord() { }
        public CallRecord(String datetime, String from,
                String to, int min, int sec)
                throws ParseException { ... }

        public CallRecord(String jsonData) throws ParseException { ... }

        /* ... Getters and setters ... */
}
```

The id field is generated automatically by the JPA implementation to store and retrieve CallRecord objects to and from a database.

The second constructor creates a CallRecord object from an entry of JSON data in the log file using the JSON Processing API. Log entries look as follows:

```
{"datetime":"03/01/2013 04:03","from":"555-0101",
"to":"555-0114","length":"03:39"}
```

The PhoneBill entity is defined as follows:

```
@Entity
public class PhoneBill implements Serializable {
    @Id
    private String phoneNumber;
    @OneToMany(cascade = CascadeType.PERSIST)
    @OrderBy("datetime ASC")
    private List<CallRecord> calls;
    private BigDecimal amountBase;
    private BigDecimal taxRate;
    private BigDecimal tax;
    private BigDecimal amountTotal;

    public PhoneBill() { }

    public PhoneBill(String number) {
        this.phoneNumber = number;
        calls = new ArrayList<>();
    }

    public void addCall(CallRecord call) {
        calls.add(call);
    }
```

```
public void calculate(BigDecimal taxRate) { ... }

/* ... Getters and setters ... *
}
```

The OneToMany annotation defines the relationship between a bill and its call records. The CascadeType.PERSIST parameter indicates that the elements in the call list should be automatically persisted when the phone bill is persisted. The OrderBy annotation defines an order for retrieving the elements of the call list from the database.

The batch artifacts use instances of these two entities as items to read, process, and write.

For more information on the Java Persistence API, see Chapter 8, "Introduction to the Java Persistence API." For more information on the JSON Processing API, see Chapter 19, "JSON Processing," in *The Java EE 7 Tutorial, Volume 1.*

26.9.1.3 The Call Records Chunk Step

The first step is composed of the CallRecordReader, CallRecordProcessor, and CallRecordWriter batch artifacts.

The CallRecordReader artifact reads call records from the log file:

```
@Dependent
@Named("CallRecordReader")
public class CallRecordReader implements ItemReader {
    private ItemNumberCheckpoint checkpoint;
    private String fileName;
    private BufferedReader breader;
    @Inject
    JobContext jobCtx;

    /* ... Override the open, close, readItem,
     *     and checkpointInfo methods ... */
}
```

The open method reads the log_filename property and opens the log file with a buffered reader:

```
fileName = jobCtx.getProperties().getProperty("log_file_name");
breader = new BufferedReader(new FileReader(fileName));
```

If a checkpoint object is provided, the open method advances the reader up to the last checkpoint. Otherwise, this method creates a new checkpoint object. The checkpoint object keeps track of the line number from the last committed chunk.

The `readItem` method returns a new `CallRecord` object or null at the end of the
log file:

```
@Override
public Object readItem() throws Exception {
    /* Read a line from the log file and
     * create a CallRecord from JSON */
    String callEntryJson = breader.readLine();
    if (callEntryJson != null) {
        checkpoint.nextItem();
        return new CallRecord(callEntryJson);
    } else
        return null;
}
```

The `CallRecordProcessor` artifact obtains the airtime price from the job
properties, calculates the price of each call, and returns the call object. This artifact
overrides only the `processItem` method.

The `CallRecordWriter` artifact associates each call record with a bill and stores
the bill in the database. This artifact overrides the `open`, `close`, `writeItems`, and
`checkpointInfo` methods. The `writeItems` method looks like this:

```
@Override
public void writeItems(List<Object> callList) throws Exception {

    for (Object callObject : callList) {
        CallRecord call = (CallRecord) callObject;
        PhoneBill bill = em.find(PhoneBill.class, call.getFromNumber());
        if (bill == null) {
            /* No bill for this customer yet, create one */
            bill = new PhoneBill(call.getFromNumber());
            bill.addCall(call);
            em.persist(bill);
        } else {
            /* Add call to existing bill */
            bill.addCall(call);
        }
    }
}
```

26.9.1.4 The Phone Billing Chunk Step

The second step is composed of the `BillReader`, `BillProcessor`, `BillWriter`, and
`BillPartitionMapper` batch artifacts. This step gets the phone bills from the
database, computes the tax and total amount due, and writes each bill to a text

file. Since the processing of each bill is independent of the others, this step can be partitioned and run in more than one thread.

The `BillPartitionMapper` artifact specifies the number of partitions and the parameters for each partition. In this example, the parameters represent the range of items each partition should process. The artifact obtains the number of bills in the database to calculate these ranges. It provides a partition plan object that overrides the `getPartitions` and `getPartitionProperties` methods of the `PartitionPlan` interface. The `getPartitions` method looks like this:

```
@Override
public Properties[] getPartitionProperties() {
    /* Assign an (approximately) equal number of elements
     * to each partition. */
    long totalItems = getBillCount();
    long partItems = (long) totalItems / getPartitions();
    long remItems = totalItems % getPartitions();

    /* Populate a Properties array. Each Properties element
     * in the array corresponds to a partition. */
    Properties[] props = new Properties[getPartitions()];

    for (int i = 0; i < getPartitions(); i++) {
        props[i] = new Properties();
        props[i].put("firstItem", i * partItems);
        /* Last partition gets the remainder elements */
        if (i == getPartitions() - 1) {
            props[i].put("numItems", partItems + remItems);
        } else {
            props[i].put("numItems", partItems);
        }
    }
    return props;
}
```

The `BillReader` artifact obtains the partition parameters as follows:

```
@Dependent
@Named("BillReader")
public class BillReader implements ItemReader {
    ...
    @Inject
    JobContext jobCtx;
    private Properties partParams;
    ...
    @Override
    public void open(Serializable ckpt) throws Exception {
```

```
        /* Get the parameters for this partition */
        JobOperator jobOperator = BatchRuntime.getJobOperator();
        long execID = jobCtx.getExecutionId();
        partParams = jobOperator.getParameters(execID);

        /* Get the range of items to work on in this partition */
        long firstItem0 = ((Long) partParams.get("firstItem")).longValue();
        long numItems0 = ((Long) partParams.get("numItems")).longValue();
        ...
    }
    ...
}
```

This artifact also obtains an iterator to read items from the JPA entity manager:

```
/* Obtain an iterator for the bills in this partition */
String query = "SELECT b FROM PhoneBill b ORDER BY b.phoneNumber";
Query q = em.createQuery(query)
        .setFirstResult((int)firstItem).setMaxResults((int)numItems);
iterator = q.getResultList().iterator();
```

The `BillProcessor` artifact iterates over the list of call records in a bill and calculates the tax and total amount due for each bill.

The `BillWriter` artifact writes each bill to a plain text file.

26.9.1.5 The JavaServer Faces Pages

The `index.xhtml` page contains a text area that shows the log file of call records. The page provides a button for the user to submit the batch job and navigate to the next page:

```
<body>
    <h1>The Phone Billing Example Application</h1>
    <h2>Log file</h2>
    <p>The batch job analyzes the following log file:</p>
    <textarea cols="90" rows="25"
            readonly="true">#{jsfBean.createAndShowLog()}</textarea>
    <p> </p>
    <h:form>
        <h:commandButton value="Start Batch Job"
                        action="#{jsfBean.startBatchJob()}" />
    </h:form>
</body>
```

This page calls the methods of the managed bean to show the log file and submit the batch job.

The `jobstarted.xhtml` page provides a button to check the current status of the batch job and displays the bills when the job finishes:

```
<p>Current Status of the Job: <b>#{jsfBean.jobStatus}</b></p>
<h:dataTable var="_row" value="#{jsfBean.rowList}"
            border="1" rendered="#{jsfBean.completed}">
    <!-- ... show results from jsfBean.rowList ... -->
</h:dataTable>
<!-- Render the check status button if the job has not finished -->
<h:form>
    <h:commandButton value="Check Status"
                    rendered="#{jsfBean.completed==false}"
                    action="jobstarted" />
</h:form>
```

26.9.1.6 The Managed Bean

The `JsfBean` managed bean submits the job to the batch runtime, checks on the status of the job, and reads the text files for each bill.

The `startBatchJob` method of the bean submits the job to the batch runtime:

```
/* Submit the batch job to the batch runtime.
 * JSF Navigation method (return the name of the next page) */
public String startBatchJob() {
    jobOperator = BatchRuntime.getJobOperator();
    execID = jobOperator.start("phonebilling", null);
    return "jobstarted";
}
```

The `getJobStatus` method of the bean checks the status of the job:

```
/* Get the status of the job from the batch runtime */
public String getJobStatus() {
    return jobOperator.getJobExecution(execID).getBatchStatus().toString();
}
```

The `getRowList` method of the bean creates a list of bills to be displayed on the `jobstarted.xhtml` JSF page using a table.

26.9.2 Running the phonebilling Example Application

You can use either NetBeans IDE or Maven to build, package, deploy, and run the `phonebilling` example application.

26.9.2.1 To Run the phonebilling Example Application Using NetBeans IDE

1. Make sure that GlassFish Server has been started (see Section 2.2, "Starting and Stopping GlassFish Server").

2. From the **File** menu, choose **Open Project**.

3. In the Open Project dialog box, navigate to:

   tut-install/examples/batch

4. Select the phonebilling folder.

5. Click **Open Project**.

6. In the **Projects** tab, right-click the phonebilling project and select **Run**.

   This command builds and packages the application into a WAR file, phonebilling.war, located in the target/ directory; deploys it to the server; and launches a web browser window at the following URL:

   http://localhost:8080/phonebilling/

26.9.2.2 To Run the phonebilling Example Application Using Maven

1. Make sure that GlassFish Server has been started (see Section 2.2, "Starting and Stopping GlassFish Server").

2. In a terminal window, go to:

   tut-install/examples/batch/phonebilling/

3. Enter the following command to deploy the application:

   mvn install

4. Open a web browser window at the following URL:

   http://localhost:8080/phonebilling/

26.10 Further Information about Batch Processing

For more information on batch processing in Java EE, see the Batch Applications for the Java Platform specification:

http://www.jcp.org/en/jsr/detail?id=352

27

Concurrency Utilities for Java EE

This chapter describes Concurrency Utilities for Java EE, which are specified by JSR 236.

This chapter covers the following topics:

- Concurrency Basics
- Main Components of the Concurrency Utilities
- Concurrency and Transactions
- Concurrency and Security
- The jobs Concurrency Example
- The taskcreator Concurrency Example
- Further Information about the Concurrency Utilities

27.1 Concurrency Basics

Concurrency is the concept of executing two or more tasks at the same time (in parallel). Tasks may include methods (functions), parts of a program, or even other programs. With current computer architectures, support for multiple cores and multiple processors in a single CPU is very common.

The Java Platform has always offered support for concurrent programming, which was the basis for implementing many of the services offered by Java EE containers. At Java SE 5, additional high-level API support for concurrency was provided by the `java.util.concurrent` package.

Prior to Java EE 7, there were no specific APIs that allowed enterprise developers to use concurrency utilities in a safely standard manner. The Java EE web and EJB containers instantiate objects using container-managed thread pools. Therefore, using Java SE concurrent APIs to instantiate `Thread` objects was strongly discouraged. If a developer creates a new (non-managed) `Thread` object, the container could not guarantee that other Java EE platform services (for example, transactions and security) would be part of this `Thread`.

27.1.1 Threads and Processes

The two main concurrency concepts are **processes** and **threads**.

Processes are primarily associated with applications running on the operating system (OS). A process has specific runtime resources to interact with the underlying OS and allocate other resources, such as its own memory, just as the JVM process does. A JVM is in fact a process.

The Java programming language and platform are primarily concerned with threads.

Threads share some features with processes, since both consume resources from the OS or the execution environment. But threads are easier to create and consume many fewer resources than a process.

Because threads are so lightweight, any modern CPU that has a couple of cores and a few gigabytes of RAM can handle thousands of threads in a single JVM process. The precise number of threads will depend on the combined output of the CPU, OS, and RAM available, as well as on correct configuration (tuning) of the JVM.

Although concurrent programming solves many problems and can improve performance for most applications, there are a number of situations where multiple execution lines (threads or processes) can cause major problems. These situations include the following:

- Deadlocks
- Thread starvation
- Concurrent accessing of shared resources
- Situations when the program generates incorrect data

27.2 Main Components of the Concurrency Utilities

Concurrent resources are managed objects that provide concurrency capabilities to Java EE applications. In GlassFish Server, you configure concurrent resources and then make them available for use by application components such as servlets and enterprise beans. Concurrent resources are accessed through JNDI lookup or resource injection.

The primary components of the concurrency utilities are as follows.

- `ManagedExecutorService`: A managed executor service is used by applications to execute submitted tasks asynchronously. Tasks are executed on threads that are started and managed by the container. The context of the container is propagated to the thread executing the task.

  For example, by using an `ManagedExecutorService.submit()` call, a task, such as the GenerateReportTask, could be submitted to execute at a later time and then, by using the `Future` object callback, retrieve the result when it becomes available.

- `ManagedScheduledExecutorService`: A managed scheduled executor service is used by applications to execute submitted tasks asynchronously at specific times. Tasks are executed on threads that are started and managed by the container. The context of the container is propagated to the thread executing the task. The API provides the scheduling functionality that allows users to set a specific date/time for the Task execution programmatically in the application.

- `ContextService`: A context service is used to create dynamic proxy objects that capture the context of a container and enable applications to run within that context at a later time or be submitted to a Managed Executor Service. The context of the container is propagated to the thread executing the task.

- `ManagedThreadFactory`: A managed thread factory is used by applications to create managed threads. The threads are started and managed by the container. The context of the container is propagated to the thread executing the task. This object can also be used to provide custom factories for specific use cases (with custom Threads) and, for example, set specific/proprietary properties to these objects.

27.3 Concurrency and Transactions

The most basic operations for transactions are commit and rollback, but, in a distributed environment with concurrent processing, it can be difficult to guarantee that commit or rollback operations will be successfully processed, and the transaction can be spread among different threads, CPU cores, physical machines, and networks.

Ensuring that a rollback operation will successfully execute in such a scenario is crucial. Concurrency Utilities relies on the Java Transaction API (JTA) to

implement and support transactions on its components through
javax.transaction.UserTransaction, allowing application developers to
explicitly manage transaction boundaries. More information is available in the
JTA specification.

Optionally, context objects can begin, commit, or roll back transactions, but these
objects cannot enlist in parent component transactions.

The following code snippet illustrates a Runnable task that obtains a
UserTransaction and then starts and commits a transaction while interacting
with other transactional components, such as an enterprise bean and a database:

```
public class MyTransactionalTask implements Runnable {

    UserTransaction ut = ... // obtained through JNDI or injection

    public void run() {

        // Start a transaction
        ut.begin();

        // Invoke a Service or an EJB
        myEJB.businessMethod();

        // Update a database entity using an XA JDBC driver
        myEJB.updateCustomer(customer);

        // Commit the transaction
        ut.commit();

    }
}
```

27.4 Concurrency and Security

Concurrency Utilities for Java EE defers most security decisions to the application
server implementation. If, however, the container supports a security context, that
context can be propagated to the thread of execution. The ContextService can
support several runtime behaviors, and the security attribute, if enabled, will
propagate the container security principal.

27.5 The jobs Concurrency Example

This section describes a very basic example that shows how to use some of the
basic concurrency features in an enterprise application. Specifically, this example

uses one of the main components of Concurrency Utilities for Java EE, a Managed Executor Service.

The example demonstrates a scenario where a RESTful web service, exposed as a public API, is used to submit generic jobs for execution. These jobs are processed in the background. Each job prints a "Starting" and a "Finished" message at the beginning and end of the execution. Also, to simulate background processing, each job takes 10 seconds to execute.

The RESTful service exposes two methods:

- `/token`: Exposed as a GET method that registers and returns valid API tokens

- `/process`: Exposed as a POST method that receives a `jobID` query parameter, which is the identifier for the job to be executed, and a custom HTTP header named `X-REST-API-Key`, which will be used internally to validate requests with tokens

The token is used to differentiate the Quality of Service (QoS) offered by the API. Users that provide a token in a service request can process multiple concurrent jobs. However, users that do not provide a token can process only one job at a time. Since every job takes 10 seconds to execute, users that provide no token will be able to execute only one call to the service every 10 seconds. For users that provide a token, processing will be much faster.

This differentiation is made possible by the use of two different Managed Executor Services, one for each type of request.

27.5.1 Running the jobs Example

After configuring GlassFish Server by adding two Managed Executor Services, you can use either NetBeans IDE or Maven to build, package, deploy, and run the `jobs` example.

27.5.1.1 To Configure GlassFish Server for the Basic Concurrency Example

To configure GlassFish Server, follow these steps.

1. Make sure that GlassFish Server is has been started (see Section 2.2, "Starting and Stopping GlassFish Server").

2. Open the Administration Console at `http://localhost:4848`.

3. Expand the **Resources** node.

4. Expand the **Concurrent Resources** node.

5. Click **Managed Executor Services**.

6. On the Managed Executor Services page, click **New** to open the New Managed Executor Services page.

7. In the **JNDI Name** field, enter MES_High to create the high-priority Managed Executor Service. Use the following settings (keep the default values for other settings):

   ▪ **Thread Priority**: 10

   ▪ **Core Size**: 2

   ▪ **Maximum Pool Size**: 5

   ▪ **Task Queue Capacity**: 2

8. Click OK.

9. On the On the Managed Executor Services page, click **New** again.

10. In the **JNDI Name** field, enter MES_Low to create the low-priority Managed Executor Service. Use the following settings (keep the default values for other settings):

    ▪ **Thread Priority**: 1

    ▪ **Core Size**: 1

    ▪ **Maximum Pool Size**: 1

    ▪ **Task Queue Capacity**: 0

11. Click OK.

27.5.1.2 To Build, Package, and Deploy the jobs Example Using NetBeans IDE

1. Make sure that GlassFish Server has been started (see Section 2.2, "Starting and Stopping GlassFish Server").

2. From the **File** menu, choose **Open Project**.

3. In the Open Project dialog box, navigate to:

   tut-install/examples/concurrency

4. Select the jobs folder.

5. Click **Open Project**.

6. In the **Projects** tab, right-click the jobs project and select **Build**.

   This command builds and deploys the application.

27.5.1.3 To Build, Package, and Deploy the jobs Example Using Maven

1. Make sure that GlassFish Server has been started (see Section 2.2, "Starting and Stopping GlassFish Server").

2. In a terminal window, go to:

    tut-install/examples/concurrency/jobs/

3. Enter the following command to build and deploy the application:

    ```
    mvn install
    ```

27.5.1.4 To Run the jobs Example and Submit Jobs with Low Priority

To run the example as a user who submits jobs with low priority, follow these steps.

1. In a web browser, enter the following URL:

    ```
    http://localhost:8080/jobs
    ```

2. In the Jobs Client page, enter the value 1 in the **Enter a JobID** field, enter nothing in the **Enter a Token** field, then click **Submit Job**.

    The following message should be displayed at the bottom of the page:

    ```
    Job 1 successfully submitted
    ```

    The server log includes the following messages:

    ```
    INFO:    Invalid or missing token!
    INFO:    Task started LOW-1
    INFO:    Job 1 successfully submitted
    INFO:    Task finished LOW-1
    ```

    You submitted a job with low priority. This means that you cannot submit another job for 10 seconds. If you try to do so, the RESTful API will return a service unavailable (HTTP 503) response and the following message will be displayed at the bottom of the page:

    ```
    Job 2 was NOT submitted
    ```

    The server log will include the following messages:

    ```
    INFO:    Invalid or missing token!
    INFO:    Job 1 successfully submitted
    INFO:    Task started LOW-1
    INFO:    Invalid or missing token!
    INFO:    Job 2 was NOT submitted
    INFO:    Task finished LOW-1
    ```

27.5.1.5 To Run the jobs Example and Submit Jobs with High Priority

To run the example as a user who submits jobs with high priority, follow these steps.

1. In a web browser, enter the following URL:

    ```
    http://localhost:8080/jobs
    ```

2. In the Jobs Client page, enter a value of one to ten digits in the **Enter a JobID** field.

3. Click the **here** link on the line "Get a token here" to get a token. The page that displays the token will open in a new tab.

4. Copy the token and return to the Jobs Client page.

5. Paste the token in the **Enter a Token** field, then click **Submit Job**.

    A message like the following should be displayed at the bottom of the page:

    ```
    Job 11 successfully submitted
    ```

    The server log includes the following messages:

    ```
    INFO:   Token accepted. Execution with high priority.
    INFO:   Task started HIGH-11
    INFO:   Job 11 successfully submitted
    INFO:   Task finished HIGH-11
    ```

    You submitted a job with high priority. This means that you can submit multiple jobs, each with a token, and not face the 10 second per job restriction that the low priority submitters face. If you submit 3 jobs with tokens in rapid succession, messages like the following will be displayed at the bottom of the page:

    ```
    Job 1 was submitted
    Job 2 was submitted
    Job 3 was submitted
    ```

    The server log will include the following messages:

    ```
    INFO:   Token accepted. Execution with high priority.
    INFO:   Task started HIGH-1
    INFO:   Job 1 successfully submitted
    INFO:   Token accepted. Execution with high priority.
    ```

```
INFO:   Task started HIGH-2
INFO:   Job 2 successfully submitted
INFO:   Task finished HIGH-1
INFO:   Token accepted. Execution with high priority.
INFO:   Task started HIGH-3
INFO:   Job 3 successfully submitted
INFO:   Task finished HIGH-2
INFO:   Task finished HIGH-3
```

27.6 The taskcreator Concurrency Example

The taskcreator example demonstrates how to use Concurrency Utilities for Java EE to run tasks immediately, periodically, or after a fixed delay. This example provides a JavaServer Faces interface that enables users to submit tasks to be executed and displays information messages for each task. The example uses the Managed Executor Service to run tasks immediately and the Managed Scheduled Executor Service to run tasks periodically or after a fixed delay. (See Section 27.2, "Main Components of the Concurrency Utilities," for information about these services.)

The taskcreator example consists of the following components.

■ A JavaServer Faces page (index.xhtml) that contains three elements: a form to submit tasks, a task execution log, and a form to cancel periodic tasks. This page submits Ajax requests to create and cancel tasks. This page also receives WebSocket messages, using JavaScript code to update the task execution log.

■ A CDI managed bean (TaskCreatorBean) that processes the requests from the JavaServer Faces page. This bean invokes the methods in TaskEJB to submit new tasks and to cancel periodic tasks.

■ An enterprise bean (TaskEJB) that obtains executor service instances using resource injection and submits tasks for execution. This bean is also a JAX-RS web service endpoint. The tasks send information messages to this endpoint.

■ A WebSocket endpoint (InfoEndpoint) that the enterprise bean uses to send information messages to the clients.

■ A task class (Task) that implements the Runnable interface. The run method in this class sends information messages to the web service endpoint in TaskEJB and sleeps for 1.5 seconds.

Figure 27–1 shows the architecture of the taskcreator example.

Figure 27–1 Architecture of the taskcreator Example

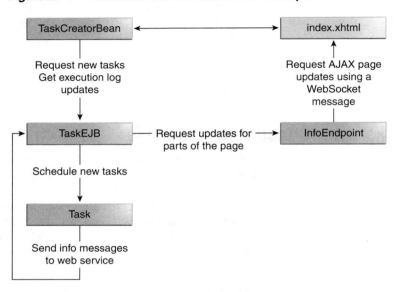

The TaskEJB class obtains the default executor service objects from the application server as follows:

```
@Resource(name="java:comp/DefaultManagedExecutorService")
ManagedExecutorService mExecService;

@Resource(name="java:comp/DefaultManagedScheduledExecutorService")
ManagedScheduledExecutorService sExecService;
```

The submitTask method in TaskEJB uses these objects to submit tasks for execution as follows:

```
public void submitTask(Task task, String type) {
    /* Use the managed executor objects from the app server */
    switch (type) {
        case "IMMEDIATE":
            mExecService.submit(task);
            break;
        case "DELAYED":
            sExecService.schedule(task, 3, TimeUnit.SECONDS);
            break;
        case "PERIODIC":
            ScheduledFuture<?> fut;
            fut = sExecService.scheduleAtFixedRate(task, 0, 8,
                    TimeUnit.SECONDS);
```

```
                    periodicTasks.put(task.getName(), fut);
                    break;
        }
}
```

For periodic tasks, `TaskEJB` keeps a reference to the `ScheduledFuture` object, so that the user can cancel the task at any time.

27.6.1 Running the taskcreator Example

This section describes how to build, package, deploy, and run the `taskcreator` example using NetBeans IDE or Maven.

27.6.1.1 To Build, Package, and Deploy the taskcreator Example Using NetBeans IDE

1. Make sure that GlassFish Server has been started (see Section 2.2, "Starting and Stopping GlassFish Server").

2. From the **File** menu, choose **Open Project**.

3. In the Open Project dialog box, navigate to:

   tut-install/examples/concurrency

4. Select the `taskcreator` folder.

5. Click **Open Project**.

6. In the **Projects** tab, right-click the `taskcreator` project and select **Build**.

   This command builds and deploys the application.

27.6.1.2 To Build, Package, and Deploy the taskcreator Example Using Maven

1. Make sure that GlassFish Server has been started (see Section 2.2, "Starting and Stopping GlassFish Server").

2. In a terminal window, go to:

   tut-install/examples/concurrency/taskcreator/

3. Enter the following command to build and deploy the application:

   ```
   mvn install
   ```

27.6.1.3 To Run the taskcreator Example

1. Open the following URL in a web browser:

   ```
   http://localhost:8080/taskcreator/
   ```

   The page contains a form to submit tasks, a task execution log, and a form to cancel periodic tasks.

2. Select the **Immediate** task type, enter a task name, and click the **Submit** button. Messages like the following appear in the task execution log:

   ```
   12:40:47 - IMMEDIATE Task TaskA finished
   12:40:45 - IMMEDIATE Task TaskA started
   ```

3. Select the **Delayed (3 sec)** task type, enter a task name, and click the **Submit** button. Messages like the following appear in the task execution log:

   ```
   12:43:26 - DELAYED Task TaskB finished
   12:43:25 - DELAYED Task TaskB started
   12:43:22 - DELAYED Task TaskB submitted
   ```

4. Select the **Periodic (8 sec)** task type, enter a task name, and click the **Submit** button. Messages like the following appear in the task execution log:

   ```
   12:45:25 - PERIODIC Task TaskC finished run #2
   12:45:23 - PERIODIC Task TaskC started run #2
   12:45:17 - PERIODIC Task TaskC finished run #1
   12:45:15 - PERIODIC Task TaskC started run #1
   ```

   You can add more than one periodic task. To cancel a periodic task, select it from the form and click **Cancel Task**.

27.7 Further Information about the Concurrency Utilities

For more information about concurrency, see

- Concurrency Utilities for Java EE specification:

  ```
  http://jcp.org/en/jsr/detail?id=236
  ```

- Concurrency Utilities specification:

  ```
  http://jcp.org/en/jsr/detail?id=166
  ```

- Concurrency Lesson in The Java Tutorials:

  ```
  http://docs.oracle.com/javase/tutorial/essential/
  concurrency/
  ```

Part VII

Case Studies

Part VII presents case studies that use a variety of Java EE technologies. This part contains the following chapters:

- Chapter 28, "Duke's Bookstore Case Study Example"
- Chapter 29, "Duke's Tutoring Case Study Example"
- Chapter 30, "Duke's Forest Case Study Example"

28

Duke's Bookstore Case Study Example

The Duke's Bookstore example is a simple e-commerce application that illustrates some of the more advanced features of JavaServer Faces technology in combination with Contexts and Dependency Injection for Java EE (CDI), enterprise beans, and the Java Persistence API. Users can select books from an image map, view the bookstore catalog, and purchase books. No security is used in this application.

The following topics are addressed here:

- Design and Architecture of Duke's Bookstore
- The Duke's Bookstore Interface
- Running the Duke's Bookstore Case Study Application

28.1 Design and Architecture of Duke's Bookstore

Duke's Bookstore is a simple web application that uses many features of JavaServer Faces technology, in addition to other Java EE 7 features:

- JavaServer Faces technology, as well as Contexts and Dependency Injection for Java EE (CDI)
  - A set of Facelets pages, along with a template, provides the user interface to the application.
  - CDI managed beans are associated with each of the Facelets pages.

- A custom image map component on the front page allows you to select a book to enter the store. Each area of the map is represented by a JavaServer Faces managed bean. Text hyperlinks are also provided for accessibility.

- Action listeners are registered on the image map and the text links. These listeners retrieve the ID value for the selected book and store it in the session map so it can be retrieved by the managed bean for the next page.

- The h:dataTable tag is used to render the book catalog and shopping cart contents dynamically.

- A custom converter is registered on the credit card field on the checkout page, bookcashier.xhtml, which also uses an f:validateRegEx tag to ensure that the input is correctly formatted.

- A value-change listener is registered on the name field on bookcashier.xhtml. This listener saves the name in a parameter so the following page, bookreceipt.xhtml, can access it.

- Enterprise beans: Local, no-interface-view stateless session bean and singleton bean

- A Java Persistence API entity

The packages of the Duke's Bookstore application, located in the *tut-install/* examples/case-studies/dukes-bookstore/src/main/java/javaeetutorial/ dukesbookstore/ directory, are as follows:

- components: Includes the custom UI component classes, MapComponent and AreaComponent

- converters: Includes the custom converter class, CreditCardConverter

- ejb: Includes two enterprise beans:

    - A singleton bean, ConfigBean, that initializes the data in the database

    - A stateless session bean, BookRequestBean, that contains the business logic to manage the entity

- entity: Includes the Book entity class

- exceptions: Includes three exception classes

- listeners: Includes the event handler and event listener classes

- model: Includes a model JavaBeans class

- renderers: Includes the custom renderers for the custom UI component classes

- `web.managedbeans`: Includes the managed beans for the Facelets pages
- `web.messages`: Includes the resource bundle files for localized messages

28.2 The Duke's Bookstore Interface

This section provides additional detail regarding the components of the Duke's Bookstore example and how they interact.

28.2.1 The Book Java Persistence API Entity

The `Book` entity, located in the `dukesbookstore.entity` package, encapsulates the book data stored by Duke's Bookstore.

The `Book` entity defines attributes used in the example:

- A book ID
- The author's first name
- The author's surname
- The title
- The price
- Whether the book is on sale
- The publication year
- A description of the book
- The number of copies in the inventory

The `Book` entity also defines a simple named query, `findBooks`.

28.2.2 Enterprise Beans Used in Duke's Bookstore

Two enterprise beans located in the `dukesbookstore.ejb` package provide the business logic for Duke's Bookstore.

- `BookRequestBean` is a stateful session bean that contains the business methods for the application. The methods create, retrieve, and purchase books, and update the inventory for a book. To retrieve the books, the `getBooks` method calls the `findBooks` named query defined in the `Book` entity.
- `ConfigBean` is a singleton session bean used to create the books in the catalog when the application is initially deployed. It calls the `createBook` method defined in `BookRequestBean`.

28.2.3 Facelets Pages and Managed Beans Used in Duke's Bookstore

The Duke's Bookstore application uses Facelets and its templating features to display the user interface. The Facelets pages interact with a set of CDI managed beans that act as backing beans, providing the underlying properties and methods for the user interface. The front page also interacts with the custom components used by the application.

The application uses the following Facelets pages, which are located in the *tut-install*/examples/case-studies/dukes-bookstore/src/main/webapp/ directory.

- bookstoreTemplate.xhtml: The template file, which specifies a header used on every page as well as the style sheet used by all the pages. The template also retrieves the language set in the web browser.

  Uses the LocaleBean managed bean.

- index.xhtml: Landing page, which lays out the custom map and area components using managed beans configured in the faces-config.xml file and allows the user to select a book and advance to the bookstore.xhtml page.

- bookstore.xhtml: Page that allows the user to obtain details on the selected book or the featured book, to add either book to the shopping cart, and to advance to the bookcatalog.xhtml page.

  Uses the BookstoreBean managed bean.

- bookdetails.xhtml: Page that shows details on a book selected from bookstore.xhtml or other pages and allows the user to add the book to the cart and/or advance to the bookcatalog.xhtml page.

  Uses the BookDetailsBean managed bean.

- bookcatalog.xhtml: Page that displays the books in the catalog and allows the user to add books to the shopping cart, view the details for any book, view the shopping cart, empty the shopping cart, or purchase the books in the shopping cart.

  Uses the BookstoreBean, CatalogBean, and ShoppingCart managed beans.

- bookshowcart.xhtml: Page that displays the contents of the shopping cart and allows the user to remove items, view the details for an item, empty the shopping cart, purchase the books in the shopping cart, or return to the catalog.

  Uses the ShowCartBean and ShoppingCart managed beans.

- `bookcashier.xhtml`: Page that allows the user to purchase books, specify a shipping option, subscribe to newsletters, or join the Duke Fan Club with a purchase over a certain amount.

  Uses the `CashierBean` and `ShoppingCart` managed beans.

- `bookreceipt.xhtml`: Page that confirms the user's purchase and allows the user to return to the catalog page to continue shopping.

  Uses the `CashierBean` managed bean.

- `bookordererror.xhtml`: Page rendered by `CashierBean` if the bookstore has no more copies of a book that was ordered.

The application uses the following managed beans, which are located in the *tut-install*/examples/case-studies/dukes-bookstore/src/main/java/javaeetutorial/dukesbookstore/web/managedbeans/ directory.

- `AbstractBean`: Contains utility methods called by other managed beans.

- `BookDetailsBean`: Backing bean for the `bookdetails.xhtml` page. Specifies the name `details`.

- `BookstoreBean`: Backing bean for the `bookstore.xhtml` page. Specifies the name `store`.

- `CashierBean`: Backing bean for the `bookcashier.xhtml` and `bookreceipt.xhtml` pages.

- `CatalogBean`: Backing bean for the `bookcatalog.xhtml` page. Specifies the name `catalog`.

- `LocaleBean`: Managed bean that retrieves the current locale; used on each page.

- `ShoppingCart`: Backing bean used by the `bookcashier.xhtml`, `bookcatalog.xhtml`, and `bookshowcart.xhtml` pages. Specifies the name `cart`.

- `ShoppingCartItem`: Contains methods called by `ShoppingCart`, `CatalogBean`, and `ShowCartBean`.

- `ShowCartBean`: Backing bean for the `bookshowcart.xhtml` page. Specifies the name `showcart`.

28.2.4 Custom Components and Other Custom Objects Used in Duke's Bookstore

The map and area custom components for Duke's Bookstore, along with associated renderer, listener, and model classes, are defined in the following packages in the *tut-install*/examples/case-studies/dukes-bookstore/src/main/ java/javaeetutorial/dukesbookstore/ directory.

- components: Contains the MapComponent and AreaComponent classes. See Section 15.4, "Creating Custom Component Classes," in *The Java EE 7 Tutorial, Volume 1.*

- listeners: Contains the AreaSelectedEvent class, along with other listener classes. See Section 15.7, "Handling Events for Custom Components," in *The Java EE 7 Tutorial, Volume 1.*

- model: Contains the ImageArea class. See Section 15.2.4, "Configuring Model Data," in *The Java EE 7 Tutorial, Volume 1.*

- renderers: Contains the MapRenderer and AreaRenderer classes. See Section 15.5, "Delegating Rendering to a Renderer," in *The Java EE 7 Tutorial, Volume 1.*

The *tut-install*/examples/case-studies/dukes-bookstore/src/main/java/ dukesbookstore/ directory also contains a custom converter and other custom listeners not specifically tied to the custom components.

- converters: Contains the CreditCardConverter class. See Section 15.10, "Creating and Using a Custom Converter," in *The Java EE 7 Tutorial, Volume 1.*

- listeners: Contains the LinkBookChangeListener, MapBookChangeListener, and NameChanged classes. See Section 15.6, "Implementing an Event Listener," in *The Java EE 7 Tutorial, Volume 1.*

28.2.5 Properties Files Used in Duke's Bookstore

The strings used in the Duke's Bookstore application are encapsulated into resource bundles to allow the display of localized strings in multiple locales. The properties files, located in the *tut-install*/examples/case-studies/ dukes-bookstore/src/main/java/javaeetutorial/dukesbookstore/web/ messages/ directory, consist of a default file containing English strings and three additional files for other locales. The files are as follows:

- Messages.properties: Default file, containing English strings

- Messages_de.properties: File containing German strings

- Messages_es.properties: File containing Spanish strings

- Messages_fr.properties: File containing French strings

The language setting in the user's web browser determines which locale is used. The `html` tag in `bookstoreTemplate.xhtml` retrieves the language setting from the `language` property of `LocaleBean`:

```
<html lang="#{localeBean.language}"
...
```

For more information about resource bundles, see Chapter 20, "Internationalizing and Localizing Web Applications," in *The Java EE 7 Tutorial, Volume 1*.

The resource bundle is configured as follows in the `faces-config.xml` file:

```
<application>
    <resource-bundle>
        <base-name>
            javaeetutorial.dukesbookstore.web.messages.Messages
        </base-name>
        <var>bundle</var>
    </resource-bundle>
    <locale-config>
        <default-locale>en</default-locale>
        <supported-locale>de</supported-locale>
        <supported-locale>es</supported-locale>
        <supported-locale>fr</supported-locale>
    </locale-config>
</application>
```

This configuration means that in the Facelets pages, messages are retrieved using the prefix `bundle` with the key found in the `Messages_`*locale*`.properties` file, as in the following example from the `index.xhtml` page:

```
<h:outputText style="font-weight:bold"
            value="#{bundle.ChooseBook}" />
```

In `Messages.properties`, the key string is defined as follows:

```
ChooseBook=Choose a Book from our Catalog
```

28.2.6 Deployment Descriptors Used in Duke's Bookstore

The following deployment descriptors are used in Duke's Bookstore:

- `src/main/resources/META-INF/persistence.xml`: The Java Persistence API configuration file

- `src/main/webapp/WEB-INF/bookstore.taglib.xml`: The tag library descriptor file for the custom components

- `src/main/webapp/WEB-INF/faces-config.xml`: The JavaServer Faces configuration file, which configures the managed beans for the map component as well as the resource bundles for the application

- `src/main/webapp/WEB-INF/web.xml`: The web application configuration file

28.3 Running the Duke's Bookstore Case Study Application

You can use either NetBeans IDE or Maven to build, package, deploy, and run the Duke's Bookstore application.

28.3.1 To Build and Deploy Duke's Bookstore Using NetBeans IDE

1. Make sure that GlassFish Server has been started (see Section 2.2, "Starting and Stopping GlassFish Server").

2. From the **File** menu, choose **Open Project**.

3. In the Open Project dialog box, navigate to:

   tut-install/examples/case-studies

4. Select the `dukes-bookstore` folder.

5. Click **Open Project**.

6. In the **Projects** tab, right-click the `dukes-bookstore` project and select **Build**.

   This will build, package, and deploy Duke's Bookstore to GlassFish Server.

28.3.2 To Build and Deploy Duke's Bookstore Using Maven

1. Make sure that GlassFish Server has been started (see Section 2.2, "Starting and Stopping GlassFish Server"), as well as the database server (see Section 2.4, "Starting and Stopping the Java DB Server").

2. In a terminal window, go to:

   tut-install/examples/case-studies/dukes-bookstore/

3. Enter the following command:

   ```
   mvn install
   ```

   This command builds the application and packages it in a WAR file in the *tut-install*/examples/case-studies/dukes-bookstore/target/ directory. It then deploys the application to GlassFish Server.

28.3.3 To Run Duke's Bookstore

1. In a web browser, enter the following URL:

   `http://localhost:8080/dukes-bookstore/`

2. On the Duke's Bookstore main page, click a book in the graphic, or click one of the links at the bottom of the page.

3. Use the pages in the application to view and purchase books.

29

Duke's Tutoring Case Study Example

The Duke's Tutoring example application is a tracking system for a tutoring center for students. Students can be checked in and out and can visit the park. The tutoring center can track attendance and status updates and can store contact information for guardians and students. Administrators can maintain the tutoring center system.

The following topics are addressed here:

- Design and Architecture of Duke's Tutoring

- Main Interface

- Administration Interface

- Running the Duke's Tutoring Case Study Application

29.1 Design and Architecture of Duke's Tutoring

Duke's Tutoring is a web application that incorporates several Java EE technologies. It exposes both a main interface (for students, guardians, and tutoring center staff) and an administration interface (for staff to maintain the system). The business logic for both interfaces is provided by enterprise beans. The enterprise beans use the Java Persistence API to create and store the application's data in the database. Figure 29–1 illustrates the architecture of the application.

Figure 29–1   Architecture of the Duke's Tutoring Example Application

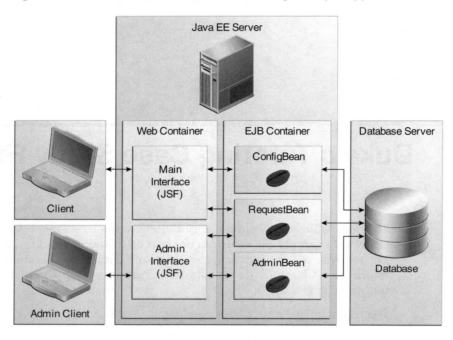

The Duke's Tutoring application is organized into two main projects: the
dukes-tutoring-common library and the dukes-tutoring-war web application.
The dukes-tutoring-common library project contains the entity classes and helper
classes used by the dukes-tutoring-war web application, and
dukes-tutoring-common is packaged and deployed with dukes-tutoring-war.
The library JAR file is useful for allowing the entity classes and helper classes to
be reused by other applications, such as a JavaFX client application.

Duke's Tutoring uses the following Java EE 7 platform features:

- Java Persistence API entities

  - A custom Bean Validation annotation, @Email, for validating email
    addresses

  - A standard jta-data-source definition that will create the JDBC resource
    on deployment

  - A standard property in the persistence.xml deployment descriptor to
    automatically and portably create and delete the tables in the
    jta-data-source

- Enterprise beans
  - Local, no-interface view session and singleton beans
  - JAX-RS resources in a session bean
  - Java EE security constraints on the administrative interface business methods
  - All enterprise beans packaged within the WAR
- WebSocket
  - A WebSocket server endpoint that automatically publishes the status of students to client endpoints
- Contexts and Dependency Injection
  - A CDI event that is fired when the status of a student changes
  - Handler methods for updating the application once the status event is fired
  - CDI managed beans for Facelets pages
  - Bean Validation annotations in the CDI managed beans
- JavaServer Faces technology, using Facelets for the web front end
  - Templating
  - Composite components
  - A custom formatter, `PhoneNumberFormatter`
  - Security constraints on the administrative interface
  - Ajax-enabled Facelets components

The Duke's Tutoring application has two main user interfaces, both packaged within a single WAR file:

- The main interface, for students, guardians, and staff
- The administrative interface used by the staff to manage the students and guardians, and to generate attendance reports

29.2 Main Interface

The main interface allows students and staff to check students in and out, and record when students are outside at the playground.

29.2.1 Java Persistence API Entities Used in the Main Interface

The following entities used in the main interface encapsulate data stored and manipulated by Duke's Tutoring, and are located in the dukestutoring.entity package in the dukes-tutoring-common project.

- Person: The Person entity defines attributes common to students and guardians tracked by the application. These attributes are the person's name and contact information, including phone numbers and email address. This entity has two subclasses, Student and Guardian.

- PersonDetails: The PersonDetails entity is used to store additional data common to all people, such as attributes like pictures and the person's birthday, which aren't included in the Person entity for performance reasons.

- Student and Guardian: The Student entity stores attributes specific to the students who come to tutoring. This includes information like the student's grade level and school. The Guardian entity's attributes are specific to the parents or guardians of a Student. Students and guardians have a many-to-many relationship. That is, a student may have one or more guardians, and a guardian may have one or more students.

- Address: The Address entity represents a mailing address and is associated with Person entities. Addresses and people have a many-to-one relationship. That is, one person may have many addresses.

- TutoringSession: The TutoringSession entity represents a particular day at the tutoring center. A particular tutoring session tracks which students attended that day, and which students went to the park.

- StatusEntry: The StatusEntry entity, which logs when a student's status changes, is associated with the TutoringSession entity. Students' statuses change when they check in to a tutoring session, when they go to the park, and when they check out. The status entry allows the tutoring center staff to track exactly which students attended a tutoring session, when they checked in and out, which students went to the park while they were at the tutoring center, and when they went to and came back from the park.

For information on creating Java Persistence API entities, see Chapter 8, "Introduction to the Java Persistence API." For information on validating entity data, see Section 8.1.2.4, "Validating Persistent Fields and Properties," in this book, and Chapter 22, "Bean Validation: Advanced Topics," in *The Java EE 7 Tutorial, Volume 1.*

29.2.2 Enterprise Beans Used in the Main Interface

The following enterprise beans used in the main interface provide the business logic for Duke's Tutoring, and are located in the `dukestutoring.ejb` package in the `dukes-tutoring-war` project.

- `ConfigBean` is a singleton session bean used to create the default students when the application is initially deployed, and to create an automatic EJB timer that creates tutoring session entities every weekday.

- `RequestBean` is a stateless session bean containing the business methods for the main interface. The bean also has business methods for retrieving lists of students. These business methods use strongly typed Criteria API queries to retrieve data from the database. `RequestBean` also injects a CDI event instance, `StatusEvent`. This event is fired from the business methods when the status of a student changes.

For information on creating and using enterprise beans, see Part II, "Enterprise Beans." For information on creating strongly typed Criteria API queries, see Chapter 11, "Using the Criteria API to Create Queries." For information on CDI events, see Section 25.5, "Using Events in CDI Applications," in *The Java EE 7 Tutorial, Volume 1*.

29.2.3 WebSocket Endpoint Used in the Main Interface

The `javaeetutorial.dukestutoring.web.websocket.StatusEndpoint` class is a WebSocket server endpoint that returns students and their status to client endpoints. The `StatusEndpoint.updateStatus` method is a CDI observer method for the `StatusEvent` event. When a student's status changes in the main interface, a `StatusEvent` is fired. The `updateStatus` observer method is called by the container, and pushes out the status change to all the client endpoints registered with `StatusEndpoint`.

The `index.xhtml` JavaServer Faces page contains JavaScript code to connect to the WebSocket endpoint. The `onMessage` method on this page clicks a JavaServer Faces button, which makes an Ajax request to refresh the table that shows the current status of the students.

For more information on WebSocket endpoints, see Chapter 18, "Java API for WebSocket," in *The Java EE 7 Tutorial, Volume 1*. For information on CDI events, see Section 25.5, "Using Events in CDI Applications," in *The Java EE 7 Tutorial, Volume 1*.

29.2.4 Facelets Files Used in the Main Interface

The Duke's Tutoring application uses Facelets to display the user interface, making extensive use of the templating features of Facelets. Facelets, the default display technology for JavaServer Faces, consists of XHTML files located in the *tut-install*/examples/case-studies/dukes-tutoring-war/src/main/webapp/ directory.

The following Facelets files are used in the main interface:

- `template.xhtml`: Template file for the main interface
- `error.xhtml`: Error file if something goes wrong
- `index.xhtml`: Landing page for the main interface
- `park.xhtml`: Page showing who is currently at the park
- `current.xhtml`: Page showing who is currently in today's tutoring session
- `statusEntries.xhtml`: Page showing the detailed status entry log for today's session
- `resources/components/allStudentsTable.xhtml`: A composite component for a table displaying all active students
- `resources/components/allInactiveStudentsTable.xhtml`: A composite component for a table displaying all inactive students
- `resources/components/currentSessionTable.xhtml`: A composite component for a table displaying all students in today's session
- `resources/components/parkTable.xhtml`: A composite component for a table displaying all students currently at the park
- `WEB-INF/includes/mainNav.xhtml`: XHTML fragment for the main interface's navigation bar

For information on using Facelets, see Chapter 8, "Introduction to Facelets," in *The Java EE 7 Tutorial, Volume 1.*

29.2.5 Helper Classes Used in the Main Interface

The following helper classes, found in the `dukes-tutoring-common` project's `dukestutoring.util` package, are used in the main interface.

- `CalendarUtil`: A class that provides a method to strip the unnecessary time data from `java.util.Calendar` instances.
- `Email`: A custom Bean Validation annotation class for validating email addresses in the `Person` entity.

- `StatusType`: An enumerated type defining the different statuses that a student can have. Possible values are `IN`, `OUT`, and `PARK`. `StatusType` is used throughout the application, including in the `StatusEntry` entity, and throughout the main interface. `StatusType` also defines a `toString` method that returns a localized translation of the status based on the locale.

29.2.6 Properties Files

The strings used in the main interface are encapsulated into resource bundles to allow the display of localized strings in multiple locales. Each of the properties files has locale-specific files appended with locale codes, containing the translated strings for each locale. For example, `Messages_es.properties` contains the localized strings for Spanish locales.

The `dukes-tutoring-common` project has the following resource bundle under `src/main/resources/`.

- `javaeetutorial/dukestutoring/util/StatusMessages.properties`: Strings for each of the status types defined in the `StatusType` enumerated type for the default locale. Each supported locale has a property file of the form `StatusMessages_locale prefix.properties` containing the localized strings. For example, the strings for Spanish-speaking locales are located in `StatusMessages_es.properties`.

The `dukes-tutoring-war` project has the following resource bundles under `src/main/resources/`.

- `ValidationMessages.properties`: Strings for the default locale used by the Bean Validation runtime to display validation messages. This file must be named `ValidationMessages.properties` and located in the default package as required by the Bean Validation specification. Each supported locale has a property file of the form `ValidationMessages_locale prefix.properties` containing the localized strings. For example, the strings for German-speaking locales are located in `ValidationMessages_de.properties`.

- `javaeetutorial/dukestutoring/web/messages/Messages.properties`: Strings for the default locale for the main and administration Facelets interface. Each supported locale has a property file of the form `Messages_locale prefix.properties` containing the localized strings. For example, the strings for simplified Chinese-speaking locales are located in `Messages_zh.properties`.

For information on localizing web applications, see Section 16.5, "Registering Application Messages," in *The Java EE 7 Tutorial, Volume 1*.

29.2.7 Deployment Descriptors Used in Duke's Tutoring

Duke's Tutoring uses these deployment descriptors in the `src/main/webapp/WEB-INF` directory of the `dukes-tutoring-war` project:

- `faces-config.xml`: The JavaServer Faces configuration file
- `glassfish-web.xml`: The configuration file specific to GlassFish Server, which defines security role mapping
- `web.xml`: The web application configuration file

Duke's Tutoring also uses the following deployment descriptor in the `src/main/resources/META-INF` directory of the `dukes-tutoring-common` project:

- `persistence.xml`: The Java Persistence API configuration file

No enterprise bean deployment descriptor is used in Duke's Tutoring. Annotations in the enterprise bean class files are used for the configuration of enterprise beans in this application.

29.3 Administration Interface

The administration interface of Duke's Tutoring is used by the tutoring center staff to manage the data employed by the main interface: the students, the students' guardians, and the addresses. The administration interface uses many of the same components as the main interface. Additional components that are only used in the administration interface are described here.

29.3.1 Enterprise Beans Used in the Administration Interface

The following enterprise bean, in the `dukestutoring.ejb` package of the `dukes-tutoring-war` project, is used in the administration interface.

- `AdminBean`: A stateless session bean for all the business logic used in the administration interface. Calls security methods to allow invocation of the business methods only by authorized users.

29.3.2 Facelets Files Used in the Administration Interface

The following Facelets files, under `src/main/webapp/`, are used in the administration interface:

- `admin/adminTemplate.xhtml`: Template for the administration interface
- `admin/index.xhtml`: Landing page for the administration interface
- `login.xhtml`: Login page for the security-constrained administration interface

- `loginError.xhtml`: Page displayed if there are errors authenticating the administration user

- `admin/address` directory: Pages that allow you to create, edit, and delete `Address` entities

- `admin/guardian` directory: Pages that allow you to create, edit, and delete `Guardian` entities

- `admin/student` directory: Pages that allow you to create, edit, and delete `Student` entities

- `resources/components/formLogin.xhtml`: Composite component for a login form using Java EE security

- `WEB-INF/includes/adminNav.xhtml`: XHTML fragment for the administration interface's navigation bar

29.3.3 CDI Managed Beans Used in the Administration Interface

The CDI managed beans used in the administration interface are located in the `dukestutoring.web` package in the `dukes-tutoring-war` project.

- `StudentBean.java`: A managed bean for the Facelets pages used to create and edit students. The first and last names have Bean Validation annotations that require the fields to be filled in. The phone numbers have Bean Validation annotations to ensure that the submitted data is well-formed.

- `GuardianBean.java`: A managed bean for the Facelets pages used to create guardians for and assign guardians to students. The first and last names have Bean Validation annotations that require the fields to be filled in. The phone numbers have Bean Validation annotations to ensure that the submitted data is well-formed.

- `AddressBean.java`: A managed bean for the Facelets pages used to create addresses for students. The street, city, province, and postal code attributes have Bean Validation annotations that require the fields to be filled in, and the postal code attribute has an additional annotation to ensure that the data is properly formed.

29.3.4 Helper Classes Used in the Administration Interface

The following helper classes, found in the `dukes-tutoring-war` project's `dukestutoring.web.util` package, are used in the administration interface.

- `EntityConverter`: A parent class to `StudentConverter` and `GuardianConverter` that defines a cache to store the entity classes when converting the entities for use in JavaServer Faces user interface components. The cache helps increase performance. The cache is stored in the JavaServer Faces context.

- `StudentConverter`: A JavaServer Faces converter for the `Student` entity class. This class contains methods to convert `Student` instances to strings and back again, so they can be used in the user interface components of the application.

- `GuardianConverter`: Similar to `StudentConverter`, this class is a converter for the `Guardian` entity class.

29.4 Running the Duke's Tutoring Case Study Application

This section describes how to build, package, deploy, and run the Duke's Tutoring application.

29.4.1 Running Duke's Tutoring

You can use either NetBeans IDE or Maven to build, package, deploy, and run Duke's Tutoring.

29.4.1.1 To Build and Deploy Duke's Tutoring Using NetBeans IDE

1. Make sure that GlassFish Server has been started (see Section 2.2, "Starting and Stopping GlassFish Server").

2. If the database server is not already running, start it as described in Section 2.4, "Starting and Stopping the Java DB Server."

3. From the **File** menu, choose **Open Project**.

4. In the Open Project dialog box, navigate to:

   tut-install/examples/case-studies

5. Select the `dukes-tutoring` folder.

6. Select the **Open Required Projects** check box and click **Open Project**.

   Note: The first time you open Duke's Tutoring in NetBeans, you will see error glyphs in the **Projects** tab. This is expected, as the metamodel files used by the enterprise beans for Criteria API queries have not yet been generated.

   ---

7. In the **Projects** tab, right-click the `dukes-tutoring` project and select **Build**.

This command creates a JDBC security realm named `tutoringRealm`, builds and packages the `dukes-tutoring-common` and `dukes-tutoring-war` projects, and deploys `dukes-tutoring-war` to GlassFish Server, starting the Java DB database and GlassFish Server if they have not already been started.

29.4.1.2 To Build and Deploy Duke's Tutoring Using Maven

1. Make sure that GlassFish Server has been started (see Section 2.2, "Starting and Stopping GlassFish Server").

2. If the database server is not already running, start it as described in Section 2.4, "Starting and Stopping the Java DB Server."

3. In a terminal window, go to:

   `tut-install/examples/case-studies/dukes-tutoring/`

4. Enter the following command:

   ```
   mvn install
   ```

   This command creates a JDBC security realm named `tutoringRealm`, builds and packages the `dukes-tutoring-common` and `dukes-tutoring-war` projects, and deploys `dukes-tutoring-war` to GlassFish Server.

29.4.1.3 Using Duke's Tutoring

Once Duke's Tutoring is running on GlassFish Server, use the main interface to experiment with checking students in and out or sending them to the park.

To Use the Main Interface of Duke's Tutoring

1. In a web browser, open the main interface at the following URL:

   `http://localhost:8080/dukes-tutoring-war/`

2. Use the main interface to check students in and out, and to log when the students go to the park.

To Use the Administration Interface of Duke's Tutoring

Follow these instructions to log in to the administration interface of Duke's Tutoring and add new students, guardians, and addresses.

1. From the main interface, open the administration interface by clicking **Administration main page** in the left menu.

   This redirects you to the login page at the following URL:

   `http://localhost:8080/dukes-tutoring-war/admin/index.xhtml`

2. On the login page, enter admin@example.com in the **User name** field, and enter javaee in the **Password** field.

3. Use the administration interface to add or modify students, add guardians, or add addresses.

   ■ To add a new student, click **Create new student** in the left menu, fill in the fields (two are required) in the form that opens, and click **Submit**. The **Email**, **Home phone**, and **Mobile phone** fields have formatting requirements enforced by HTML5 pass-through or by Bean Validation constraints.

   ■ To modify a student, click **Edit** next to the student's name, modify the fields in the form that opens, and click **Submit**. To edit another student, select the student from the drop-down list at the top of the page and click **Change student**.

   ■ To remove a student, click **Remove** next to the student's name, then click **Confirm** in the page that appears. This action removes the student from the tutoring session but does not remove the student from the database. To add the student to the tutoring session again, click **Activate student** in the left menu, then click **Activate** next to the student's name in the page that appears.

   ■ To add a guardian for a student, click **Add guardian** next to the student's name. The page that appears shows the student's name, the available guardians, and the current guardians for the student, if any. To add an existing guardian for that student, select the guardian from the list and click **Add guardian**. To create a new guardian for the student, fill in the fields and click **Submit**. To remove a guardian from a student, select one of the student's current guardians from the list and click **Remove guardian**.

   ■ To add an address for a student, click **Add address** next to the student's name. In the page that appears, fill in the appropriate fields in the form that appears, and click **Submit**. Four fields are required.

The administration interface is not fully implemented. It is not possible to edit a guardian or to view or edit an address, although Facelets pages exist for these features. The application also makes no use of the properties in the PersonDetails entity. Feel free to modify the application to add these features.

30

Duke's Forest Case Study Example

Duke's Forest is a simple e-commerce application that contains several web applications and illustrates the use of multiple Java EE 7 APIs:

- JavaServer Faces technology, including Ajax
- Contexts and Dependency Injection for Java EE (CDI)
- Java API for RESTful Web Services (JAX-RS)
- Java Persistence API (JPA)
- Java API for JavaBeans Validation (Bean Validation)
- Enterprise JavaBeans (EJB) technology
- Java Message Service (JMS)

The application consists of the following projects.

- Duke's Store: A web application that has a product catalog, customer self-registration, and a shopping cart. It also has an administration interface for product, category, and user management. The project name is `dukes-store`.

- Duke's Shipment: A web application that provides an interface for order shipment management. The project name is `dukes-shipment`.

- Duke's Payment: A web service application that has a RESTful web service for order payment. The project name is `dukes-payment`.

- Duke's Resources: A simple Java archive project that contains all resources used by the web projects. It includes messages, CSS style sheets, images, JavaScript files, and JavaServer Faces composite components. The project name is `dukes-resources`.

- Entities: A simple Java archive project that contains all JPA entities. This project is shared among other projects that use the entities. The project name is `entities`.

- Events: A simple Java archive project that contains a POJO class that is used as a CDI event. The project name is `events`.

The following topics are addressed here:

- Design and Architecture of Duke's Forest
- Building and Deploying the Duke's Forest Case Study Application
- Running the Duke's Forest Application

30.1 Design and Architecture of Duke's Forest

Duke's Forest is a complex application consisting of three main projects and three subprojects. Figure 30–1 shows the architecture of the three main projects that you will deploy: Duke's Store, Duke's Shipment, and Duke's Payment. It also shows how Duke's Store makes use of the Events and Entities projects.

Duke's Forest uses the following Java EE 7 platform features:

- Java Persistence API entities
    - Bean Validation annotations on the entities for verifying data
    - XML annotations for Java API for XML binding (JAXB) serialization
- Web services
    - A JAX-RS web service for payment, with security constraints
    - A JAX-RS web service that is EJB based
- Enterprise beans
    - Local session beans
    - All enterprise beans packaged within the WAR
- Contexts and Dependency Injection (CDI)
    - CDI annotations for JavaServer Faces components
    - A CDI managed bean used as a shopping cart, with conversation scoping
    - Qualifiers
    - Events and event handlers

Figure 30–1   Architecture of the Duke's Forest Example Application

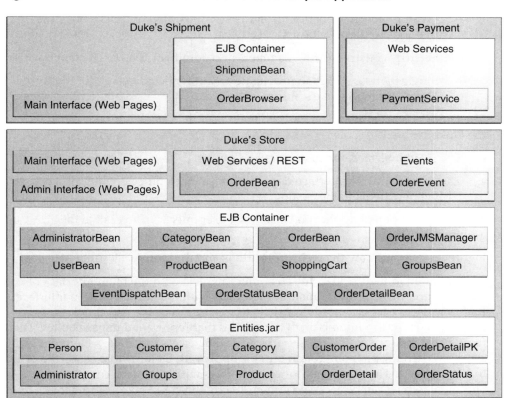

- Servlets
  - A servlet for dynamic image presentation
- JavaServer Faces 2.2 technology, using Facelets for the web front end
  - Templating
  - Composite components
  - File upload
  - Resources packaged in a JAR file so they can be found in the classpath

- Security
  - Java EE security constraints on the administrative interface business methods (enterprise beans)
  - Security constraints for customers and administrators (web components)
  - Single Sign-On (SSO) to propagate an authenticated user identity from Duke's Store to Duke's Shipment

The Duke's Forest application has two main user interfaces, both packaged within the Duke's Store WAR file:

- The main interface, for customers and guests
- The administrative interface used to perform back office operations, such as adding new items to the catalog

The Duke's Shipment application also has a user interface, accessible to administrators.

Figure 30–2 shows how the web applications and the web service interact.

As illustrated in Figure 30–2, the customer interacts with the main interface of Duke's Store, while the administrator interacts with the administration interface. Both interfaces access a façade consisting of managed beans and stateless session beans, which in turn interact with the entities that represent database tables. The façade also interacts with web services APIs that access the Duke's Payment web service. When the payment for an order is approved, Duke's Store sends the order to a JMS queue. The administrator also interacts with the interface of Duke's Shipment, which can be accessed either directly through Duke's Shipment or from the administration interface of Duke's Store by means of a web service. When the administrator approves an order for shipping, Duke's Shipment consumes the order from the JMS queue.

The most fundamental building blocks of the application are the Events and Entities projects, which are bundled into Duke's Store and Duke's Shipment along with the Duke's Resources project.

30.1.1 The events Project

Events are one of the core components of Duke's Forest. The events project, included in all three of the main projects, is the most simple project of the application. It has only one class, OrderEvent, but this class is responsible for most of the messages between objects in the application.

Figure 30–2   Interactions between Duke's Forest Components

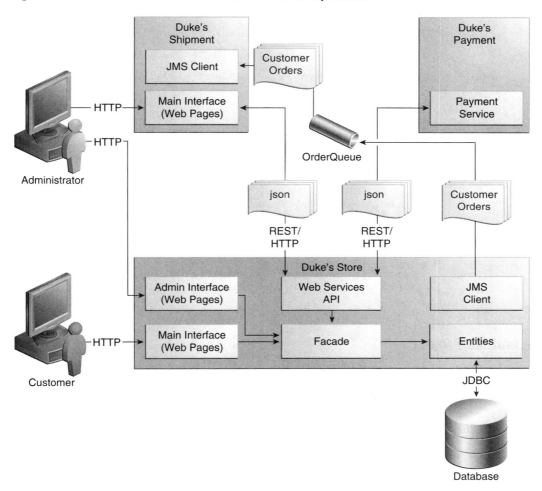

The application can send messages based on events to different components and react to them based on the qualification of the event. The application supports the following qualifiers:

- `@LoggedIn`: For authenticated users
- `@New`: When a new order is created by the shopping cart
- `@Paid`: When an order is paid for and ready for shipment

The following code snippet from the `PaymentHandler` class of Duke's Store shows how the `@Paid` event is handled:

```
@Inject @Paid Event<OrderEvent> eventManager;

...
public void onNewOrder(@Observes @New OrderEvent event) {

    if (processPayment(event)) {
        orderBean.setOrderStatus(event.getOrderID(),
            String.valueOf(OrderBean.Status.PENDING_PAYMENT.getStatus()));
        logger.info("Payment Approved");
        eventManager.fire(event);
    } else {
        orderBean.setOrderStatus(event.getOrderID(),
            String.valueOf(OrderBean.Status.CANCELLED_PAYMENT.getStatus()));
        logger.info("Payment Denied");
    }
}
```

To enable users to add more events to the project easily or update an event class with more fields for a new client, this component is a separate project within the application.

30.1.2 The entities Project

The `entities` project is a Java Persistence API (JPA) project used by both Duke's Store and Duke's Shipment. It is generated from the database schema shown in Figure 30–3 and is also used as a base for the entities consumed and produced by the web services through JAXB. Each entity has validation rules based on business requirements, specified using Bean Validation.

Figure 30–3   Duke's Forest Database Tables and Their Relationships

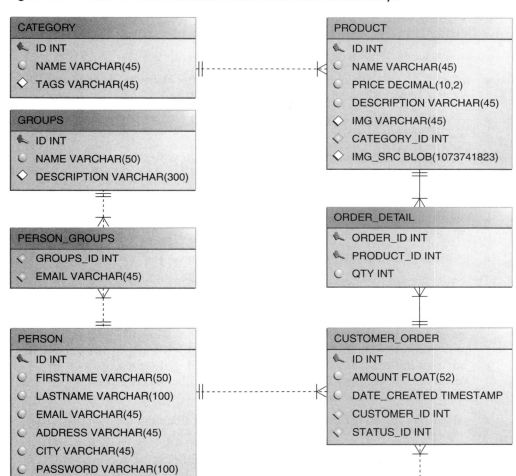

CATEGORY
- 🔑 ID INT
- ⚪ NAME VARCHAR(45)
- ◇ TAGS VARCHAR(45)

GROUPS
- 🔑 ID INT
- ⚪ NAME VARCHAR(50)
- ◇ DESCRIPTION VARCHAR(300)

PERSON_GROUPS
- ◇ GROUPS_ID INT
- ◇ EMAIL VARCHAR(45)

PERSON
- 🔑 ID INT
- ⚪ FIRSTNAME VARCHAR(50)
- ⚪ LASTNAME VARCHAR(100)
- ⚪ EMAIL VARCHAR(45)
- ⚪ ADDRESS VARCHAR(45)
- ⚪ CITY VARCHAR(45)
- ⚪ PASSWORD VARCHAR(100)
- ◇ DTYPE VARCHAR(31)

PRODUCT
- 🔑 ID INT
- ⚪ NAME VARCHAR(45)
- ⚪ PRICE DECIMAL(10,2)
- ⚪ DESCRIPTION VARCHAR(45)
- ◇ IMG VARCHAR(45)
- ◇ CATEGORY_ID INT
- ◇ IMG_SRC BLOB(1073741823)

ORDER_DETAIL
- 🔑 ORDER_ID INT
- 🔑 PRODUCT_ID INT
- ⚪ QTY INT

CUSTOMER_ORDER
- 🔑 ID INT
- ⚪ AMOUNT FLOAT(52)
- ⚪ DATE_CREATED TIMESTAMP
- ◇ CUSTOMER_ID INT
- ◇ STATUS_ID INT

ORDER_STATUS
- 🔑 ID INT
- ⚪ STATUS VARCHAR(45)
- ◇ DESCRIPTION VARCHAR(200)

- 🔑 Primary key
- ⚪ Required field
- ◆ Foreign key
- ◇ Field

The database schema contains eight tables:

- PERSON, which has a one-to-many relationship with PERSON_GROUPS and CUSTOMER_ORDER

- GROUPS, which has a one-to-many relationship with PERSON_GROUPS

- PERSON_GROUPS, which has a many-to-one relationship with PERSON and GROUPS (it is the join table between those two tables)

- PRODUCT, which has a many-to-one relationship with CATEGORY and a one-to-many relationship with ORDER_DETAIL

- CATEGORY, which has a one-to-many relationship with PRODUCT

- CUSTOMER_ORDER, which has a one-to-many relationship with ORDER_DETAIL and a many-to-one relationship with PERSON and ORDER_STATUS

- ORDER_DETAIL, which has a many-to-one relationship with PRODUCT and CUSTOMER_ORDER (it is the join table between those two tables)

- ORDER_STATUS, which has a one-to-many relationship with CUSTOMER_ORDER

The entity classes that correspond to these tables are as follows.

- Person, which defines attributes common to customers and administrators. These attributes are the person's name and contact information, including street and email addresses. The email address has a Bean Validation annotation to ensure that the submitted data is well-formed. The generated table for the Person entity also has a DTYPE field that represents the discriminator column. Its value identifies the subclass (Customer or Administrator) to which the person belongs.

- Customer, a specialization of Person with a specific field for CustomerOrder objects.

- Administrator, a specialization of Person with fields for administration privileges.

- Groups, which represents the group (USERS or ADMINS) to which the user belongs.

- Product, which defines attributes for products. These attributes include name, price, description, associated image, and category.

- Category, which defines attributes for product categories. These attributes include a name and a set of tags.

- CustomerOrder, which defines attributes for orders placed by customers. These attributes include an amount and a date, along with id values for the customer and the order detail.

- `OrderDetail`, which defines attributes for the order detail. These attributes include a quantity and id values for the product and the customer.

- `OrderStatus`, which defines a status attribute for each order.

30.1.3 The dukes-payment Project

The `dukes-payment` project is a web project that holds a simple Payment web service. Since this is an example application, it does not obtain any real credit information or even customer status to validate the payment. For now, the only rule imposed by the payment system is to deny all orders above $1,000. This application illustrates a common scenario where a third-party payment service is used to validate credit cards or bank payments.

The project uses HTTP Basic Authentication and JAAS (Java Authentication and Authorization Service) to authenticate a customer to a JAX-RS web service. The implementation itself exposes a simple method, `processPayment`, which receives an `OrderEvent` to evaluate and approve or deny the order payment. The method is called from the checkout process of Duke's Store.

30.1.4 The dukes-resources Project

The `dukes-resources` project contains a number of files used by both Duke's Store and Duke's Shipment, bundled into a JAR file placed in the classpath. The resources are in the `src/main/resources` directory:

- `META-INF/resources/css`: Two style sheets, `default.css` and `jsfcrud.css`

- `META-INF/resources/img`: Images used by the projects

- `META-INF/resources/js`: A JavaScript file, `util.js`

- `META-INF/resources/util`: Composite components used by the projects

- `bundles/Bundle.properties`: Application messages in English

- `bundles/Bundle_es.properties`: Application messages in Spanish

- `ValidationMessages.properties`: Bean Validation messages in English

- `ValidationMessages_es.properties`: Bean Validation messages in Spanish

30.1.5 The Duke's Store Project

Duke's Store, a web application, is the core application of Duke's Forest. It is responsible for the main store interface for customers as well as the administration interface.

The main interface of Duke's Store allows the user to perform the following tasks:

- Browse the product catalog
- Sign up as a new customer
- Add products to the shopping cart
- Check out
- View order status

The administration interface of Duke's Store allows administrators to perform the following tasks:

- Product maintenance (create, edit, update, delete)
- Category maintenance (create, edit, update, delete)
- Customer maintenance (create, edit, update, delete)
- Group maintenance (create, edit, update, delete)

The project also uses stateless session beans as façades for interactions with the JPA entities described in Section 30.1.2, "The entities Project," and CDI managed beans as controllers for interactions with Facelets pages. The project thus follows the MVC (Model-View-Controller) pattern and applies the same pattern to all entities and pages, as in the following example.

- `AbstractFacade` is an abstract class that receives a `Type<T>` and implements the common operations (CRUD) for this type, where `<T>` is a JPA entity.

- `ProductBean` is a stateless session bean that extends `AbstractFacade`, applying `Product` as `Type<T>`, and injects the `PersistenceContext` for the `EntityManager`. This bean implements any custom methods needed to interact with the `Product` entity or to call a custom query.

- `ProductController` is a CDI managed bean that interacts with the necessary enterprise beans and Facelets pages to control the way the data will be displayed.

`ProductBean` begins as follows:

```
@Stateless
public class ProductBean extends AbstractFacade<Product> {
    private static .final Logger logger =
        Logger.getLogger(ProductBean.class.getCanonicalName());

    @PersistenceContext(unitName="forestPU")
    private EntityManager em;
```

```
@Override
protected EntityManager getEntityManager() {
    return em;
}
...
```

30.1.5.1 Enterprise Beans Used in Duke's Store

The enterprise beans used in Duke's Store provide the business logic for the application and are located in the `com.forest.ejb` package. All are stateless session beans.

`AbstractFacade` is not an enterprise bean but an abstract class that implements common operations for `Type<T>`, where `<T>` is a JPA entity.

Most of the other beans extend `AbstractFacade`, inject the `PersistenceContext`, and implement any needed custom methods:

- `AdministratorBean`

- `CategoryBean`

- `EventDispatcherBean`

- `GroupsBean`

- `OrderBean`

- `OrderDetailBean`

- `OrderJMSManager`

- `OrderStatusBean`

- `ProductBean`

- `ShoppingCart`

- `UserBean`

The `ShoppingCart` class, although it is in the `ejb` package, is a CDI managed bean with conversation scope, which means that the request information will persist across multiple requests. Also, `ShoppingCart` is responsible for starting the event chain for customer orders, which invokes the RESTful web service in `dukes-payment` and publishes an order to the JMS queue for shipping approval if the payment is successful.

30.1.5.2 Facelets Files Used in the Main Interface of Duke's Store

Like the other case study examples, Duke's Store uses Facelets to display the user interface. The main interface uses a large number of Facelets pages to display different areas. The pages are grouped into directories based on which module they handle.

- `template.xhtml`: Template file, used for both main and administration interfaces. It first performs a browser check to verify that the user's browser supports HTML5, which is required for Duke's Forest. It divides the screen into several areas and specifies the client page for each area.

- `topbar.xhtml`: Page for the login area at the top of the screen.

- `top.xhtml`: Page for the title area.

- `left.xhtml`: Page for the left sidebar.

- `index.xhtml`: Page for the main screen content.

- `login.xhtml`: Login page specified in `web.xml`. The main login interface is provided in `topbar.xhtml`, but this page appears if there is a login error.

- `admin` directory: Pages related to the administration interface, described in Section 30.1.5.3, "Facelets Files Used in the Administration Interface of Duke's Store."

- `customer` directory: Pages related to customers (`Create.xhtml`, `Edit.xhtml`, `List.xhtml`, `Profile.xhtml`, `View.xhtml`).

- `order` directory: Pages related to orders (`Create.xhtml`, `List.xhtml`, `MyOrders.xhtml`, `View.xhtml`).

- `orderDetail` directory: Popup page allowing users to view details of an order (`View_popup.xhtml`).

- `product` directory: Pages related to products (`List.xhtml`, `ListCategory.xhtml`, `View.xhtml`).

30.1.5.3 Facelets Files Used in the Administration Interface of Duke's Store

The Facelets pages for the administration interface of Duke's Store are found in the `web/admin` directory:

- `administrator` directory: Pages related to administrator management (`Create.xhtml`, `Edit.xhtml`, `List.xhtml`, `View.xhtml`)

- `category` directory: Pages related to product category management (`Create.xhtml`, `Edit.xhtml`, `List.xhtml`, `View.xhtml`)

- `customer` directory: Pages related to customer management (`Create.xhtml`, `Edit.xhtml`, `List.xhtml`, `Profile.xhtml`, `View.xhtml`)

- `groups` directory: Pages related to group management (`Create.xhtml`, `Edit.xhtml`, `List.xhtml`, `View.xhtml`)

- order directory: Pages related to order management (Create.xhtml, Edit.xhtml, List.xhtml, View.xhtml)

- orderDetail directory: Popup page allowing the administrator to view details of an order (View_popup.xhtml)

- product directory: Pages related to product management (Confirm.xhtml, Create.xhtml, Edit.xhtml, List.xhtml, View.xhtml)

30.1.5.4 Managed Beans Used in Duke's Store

Duke's Store uses the following CDI managed beans, which correspond to the enterprise beans. The beans are in the com.forest.web package:

- AdministratorController

- CategoryController

- CustomerController

- CustomerOrderController

- GroupsController

- OrderDetailController

- OrderStatusController

- ProductController

- UserController

30.1.5.5 Helper Classes Used in Duke's Store

The CDI managed beans in the main interface of Duke's Store use the following helper classes, found in the com.forest.web.util package:

- AbstractPaginationHelper: An abstract class with methods used by the managed beans

- ImageServlet: A servlet class that retrieves the image content from the database and displays it

- JsfUtil: Class used for JavaServer Faces operations, such as queuing messages on a FacesContext instance

- MD5Util: Class used by the CustomerController managed bean to generate an encrypted password for a user

30.1.5.6 Qualifiers Used in Duke's Store

Duke's Store defines the following qualifiers in the `com.forest.qualifiers` package:

- `@LoggedIn`: Qualifies a user as having logged in
- `@New`: Qualifies an order as new
- `@Paid`: Qualifies an order as paid

30.1.5.7 Event Handlers Used in Duke's Store

Duke's Store defines event handlers related to the `OrderEvent` class packaged in the `events` project (see Section 30.1.1, "The events Project"). The event handlers are in the `com.forest.handlers` package.

- `IOrderHandler`: The `IOrderHandler` interface defines a method, `onNewOrder`, implemented by the two handler classes.
- `PaymentHandler`: The `ShoppingCart` bean fires an `OrderEvent` qualified as `@New`. The `onNewOrder` method of `PaymentHandler` observes these events and, when it intercepts them, processes the payment using the Duke's Payment web service. After a successful response from the web service, `PaymentHandler` fires the `OrderEvent` again, this time qualified as `@Paid`.
- `DeliveryHandler`: The `onNewOrder` method of `DeliveryHandler` observes `OrderEvent` objects qualified as `@Paid` (orders paid and ready for delivery) and modifies the order status to `PENDING_SHIPMENT`. When an administrator accesses Duke's Shipment, it will call the Order Service, a RESTful web service, and ask for all orders in the database that are ready for delivery.

30.1.5.8 Deployment Descriptors Used in Duke's Store

Duke's Store uses the following deployment descriptors, located in the `web/WEB-INF` directory:

- `faces-config.xml`: The JavaServer Faces configuration file
- `glassfish-web.xml`: The configuration file specific to GlassFish Server
- `web.xml`: The web application configuration file

30.1.6 The Duke's Shipment Project

Duke's Shipment is a web application with a login page, a main Facelets page, and some other objects. This application, which is accessible only to administrators, consumes orders from a JMS queue and calls the RESTful web service exposed by Duke's Store to update the order status. The main page of Duke's Shipment shows a list of orders pending shipping approval and a list of shipped orders. The administrator can approve or deny orders for shipping. If approved, the order is shipped, and it appears under the Shipped heading. If denied, the order disappears from the page, and on the customer's Orders list it appears as cancelled.

There is also a gear icon on the Pending list that makes an Ajax call to the Order Service to refresh the list without refreshing the page. The code looks like this:

```
<h:commandLink>
    <h:graphicImage library="img" title="Check for new orders"
                    style="border:0px" name="refresh.png"/>
    <f:ajax execute="@form" render="@form" />
</h:commandLink>
```

30.1.6.1 Enterprise Beans Used in Duke's Shipment

The UserBean stateless session bean used in Duke's Shipment provides the business logic for the application and is located in the com.forest.shipment.session package.

Like Duke's Store, Duke's Shipment uses the AbstractFacade class. This class is not an enterprise bean but an abstract class that implements common operations for Type<T>, where <T> is a JPA entity.

The OrderBrowser stateless session bean, located in the com.forest.shipment.ejb package, has one method that browses the JMS order queue and another that consumes an order message after the administrator approves or denies the order for shipment.

30.1.6.2 Facelets Files Used in Duke's Shipment

Duke's Shipment has only one page, so it has many fewer Facelets files than Duke's Store.

- template.xhtml: The template file, like the one in Duke's Store, first performs a browser check to verify that the user's browser supports HTML5, which is required for Duke's Forest. It divides the screen into areas and specifies the client page for each area.

- topbar.xhtml: Page for the login area at the top of the screen.

- top.xhtml: Page for the title area.

- index.xhtml: Page for the initial main screen content.

- login.xhtml: Login page specified in web.xml. The main login interface is provided in topbar.xhtml, but this page appears if there is a login error.

- admin/index.xhtml: Page for the main screen content after authentication.

30.1.6.3 Managed Beans Used in Duke's Shipment

Duke's Shipment uses the following CDI managed beans, in the com.forest.shipment package:

- web.ShippingBean: Managed bean that acts as a client to the Order Service

- web.UserController: Managed bean that corresponds to the UserBean session bean

30.1.6.4 Helper Class Used in Duke's Shipment

The Duke's Shipment managed beans use only one helper class, found in the com.forest.shipment.web.util package:

- JsfUtil: Class used for JavaServer Faces operations, such as queuing messages on a FacesContext instance

30.1.6.5 Qualifier Used in Duke's Shipment

Duke's Shipment includes the @LoggedIn qualifier described in Section 30.1.5.6, "Qualifiers Used in Duke's Store."

30.1.6.6 Deployment Descriptors Used in Duke's Shipment

Duke's Shipment uses the following deployment descriptors:

- faces-config.xml: The JavaServer Faces configuration file

- glassfish-web.xml: The configuration file specific to GlassFish Server

- web.xml: The web application configuration file

30.2 Building and Deploying the Duke's Forest Case Study Application

You can use NetBeans IDE or Maven to build and deploy Duke's Forest.

30.2.1 To Build and Deploy the Duke's Forest Application Using NetBeans IDE

1. Make sure that GlassFish Server has been started (see Section 2.2, "Starting and Stopping GlassFish Server").

2. From the **File** menu, choose **Open Project**.

3. In the Open Project dialog box, navigate to:

   tut-install/examples/case-studies

4. Select the dukes-forest folder.

5. Select the **Open Required Projects** check box and click **Open Project**.

6. In the **Projects** tab, right-click the dukes-forest project and select **Build**.

   This task configures the server, creates and populates the database, builds all the subprojects, assembles them into JAR and WAR files, and deploys the dukes-payment, dukes-store, and dukes-shipment applications.

   To configure the server, this task creates a JDBC security realm named jdbcRealm, enables default principal-to-role mapping, and enables single sign-on (SSO) for the HTTP Service.

30.2.2 To Build and Deploy the Duke's Forest Application Using Maven

1. Make sure that GlassFish Server has been started (see Section 2.2, "Starting and Stopping GlassFish Server"), as well as the database server (see Section 2.4, "Starting and Stopping the Java DB Server").

2. In a terminal window, go to:

   tut-install/examples/case-studies/dukes-forest/

3. Enter the following command to configure the server, create and populate the database, build all the subprojects, assemble them into JAR and WAR files, and deploy the dukes-payment, dukes-store, and dukes-shipment applications:

   mvn install

   To configure the server, this task creates a JDBC security realm named jdbcRealm, enables default principal-to-role mapping, and enables single sign-on (SSO) for the HTTP Service.

30.3 Running the Duke's Forest Application

Running the Duke's Forest application involves several tasks:

- Registering as a customer of Duke's Store

- As a customer, purchasing products

- As an administrator, approving or denying shipment of a product
- As an administrator, creating a new product, customer, group, or category

30.3.1 To Register as a Duke's Store Customer

1. In a web browser, enter the following URL:

   `http://localhost:8080/dukes-store`

   The Duke's Forest - Store page opens.

2. Click **Sign Up** at the top of the page.

3. Fill in the form fields, then click **Save**.

   All fields are required, and the **Password** value must be at least 7 characters in length.

30.3.2 To Purchase Products

1. To log in as the user you created, or as one of two users already in the database, enter the user name and password and click **Log In**.

   The preexisting users have the user names `jack@example.com` and `robert@example.com`, and they both have the same password, `1234`.

2. Click **Products** in the left sidebar.

3. On the page that appears, click one of the categories (**Plants**, **Food**, **Services**, or **Tools**).

4. Choose a product and click **Add to Cart**.

   You can order only one of any one product, but you can order multiple *different* products in multiple categories. The products and a running total appear in the Shopping Cart in the left sidebar.

5. When you have finished choosing products, click **Checkout**.

   A message appears: "Your order is being processed. Check the Orders page to see the status of your order."

6. Click **Orders** in the left sidebar to verify your order.

   If the total of the order exceeds $1,000, the status of the order is "Order cancelled," because the Payment web service denies orders over that limit. Otherwise, the status is "Ready to ship."

7. When you have finished placing orders, click **Logout** at the top of the page.

30.3.3 To Approve Shipment of a Product

1. Log in to Duke's Store as an administrator.

   Your user name is `admin@example.com`, and your password is `1234`.

   The main administration page allows you to view categories, customers, administrators, groups, products, and orders, and to create new objects of all types except orders.

2. At the bottom of the page, click **Approve Shipment**.

   This action takes you to Duke's Shipment, retaining your administrator login.

3. On the **Pending** list, click **Approve** to approve an order and move it to the **Shipped** area of the page.

   If you click **Deny**, the order disappears from the page. If you log in to Duke's Store again as the customer, it will appear in the Orders list as "Order cancelled."

   To return to Duke's Store from Duke's Shipment, click **Return to Duke's Store**.

30.3.4 To Create a New Product

You can create other kinds of objects as well as products. Creating products is more complex than the other creation processes, so it is described here.

1. Log in to Duke's Store as an administrator.

2. On the main administration page, click **Create New Product**.

3. Enter values in the **Name**, **Price**, and **Description** fields.

4. Select a category, then click **Next**.

5. On the Upload the Product Image page, click **Browse** to locate an image on your file system using a file chooser.

6. Click **Next**.

7. On the next page, view the product fields, then click **Done**.

8. Click **Products** in the left sidebar, then click the category to verify that the product has been added.

9. Click **Administration** at the top of the page to return to the main administration page, or click **Logout** to log out.

Index

Symbols

@AccessTimeout annotation, 84
@ActivationConfigProperty annotation, 293
@AroundConstruct annotation, 498
@AroundInvoke annotation, 498
@AroundTimeout annotation, 498
@Asynchronous annotation, 114
@ConcurrencyManagement annotation, 83
@DeclareRoles annotation, 415, 423
@DenyAll annotation, 416
@DependsOn annotation, 81
@DiscriminatorColumn annotation, 138
@DiscriminatorValue annotation, 138
@Embeddable annotation, 135
@EmbeddedId annotation, 130
@Entity annotation, 124
@HttpConstraint annotation, 385, 403
@HttpMethodConstraint annotation, 385, 403
@Id annotation, 130
@IdClass annotation, 130
@Interceptor annotation, 498
@Interceptors annotation, 498
@JMSConnectionFactoryDefinition
    annotation, 288
@JMSDestinationDefinition annotation, 288
@Local annotation, 58, 74
@Lock annotation, 83
@ManyToMany annotation, 132, 133
@ManyToOne annotation, 132
@MessageDriven annotation, 293, 343
@NamedQuery annotation, 180
@OneToMany annotation, 132, 133, 134
@OneToOne annotation, 132, 133, 134
@PermitAll annotation, 416
@PersistenceContext annotation, 141

@PersistenceUnit annotation, 142
@PostActivate annotation, 75, 77
@PostConstruct annotation, 63, 75, 77, 498
@PreDestroy annotation, 63, 75, 77, 498
@PrePassivate annotation, 75, 77
@Remote annotation, 58, 74
@Remove annotation, 64, 75, 78
@Resource annotation
    JMS resources, 262, 263, 337
@RolesAllowed annotation, 415, 423
@RunAs annotation, 420
@Schedule and @Schedules annotations, 97
@ServletSecurity annotation, 385, 403
@Singleton annotation, 81
@Startup annotation, 81
@Stateful annotation, 75
@Timeout annotation, 95
@Timeout method, 96, 98
@Transient annotation, 126
@WebMethod annotation, 78

A

abstract schemas, 180
access control, 364
acknowledge method, 280
acknowledging messages. *See* message
    acknowledgment
administered objects, 262
    creating and removing, 302
    definition, 257
    See also connection factories, destinations
Administration Console, 34
    starting, 40
afterBegin method, 464
afterCompletion method, 464

    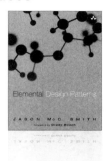

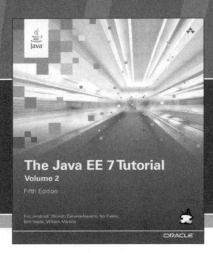

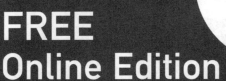

FREE
Online Edition

Your purchase of *The Java EE 7 Tutorial, Volume 2*, includes access to a free online edition for 45 days through the **Safari Books Online** subscription service. Nearly every Addison-Wesley Professional book is available online through **Safari Books Online**, along with thousands of books and videos from publishers such as Cisco Press, Exam Cram, IBM Press, O'Reilly Media, Prentice Hall, Que, Sams, and VMware Press.

Safari Books Online is a digital library providing searchable, on-demand access to thousands of technology, digital media, and professional development books and videos from leading publishers. With one monthly or yearly subscription price, you get unlimited access to learning tools and information on topics including mobile app and software development, tips and tricks on using your favorite gadgets, networking, project management, graphic design, and much more.

Activate your FREE Online Edition at
informit.com/safarifree

STEP 1: Enter the coupon code: KDXGNCB.

STEP 2: New Safari users, complete the brief registration form.
Safari subscribers, just log in.

If you have difficulty registering on Safari or accessing the online edition,
please e-mail customer-service@safaribooksonline.com